MW01473894

PERFECTION
Makes Practice

PERFECTION Makes Practice

Learning, Emotion, and the Recited Qur'ān in Indonesia

Anna M. Gade

University of Hawai'i Press
Honolulu

© 2004 University of Hawai'i Press
All rights reserved
Printed in the United States of America
09 08 07 06 05 04 6 5 4 3 2 1

Library of Congress Cataloging-in-Publication Data
Gade, Anna M.
Perfection makes practice : learning, emotion, and the recited Qur'ān in Indonesia /
Anna M. Gade.
p. cm.
Includes bibliographical references and index.
ISBN 0-8248-2599-3 (hardcover : alk. paper)
1. Koran—Study and teaching—Indonesia. 2. Koran—Appreciation—Indonesia.
3. Islamic renewal—Indonesia. 4. Koran—Recitation. I. Title.
BP130.78.I5G33 2004
297.7'7'09598—dc22

2003019695

University of Hawai'i Press books are printed on acid-free
paper and meet the guidelines for permanence and durability
of the Council on Library Resources.

Designed by the University of Hawai'i Press production staff
Printed by The Maple-Vail Book Manufacturing Group

Contents

Abbreviations vii
Acknowledgments ix

1. Introduction: Practice and Perfection 1
2. Memorizing: Attentive Modes of Preserving the Qur'ān 60
3. Reading: Affective ABCs of Learning 114
4. Expression: Emotional Projects of Performance and Pedagogy 164
5. Competing: Promoting Motivated Participation 216
6. Conclusion: An Envy of Goodness 267

Notes 279
Selected Bibliography 311
Index 337

Abbreviations

AMM	Angkatan Muda Masjid & Mushalla (Youth Generation of Mosques and Places of Worship)
BKPRMI	Badan Komunikasi Pemuda Remaja Masjid Indonesia (Organizing Body for the Youth Groups of Indonesian Mosques)
IAIN	Institut Agama Islam Negeri (National Islamic University)
IIQ	Institut Ilmu Al-Quran
KKN	Kulia Kerja Nyata
LBIQ	Lembaga Bahasa dan Ilmu Al-Quran
LPTQ	Lembaga Pengembangan Tilawatil Quran (Institute for the Development of the Recitation of the Qur'ān)
MTQ	Musabaqah Tilawatil Quran (Qur'ān Recitation Contest)
NU	Nahdlatul Ulama
PTIQ	Perguruan Tinggi Ilmu Al-Quran
RRI	Radio Republik Indonesia
STAI	Sekolah Tinggi Agama Islam
TKA	Taman Kanak-kanak Al-Quran
TPA	Taman Pendidikan Al-Quran
TVRI	Televisi Republik Indonesia

Acknowledgments

I WOULD LIKE to acknowledge with gratitude the faculty, staff, and students of IAIN Alauddin, Ujung Pandang (Makassar). I am grateful to the students of STAI "Al-Furqan" in Ujung Pandang. In Jakarta, I would like to acknowledge the assistance of faculty, staff, and students of IIQ and PTIQ, especially the national coaches who were so generous with their time. I would also like to thank members of Team Tadarus "AMM" in Kotagede, Yogyakarta, for their time and gracious assistance, as well as the staff of the LBIQ in Jakarta for their helpful cooperation. At the national Ministry of Religious Affairs (Penerangan Islam section) and at the national LPTQ, I received special kindness and assistance, as I did at the Provincial Ministry of Religious Affairs, South Sulawesi. I express my thanks also to the Kotamadya Ministry of Religious Affairs, Ujung Pandang. Thanks, warmth, and respect go to the young people who trained at Mesjid Raya during 1996–1997, who graciously allowed me to join their coaching sessions. I would also like to thank the corporate employees and affiliates who extended similar hospitality.

I would like to thank the Panitia MTQ ke-18 in Jambi, Kafila Irian Jaya, and the administration of IAIN Sultan Thaha Saifuddin, Jambi, for hospitality and assistance. I would also like to thank the TVRI and RRI stations and studio staff in Ujung Pandang as well as the radio station Al-Ikhwan, in Ujung Pandang. The women who met at Majelis Ta'lim Mappanyuki and Masjid "Al-Markaz Al-Islami" (Yayasan Islamic Center) were exceedingly kind and forthcoming. In Bone, I thank the faculty and staff of Pondok Pesantren "Mahadul Hadits." Also in Bone, I acknowledge the girls from Pondok Pesantren "Athira" as well as their teachers. The staff, teachers, and students at Masjid "Al-Markaz" have my heartfelt gratitude for their welcoming support, day in and day out.

Philip Bohlman, Frederick Denny, and Mark Woodward expertly and energetically provided ideas and guidance from the project's initial exploration stage to its completion in 1999 as the doctoral dissertation "An Envy of Goodness: Learning to Recite the Qur'an in Modern Indonesia." Their knowledge, support, and example have been indispensable, their understanding often undeserved, and I have taken far too much from each one of them. Frank Reynolds has been absolutely the finest mentor there ever was.

At the University of Chicago, I thank the Anthropology and Education Workshop for discussion. I would also like to express my gratitude to Wendy Doniger, Daniel Gold, Wadad Kadi, and Donald K. Swearer for enduring inspiration. At the Department of Near Eastern Studies and the Religious Studies Program at Cornell University, I thank my supportive colleagues; also at Cornell, my debt to the Southeast Asia Studies Program and particularly to John Wolff is long-standing. I would also like to thank Gary Ebersole, Howard Federspiel, Hendrik M. K. Maier, Michael Sells, Jonathan Z. Smith, and R. Anderson Sutton. I would never have gotten anywhere without the assistance of Richard Rosengarten, Sandy Norbeck, and Nelly Polhaupessy. Clarissa Burt, Pierre Cacchia, John Eisele, and Farouk Mustafa introduced me to the Arabic language and its appreciation, and I believe that the privilege of having been their student helped determine the choice to craft an entire research project around the project of how it feels to try to learn Arabic.

I also thank Niken Adisasmito, Robin Aronson, Alex Bardsley, William and Kiersty Cummings, Seemi Bushra Ghazi, Marion Katz, Noor Aiman Khan, Mulyadhi Kartanegara, Tariq Quadir, Omid Safi, Jonathan Wyn Schofer, and Bill Stratford. Greg Downey's many profound contributions are singular. I also thank R. Michael Feener and Paul R. Powers; their information, help, and humor have been an essential part of the project from start to finish. I know of no other way to express gratitude to the eminent reciter in Makassar who assisted so much in the research than to state: this book would not have been possible without his abundant expertise and insight. There are many others in Makassar not mentioned here but whom I hope know that they are always gratefully remembered. Among them, I owe a weighty debt to my host family.

The Department of Near Eastern Languages and Civilizations and the Middle East Studies Program at the University of Chicago facilitated and supported language study in Arabic. The Southeast Asian Studies Summer Institute (SEASSI) at the University of Washington in 1993 as well as Cornell University's Foreign Asian Language Concentration Program (FALCON) in 1994–1995 supported study in Bahasa Indonesia. The Committee on Southern Asian Studies (COSAS) at the University of Chicago provided support. Field research was carried out under a Fulbright fellowship to Indonesia in 1996–

1997. Research in Indonesia was undertaken with official sponsorship from IAIN Alauddin, Ujung Pandang (Makassar), and with formal permission from the Lembaga Ilmu Pengetahuan Indonesia (LIPI), for which I am grateful. The dissertation was completed under a Charlotte W. Newcombe Dissertation Fellowship in 1998–1999. Revisions were made with support of the Center for the Study of Religion at Princeton University in 1999–2000 as a part of the Thematic Project "Songs of the Spirit: World Traditions of Religions Chant."

At Princeton, I thank Ra'anan Abusch, Ramsey El-Assal, Peter Jeffery, Anita Kline, Simon M. Morrison, Robert Wuthnow, as well as a friend who also found her way to Oberlin, Deborah J. Schildkraut. Warm thanks to Michael Kodysz, Pablo Reid Mitchell, Paula Richman, James Dobbins, and the rest of the Religion Department at Oberlin. Kenneth M. George offered essential encouragement, and provided valuable comments on the manuscript. Many thanks to University of Hawai'i Press and especially to an outstanding, patient, and meticulous team: Cheri Dunn, Pamela Kelley, and Susan Stone. The two readers at the press were wonderfully informative and insightful with thorough and thoughtful comments on the manuscript, and I thank them. Any and all errors and omissions are entirely my own responsibility, and I apologize for them in advance.

Parts of chapter 2 on ritual experience of Qur'ānic structure and an overview of emotion theory were presented at the University of Chicago in 1996; material drawn from chapters 4 and 5 was presented at the American Academy of Religion (1997), Cornell University (1998), Middle East Studies Association (1999, along with the visit of Hj. Maria Ulfah to the United States), Princeton University (1999–2000), Yale University (2000), the University of Chicago Divinity School (2001), the University of Michigan at Ann Arbor (2001), the University of Wisconsin at Madison (2002), and elsewhere. I am grateful for feedback I received. Parts of this work have also been published in *History of Religions* as "Taste, Talent and the Problem of Internalization: A Qur'ānic Study in Religious Musicality from Southeast Asia" (2002) and in *Journal of Ritual Studies* as "Motivating Qur'ānic Practice in Indonesia by 'Competing in Goodness'" (forthcoming, 2004).

Finally, I thank my student-friends at Oberlin College, who carry forward a mission of committed "perfectionism" in higher education; they can't know how proud they make me or how much they they have given me by imagining that somehow this work might someday help *them* to explain the diversity of global religious systems to others. In that spirit, I dedicate this book to teachers: to my parents, both of whom devoted their careers to the practice and understanding of education; to my Indonesian host family, also a family of educators, who sincerely wished that through this work an English-speaking audience would appreciate Islam in Qur'ānic Indonesia; to the master teacher Frank Reynolds, who has coached more than one generation of historians of religions for conversation and collaboration; and, finally, to the inspired scholars and teachers with whom I have had the privilege to work in Indonesia and at Oberlin. I envy their example.

Note: Indonesian words of Arabic origin are transliterated from Bahasa Indonesia. The Arabic character ʻayn is indicated by a single open quote mark and the hamzah by an apostrophe. Informants are anonymous or are given pseudonyms in the text, except for names in published sources. All the institutional and place names are real. Photographs are by the author.

CHAPTER 1

INTRODUCTION

Practice and Perfection

THE STUDY OF the Arabic Qur'ān is the foundation of religious learning throughout the Islamic world, including Southeast Asia. The Muslim population of Indonesia alone is almost the same size as that of the Arabic-speaking Muslim world, and Indonesian Muslims comprise about a quarter of the 80 percent of Muslims worldwide who are not native Arabic speakers. In Indonesia in the mid-1990s, programs and projects of Islamic revitalization focused intensively on the recited Qur'ān, emphasizing participation in perfecting various modes of its reading. Overall, Indonesian Muslims are known worldwide for the depth of their piety in general and for heightened skill in reading the Qur'ān in particular. Evidence of this includes the international profile in the late 1990s of the woman reciter from Jakarta Dra. Hj. Maria Ulfah.[1] In Indonesia in the mid-1990s, a broad segment of the Muslim population enthusiastically pursued the improvement of vocal reading of the Qur'ān, representing a distinctive and energetic expression of a transnational phenomenon of "Islamic awakening." The trend enrolled active and enthusiastic participation from persons who were opting to become not only committed practitioners of reading and reciting the Qur'ān, but also its teachers and students. This book explains the ongoing and escalating aspects of Indonesian Qur'ānic piety in this period in terms of developmental religious processes and projects of learning and feeling among Muslim groups and individuals.

The widespread phenomenon of Qur'ānic learning and engagement was not limited to young people in Indonesia in the 1990s; it also included mature Muslims who labeled themselves as "learners." As part of a resurgent movement in the "fundamentals" of religious practice in Indonesia during the last months of Indonesia's "New Order" under former president Suharto, religiously oriented individuals actively adopted and promoted projects such as local and national Qur'ān recitation competitions, a widespread movement in "Qur'ān kindergartens," revitalized efforts to memorize the Qur'ān, and a lively women's mosque movement trained on the development of reading skills.[2] Qur'ān reading and the "Islamic arts" were a key focus of Islamist, nationalist, and developmentalist programs, blending with compatible goals such as mainstream Islamic "*da'wah*," or Muslim outreach. These projects of performance and education met with public and official support, although it would be a mistake to identify the movement as a top-down imposition of ideological interest. The affective and educative aspects of the system were subject to continuous feedback among individual projects of self-cultivation and the collective interests of community-building.

The emphasis of the Qur'ānic movement in Indonesia in the mid-1990s was on processes of enhanced learning, participation, and engagement. Even performances by experts in Indonesia primarily served as pedagogy, potentially for all. As a result, many Muslims were coming to pursue the standard of a world-class virtuoso as a model of ordinary piety. The phenomenon of performances doubling as pedagogy was especially apparent, for example, in broadcast media, which pervasively cast the recited Qur'ān as participatory and educational. Although there were recitation segments by trained performers aired on television and radio at designated times of the day, especially in locally taped spots broadcast during the month of Ramadan, recitation on the air was most often structured as a form of educational programming. The format of a wide variety of shows was a virtual learning space, and the representation of the very activity of learning itself was a critical aspect of teaching. The depiction of learning through voices and presences of virtual students on broadcast and cassette allowed real students at home to follow along with studio performers, teachers as well as their mock students.

For example, a call-in radio show for Qur'ān recitation in the city of research, Makassar, South Sulawesi, was not primarily construed as an opportunity to recite on the air. It was instead understood to be a forum for the presentation of Qur'ānic learning. The show "Bimbingan Tadarusan al-Qur'ān" was broadcast by Radio Al-Ikhwan (with the station identification "Voice of Moslem," after "Voice of America"), and a local Qur'ān kindergarten instructor was the host. When I first heard about the show, and even when I first listened to broadcasts, I assumed that the show was, for callers, chiefly an opportunity to be heard performing on the air (like a sort of ritual "open mike"). I was missing the expressed purpose of the activity for participants. As the show's title "Bimbingan" (Guidance) implies, this was not just an opportunity to be heard reciting on the radio, but, more important to those involved, the show was intended to provide listeners with the guidance of a teacher who would correct callers' recitational mistakes. On-air broadcast was explained by station directors to be incidental, practically expedient, to the actual purpose of the program. Callers gained access, producers explained, to a qualified teacher who assisted the entire listening audience through his corrections and comments. The call-in radio show was one of countless examples in Indonesia in the mid-1990s in which pedagogy was not for the sake of a final performance as much as performances were used as a form of pedagogy.

A widespread assumption in this period was that a desire to practice and to learn was a primary reason for Muslims to want to listen to performances of the recited Qur'ān. The dominant model of pedagogy and performance conveyed that not only were all kinds of voices supposed to participate in reading the Qur'ān aloud, but one ought to select the voice closest to one's own from among a group of surrogate participants in order to personalize and maximize efforts to improve. For example, when I first asked for cassettes of "recitation" *(pengajian)* at a local shop, the owner asked whether I wanted recitation by a woman or a man. As he did this, he was already reaching for Dra. Hj. Maria Ulfah's cassette recording of performed recitation, effectively answering his own question. He seemed to approach our exchange with the idea that I would be listening to the recited Qur'ān expressly in order to learn how to recite better myself and that, as a woman, I naturally would want to listen to and learn from another woman's voice. Cassette tapes that were explicitly geared toward learning, such as those distributed by a popular program for the memorization of the final *juz'*, or thirtieth, of the Qur'ān, as well as other "*hafalan*" (memorizational) material for children suggested a similar logic. One will learn best by listening to a member of one's own group *(golongan)*, in terms of gender as well as age; a child's voice would be heard on instructional materials for children, for example.

Sustained or escalating Qur'ānic piety within diverse Muslim religious domains in Indonesia in the 1990s used affect, or feeling, as both a strategy and a recognition of piety within projects of Muslim learning and community-building. Pious Muslims eagerly sought the sense of being "able to" engage the voiced Qur'ān correctly, beautifully, and better through the development of abilities such as reading from memory, vocalizing the text correctly according to normative rules and culture-bound assessments, reciting with standardized melody types based on the performances of nationally or world-renowned experts, and competing in all of these practices in events that were widely understood to be a program for further religious inspiration. Practitioners self-consciously aligned religious ideals with the particularities of practice within their projects of learning and feeling, and this occurred on both personal and social levels. When Indonesian Muslims studied forms of reciting the Qur'ān according to shared norms, they enhanced self-consciously a widespread affective dynamic of escalating engagement. These processes changed not only how Indonesian Muslims recited the Qur'ān, but also who they understood themselves to be. The result for many Muslims was an ongoing transformation of religious subjectivities into being and becoming ongoing Qur'ānic practitioners.

Piety is progressive, and repeated religious activity is necessarily a learning process over time, whether understood self-consciously as such or not. In Indonesia, individual and collective projects of acquiring, perfecting, and sustaining abilities related to reading the Qur'ān formed a widespread system of continuous motivated involvement. In different kinds of Qur'ānic projects, learners and practitioners initially took on the development of an objectified aptitude or named process, such as becoming or remaining "holders" of the Qur'ān in memory, applying a curriculum for learning how to vocalize the Qur'ān, or analyzing their own feelings during or about the performance of Qur'ān recitation itself. They subsequently applied strategies of affect that interacted with specifics of Qur'ānic practice as well as the shared norms of social systems. The ongoing nature of these projects was usually a given for practitioners who undertook or sustained them; the religious subjectivities that emerged as a result of these processes, however, were not always what had been envisioned at the outset. Often the involvement comprised a compelling pull that practitioners themselves may not have anticipated. Combining with social frameworks and technical and theological aspects of the recited Qur'ān, the process of the acquisition of enhanced Qur'ānic practical abilities within projects of self-cultivation led to an ongoing and sometimes even unexpected transformation of Qur'ānic practitioners.

Pious Muslims in Indonesia greatly valued the opportunities for self-improvement and contribution to community offered by the practice of the recited Qur'ān in the 1990s. Institutions and public programs (such as Qur'ān recitation contests) energetically promoted these goals, while individuals simultaneously applied personal projects to pursue enhanced Qur'ānic ability. Desired abilities took the form of the comprehension of the meanings of the Arabic text, the maintenance of parts of the Qur'ān that had already been memorized, the ability to make the ever-present choices in phrasing that are stipulated within the orthoprax rules of recitation *(tajwīd),* as well as mastery of the improvisatory system of melodic modes for recitation. Each of these practices engendered a motivation (Ind. *motivasi*) to enhance ability that the educationally oriented curricula, media, and practices of the recited Qur'ān in Indonesia in the 1990s shaped and amplified. During fieldwork, there were many instances in which a person attempted self-consciously to acquire a particular skill or ability, and found that the open-endedness of Qur'ānic practice offered new compelling horizons for potential competence and mastery.

For example, at an intensive training session for a corporate competition, I met an executive who said that he first undertook recitation study for competition in a markedly disinterested way. He said that he began to study recitation only in order to improve his employee profile for promotion (he had also taken up folk dance). He himself was amused at the irony, however, that after he began to study Qur'ān recitation, he became deeply involved with it (and he subsequently quit folk dancing). He found himself unable even to take a break from his recitation practice. He would hum the melodic modes he was studying when he was on his motorcycle to and from work, he said, and then also at work as well as at home, and he also found himself seeking out more places in which to study and practice. A horizon of possibility had opened up for him through discovery of the improvisatory and aesthetic dimensions of normative practice. The compelling project of acquiring competence in a ritual practice had become, as he said, "*ibadah*," a practice of religious piety. As predicted by the Qur'ān itself, such developmental "moods and motivations" of the recited Qur'ān cycled with sustained or intensifying force among individuals and within Qur'ānic communities in Indonesia in the 1990s; these affective dynamics of learning and practice generated escalating dynamics of ongoing religious engagement. A widespread movement of religious change in the world's most populous Muslim-majority nation was the result.

Energetic systems of Qur'ānic engagement in Indonesia in the 1990s were based on norms of person, practice, and piety. These determined the goals, structures, and methods of practice and performance, and also fueled their escalation. The overall phenomenon suggested that a large-scale movement of "Islamic revitalization" could be interpreted as the collective face of individuals pursuing such goals, their agency shaping social structure just as social systems reciprocally informed the context for practice. In addition, social and religious structures conveyed salient norms. Because authoritative religious structures and ideals could not possibly explicitly encompass everything one would want or need to know to practice piety in every situation or to improve technical expertise, however, such norms were also sought actively and developed directly within projects of learning and practice. In some cases the authority of such modes or models was understood to extend directly from the Qur'ān, sharing in an ontology of revelation; in other cases this legitimacy was seen to emerge from historically contingent and socially specific systems. Most norms were multiply determined: they were understood to be universal as well as emergent for practitioners within their specific trajectories of learning and repetition. As such, they were pragmatically approached and piously deployed.

This book analyzes how Indonesian Muslims exerted efforts self-consciously to develop and to enhance normative Qur'ānic abilities in dynamics of increasing or escalating engagement. Building on the recognition that learning is an aspect of all human activity and that religious practice in particular lends itself to long-term projects of self-cultivation, each of the book's chapters demonstrates affective patterns and proclivities that sustained or intensified long-term practices of piety, especially through modes of feeling. Qur'ānic performative and pedagogical pursuits and their affective dynamics generated all of the following in Indonesia in the 1990s: selves recognized for a practice explicitly characterized as being ongoing (chapter 2), Qur'ānic "learners" engaged with continuous study (chapter 3), discoverers of unrealized potential within open-ended projects of learning (chapter 4), and "motivated" subjects who self-consciously developed their own and others' motivations for Islamic practice (chapter 5).

The argument of each chapter is based on the study of one of four Qur'ānic practical abilities, with particular emphasis on how affect was deployed in direct engagement with the Qur'ān and in understandings of self with respect to processes of Qur'ānic learning, rehearsal, and repetition. Rather than attempting to unravel the tightly woven reciprocity of individual and social structure, each chapter considers the modes that sustain and compel such projects on individual and collective levels. Chapter 2 highlights social, cognitive, and especially affective aspects of Qur'ān memorization in terms of formal properties of the recited Qur'ān as well as strategies of feeling applied in social interaction in order to "manage" the moral demands of maintaining memory. Chapter 3 demonstrates how learning to read correctly generated new subjectivities for ongoing learners in reference to affective aspects of teaching curricula. The main argument of chapter 4 is that the attempt to recite the Qur'ān according to expansive norms for technical artistry, grounded in systems of feeling, made individual potential and increased competence self-conscious objects of cultivation. Finally, chapter 5, which presents influential tournaments in Qur'ānic practices, shows that in Indonesia in this period competing was a form of religious and educative practice, undertaken in the service of collective as well as individual interests; among the norms and standards that the competition system conveyed to Indonesian Muslims were affective strategies oriented toward enhancing "*motivasi*" for Qur'ānic practices in the self and among others. In each of these chapters, subjectivities of ongoing practice (which, naturally, reflect and refract social schemas) are shown to emerge through the affective dynamics of learning and repeated activity.

Qur'ānic Reading in Context

The ethnographic data for this book come primarily from the province of South Sulawesi (Ind. Sulawesi Selatan) and especially its capital city, Ujung Pandang (formerly known as Makassar and since the end of the New Order called Makassar once more). The size of the city (approximately one million inhabitants at the time of fieldwork) offered an opportunity to observe engagement with the Qur'ān on multiple educative levels and in a representative variety of institutional contexts. For example, regular visits over a period of ten months to the newly dedicated main mosque known as Masjid "Al-Markaz Al-Islami" (or Yayasan Islamic Center), which opened as a showcase to all of Indonesia in 1996, allowed me to observe Qur'ān recitation instruction and performance on a number of levels, from beginner to advanced. The observations of teaching and learning there, and elsewhere, point to social networks and interconnections among institutions, groups, and individuals that supported an energetic upsurge in Qur'ānic practice and education in the mid-1990s in South Sulawesi and also throughout Indonesia more generally.

The data represent linkages that connect Qur'ānic practices in Makassar to influences that originate elsewhere. With the exception of some modes of non-Qur'ānic Arabic recitation (described below), Islamic revitalization movements of Qur'ān reading in South Sulawesi were continuous with national and transnational networks, in contrast to and often disjunct from the distinctive local traditions of Bugis and Makassarese South Sulawesi. In portraying salient textual and social systems that cut across time and space in Muslim experience, I use the local context of South Sulawesi as the center to which other threads relate. I do not attempt to describe or compare the structure of Qur'ānic practices in other Islamicized areas of Southeast Asia such as Malaysia. Beginning in South Sulawesi, analysis considers networks that radiate out from this center: in space, to sites as near as Jakarta and as far as Mecca and Cairo; and, in time, spanning the recent past as well as the more distant past, including the thought and practice of the early Muslim Community, which Muslims of all historical periods have rendered a part of lived experience. Because the connections drawn sometimes mirror my own contacts and friendships, the picture naturally evidences chance, personal networks, and a Sulawesi-centric view. Ethnographic data from field research in Indonesia are supplemented by textual sources, including "classical" Arabic writings. Some of these materials are known in South Sulawesi (such as the writings of al-Ghazzālī, for example) and thus can be said to form a part of "Indonesian" or even "South Sulawesi" tradition.[3] Rather than emphasizing the political conditions of the "New Order" as an overarching interpretive frame, this work

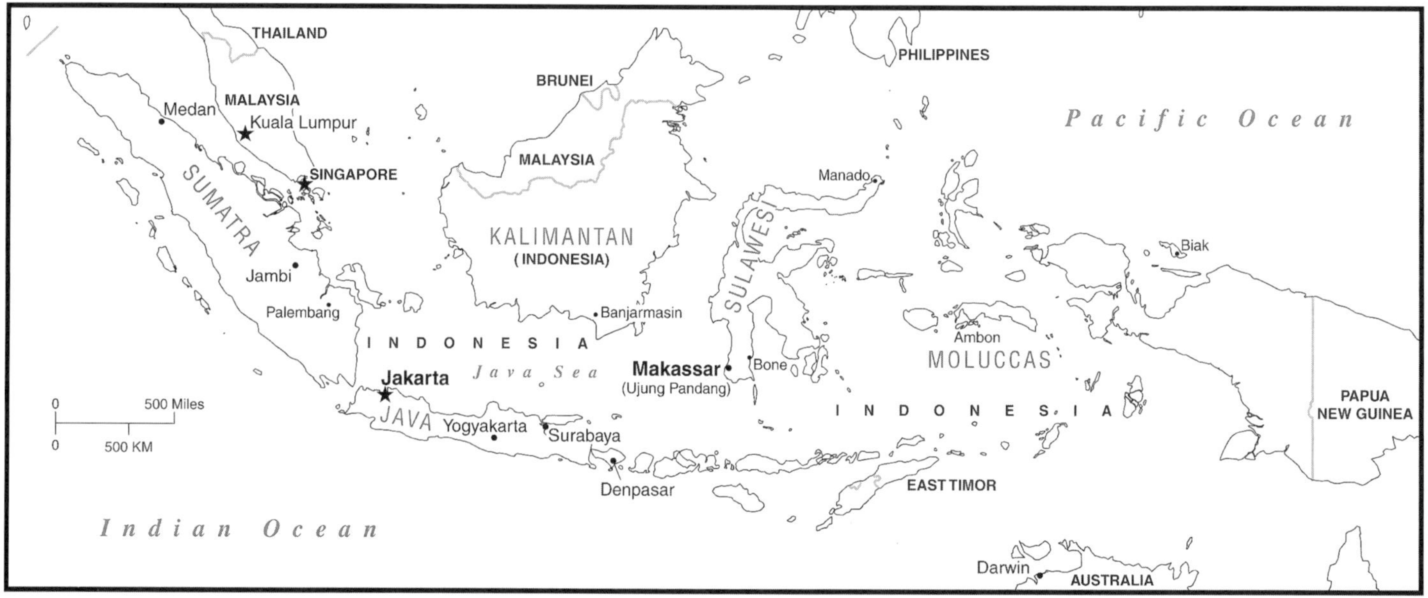

The Indonesian archipelago (Map by Michael Kodysz)

applies instead a method and approach that could explain Arabic-language practices in Indonesia by locating them within the larger continuities of the Islamic religious tradition.[4]

The primary linguistic and ethnic groups of South Sulawesi represented in the urban area of Makassar are Bugis and Makassarese, with a sizable Mandar and Torajan influence originating from northern areas. As it has been for centuries, Makassar is still said to be the "gateway" to the eastern archipelago. This is the case not only with respect to the movement of goods (such as spices from the eastern islands of Moluku moving west and south), but also for the dissemination of ideas. For example, during the time of the field research, the State Islamic University (Institut Agama Islam Negeri, or IAIN, on one of whose campuses I lived) was responsible for overseeing all of the smaller satellite campuses throughout the eastern archipelago. Many individuals who were influential in the systems of formal and informal Qur'ānic education in Makassar were not originally from Sulawesi but from elsewhere in the eastern archipelago (such as Bima, Ambon) or from Java, evidencing the translocal character of Islamic networks in the region in the present as well as the past.

The early Islamicized states of Gowa (ethnically Makassarese) and its Bugis rival across the peninsula in the region of Bone were important historical influences in the development of structures of power in the eastern archipelago.[5] Dutch policies in the later seventeenth century irrevocably changed their relations as well as their influence among their neighbors. A turning point was the treaty of 1669, in which the Bugis leader Arung Palakka, in alliance with the Dutch, overtook the Makassarese kingdom of Gowa, which was centered near present-day Makassar. The Bugis ethnic group is especially well known throughout the Indonesian archipelago as a maritime diaspora.[6] At times the outward-reaching aspects of South Sulawesi's historical tradition refracted back into the area; figures in the anti-Dutch resistance who were sent to South Sulawesi included the Javanese Prince Diponogoro, famous for his leadership in the Java War of the nineteenth century, as well as the celebrated figure from Makassar Sheikh Yusuf, to whom is credited, among other things, the Islamization of South Africa during his period of exile there.[7]

In the twentieth century, a pattern of resistance to centralized control from outside the island continued to be associated with the area, particularly in the case of a rebellion against postcolonial federal governance. Under the insurrection led by Kahar Muzakkar starting in the 1950s, South Sulawesi came under an Islamist government that, like counterparts in West Java and Aceh (north Sumatra), claimed to be an "Islamic state" under the Darul Islam movement. This period lasted from 1950 to 1965, with parts of South Sulawesi coming under the political control of the movement from the mid-1950s to the mid-1960s.[8] Eventually, the central administration in Jakarta brought South Sulawesi back under its political and military jurisdiction. South Sulawesi is famous throughout Indonesia for its traditions of committed Islamic piety (along with, the visitor is often told, its hot weather, shipbuilding, and tasty fish). As is announced at every national Qur'ān recitation competition, the first Qur'ān recitation competition called "national" was held in 1968 in Makassar.

Qur'ān recitation always occurs within a context, and to describe the recited Qur'ān in modern Indonesia in terms of overly idealized performances dislocates it from realities of lived, historical systems and may distort the experience and everyday activities of lived practice. As is the case throughout the Muslim-majority and Muslim-minority worlds, the most common context for Qur'ān recitation in Indonesian Muslims' lifeworlds is not the appreciation of heightened performance styles such as those heard on recordings of highly trained *qāri*'s (reciters) but the daily situated recitation performed multiple times within each canonical act of worship *(ṣalāt)*. Although *ṣalāt* is often performed alone, when following the recommendation to pray with others, an *imām* (prayer leader) may recite for the entire group. This requirement guarantees that all practicing Muslims will have memorized at least some of the Qur'ān.

During Ramadan, standard daily worship is enhanced and amplified, as more people attend mosques (hundreds, for example, come for morning and evening prayers at Masjid "Al-Markaz"), and supererogatory worship often follows canonical prayers. During Ramadan, an evening prayer cycle called "*tarāwīḥ*" (Ind. *tarwih*) is observed in which the entire Qur'ān is read through over the course of the month. *Tarwih* imams must have memorized the Qur'ān in order to lead the prayers, in which a *juz'* (one-thirtieth of the Qur'ān) is read each night. *Tarwih* prayers are held at mosques in Indonesia as well as in homes. There was, for example, a "*tarwih keliling*," or "traveling *tarwih*," that moved from house to house among a circle of associates of the family with whom I lived; the night it was at my house, a preacher *(penceramah)* also came to speak to the crowd assembled in the living room. Every night during Ramadan, the *tarwih* prayers from Mecca were also broadcast live on television. Especially in the last days of Ramadan, some observed the Islamic tradition of staying in the mosque all night. The city's main mosque, Al-Markaz, was busy with Ramadan celebrants who rested on blankets, rugs, and mats in the cool, quiet building. Men and women read the Qur'ān and other religious texts all night long; they snacked, chatted, and napped but were mostly quiet with their own thoughts until crowds began to gather in and around the mosque for the busy dawn prayer.

Non-Qur'ānic Islamic performances were another context for performances of Arabic-language piety in South Sulawesi. In Indonesia in the mid-1990s, systems of religious performance in the Arabic language, not just the recitation of the Qur'ān itself, were shifting and evolving along with Muslim recitation traditions in Indonesian languages. This was especially the case with devotional readings dedicated to the Prophet Muḥammad (which have been heatedly controversial at times, including in Indonesia).[9] These non-Qur'ānic Arabic-language texts were often read communally, highlighting the participatory and social aspects of Arabic-language piety. Such texts have been commonly recited in "*dhikr*" observances and on life-cycle celebrations such as circumcisions, occasions that mark that a young person has "*tammat*" (completed a first reading of all or part of the Qur'ān), weddings, departures for Hajj, as well as holidays such as the Birthday of the Prophet (Mawlid al-Nabī) and the commemoration of the Isrā' and the Mi'rāj (the Prophet's "Night Journey" and "Ascent"). In addition, these texts may be recited in the home, especially on a Thursday night at any time of the year.

Many of these devotional texts comprised praise of the Prophet, often based on *sīrah* (hagiographical) literature, and, dating back to the early period of Islam, they have variants throughout the Islamic world. One of the best known, and earliest to appear in the Malay-speaking world, is the "Burdah" or "Mantle Ode" of the Egyptian al-Busīrī (thirteenth century). In the early nineteenth century, a cycle composed in the previous century known popularly as the "Barzanji" (which includes texts in the "Mawlid al-Nabi," or "Birth of the Prophet," cycle) came to Southeast Asia and became one of the most popular texts for recitations after that time.[10] Both archival and ethnographic evidence point to the fact that the Barzanji tradition has been especially popular in the Muslim religious history of eastern Indonesia, including South Sulawesi. Like other "Mawlid" texts, it narrates events in the Prophet's life (especially his birth), and it also includes sections of praise. In contemporary Indonesia, several readings are often found bound together as a single "Barzanji" text: "Mawlid Diba'ī," the Barzanji (of several variants), "Sharif al-'Anām," and the "Burdah."[11] The texts are sometimes rendered into local languages (such as Makassarese or Buginese), and Arabic-language variants are identified in terms of the influence of regional and vernacular versions.

The texts are almost always recited by a group in monophonic unison, often under the direction of a leader, with reading alternating between soloist and group. Leaders may choose selectively which sections to read and may also extend the reading of some sections, such as praise of God, into a *dhikr*-like performance. Instrumentation, when used, consists of membranophones such as tambourines and drums. There are regional variants to Barzanji practices, in terms of the melodies used and the relative participation of men and women.

In Ambon (Moluku), for example, there was said to have been special instruction in the Barzanji (for men and women), and persons of both genders would recite together at observances; elsewhere in Indonesia this has not been the case. The melodic structures for Barzanji reading are also sometimes taught in semiformal instruction, and in areas such as central Java there were known to be several named melodic variants. Readings in Sumatra, Java, and Sulawesi were different in their musical and performative qualities. Even readings in the city of Makassar showed great variation; a performance by a semiprofessional troupe from Banjarmasin at a housewarming contrasted significantly with a reading in the home of a *kiai* (religious teacher) whose relative was away on Hajj, for example.

When recited in Arabic, there is a strong vernacular flavor to the style of reading these texts, unlike the recited Qur'ān, and within South Sulawesi during my fieldwork the differences between the recitations of Bugis and Makassarese readers were apparent. This is an expected aspect of the style of these non-Qur'ānic Arabic performances. A self-conscious deployment of regional style and language was especially clear, for example, at a special observance at the old royal palace of the Makassarese kings of Gowa (Ballalampoa) dedicated to reading a text in the cycle.[12] Before the performance, the sister of the last king of Gowa lit incense and invited ancestral spirits to bless bananas that were distributed to the group after the occasion; when reciting, the soloist read from one text mounted on a pillow, while others joined in ensemble portions of the reading, holding saucers over their mouths during the two-hour event. The Makassar-language influence on the Arabic text and a stylized form of reading were so elaborated that the recitation was virtually unrecognizable as Arabic. Remarkably, the performers at Ballalampoa erased such vernacular influences when reciting the Qur'ān at the end of the performance, indicating a self-consciousness about registers of vernacularization of the articulation of Arabic sound depending on what text was being recited.

On a performative as well as an ontological level, there are clear distinctions between Arabic-language texts that Indonesians recited and the recited Qur'ān, as well as particular ways that Indonesians construed these continuities and contrasts.[13] When discussing the difference in situated terms (rather than theologically), Indonesians usually compared the modes of learning the devotional readings with the normative pedagogy for learning to read the Qur'ān. While they are often exposed to both kinds of Arabic-language readings from an early age, the method of acquisition of competence in devotional readings resembles what Jean Lave has termed "legitimate peripheral participation" (rather than formal schooling).[14] A statement made by a respected educator summarizes perceptions of difference based on learning and expectations of established orthopraxy; when clarifying the distinction of Qur'ānic and non-Qur'ānic recitation, he began by explaining that, in reading the Barzanji (unlike reciting the Qur'ān), one does not have to apply the Qur'ānic rules of *tajwīd* for vocalization, and when people make mistakes, they are not corrected (as they must be in the Qur'ānic case).

Both Qur'ānic and non-Qur'ānic Arabic religious performance were promoted as part of the revitalization in Islamic piety in Indonesia the 1980s and 1990s. Performances of Arabic-language devotional texts were undergoing an upsurge in interest, evidenced in new media for their performance (such as competitions and television broadcast). The passing away of the first lady, Madame Ibu Thien, in 1996 added to what was already an energetic movement in reading Arabic-language texts. Her "*tahlil*" funerary observances were the focus of national attention for a full year. Copies of Sūrat 36 Yā Sīn along with standard prayers for the dead were in great supply in book shops. The religious observance on the anniversary of her death was broadcast nationally on every television station, showing the president with his family members and cabinet wearing simple clothes as they recited on television under the direction of a *shaikh*. The standard texts for this sort of recitation provide each line of Arabic text with interlinear romanized transliteration and Indonesian translation, greatly assisting those whose confidence or competence is not yet complete. Not surprisingly, the sudden requirement placed on government officials to recite Arabic publicly was noted with some sympathetic irony by Muslim intellectuals and educators.

Diverse religious influences in this period rendered the recited Qur'ān increasingly developed and standardized in terms of its pedagogy and popularity, leading to the disappearance of some local styles of recitation. At the same time, however, there was also a reappearance of other "traditional" Muslim practices, such as the recitation of devotional readings in Arabic that valorized localness and regionalism. Until the early 1990s, for example, it seemed to many that Barzanji recitation was dying out across the archipelago. However, by the mid-1990s, a Barzanji revival was actually under way (surprising even many Barzanji readers themselves). A prominent *kiai* (religious scholar and teacher) in Makassar who ran a special *pesantren* (Islamic school) for Qur'ānic memorization and study still led a Barzanji group, as he had for decades, while at the same time a new phenomenon began in which champion Qur'ān reciters from the region increasingly rehearsed and performed Barzanji at public events. Cassettes were beginning to appear, to the expressed amazement of some who had never associated the "traditional" context of Barzanji reading with a commodity like a cassette. Barzanji reading had come to be included among the required activities at one of the Qur'ānic institutes in Jakarta, and it was not unusual for Qur'ān recitation teachers working with beginning and intermediate-level readers in popular new study circles to teach "Salawat Nabi" ("Prayers on the Prophet," including also devotional songs such as the famous "Tolal Al-Badru") and the Barzanji, along with Egyptian-inspired religious songs, or "*qasida*," to their classes. When I was in Makassar, a local businessman paid for soccer tickets for such a group of older women who attended Qur'ān reading groups so that they could go to the game and recite prayers on the Prophet in the stands (in order to support the home team, it was explained)—and the only controversy I heard was that the husbands complained they didn't get tickets to see the game too. In general, in the Muslim public culture of the late New Order years, such devotional reading was becoming increasingly accepted and, in many contexts of "Islamic" performance, expected.

An example of the upsurge in new interest in reading Arabic-language religious texts and hearing them read was a Barzanji-reading contest sponsored by a South Sulawesi corporation in 1996. In contrast to the national Qur'ān-reciting tournament, which tended to have a minimizing effect on the diversity of regional expression, the revival of the reading of Arabic-language Barzanji was being explicitly promoted at the contest as an appreciation of the range of regional variation (all within one province). For example, the organizers of this competition stated that they intended to add to the Barzanji event the following year a required translation of the reading into any one of the four principal regional languages (i.e., Bahasa Bugis, Bahasa Makassar, Bahasa Mandar, and Bahasa "Tator" [Tana Toraja]). Whether the end result was the promotion or the diminishment of local variations in practice (or both), competition practices were having powerful effects on Qur'ānic and non-Qur'ānic Arabic-language recitation in South Sulawesi.

Another popularizing mode of the resurgence of Arabic-language devotional reading, song, and piety was performances broadcast during Ramadan. These were usually some form of a group reading of religious songs, with characteristic lighting and staging effects. An example was a "TV Takbir" broadcast from the capital on the eve of "'Idul Fitri" (Hari Raya) at the end of Ramadan in 1997, which was attended by the president and his family as spectator-stars of the show. It featured performances by the great *dangdut* (Muslim pop music) and movie star Rhoma Irama as well as the well-known and respected poet and performer Emha Ainun Najib, whose not-for-profit album *Kado Muhammad* was being circulated widely among Muslim youth at the time. This program's dramatic structure highlighted emotional modulation in its musicality and "stadium rock" smoke and lighting effects in its staging. The material drew on revitalized aspects of Indonesian performance traditions, such as excerpts from the Barzanji and "Salawat Nabi" genre known across the Muslim world, chanting and singing by students from the flagship Qur'ān institute in Jakarta (Institut Pengembangan Tilawah dan Ilmu Al-Quran, or PTIQ), the drumming characteristic of 'Idul Fitri celebrations across Indonesia, plaintive wept speech by a female vocalist imploring God's mercy, and accompaniment by a Javanese gamelan ensemble. Viewers in Makassar (those who stayed home rather than attending the great float parade in the main square or joining in the drumming and chanting of "Takbir" celebrations at mosques) enjoyed identifying the excerpts of devotional chants in the broadcast, such as the ever-recapitulating "Salawat Nabi"; everybody in my house that night was singing along. Other performances broadcast nationally in Ramadan 1997 included Barzanji groups from Jakarta, although nothing matched the spectacular production effects of "TV Takbir."

On the campus of the Islamic university where I lived, the tambourines and drums from the Fakultas Dakwah departmental building reverberated through quiet afternoons, and I would occasionally come across groups of students sitting informally in classrooms, practicing songs for performance rehearsal or just for fun. At the city's Qur'ān college, the advanced Qur'ān readers who competed at national competitions would spend hours practicing *programs* in devotional readings, Barzanji as well as arrangements of the recited Qur'ān that were to be performed at public and private occasions in mosques, homes, the residence of the provincial governor, and elsewhere. At rehearsals, key criteria for composition and arrangement included aesthetic balances of "high and low" and male and female voices as well as the expressive dynamics of soloist-group modulation. An example of this kind of performance was the great celebration at the Department of Motor Vehicles in Makassar on the occasion of the bureau having achieved its annual revenue goals. There, the performing group from the local Qur'ān college (some of the best regional talent at the national level and one international champion reciter) wore special yellow attire (signifying the Golkar party of former president Suharto) and sat in a special room that was designated for "Islamic" performance (in distinction to other parts of the complex, which featured marching bands and local "traditional" dance).[15] They had rehearsed the program of "Salawat Nabi" in advance, and discussions in these rehearsals included the question of timing the musical climax with the official entrance of the provincial governor into the space.

The recited Qur'ān was embedded within such contexts of revitalized Islamic piety, which included the reading of many Arabic-language texts. The Qur'ān was, however, always recognized to be a religiously and ontologically unique performance. The recited Qur'ān and other Arabic-language religious performances were readily combined in new modes of performance in Muslim

Indonesia in this period. Muslims elaborated programs in these kinds of performances not primarily because of their shared linguistic and cultural basis as "Arabic" or "Arab," although they were certainly valorized on these grounds, but more significantly because of an embracing recognition of the accessibility and effectiveness of such modes of participatory piety for individual and collective projects of *da'wah*.

Global Qur'ānic Revitalization and Mainstream Qur'ānic *Da'wah* in Indonesia

"*Da'wah*" is a Qur'ānic term interpreted and applied in different ways in different global contexts and even in Indonesia itself. Most basically, the term means a "call" to deepen one's own or encourage others' Islamic piety; it has been a crucial concept in the historical propagation of the Islamic religious tradition and especially for certain historical traditions. It is also one of the more misunderstood categories in the contemporary academic study of Islam because of its wide range of connotations as well as its differing theory and practice in diverse parts of the Muslim-majority and Muslim-minority worlds. In Indonesia during the New Order, mainstream *da'wah* was understood to be an "invitation" to voluntary Islamic piety issued only to Muslims and not to other faith communities.[16] This was consistent with the policy of the Ministry of Religious Affairs in much of the 1980s and 1990s, which was to promote ideals of religious pluralism among faith communities as a part of mainstream Islamic *da'wah*. This approach emphasized the Qur'anic value of "*li'ta'ārifū*," derived from 49 al-Ḥujurāt 13, which expresses the idea that differing groups have been placed on earth in order to "get to know one another" and, by extension, to vie in their good works, in a context of human and religious pluralism.

The work of K. H. Zainuddin M.Z., an orator of undisputed star status in Indonesia, could be seen to be paradigmatic of the popular attitudes and popularizing aspects of mainstream Indonesian Islamic *da'wah* in this period. His book (the title of which translates as "Secrets to the Success of K. H. Zainuddin M.Z.'s *Dakwah*") surveys uses of the term "*da'wah*" (Ind. *dakwah*) in Qur'ān and *ḥadīth* material before it offers no less than six distinctively Indonesian definitions of "*dakwah*." Each of these conforms to the mainstream, nationalist, and pluralist Pancasila ideology of the time. Deploying categories of "general" and "specific" application, common to the logic of the Qur'ānic sciences, these definitions divide the concept "*dakwah*" into its "restricted" form (for within Islam) and its "open" form (for all of humanity). *Da'wah*, according to this framework, carries the basic meaning of persuading people to commit to Islamic values and, by extension, to the improvement of the human condition.

The latter reflects developmentalist and nationalist goals that both Muslim and non-Muslim Indonesians were expected to share in this period.[17]

Another kind of conceptualization of the goals of *da'wah*, such as that emphasized in the curriculum of *da'wah* programs in state-run Islamic universities (IAINs), is more instrumental than ideational in its focus. The programmatic statement that follows, typical of this curriculum, is characteristically straightforward; also characteristic is that *da'wah* is conceptualized as a means to a goal, constituted in terms of its final ends:

1. Overall Objective (Major Goal). The first objective of *dakwah* is the final value/result that is intended or applied by each [successive] step of *dakwah*. In order to reach this goal, every arrangement and action must be aimed and directed toward it. The first goal of *dakwah* is to realize well-being and prosperity for human existence in this world and the next, as bestowed by God.
2. Administrative Objective (Minor Goal). The administrative [departmental] objective of *dakwah* is to give shape to the goals of the agent [*perantara*, lit. "intermediary"]. For the agent, the goal at its very basis is none other than the [moral] values that can bring about well-being and prosperity that are bestowed by God, each [value] in accordance with the area or part *(segi atau bidang)* of life being developed. For example, well-being and prosperity in the field of education is marked by the readiness of adequate resources *(sarana)* and administration of the educational system in order to shape a pious people *(manusia bertakwa)*. In the area of religious social organizations, it is marked by the existence of religious activities, such as religious lectures and instruction [*pengajian*, a term also denoting "Qur'ān recitation"], based on piety *(taqwa)* toward God.[18]

The circularity of the statement (the overall goal of *da'wah* is defined as that which each particular strategy of *da'wah* attempts to achieve) casts *da'wah* activities as absolutely instrumental: means are dominated (and certainly justified) by their ends. This logic supported an enormous creativity in mainstream Indonesian *da'wah* in the New Order years as well as an Indonesian emphasis on the appreciation of beauty and enjoyable activities as the most effective means to "motivate" *(memotivasikan)* people to deepen mainstream Muslim piety.

Aesthetics and performance have been primary modes by which Indonesian Muslims have approached the project of contemporary mainstream *da'wah*. An example of a *da'wah* performance that was presented explicitly as such is the play staged by the group El Bitrul at the 1997 National Qur'ān Recitation Contest (Musabaqah Tilawatil Quran or MTQ). The group was a part of the national oil company's Badan Dakwah Islam Unit Korpri Pertamina. The performance was titled "Taubah"; possible English translations could be "Repentance" or "Change of Heart," but neither captures the profound Qur'ānic, Islamic revivalist, and Sufi overtones of the term. It was a morality play about a pious blind singer and the drunken sinner she reformed, and it included production numbers in the *tarian massal* choerographical genre as well as dazzling stage effects. A glossy printed program introduces the performance in terms of its *da'wah:*

> This stage presentation is always [intended to be] related to the cultivation and development of the people of Indonesia as a unity. The development that is occurring at this time does not only take the form of media and projects in the physical sense but is also the development of humanity itself, that is, *spiritual* development. With this artistic performance, we may carry out *dakwah* and introduce elements of spiritual *(spiritual dan rohani)* life into the forms of *drama*, song, and dance. This presentation is centered not only on the arts *(seni)* that appear but even more intensely on the content conveyed within it. Because most of the performers are (male and female) employees of Pertamina [the national oil company], we are aware that the work and its performance are still in progress at this time, and for this we "*mohon maaf*" [ask for your forgiveness].[19]

This statement suggests that, within the outer form of the presentation, there is held *(terkandung)* a hidden, pure essence. As long as this essence remains pure and protected, it is implied, the material form *(rupa)* of the effort *(upaya)* applied is actually immaterial. Aesthetic means, including Qur'ānic frameworks like competitions, could be seen to collapse into ends in the mainstream Indonesian logic of *dakwah* in the mid-1990s. Among other effects, one result of this logic was the erasure of possible objections to some media of *da'wah* (such as musical theater) just as long as the ultimate ends were deemed appropriate and desirable.

Instrumentality was at the core of discussions over other modes of Islamic piety, embracing not just new forms of for *da'wah* but also "traditional" practices that had first propagated Islam in the archipelago. Performances such as the public reading of Barzanji texts or "Mawlid al-Nabi" had been controversial earlier in the century, along with gravesite commemoration *(tahlil)* and other observances, coming under attack by Muslim modernists in Indonesia as well as reformers elsewhere in the Muslim world. An idea underlying these social and legal disputes was criticism of the potentially confused instrumental goals that might be motivating activity (in Islamic terminology, the "*niyya*" or intent by which actions are assessed) as well as questionable implied notions of spiritual agency.[20] With the ends recast, however, the means were resurfacing in Indonesia in the 1990s, as in the case of the Barzanji revival. When discussing the occasions of reading the Barzanji, one modernist, prominent educator and university administrator, and member of the "modernist" Muhammadiyya organization made an offhand comment that perhaps he himself should hold a Barzanji reading in his home. He explained that where he came from in the eastern archipelago, such a reading that was not associated with a specific life-passage event would be said to be for the sake of "venerating the ancestors' spirits, or suchlike"; this one, he went on, would be said just to be "for the benefit of Muslims everywhere." Implied was that there was no problem with a Barzanji reading in itself, only a potential problem in intention and potential ends—who or what it was said to be for. The means-ends logic of mainstream Indonesian *da'wah* in the mid-1990s was critical for the acceptance of practices, such as competitions, that might otherwise have been controversial.[21]

At the forefront of reinvigorated Indonesian *da'wah* projects was often the appreciation of aesthetic features of religious practice, referred to as "arts with an Islamic flavor" *(kesenian yang bernafaskan Islam)*. While a range of practices and performances had come potentially to be understood as *da'wah*, occurring in similar settings and with the same performers or agents, the routes by which non-Qur'ānic practices and Qur'ān recitation activities (such as competitions) had become a part of mainstream Islam in Indonesia had differed. Similarly, the imagined reach and scope of Qur'ānic and non-Qur'ānic *da'wah* efforts differed, from local to national spheres and beyond. The logic underlying the acceptance of Qur'ān recitation competitions, for example—while sharing in the "aesthetic" framework—went beyond appreciation or expression of regional identity as emblematically Muslim or as a part of Indonesian collective nationhood. Contests resonated more deeply with a framework of piety located within what was imagined to be a "globalized" (a key term in New Order rhetoric in the late 1990s was "*globilisasi*") and universal Islamic Message.

The mainstream conceptualization of promoting Islamic *da'wah* in Indonesia was increasingly expanding toward ideals of internationalization in 1996–1997 (on the eve of the sweeping social change Indonesia was to experience within a year). A pivotal event in the development of mainstream Qur'ānic revitalization in the later New Order years was the "Festival Istiqlal," held for one month in Jakarta in 1991; it was aimed at representing and celebrating the "Islamic culture" of Indonesia. As one English-language source published by the Ministry of Religious Affairs explains, "Different from the World of Islam Festival in London April–October 1976, which showed Islamic culture in Middle East region and exhibition moving artefact from museum,

Istiqlal Festival pointed out daily activity and art performa which have Islamic value from entire Indonesia region" *[sic]*.[22] This statement puts the festival in the context of an international event, while also demonstrating the value of representing "unity and diversity" in Indonesian (Muslim) "culture." One of the main attractions of the festival activities was the project of the great *muṣḥaf* (written text) of the Qur'ān, purportedly the largest in the world (it was completed in 1995, with "Festival Istiqlal II"), in addition to a magnificent illuminated *muṣḥaf* known as the "Mushaf Istiqlal."[23] There were also exhibitions of Islamic calligraphy, decorative arts (especially textiles), and mosque architecture, Qur'āns from all over the world, as well as performances (representing "regional culture" with "Islamic value") that included a competition in *ādhān* (call to prayer) for children and youth and a calligraphy contest open to all ages. Another highlight was an "Intellectual Forum" the official theme of which was "Islam and Indonesian Culture: The Past, the Present, and the Future," with topics subdivided according to the headings "Aesthetic Expression in Islam in Indonesia," "Islamic Tradition and Innovation in Indonesian Culture," and "Islam and the Future of World Civilization."[24] The festival promoted the idea of Indonesian Islam as a showcase to the world, especially in terms of its Qur'ānic visual arts.

The Indonesian movement to represent Islamic practice on a massive scale in this period featured especially the Qur'ān and its recitation. In early 1997, for example, the latest exhibit was inaugurated at Taman Mini Indonesia Indah, the amusement park outside Jakarta that is known for its Disney-like "*fantasi*" castle and the scale model of the Borobudur Buddhist monument. Another of Madame Ibu Thien's projects, the last before she passed away, the Baitul Quran (House of the Qur'ān) shows an overwhelming maximalization of scale, reversing the "miniaturization" of "beautiful Indonesia" that John Pemberton describes in his article on Taman Mini.[25] If the immensity of Indonesia's culture-scape is shrunk to an individual scale in the park's other exhibits, the Baitul Quran blows up representation of text and individual practice to epic dimensions.

As one enters the Baitul Quran, whose roof is a gigantic model of a Qur'ān recitation stand (so that, it was said, Hajjis traveling to and from the Middle East via Jakarta's international airport would see it as they passed overhead), one is immediately confronted with what is reputedly the biggest *muṣḥaf*, or Qur'ān text, in the world and the one featured at Festival Istiqlal II (made at a *pesantren* in Wonosobo, Central Java). There is also a giant video screen showing a Qur'ān recitation class in progress, the booming sounds of more children reciting on the sound system, and, further inside, halls full of huge reproductions of Qur'ān pages. The illuminated pages are from the "Mushaf Sundawi" (which had a float and special booth at the fair at the 1997 National Recitation Contest, or MTQ); designers, calligraphers, and artists from West Java used indigenous motifs inspired by regional flora and local textiles.[26] The exhibit within an adjoining hall, called the Museum Istiqlal, houses the Qur'ānic and Islamic texts from all over the world that had been displayed at the festivals in previous years. A museum official explained that the planners of these exhibits wanted there to be an example of a House of the Qur'ān of massive proportions to suggest to visitors that all Muslim houses are potentially "houses of the Qur'ān" and that the Qur'ān should always be cared for at home just as it is in the park's exhibit.

The enhancement of Qur'ānic practice in Indonesia as a form of *da'wah* in the 1990s was increasingly linked to an educational discourse that drew on aesthetics; local, national, and global identity; Muslim personal piety; the improvement of collective moral character; and other ideals. *Da'wah* efforts related to the recited Qur'ān comprised a new kind of educational movement that was sweeping Muslim Indonesia, as shown by the enthusiastic growth of semiformal settings for Qur'ān reading education that were to be found in or near almost any urban block. Educational institutions, including special training institutes for memorizers and new "Qur'ān kindergartens," were proliferating rapidly in the 1990s. Recitation competitions, too, were viewed as a form

Exterior of Baitul Quran in the amusement park Taman Mini Indonesia Indah, Jakarta

of religious education within a wide variety of institutions and programs. I observed, for example, Qur'ān recitation competitions in settings as diverse as a corporate headquarters of the national communications company, a prison, several schools and ladies' clubs, mosques, and, finally, the annual MTQ, a weeklong event with national attention in July 1997. In all of these settings, promotional and participatory rhetoric linked competing in the recited Qur'ān to personal, social, and institutional edification and improvement.

The increasing popularity of Qur'ān reciting and recitation contests and, since 1977, their promotion by the LPTQ (Lembaga Pengembangan Tilawatil Quran or Institute for the Development of the Recitation of the Qur'ān) and other organizations contributed to an explosion of interest, and new media and techniques, for the study and appreciation of the recited Qur'ān. Recitation tournaments had come to be viewed by many in Indonesia as an avenue for "*syi'ar Islam*," or the propagation and deepening of Islamic practice through an appreciation of Qur'ānic knowledge and ability, as well as an avenue for the expression of distinctive aspects of Indonesian Islamic piety within the context of the global Muslim community. Competitions, as *syi'ar Islam*, were understood to be simultaneously a form of education and an invitation to Muslim practice. Contests, especially the MTQ, also had far-reaching effects in shaping the way that recitation was studied and evaluated in modern Indonesia for practically all dimensions of practice and levels of ability by way of the dissemination of preparatory materials through cassette tapes and broadcast technology.

The MTQ, featuring various competitional and noncompetitional events, highlighted especially performances in "melodic" recitation in a virtuosic style known in Egypt as "*mujawwad*" and in Indonesia as "*tilawah*." In the Muslim-majority and Muslim-minority worlds of Islam in the late twentieth century, Egyptian reciters (many of whom trained in classical Arabic music) were the most influential; the recitation recordings of a handful of Egyptian reciters became the models for reciters globally. In the 1960s and 1970s, the Egyptian government, with official Indonesian support, sponsored many of the most renowned Egyptian reciters to come to Indonesia to teach and perform. Their methods and techniques were prevalent at the time of research, although they had also been transformed by Indonesian reception. In Indonesia in the mid-1990s, virtuosic readings in the *mujawwad* style were not appreciated most intensively for inducing heightened experiential states but for the tendency of listeners to attempt actively and effortfully to emulate those very performances. In Indonesia, expert performances from the Arab world and by Indonesians doubled as pedagogy for ordinary practitioners, disseminated and mediated by competition frameworks and other programs and interests, both individual and collective. Under these educationally oriented influences, a great variety of material—including the recordings of great Egyptian reciters—became in Indonesia educational "*kurikulum*."

The educational trend in Qur'ān recitation resonated with Indonesian social and cultural patterns of many types. It elaborated, for example, a characteristic valorization of group "participation" that had a distinctive form in Indonesia. It also included the valuation of self-improvement through supererogatory piety, which was strengthened by long-standing traditions of Sufi-oriented devotional piety in the archipelago. The key idea of "education" for the moral and material improvement of society (a critical aspect of colonial policy under the Dutch in earlier times as well as an ideology enthusiastically promoted throughout the New Order in the name of "national development") combined with the gravity of the traditions of education and the ideals of the search for knowledge that are central to the Islamic religious tradition. These influences, regional and transnational, old and new, formed a constellation of educational values and experiences around the recited Qur'ān in South Sulawesi and greater Muslim Indonesia in the context of global Islamic religious revitalization.

As the experience of recitation changed in modern Indonesia in the late twentieth century owing to diverse influences, a new prominence of Qur'ān recitation affected Indonesian reciters and memorizers of the Qur'ān. Many Muslims in Indonesia self-consciously promoted Qur'ānic practice (rather than other religious activities that are less Qur'ān-focused or practice-oriented) specifically as a form of *da'wah*, recognizing the power of the Qur'ānic practices to fascinate, engage, and transform religious subjectivities. The key idea of *syiar Islam* (the "glorification of Islam") conveyed a compelling power to invite other Muslims to participate in Qur'ānic piety. Indonesian strategies of Qur'ānic *da'wah*, such as recitation competitions, were elaborations on pre-existing religious, Qur'ānic, and psychological dynamics. The educational aspect of recitation practice also made Qur'ān recitation appealing to those who had compatible nationalist, developmentalist, or otherwise instrumental commitments. It would be no more true, however, to say that these interests had "appropriated" the Qur'ān than to say that these interests, eager to align with widening circles of power in any form, became susceptible to and ultimately were themselves "appropriated" by a powerful Qur'ānic system.[27]

The Recitation of the Qur'ān in Muslim Indonesia

As many in the fields of Islamic and Qur'ānic studies have noticed, the Qur'ān is often better understood in Muslim religious lifeworlds as an activity and an experience over and above a written "text."[28] Qur'ān recitation is best under-

In the studio during the live broadcast of a call-in recitation show, Radio Al-Ikhwan, Makassar

Studio taping session for a televised recitation show featuring *lagu*, TVRI Makassar

stood not as an oral performance based on a text, but as participation in a divine revelation whose primary medium is voice. The word "*qur'ān*" is almost always said to be a nominalized form of the verb "to read" (i.e., "reading," "reciting"). In order to explain the energetic surge in Qur'ānic practice in Indonesia in the mid-1990s and the religious affect that accompanied it, the recited Qur'ān itself must be recognized not only as an object, but also as a verb—if not an acting subject in itself.

Frederick Denny has pointed out that the word "*qur'ān*" itself means "reading," in both the senses of "reading aloud" and "reading for discursive content."[29] Until recently, however, the latter aspect has been emphasized in the fields of Islamic and religious studies; musicologists and linguists have not tended to take an ethnographic approach in considerations of Qur'ān recitation until relatively recently.[30] Among anthropologists working in Indonesia, Clifford Geertz did treat the significance of Qur'ān recitation but described it in terms of categories and values pertaining to social and political situations. Historian of religions Frederick Denny was the first to break ground in English-language scholarship on the recited Qur'ān in Indonesia in several important respects, writing on methods of instruction, normative ideals *(adab)*, and history, as well as undertaking ethnography on Java. The present study also builds on the seminal work of Kristina Nelson, whose book *The Art of Reciting the Qur'ān* treats perceptions of "ideal" performance in Egypt as well as training and performance among highly accomplished professional reciters.[31] The present work draws on Nelson's study directly to the degree that recorded performances in the 1980s by the reciters with whom she worked in Egypt were the models to which Indonesian reciters aspired in the 1990s. This study is not only about accomplished Indonesian reciters, however; my primary concerns are the educative, lived, and psychological aspects of practices of the recited Qur'ān among ordinary Indonesian Muslims, highlighting its centrality in personal projects of piety and within a regional, national, and transnational movement of Islamic "awakening."

Qur'ān recitation has been a primary mode of Islamic piety since the coming of Islam. From the moment of the initial revelation of the Qur'ān to the Prophet Muḥammad, its recitation has existed alongside—in fact it historically preceded—the orthographic representation of the text. The oral transmission of correct recitation is understood to have begun in the time of the Prophet, as he learned recitation along with the Qur'ān itself from the Angel Jibrā'il (Gabriel), who related it from God. The Prophet Muḥammad is thus the first—chronologically and authoritatively—in reciting the Qur'ān in Islamic tradition. While technical written works on recitation systematizing and theorizing this practice appeared some centuries later, the transmission of the recited Qur'ān was supported by the Prophet's normative precedent of careful study, documented by accounts of his meticulously repeating parts of it with his Companions. Many early figures were identified specifically as Qur'ān readers and transmitters.[32] Since the earliest times, the "preservation" of the Qur'ān was a social, community activity. As related in *ḥadīth* traditions, some of the Companions of the Prophet transmitted the proper technique of recitation and interpretation of the text to others, and it was subsequently preserved in tradition. Muslims who follow the Prophet in reading the Qur'ān are understood to be aided by God in the accurate preservation of the Qur'ān in an unbroken chain.[33]

Between the time that the Prophet Muḥammad passed away in 632 C.E. and the appearance of the official recension of the text of the Qur'ān under the Caliph 'Uthmān in 653 C.E., according to religious historians, early members of the Muslim community had compiled several collections of the written Qur'ān. A first recension effort had been attempted under the caliph Abū Bakr (after the Battle of Yamāma in 633, a year after the Prophet's death), using various materials available; this codex was the version on which the authoritative 'Uthmānic recension was later to be based approximately twenty years later. According to Islamic historians, the recension compiled under the Caliph 'Uthmān standardized the collection into the perfect text (as revealed in the dialect of the Quraysh tribe of the Prophet).[34] It is important, however, not to overemphasize the textual-critical aspects of the preservation of the Qur'ān at the cost of neglecting the performative aspects. As Frederick Denny shows in his article "Exegesis and Recitation," the establishment of the oral transmission of the Qur'ān not only preceded textual standardization, but oral recitation was a key criterion for the determination of uniform parameters of textual diversity in efforts to develop the rigorous sciences of the text and its "readings."

Although the 'Uthmānic recension standardized the written text, it was rendered without markings that would later come to be considered standard (such as declensional and other vowels, *i'rāb*). For this reason, variant ways of vocalizing the 'Uthmānic text continued even though Muslims in a rapidly expanding empire were reading with the same written text as their referent. Over a period of approximately two hundred years, starting from the middle of the second Islamic century, the standard, voweled text of the Qur'ān emerged, along with "preferences" *(ikhtiyārāt)* for the vocal rendering of the Qur'ān. In this period, it was expected that reciters, while exercising such "preferences," would be following the standard 'Uthmānic *muṣḥaf*, or written text, along with the grammatical rules of Arabic (which were being formalized during the same period) and that the reading would soundly be derived from past authority.[35] Such systems of vocalization are known as "*qirā'āt*," a term that means "readings" in several senses; the term conveys a technical and specific meaning in the Qur'ānic sciences denoting "variant readings" or slight differences in vocalizations of the standard text. These "readings" are understood together to provide enhanced information about the meanings of particular verses or terms in a text understood to be "multifaceted" *(dhū wujūh)*. The variant readings also include differences in permissible sectioning, which can influence shades of meaning as well. However, the "variant readings" do not cover pitch variation, a topic that is not treated in the Qur'ānic sciences.

Abū Bakr b. Mujāhid (d. A.H. 324) is credited with establishing the accepted range of variations in "readings" of the text.[36] There are seven accepted "readings" in this system. The number 7 correlates with a well-known *ḥadīth* (that the Prophet said, "This Qur'ān has been revealed to be recited in seven different modes *[aḥrūf]*, so recite of it whichever is easiest for you," a report open to a variety of interpretations).[37] The expectation of a fixed number for the "readings" was reconciled with the varying content of actual enumerated lists. The seven readings that were standardized in Ibn Mujāhid's time as the accepted *qirā'āt* represented prominent schools of reading in five centers of Muslim transmission of learning in that period, Medina, Mecca, Damascus, Basra, and Kufa. The rationale for this selection was to derive a single authoritative system from independent lines of transmission. There was some controversy over the authority of this selection even at the time. It is also clear that there was continued development in the "variant readings" after that time, since the later influential scholar Ibn al-Jazarī (d. A.H. 823), describes ten readings, and other scholars cite fourteen. Despite this variation, Ibn Mujāhid's system of seven readings continued to prevail and is now standard throughout the Muslim world. Denny writes that the work of Ibn Mujāhid led to a development that was like the contemporaneous "closing of the gate of *ijtihād* [independent opinion]" in jurisprudence; from this time on, readers were expected not to deviate from set "readings."[38]

The word most often used for "recitation" is "*tilāwah*," from a semantic root connoting meanings of following, rehearsing, reading, declaring, and mediating.[39] *Tilāwah* embraces both the technical and evocative dimensions of recitation. Richard Martin describes it as follows: "*Tilāwah* is . . . a meaningful speech act governed by rules that situate the speaker and the addressee within the sacred paradigm of God's address to humankind. . . . *Tilāwah* as an Islamic cultural framework embraces not only the sounds but also the cognitive processes of meaning and the emotional responses appropriate to this symbol of divine manifestation."[40] The difference, Denny writes, between "*tilāwah*" (following) and "*qirā'ah*" (reading) is the dimension of the meaning of the term "*tilāwah*" that corresponds to the sense of "conforming to" the Qur'ān's Message.[41] For example, in his treatise on recitation, al-Ghazzālī treats *tilāwah* as an activity that is as much affective and cognitive as it is performative and technical, an activity in which the "tongue, heart, and mind" are equally engaged.

Technical components of the general concept of *tilāwah* convey theory and practice for the technical aspects of proper recitation in the Qur'ānic sciences. While not easily translated, there are two key terms for formal aspects of the recited Qur'ān: "*tartīl*" and "*tajwīd*." The terms are closely related; for example, the Qur'ān's instruction "Recite the Qur'ān with *tartīl*" (73 al-Muzammil 4) is often interpreted as "Recite the Qur'ān according to the rules of *tajwīd*." Denny defines "*tartīl*" as the accurate and precise recitation of the words and phrases of the Qur'ān, providing a definition familiar from classical and authoritative Islamic sources: "measuring them [words and phrases] out properly in relation to each other, in correct sequence and without haste."[42] Although it had other popular Indonesian usages, the term "*tajwīd*" refers to the rigorous system that establishes the vocalization of correct recitation, thereby determining its actual sound. The root of the word *tajwīd* carries meanings pertaining to "making correct" and "beautifying." For the Qur'ān reciter, the system of *tajwīd* includes instructions on fixed rules such as the correct articulation of phonetic sounds, the assimilation of juxtaposed vowels or consonants, and the proper rhythmic duration of vowel sounds. *Tajwīd* also determines the parameters for nonmelodic improvisational flexibility. For example, pausing and restarting in reciting, among the practices covered by the rules of *tajwīd*, allow the reciter to emphasize specific words, phrases, or sections. *Tajwīd* shapes the rhythm and cadences of Qur'ān recitation and "musicalizes" it, although the recited Qur'ān is not to be understood in terms of a human product such as music.

The term "*tajwīd*" does not appear in the Qur'ān. However, the practice of recitation according to such guidelines, no matter what they were called, is understood to have been a central dimension of Islamic piety since the beginning of the Prophet's mission. Recitation manuals certainly consolidated what had been long-accepted techniques and definitions. As with the other Qur'ānic sciences such as *tafsīr* (commentary), systematic treatises on *tajwīd* (such as those of Ibn Mujāhid, al-Makkī, and al-Danī) appeared in the fourth century A.H. and were circulated widely. After al-Dānī (d. A.H. 444), *tajwīd* was fully developed and qualified as both a term and a practice, particularly with the work of Ibn al-Jazarī. Most manuals and discussions after the time of al-Jazarī follow his systematization.[43]

Just as in the development of "sciences" and methods of jurisprudence (*fiqh*), throughout the formative history of development of the sciences of "readings" and *tajwīd* and up to the present day, Muslims across space and over time have continued to base theory and practice of the recited Qur'ān on principles from the most authoritative sources: the Qur'ān itself as well as authoritative accounts of the practice of the Prophet (*ḥadīth*) and his Companions. *Ḥadīth* reports, such as that the Prophet spent a whole night repeating a particular verse, relate the ideal intensity of Qur'ānic engagement through a mode of ethicolegal injunction to follow the model of the Prophet (*sunnah*). *Ḥadīth* accounts preserve such information about how the Prophet recited, including the suggestion that he valued beautiful voices, such as in the following reports of statements of the Prophet (transmitted by Bukhārī and others): "He is not one of us who does not sing (*yataganni*) the Qur'ān," and "Allāh has not heard anything more pleasing than listening to a Prophet reciting the Qur'ān in a sweet loud voice."[44] Al-Bukhārī and other compilers of such traditions relate accounts of the Prophet's reaction to hearing the Qur'ān, such as shedding tears. *Ḥadīth* material also includes detailed information about particular *sūrahs*, reporting, for example, which *sūrahs* the Prophet tended to favor at what times of day. In general, such accepted *ḥadīth* accounts emphasize the occasions and merits of recitation based on the prophetic model rather than practical technique.

Later authorities continued the precedent of collecting information about the recitational practice of the Prophet Muḥammad and also compiled further information about the recitation habits of pious Muslims who followed him. One issue that recurs in recitational literature such as this is the question of how rapidly to recite and the proper amount of the Book to complete in a given amount of time; one report transmitted on the authority of Abū Dāūd and al-Tirmīdhī, for example, states, "Whoever recites the Qur'ān in less than three days does not understand it." Material on the proper comportment (*adab*) of recitation recounts the recitational practices of famous religious figures, such as the first four caliphs in Sunni tradition, and addresses matters such as the desirability of completing recitation of the entire Qur'ān at nightfall, daybreak, and just before prayer times, along with common challenges that reciters face, like confusing pauses and starts in sectioning.

As Muslims recognize, the recited Qur'ān is remarkably reflexive in its content and continually self-referencing in its practice. In significant respects, the recited Qur'ān may be approached as a robust, ritually closed system: instruction for how to recite the Qur'ān is in the Qur'ān, making it difficult to identify the prescribed aesthetic dimensions of Qur'ān recitation in non-Qur'ānic terms. For example, in 75 al-Qiyāmah 16–19, God instructs the Prophet on recitational technique: "Do not move your tongue with it [the Qur'ān] in order to be able to repeat it quickly. It is for Us [God] to see to its arrangement and recitation. So after We have recited it, then you, in your turn, recite it." An experiential sense of the recursiveness of Qur'ānic practice reinforces expectations and anticipations through repeated practice. This is supported by the structure of Qur'ān as well as the ways that the Qur'ān discursively and reflexively prescribes its own performance. Since the rules of *tajwīd* build on the rules of Arabic grammar, the performative aesthetics of Qur'ānic vocalization and its technical artistry are based on its syntax in a natural way. The stipulated improvisation and optionality of orthoprax recitation (as in, for example, the requirement to improvise with respect to melody or pitch variation, or even the necessity to make choices among the "options" for phrasing) works in tension with perceptions and expectations of performative "closure," drawing the practitioner further into the repetition of practice in a poetics of attention.

Other normative "rules" of recitation not given in or as the text are also the "recited Qur'ān." Beyond vocalization rules of *tajwīd*, there are such rules, for example, about the proper occasions for recitation (canonical prayer, for example); rules for appropriate context (ritual purity, for example); and rules for proper conduct during recitation, including opening and closing formulae, respectful silence, and prostration when certain verses are recited. These make up what is known as the "*adab*," or normative comportment, of recitation.[45]

Instruction in the orthoprax vocalization of the Qur'ān (in accord with the rules of *tajwīd*) is often the first kind of formal or semiformal religious instruction Muslims receive. This has been and still remains the case in Indonesia. In the contemporary Muslim world, there are said to be two principal styles of recitation, both called *tilāwah* and both conforming to the rules of *tajwīd*: *murattal* and *mujawwad*. *Murattal* is straightforward, often rapid in pace, and appropriate for individual worship and private reading as well as for recitation of large portions of the Qur'ān from memory. This is the style in which children learn to recite the Qur'ān, for example. It is also sometimes called "*tartīl*," or in Indonesia "*tadarus*." *Mujawwad* (a noun with the same root as the derived form "*tajwīd*") is a more melodious and ornate style of recitation, often much slower, and is generally performed by trained or professional reciters for religious occasions and public events. In Indonesia in the 1990s, the term "*mujawwad*" was not widely known, and during the course of field research, I did not hear it used. Instead, "*tilawah*" or, among nonspecialists, "*tajwid*" (at times somewhat confusingly) often denoted the slower, more ornamental style.[46]

Recitation of the Qur'ān is an essential component of canonical worship (*ṣalāt*). It is also a valued practice of supererogatory piety. Both Sufi-influenced and contemporary revivalist modes of piety draw on the same early historical traditions to emphasize effortful, personalized, voluntary Qur'ānic practice. Sometimes influenced by the stress that Sufi traditions have placed on the cultivation of internal states, there is a highly developed literature on the technical artistry of recitation and the affective aesthetics of performance, associated with "*samā*ʿ" (practices of the "audition" of aesthetic reading, sometimes controversial for non-Qur'ānic and even Qur'ānic performances). Such aesthetic and moral assessments persist, although in reinvigorated forms of mainstream Islamic revitalization their "Sufi" indentification has disappeared. Appreciation of compelling, affecting Qur'ānic performance in modes that are consistent with the moralized aesthetics of Sufi systems is rarely controversial and is by no means limited to "Sufi" contexts, as Nelson's work in modern Egypt demonstrates.

In Indonesia, what limited historical data there are from the period of the coming of Islam suggest that Qur'ān recitation has been popular since the time of the earliest Islamic states. Historian of early modern Makassar William Cummings discusses such textual reception of Islamic and Arabic-language materials in reference to changing modes of authority, reading, and literacy in the early modern era in his book, *Making Blood White*. Regional court chronicle literature across the Malay-speaking maritime world (which extends from the Malaysian peninsula in the west to Ambon in the east), such as the *Sejarah Melayu*, refer to Qur'ānic as well as *ḥikāyāt* (Muslim narrative) recitation in foundational accounts. Some narratives of conversion in these court chronicles actually identify the pivotal event of the coming of Islam as the sudden ability of a local ruler to recite the Book, suggesting the significance of Qur'ānic practice to the Islamization of the archipelago since the earliest times, in myth and probably also in practice. Early sources, including those from South Sulawesi, indicate that at the time of the coming of Islam the Qur'ān was recited publicly on at least two kinds of occasions: funerary observances and during the fasting month of Ramadan.[47]

Historical traditions of the public recitation of the Qur'ān in the Indonesian archipelago are associated with the religious patronage of ruling elites as well as with widespread Sufi-oriented practices of piety. As the prolific work of Anthony Johns has suggested, the Muslim maritime world was a "Sufi world" for many centuries of the premodern era, and this period coincided with the early Islamization of the Indonesian islands.[48] Sufi networks of teaching, practice, and performance complemented and overlapped the formation of other institutions and systems of education in the Muslim archipelago. Sufi-oriented concepts permeate vocabularies of Indonesian languages, resonant with the same principles of interiorized piety that have strongly influenced the historical development of the discourse and practice of Qur'ān recitation worldwide.[49]

As a commonly cited *ḥadīth* states, "Seek knowledge, even unto China." The *riḥlas*, or journeys, made in the Middle Period by travelers such as the famous figure Ibn Baṭūṭṭa (d. 1378) did in fact reach China (just as Chinese Muslims also traveled to the Middle East), and Chinese and Arab Muslims like Ibn Baṭūṭṭa stopped (sometimes permanently) in Southeast Asian ports along the way. As Muslims originating from a "center" moved to the Islamizing "periphery" in Southeast Asia, the periphery also sought out the "center." Southeast Asians traveled widely to gain new information, practices, and ways of being Muslim. Southeast Asian Muslim travelers in the Middle East were known as "Jawis" (those of "Javanese" origin, although many were ethnically Malay). They helped to sustain a vibrant Muslim network that spanned the Indian Ocean in the premodern period, forging strong connections especially between Southeast Asia and the Arabian peninsula (particularly the Yemeni coast known as the Hadramaut). "Jawi" scholars later flocked to the halls of al-Azhar University in Cairo after the opening of the Suez Canal, while many also continued to study in the "Two Holy Cities" of Mecca and Medina. The certificates that "Jawi" scholars gained came not only from institutions for the study of religious sciences such as law, but also from Sufi-oriented lineages; Southeast Asian travelers returned as new links in expanding chains of religious and spiritual authority.

"Traditional" Islamic education in Southeast Asia represents a system shared throughout the Muslim world, although Islam was felt as a social political force in the archipelago centuries after its initial flowering in the Near East. Southeast Asians who studied in institutions in the Arabic-speaking world returned to the archipelago as *kiai* (religious teachers) to transmit the memorized Qur'ān, law, and other subjects in the Islamic religious sciences. These scholars had acquired authority primarily by memorizing texts, especially the Qur'ān. Among the Qur'ān memorization teachers *(kiai)* with whom I worked, many in the older generation had begun their study in the Arab world with the memorization of the Qur'ān, and their heritage included families and networks known for memorization and connections to the Middle East in particular.

The "traditional" mode of Islamic schooling in the archipelago takes place in institutions called "*pesantren*," or "places for students." Much has been written about these institutions and the religious scholars *(kiai)* who head them. As with Islamic education more generally, a memorizational and oral-aural model dominates instruction in these schools. These institutions and the related traditions of Arabic-language teaching (associated with what are known, fondly, as "*kitab kuning*," or the "yellowed books") have been the subject of many scholarly studies in recent decades, including the work of van Bruinessen, Dhofier, Riddell, and Johns. The pattern for transmission of this material in Indonesia (and elsewhere) was for a given text to be "read" aloud by the *shaikh*, while students often copied vernacular-language interpretation of the text interlinearly into their texts. Muslims in the Malay-speaking world have excelled especially in the production of short and concise summaries and study aids associated with the transfer of knowledge and this tradition continued in the movement in Qur'ān recitation in Indonesia in the 1990s.[50]

Much of the literature about Islamic education in Indonesia, as elsewhere, highlights a division between the categories "traditional" and "modern." This was an unambiguous polarity for most in the colonial period and after, but such lines had come to blur by the end of the twentieth century. Before Indonesian independence from Dutch rule, Islamic modernist movements earlier in the century energetically sought to reform educational practices, including schooling. After the establishment of the Republic of Indonesia in 1945, and especially in the New Order after 1965, public and religious schools were sites that multiple interests sought to influence.[51] At the time of fieldwork, change was taking place in the imagination of the relationship between the models of schooling: at the primary and secondary level, public institutions were adopting the model of *pesantren* study, while at the same time, as work by Lukens-Bull and others shows, curricula in "traditional" institutions continued to respond to social change.

In higher education, national Islamic universities (IAIN) dominated Islamic higher education in Indonesia, particularly in the 1980s and after. Since the early 1970s, and in the 1980s and 1990s especially, a new kind of Qur'ānic institution, the "Qur'ān college," had also developed in Indonesia. These institutions were modeled after two prototypes in Jakarta, the IIQ (Institut Ilmu Al-Quran, for women) and the PTIQ (for men), which were, in turn, inspired by the model of the prestigious al-Azhar University in Cairo. As directors explained, these institutions were established with a primary stated goal of graduating students who had memorized the Qur'ān, like those who had attended al-Azhar. In Makassar, the Qur'ān college established on this model was called STAI (Sekolah Tinggi Agama Islam) "Al-Furqan," and it had a similar mission statement and curriculum; Qur'ān recitation and memorization coaches and Islamic studies professors would travel out to the residential college on the outskirts of the city in order to conduct classes. In addition, there were also other major Islamic and nonreligious universities in Makassar. Many students in diverse settings of Islamic higher education and Muslim colleges saw themselves as future teachers.

Education and instruction were a stated goal of a widespread movement of Islamic revitalization in Indonesia within institutional contexts that were not limited to formal and semiformal schooling for students in primary, secondary, and postsecondary education. For example, "*pesantren kilat*" (lightning *pesantren*), which were intensive, usually weeklong programs often held during the month of Ramadan, were eagerly attended by adults who met from dawn to dusk and even stayed after school for discussion, practice, and "*pengajian*" (here meaning "instruction," although this is also an expression for Qur'ān recitation in Indonesia). In small groups as well as in institutions known as "Majelis Ta'lim" across the archipelago, women especially were meeting to practice and study Qur'ān recitation earnestly and, in some cases, to enhance other kinds of Islamic learning.[52] The women with whom I worked in these popular groups were not gathering together to read the Qur'ān merely as an expression of devotional piety. They were meeting with instructors expressly in order to learn; often they would not even begin to recite if their teacher was not present. As a result of this widespread dissemination of educational practice and values, a transformation in an affective, melodic, and social system of Qur'ān recitation was occurring at the time of research and at a rate that surprised even those involved.[53]

The recitation of the Qur'ān (Ar. *qirā'ah*, *tilāwah*) is also known in Indonesia as "*seni baca al-Qur'ān*" (the "art of reciting the Qur'ān") or simply "*pengajian.*" Correct recitation of the Qur'ān follows rules of othoprax vocalization, known as *tajwīd*, which is understood to be the way that the Prophet Muḥammad repeated the revealed Message as he received it. Unlike the straightforward style of reciting the Qur'ān for worship *(ṣalāt)*, Indonesian competitions most commonly featured the *mujawwad* style of Qur'ān recitation (or "*tilawah*" in Indonesia). This is a melodically sophisticated form of vocalizing the Qur'ān with the improvisational application of Arabic musical modes known as "*maqām*" (pl. *maqāmāt*). In contrast to some other traditions of religious "chant," melodic aspects of Qur'ān recitation such as these are required by religious law to be improvised. This is necessary from a theological perspective so that human technical artistry is not associated with God's revealed Speech.

The Indonesian term "*lagu*" (which also denotes "song") is used for musical qualities of recitation, doubly conveying the ideas of scalar pitch class and melody type. In Indonesia, the competition *lagu* were based on Egyptian prototypes of *maqāmāt* known as *bayati*, *rast*, *hijaz*, *soba*, *sika*, *jiharka*, and *nahawand*. In performances and pedagogies that increasingly accepted this style as normative for all readers, especially under the influence of competitional readings and regimens, practitioners recited with these *lagu*, modulating among them, often in ten-minute loose arrangements with a progressional structure. Indonesia has a strong tradition of developing excellence in Qur'ān recitation, in part because of the popularity of perfecting recitation in this style, supported by a long-standing Southeast Asian Islamic pattern of producing short, clear, practical, and highly effective educational methods and materials. Indonesian reciters are recognized internationally for the excellence of their technical artistry and skill, now especially in the *mujawwad* style, and the vitality and versatility of local pedagogical systems has done much to bring about this achievement.

Rapid change was taking place in the experience of Qur'ānic recitational systems at the time of fieldwork. This change was audible in the transformation of recitation styles, especially their melodic aspects and their affective evaluation in informal or semiformal contexts of learning. Some "traditional *lagu*" remained in use for Qur'ān recitation in South Sulawesi, and their acceptance and assessment indexed Qur'ānic change. One type of these practices was for private, devotional reading (in the style known as *murattal*) and tended to be gendered for women (and was often heard in the women's circles of recitation). It elaborates affective textures of sadness and weeping, or *ḥuzn*. Nelson presents this feeling as a latent "ideal" in Egyptian recitation, and it was supported in Indonesia by historical Sufi-oriented traditions of affect, Qur'ānic experience, and performance in text and practice. In Indonesia, these patterns of performance had long been associated with funerary reading of the Qur'ān. In women's circles of recitation, however, participants effortfully replaced affective and melodic styles that were once heard in private, devotional reading with simple variants of the styles that had come to be applied in competitions in previous decades. For many this was the primary goal of participation in the women's mosque movement in Indonesia. With the adaptation of previous patterns of feeling and practice, a new affective system of Qur'ānic learning and performance was taking hold, evident in the stated evaluations of the performance styles.[54]

Some of the "old *lagu*" (often called "old people's *lagu*") were described as "slow, like crying"; they were also called "*lagu nangis*," or "weepy *lagu*." An anthropology professor's mother in one of the women's groups demonstrated, half-closing her eyes, reciting slowly. Then she stopped, recounting that when she was a little girl she would awaken to hear reading like that late at night, and she would stay up to listen. (She also made reference to a Qur'ānic statement relating that when people hear the Qur'ān, it increases their faith [8 al-Anfāl 2].) The women around her added that they had heard similar reading as children too, describing variants among styles, but with all apparently appreciating a congruent affective memory. I asked them, did anyone ever actually cry when the Qur'ān was recited? At once they answered, of *course* they did! Stories about grandmothers, mothers, and aunts who cried buzzed all around. When the activity died down, I remarked, but nobody cries here anymore. No, not here, not anymore, they said. One explained: "Times have changed." The women's "weepy songs" and other regional *lagu* were becoming, as a college student who was a "Qur'ān kindergarten" instructor put it, "forgotten by time" *(ketinggalan zaman)*.

"Times were changing" in a system of religious performance, and projects of teaching and learning were reconfiguring recitational theory and practice, including how practitioners understood their own relationship to the recited Qur'ān. Ny. Nurhayati, a contest judge, teacher, and national champion reciter (and leader of most of the women's circles that I attended), for instance, encouraged her students to replace old patterns of reactive feeling with another, affective system. The newer system was grounded in self-evaluation and alert, energetic engagement that inspires the self just as it may also inspire others. For example, when we were discussing the difficulty most women had with the new *lagu* (for example, *lagu bayati*) because they had known only the old styles since they were children, I asked Ny. Nurhayati whether the old *lagu* "still were any good." She answered that they could be, if they worked well *(cocok)* with the woman's voice. In fact, she would habitually point out with interest different "old *lagu*" (and often comment on their origin, as "Makassarese" or "like a *lagu* we used to have back home," for example) as they were heard in women's recitations in the groups she led. She also said just before the end of fieldwork that she was beginning to teach some of the women to recite "Salawat Nabi" as a group, with the old *lagu*, "the kind," she added, "that make you want to fall asleep." There was simultaneously an ambivalence, an aesthetic appreciation, and a nostalgia in her treatment of the women's old *lagu*. Her association of *lagu* with affective states and patterns of religiosity in musical, aesthetic, and religious terms, however, ultimately meant that the old *lagu* had to go.

Abandonment of the older styles was premised on the acceptance of a new affective system in which "interest," "motivation," and self-evaluation were integral to recitational orthopraxy. At the same time that she was sensitively nostalgic about older styles of reading, Ny. Nurhayati was ever keen to point out her students' "old" *lagu* as "boring," "depressing," or (one of her favorite expressions) "from the grave." One critical reason that Ny. Nurhayati would give for altering or "picking up" *(angkat)* the *lagu* was that the spirit *(jiwa)* is more open to the Qur'ān when *lagu* are "interesting." One is paying attention, alert, awake, open to the Qur'ān and its Message. Musical and affective styles labeled as lugubrious Ny. Nurhayati also identified with distraction, "disaffection," a weak engagement with the Qur'ān, as well as poor knowledge overall. "What?" a teacher once said, stopping a woman in her class who had begun her reading in one of the older styles of recitation. "Here's a Hajji who doesn't know *lagu*?" She meant, it seemed, that a person serious about her religion ought to know and evaluate her own practice in terms of the musical system based on Egyptian styles that was becoming increasingly identified with Qur'ānic orthopraxy and a new emotional system.

Many of the women participating in the groups were at a transition point between the system of "traditional *lagu*" and the modal system of competition *lagu*. When listening to them read, the transition in Indonesian recitation styles was sometimes rendered audible. Some women could switch between systems with a self-conscious religious "bimusicality," first demonstrating an old *lagu* ("Lagu Muhammadan," as one called the style, generically) and then a plain *murattal* version of *bayati* for comparison. At tournaments in which the women participated, it was possible to hear how older contestants were attempting a transition in styles musically: they retained a semiregular *murattal* pattern on four or five pitches, but at regular periods they would modulate this up to a higher register (even up to a squeak in some cases), evidencing a rich mixture of two musical systems. Many of them had already come to picture what was known as the "ladder of melody" *(tangga nada)* of Egyptian-derived styles of recitation, while many admitted that they were still at the stage of just starting out on the "bottom rung."

They were eager to climb up, however. One woman in a group reported that she had not long before gone to study *lagu* with a teacher ("sitting up on chairs and using a microphone") and that she was now teaching other women informally what she knew before the women's circle with the regular teacher began, displaying the earnestness that often accompanied study of the new system within these groups. Some grandmothers and others were starting to break away from the women's study circles in the mosques in order to join aspiring competition reciters in their teens, coming to identify personal styles—as one telephone operator did—with world-famous *qārī*'s such as Sh. ʿAbd al-Bāsiṭ ʿAbd al-Ṣamad. Modes of evaluation in musical and affective practice derived from the formalization of an Egyptian model had altered standards for self-perception, rendering anyone a potential virtuoso and thus rendering virtuosity a potentially salient standard for ordinary practice.

For Indonesians of diverse social locations in this period, new systems of Qur'ānic practice were taking hold, consistent with the past and with immediate and long-lasting effects on how practitioners felt and understood Qur'ānic piety as individuals and as members of Muslim groups. In Indonesian Qur'ān recitation systems in the 1990s, the shared educational goal of Islamic revitalization emphasized the direct, transformative effect of engaging the Qur'ān through projects of learning feeling. Indonesian Muslims recognized this to be the natural effect of the experience and content of the recited Qur'ān itself.

Qur'ānic Transformations

Patterns of affective experience and interaction that sustained and propelled a Qur'ānic movement in Indonesia in the 1990s were built on—and derived directly from—unique features of the recited Qur'ān. These aspects of Qur'ānic reception are embedded in aspects of Islamic tradition that are consistent over space and time. In projects of acquiring Qur'ānic abilities, the recited Qur'ān is the object, goal, and method of learning, while at the same time it is the principal criterion for evaluation and achievement. The Qur'ān's tendency to reference itself rhetorically is amplified in the ways that it also doubles back on itself in practice (containing, for example, instruction for how to recite even as it is recited). This recursive and expansive effect emerges in shared Muslim lifeworlds and within specific modes of engagement. The structure of the Qur'ān, for example, makes its memorization an especially challenging task, one mode that ensures that the Qur'ān will have the transforming effect that it claims for itself over time. Such normative processes of ongoing lived encounter with the recited Qur'ān occur on at least two levels. First, believers experience the impact of the Qur'ān immediately when reciting it and hearing it recited. Second, there are long-term and cumulative transformations that daily repeated activity of recitation may naturally and inevitably produce. The affective dynamics of the Qur'ān that the Qur'ān and authoritative Qur'ānic tradition describe, the referent for Muslim Indonesians, naturally underlie and anticipate components of the theoretical argument and ethnographic data to be presented as an explanation for intensifying Qur'ānic engagement in this book.

Although the upsurge in Qur'ān-related practices during the time of field research (1996–1997) could be analyzed solely in terms of the social conditions of Muslim Indonesia in the 1990s, it may also be recognized that the dynamics of religious motivation and practice are established in, on, and about the recited Qur'ān. Structural, syntactic, and normative characteristics of the recited Qur'ān determine open-ended and expansive qualities of the project of acquiring competence in forms of its recitation. The Qur'ān's statements about the dynamics of such affective engagement and especially about the impact of reading and hearing the Qur'ān read show how the Qur'ān claims an immediate, embodied encounter with its Message to be transformative of the enduring moral, ethical, and social characteristics of a person. In addition to presenting lasting cognitive engagement to be transformative (such as with the Qur'ān's self-characterization as a "reminder"), the Qur'ān also shows continued affective and emotional engagement to sustain long-term processes of progressive development among believers and their religious communities. This Qur'ānic discourse about its own affective power is not only descriptive, but, because the Qur'ān's Message is also a "guide," it is prescriptive as well. *Ḥadīth* accounts, which Muslims look to for guidance in the form of *sunnah* along with other extra-Qur'ānic structures, enhance this expectation.

Internal characteristics of a Qur'ānic system, which may exert a palpable and unparalleled influence both on the level of persons and within groups, determined and propagated many of the affective dynamics of the Indonesian social movement in the recited Qur'ān. The recited Qur'ān itself generates expectations of and desire for increased competence through its gripping meanings as well as through the experiential dynamics that Qur'ān readers, memorizers, and reciters develop through their ongoing practice. Although the "ritual" of reciting the Qur'ān does not change, then, the recited Qur'ān will develop over time for each reciter or memorizer. The Qur'ān discusses its own effects in terms of progressive development over time. While the text of the Qur'ān does not change, these aspects of situated practice do, whether seen in terms of individuals developing competence or in terms of historical changes in systems like melodic and aesthetic systems of recitation. Developmental patterns of affective experience and interaction that sustained and propelled a Qur'ānic movement in Indonesia in the 1990s were built on—and derived directly from—unique features of the recited Qur'ān in its own terms.

The Qur'ān makes numerous claims about its capacity to affect human experience in the present, to remake a person, reorienting him or her to moral sensitivity, social responsibility, and an appropriate relationship to the Creator.[55] Apart from and prior to interpretations grounded in traditions of esoteric piety ("Sufism," which stresses interiorized and affective experience), affective and even visceral experience are integral aspects of the Qur'ān's Message, especially evident when it refers to itself.[56] The Qur'ān's self-presentation also suggests that it works progressively and cumulatively on the hearts of beings capable of recognizing and accepting its Message. For those people, the Qur'ān describes (and thus prescribes and even proscribes) affective states.

The Qur'ān states that its recitation is a primary medium for manifesting the affecting presence of revelation. God calls people to recite the Qur'ān (as in Sūra 96 Al-'Alaq, said by many to be the first to be revealed, which opens with words that mean, "Recite! In the name of your Lord"). Believers are also to "remember," "preserve," and "read [aloud]" when engaging the Qur'ān. The reading of the Qur'ān is to occupy the full concentration of the reciter, and this activity is also shown by the Qur'ān to be one of which God, omniscient of all things, is aware (10 Yūnus 61). The actions and reactions of personal encounters with revelation, including affective and moral states, are said to be scrutinized, weighed, and ultimately judged.

The Qur'ān prescribes both immediate and enduring feeling as appropriate responses to creation and revelation, just as it construes feeling as an essential component of religious life and social conduct more generally. Feeling forms the basis of a receptivity to the Message, a message recognized "by heart." The Qur'ān teaches, for example, that God gave emotions to the beings He created. This teaching could be seen as analogous to the Qur'ān's many statements about God having provided the faculty of reason to people, another mode by which beings recognize, validate, and accept the Message of the Qur'ān. By explicitly including feeling as an aspect of creation, the Qur'ān renders the emotional capacities and thus responsibilities of persons in moral, ethical, and cosmological terms. In 32 al-Sajdah 9, for instance, after a description of God's act of revelation and creation of humanity, God gives the faculties of the senses to people so that they will remain in appropriate relation to Him: "Then He molded him [a human] and proportioned him and breathed into him from His spirit. And He made hearing and sight and feeling *(āf'idah)* for you; how little you are thankful!"[57] The Qur'ān instructs that created beings are in an emotional relationship to their Creator, obliged to Him to feel thankfulness and adoration, with hearts "turning in repentance" and patiently anticipating God's impending Judgment.[58]

The natural world that God created also evokes feeling; the Qur'ān associates the experiences that nature inspires with a moral-affective response both to creation and to revelation simultaneously. God made "hearts," bodies, and also emotions for beings so that they could—and would and should—glorify Him when beholding His Signs *(āyāt)* in nature.[59] The Qur'ān's speech often moves from the theme of the emotive power of nature to the didactic power of the Message of the Qur'ān, which, like God's Signs in the natural world, makes beings react and behave in appropriate praise and sensitivity. For example, 53 al-Najm 33–62 emphasizes that emotive receptivity is the religious reality of the righteous. Beginning with the example of someone who "turns back [to God], gives a little, then withholds," it teaches that no one can carry another's burden and that every being must strive in order to achieve reward. Sūrat al-Najm continues:

> 41: Then he will be rewarded with a full reward
> 42: And truly to your [singular] Lord is the final Goal.
> 43: And truly it is He who makes laughing and crying
> 44: And truly it is He who makes dying and living
> 45: And truly He created the pair, male and female

Here, the Qur'ān connects the contrasting pair "laughing and crying" (physical correlates of emotional states) both to the goal of the ideal relationship to divinity as well as to God's creative power in the phenomenal world. (A list of God's wonders and Signs follows, including mention of the Warners that God has sent to historical communities.) *Ayahs* 57–62 conclude the *sūrah* with the theme of direct, immediate response to the Message:

57: The Ever-approaching [Judgment] approaches.
58: None but God can make it manifest.
59: [The following three *āyahs* rhyme:] With this recital [the Qur'ān], are you [plural] not amazed?
60: And laughing? And weeping?
61: How can you [still] be arrogant?
62: So prostrate to God and worship Him.

Feeling is a mode of orientation to God; it is both motivation and means for attaining peace, righteousness, and reward. Feeling is described explicitly as a response to the recited Qur'ān in the powerful, rhyming phrase of 53 al-Najm 59–60, for example. In verses 61–62, it is also made clear that a change in moral state occurs through direct and affective engagement with the Qur'ān.

The Qur'ān employs language about feeling to assert the immediate, transformative power of its revelation. An example is the ending of 7 al-A'rāf 143, a verse that describes the event of the revelation to the Prophet Moses (Mūsā) at Sinai (Ṭūr): "When his Lord manifested His Glory on the Mount, He made it as dust, and Moses fell down in a swoon. When he recovered his senses, he said: 'Glory be to You! I turn to You in repentance, and I am the first to believe'" (7 al-A'rāf 143). The word "first" here is understood to carry intensive but not necessarily temporal comparative meaning. This *āyah* describes the compelling power of revelation, while at the same time it may act prescriptively by depicting the appropriate sensory response to the impact of revelation. It further shows that revelation effects a transformation of self as one recognizes oneself to be a Muslim "believer."

The Qur'ān provides numerous descriptions of embodied, emotive responses to itself that lead to a permanent change of moral state. Its recitation causes the senses of the faithful to react, for example, with "shivering" skin and a "trembling" heart in passages that are favorites of Sufis:

> When the Signs of the All-Merciful were recited to them [the Qur'ān, to the Prophets], they fell down prostrate, weeping. (19 Maryam 58)

> God has sent down the best discourse as a Book [the Qur'ān], fully consistent within itself, oft-repeated, whereat shiver the skins of those who fear their Lord; then their skins and hearts soften to the remembrance of God. (39 al-Zumar 23)

The related experiences of weeping, prostration, and feeling are all three connected to a recognition of the Message. Description of such embodied responses to the Qur'ān's Message is often immediately followed in the Qur'ān with a statement about a corresponding long-term or permanent change in moral state:

> When it [the Qur'ān] is recited to them, they fall down upon their faces, prostrating, and say: Glory be to our Lord! Our Lord's promise is fulfilled. And they fall down upon their faces, weeping; and it increases them in humility. (17 al-Isrā' 107–109)

> And when they hear what has been sent down to the Messenger [the Qur'ān], you see their eyes overflow with tears because of what they have recognized of Truth. They shout: Our Lord! We believe; so You will write us down among the witnesses [to the Truth]. (5 al-Mā'idah 83)

In the first case, there is an increase in faith and humility; in the second, the emotive and internal change in moral status is exteriorized to the degree that it may be "recorded," echoing the Qur'ānic idea that all matters are preserved or "accounted."

Regarding such long-terms effects, the Qur'ān provides paradigms of appropriate feelings (such as those of Prophets and other exemplars, whether humans, angels, or jinn) for believers to follow. The Qur'ān expresses the nature and purpose of these emotions in cosmological and soteriological terms, and the presence of these affective dynamics often signals a transformation into a new state. The Qur'ān shows that transformation is effected not only through the medium of the encounter with the recited Book, but also through social interactions mediated by the recited Qur'ān, whether in the case of Prophets bearing the Message or, more simply, repeated reading carried out by Muslims.

The Qur'ān prescribes ethical conduct and provides examples of moral transformation through nuanced descriptions of the emotions of exemplary groups and authoritative individuals, particularly Prophets. The Qur'ān explicitly identifies the comportment of Prophets to be *'uswāt*, examples or models, for Muslims to follow. The Qur'ān often states that God eases the emotional troubles of Prophets (such as the Prophet Moses [Mūsā], for example) and assists with the burdens of the Prophet Muḥammad. (Examples are 93 al-Ḍuḥā and 94 al-Sharḥ.) The Qur'ān highlights the Prophet Muḥammad's own emotions, and entire *sūrah*s seem to relate to his experiences.

The actions of righteous believers, Prophets, and ordinary Muslims are potential models for and influences upon others. By reading the Qur'ān aloud, the Qur'ān states, Muslims may affect others' religiosity and potentially transform them through emotional modes, as indicated in the following verse, often quoted in contemporary Qur'ānic Indonesia: "The believers are only they whose hearts tremble when God is mentioned; and, when His Signs [or 'verses,' the Qur'ān] are recited to them, they multiply in faith and put their trust in their Lord" (8 al-Anfāl 2). Just as the Prophet Muḥammad experienced the Qur'ān as coming down "in stages," the processes of ordinary believers and religious communities engaging the Qur'ān is presented in the Qur'ān to be gradual and open-ended, occurring through the cumulative effects of repeated practice. These ideals connect in reality to a potentially self-sustaining system of religious activity, continually supported by a convergence of aspects of the recited Qur'ān, the experiences of practitioners, and the social forms of religious practice. The Qur'ān does not only offer incentives and exhortations to self-betterment, but it is also the "technology" by which orthopraxy in the recited Qur'ān may be obtained. The recited Qur'ān is thus not only the objective of practice but also the method through which projects of piety may be realized.

The pious perception of this system of the Qur'ān, including its transformative power, is linked closely to the doctrine of the ontology of the text as being "miraculous" and "inimitable" revelation. *I'jāz* is a concept for the "inimitability" of the Qur'ān, central to normative Qur'ānic tradition.[60] It provides a framework to explain expansive expectations that may be internalized and embodied through Qur'ānic practice. A basis of the doctrine is what are known as the "*taḥaddī* verses," or statements in the Qur'ān that challenge those who do not accept the validity of revelation to bring a book (28 al-Qaṣaṣ 49), *sūrahs* (11 Hūd 16), or even just one *sūrah* (10 Yūnus 39) like those in the Qur'ān. The idea of *i'jāz* is related to the authenticity of the Prophet Muḥammad's mission as well as the "*mu'jizah*" or the "miracle" of the Qur'ān that was revealed to him. Another contributing factor to the development of the formal doctrine of *i'jāz* was the Mu'tazilī controversies in dialectial theology over agency and voice in Qur'ān recitation; the status of Divine Speech and its "createdness" in time, including during the "speech" of recitation, was part of the vexed issue of the "createdness" of the Qur'ān, the focus of the watershed doctrinal "inquisition" *(miḥna)* in the ninth century.[61] The theological concept of *i'jāz* developed in a critical phase of Islamic thought, when these debates over the nature of the Qur'ān (such as its "createdness") were especially heated within the tradition. The idea also became central to linguistic and literary analysis of all three categories of Arabic expression: poetry, prose, and Qur'ān, with the Qur'ān evidencing the ("inimitable") paradigm of Arabic-language expression that cannot be rendered into any other language.[62] Later, *i'jāz* also saw polemical and apologetic usage within discussions with representatives of other faith traditions, especially those who also possess a sacred Book. Finally, the understanding of the "miraculous" nature of the Qur'ān shades into the direction of popular ideas and practices of piety (with some of their aspects supported by legal scholars and with others, such as drinking water in which written Qur'ānic verses have been soaked, viewed as objectionable).

The doctrine of *i'jāz* is flexible in application and powerful for that very reason: it potentially references all Arabic language and expression to the ultimate Speech of God. It is the thus the basis of legal understandings of the relation of the words of the Qur'ān to other Qur'ānically based expression, such as "translation,"[63] exemplified in controversies that erupted in contemporary Indonesia over the works of H. B. Jassin, *Al-Quran Bacaan Mulia* and *Al-Quran Berwajah Puisi*, for example. One dispute concerned Jassin's interpretation of the Qur'ān into "poetical" Indonesian; standards of Arabic grammar were the grounds for justifying the rejection of his efforts to render the Qur'ān with "*puitisisasi*." Subsequently, the presentation of a *muṣḥaf* (text) of the Qur'ān that spaced the *āyah*s on the page in order to make them more readily recited and appreciated, though legally permissible, was nevertheless opposed by some Indonesian religious scholars. At the same time, the Mushaf Istiqlal and a Braille edition of the Qur'ān were being promoted by the Ministry of Religious Affairs as well as the official "Mushaf Standar" (standardized version) of the Qur'ān in Indonesia, further enhancing expectations for processes of textual standardization based on perceptions of ultimate ideals of perfection.[64]

Transformation and emotional engagement with lived, historical situations are expected to occur as part of and as a direct result of encounter with the Qur'ān's miraculous nature: according to the Qur'ān, the Qur'ān was revealed all at once (97 al-Qadr) *and* in stages (17 al-Isrā' 106), and in both of these modes (immediate and developmental) it is understood to affect pious persons. Muslims tend to expect all aspects of Qur'ānic practice, in whole and in part, in a moment and gradually over time, to be permeated by its "miraculous" aspects, consistent with the doctrine of *i'jāz*. In embodied, affective, and technical aspects of practice, such expectations take hold and become internalized through effortful rehearsal. One systematic and explicit mode of the internalization of Qur'ānic piety has been ascetic and aesthetic Sufi-oriented thought and practice. This tradition has generated much written material treating active and interiorized Qur'ānic piety, consistent with the perspectives of "*sharī'a*-minded" jurists and scholars with Qur'ānic commitments in the formative period. This material remains influential in diverse contemporary movements of mainstream and revitalized piety that emphasize the internalization of Qur'ān- and *ḥadīth*-based religiosity.

Salient historical patterns of "Sufism," a self-conscious organizational basis of some religious revitalization movements in contemporary Indonesia,[65] also persist implicitly in contemporary Qur'ānic resurgent movements. This is despite labeling of orientalist and Islamist colonial and postcolonial discourses and distinctions, although many figures of modern reformist systems themselves have significant "Sufi" pasts.[66] Not only are key Sufi terms like "*khushū'*" (earnest engagement) foundational to revivalist rhetorics, especially in relation to Qur'ānic piety, but contemporary modes of piety are consistent with formative "Sufi" tradition. Examples are emphasis on intensifying supererogatory involvement, their Qur'anic basis, development of criteria for moral responsibility and self-scrutiny as aspects of self-cultivation, attempts to unify religious spheres of conduct and experience, as well as a vision for social change and reform as an aspect of personal and collective piety. These were foundational for traditions of normative Qur'ānic piety in the formative period of Islam as well as in movements of reformist "neo-Sufism" long before later "Sufi"–"Anti-Sufi" polemics. Some longstanding patterns of piety consistent with "Sufism," such as Qur'ānic aesthetics and internalization (evidenced, for example, in the writings of al-Ghazzālī as well as in the thought of modern reformist thinkers such as Sayyid Qutb), remain untouched by reformist critique in the domain of contemporary revitalization programs of Qur'ānically focused education and piety.

One example of a mode of piety in which multiple Qur'ānic strains converge, including popular contemporary perceptions of *i'jāz,* is material known as "Faḍā'il al-Qur'ān" (Excellences of the Qur'ān), which forms a large and robust corpus in the Islamic tradition. This information circulated in the formative period and later, often highlighting specific *sūrah*s and the merits accrued for their recitation. This material represents an eschatological mode of devotional piety, since it connects the specifics of Qur'ānic practice to ideal perceptions and ultimate expectations. The literature expresses the relationship of Qur'ānic ideals and personal realities in terms of the results of the practice of recitation that accumulate over time. On an evident level, such material is authoritative encouragement for practice, and it also provides important information for how to conduct Qur'ānic piety. The material also evidences Muslims' understandings of a potential change in moral state that engagement with the Qur'ān may naturally bring about. Many of these traditions relate the exemplary Prophetic model *(sunnah)* to practices of Qur'ānic piety. For example, there is a well-known statement attributed to the Companion of the Prophet Ibn Mas'ūd to the effect that loving the Qur'ān is a sign that one loves the Prophet as well as the famous *ḥadīth* that relates that the Prophet said, "A man who reads the Qur'ān thereby includes prophethood between the two sides of his body. However, no revelation will be revealed to him."[67]

Rewards for reciting the Qur'ān are often accounted *sūrah* by *sūrah* in this literature; it also includes a great amount of material about the merits of particular *sūrahs*. Such rewards may even come *āyah* by *āyah*:

> From Abdullah b. ʿAmr b. al-Aṣ: The Prophet said, "The companion of the Qur'ān will be told: recite and ascend, ascend with facility as you used to recite with facility in the world. Your final abode is the height you reach at the last verse you recite." (Abū Dāūd, Tirmīdhī, Aḥmad b. Ḥanbal, Nasā'ī)

Not only *sūrah* by *sūrah*, or *āyah* by *āyah*, but there are statements that rewards may even be achieved letter by letter, such as the report transmitted by Tirmīdhī "For every letter that you read you will get tenfold reward" and:

> Ibn Masʿūd said: [The Prophet] said, "Read the Qur'ān for you will be rewarded at the rate of [the recompense of] ten good deeds for reading every letter of the Qur'ān. Take notice, I do not say that *ālif lām mīm* constitute one letter. Rather, I should say that *ālif* is one letter, *lām* is another, and *mīm* is [still] another."[68]

This statement suggests that even a little recitation is counted in one's favor; it also implies that being able to do only a little bit is not an excuse to do nothing at all. It further reveals that the practice of recitation and memorization (exemplified by the Qur'ānic phrase "*ālif-lām-mīm*") progresses little by little, and only by progressive increments does one become transformed into someone who shares in the spiritual status of the diligent and righteous Qur'ān readers. The recitation of the Qur'ān brings on both individual and collective rewards for persons and communities according to this literature, as expressed in the following statement of the Companion of the Prophet and the transmitter of many traditions Abū Huraira:

> Abū Huraira said: "Surely the house in which the Qur'an is recited provides easy circumstances for its people, its good increases, angels come to it [in order to listen to the Qur'ān] and satans leave it. The house in which the Book of God is not recited provides difficult circumstances for its people, its good decreases, angels leave it, and satans come to it."[69]

Like all rewards, the ultimate realization of transformative engagement with the Qur'ān is eschatological in this material, manifest with the final accounting on the Day of Judgment.

Religious sources assert that the Qur'ān invokes a palpable presence and agency in soteriological terms, as shown in the evocative (and also controversial) idea that the Qur'ān intercedes at Judgment on behalf of beings whose hearts "contain" it. Among pious nonspecialists in the Qur'ānic and Islamic religious sciences, it is understood that the Qur'ān is among the presences and objects (including even the physical body, as in 41 Fuṣṣilāt 20–21) that witness the accountable moral behavior of a person or group on the ultimate Day of Accounting. Some Muslim statements indicate that a relationship to the Qur'ān that has developed through continuous practice is a criterion at Judgment, asserting that the Qur'ān itself may testify on behalf of its readers in this regard. There are reports, on authority deemed both sound and questionable in tradition, that the Qur'ān "intercedes" for its readers at Judgment, a vexed issue in general; as cited in sources such as al-Ghazzālī's (d. 1111) treatise on recitation (*Iḥyā' 'Ulūm al-Dīn*, Book 8), there is the *ḥadīth* from Abū Dāūd "On the Day of Resurrection, the companion of the Qur'ān will be told to read the Qur'ān and ascend as high as the last verse he reads." It would not be a contentious assertion in any context that merit for a Qur'ān reader does not come automatically but only as a result of repeated and continuous activity.

The development of early traditions of ascetic piety lent heightened emphasis to such material within the Islamic tradition. Sufis, often presented as the heirs to this pious tradition (especially the lineages that developed some centuries later) adopted especially the practice of radical or interiorized Qur'ānic piety. Statements of well-known Sufis give the Qur'ān a palpable presence in both dreams and waking states. This presence is described as an ongoing relationship, at times framed in terms of the key Sufi concept of intimate "friendship." This is indicated by personal accounts as well as in the relation of reports, such as that the Prophet said, "Those who are concerned with the Qur'ān *(ahl al-Qur'ān)* are friends of God and are special to Him," which al-Ghazzāli relates on the authority of the collection of the great pious figure Ibn Ḥanbal. Ideally, engaging the Qur'ān through practice should be in conformity with the reciter's close and immediate experience of the text in his or her "heart." There is a well-known *ḥadīth* that supports this idea. The Prophet said: "Read the Qur'ān as long as your hearts are in harmony with it; when they are not in harmony you are not reading it, so get up and stop reading it" (Bukhārī, Muslim). The Sufi al-Makkī writes, "If they [some reciters] recited a *sūrah* and their hearts were not in it, [then they] would repeat."[70] Such ideals of Qur'ānic piety have been shared by multiple orientations in the Islamic tradition and are a location at which perspectives seen to be in opposition on other issues (such as the permissibility of some devotional practices or the human potential to recognize Divine Unity) actually merge. For pious Muslims of diverse orientations, the Qur'ān exerts a presence in the consciousness and self-consciousness of Muslims through direct and intimate engagement and practice.

Authoritative conceptions of affective engagement with the recited

Qur'ān, extending first and foremost from the recited Qur'ān and also from Prophetic *sunnah*, and from there ranging from the doctrine of *i'jāz* to understandings of soteriology and pious lifeworlds in this world and the next, continue to influence the experiences and practice of religious piety through the repeated recitation of the Qur'ān. Descriptions of the emotive and psychological dimensions of repeated practice in the past determine potentials for practice in the present and the future. Perfection, as an ontological concept and a lived project, propelled a system of increased Qur'ānic engagement in Indonesia in the 1990s through the open-endedness of ideals of the recited Qur'ān itself, connected to realities of lived affect and learning. Indonesian Muslims approached the recited Qur'ān as a mechanism for inspiration in both abstract and engaged terms. They applied the Qur'ānic idea that an inspired Qur'ānic self may inspire others. Drawing on Qur'ānic traditions, they recognized that this transaction occurs especially through the self-conscious development of modes of feeling and through ongoing projects of practice and development.

Religious "Moods and Motivations" and Sustained Projects of Piety

In general, the study of religion in the human sciences has been lacking in adequate theory to explain why people undertake long-term, voluntary projects in the practice of religious piety such as the memorization and improved reading and recitation of the Qur'ān. There is little in the academic literature to complement the Qur'ān's own representation of the dynamics of transformation and escalating engagement with itself by way of ongoing, affective encounter. Attention in a number of fields in the human sciences has tended to focus instead on patterns of cognition, categorization, and communication conveyed by religious activity. For example, treatments of practices of discipline in religious contexts (such as medieval European Christian monasticism) usually have tended to focus on the encompassing power relations instantiated through such regimens,[71] and have not placed in the foreground the question of what power the experiential dynamics of ongoing learning, practice, and performance themselves hold to engage the practitioner over time.

The system of Qur'ānic study in Indonesia is not best analyzed as a subjectivist collection of selves seeking to maximize material self-interest (as by winning a contest) or individuals pursuing other "intrinsic rewards"[72] any more than it would be satisfactorily described as a machinery of social structure. Explanation of pious engagement with the recited Qur'ān in the religious and social conditions of Indonesia in the 1990s requires a model that can embrace a social system of religious revitalization; the personal developmental trajectories of skill, feeling, and self-understanding; as well as the robust religious ontology of the recited Qur'ān. Affect stood in a dynamic relation within each of these domains of Qur'ānic practice and learning in Indonesia in the 1990s through increasingly popular modes of activity such as memorization, reading, reciting in a virtuosic style, and the activity of competing.

Feeling and learning were recognized by Indonesians as mechanisms for sustained and sustaining inspiration within the Qur'ānic movement in Indonesia in the 1990s. In Indonesia, projects promoting the recited Qur'ān explicitly supported the ongoing nature of practice through regimens of learning and rehearsal; the affective theory and practice of this phenomenon collapsed the levels of individual and social engagement. This feedback between self and system led to escalating engagement within affective and emotional contexts and interactions, which was the very goal of such programs at the outset. In some cases, continuous engagement with the recited Qur'ān under specific social conditions came to alter shared systems of practice, learning, and feeling themselves, just as they transformed the subject and his or her self-understanding. In analyzing these processes (and in contrast to a popular bias about religion and feeling, which takes "religious experience" to be idiosyncratic or exceptional), I view the intersection of affective frameworks of feeling and religious devotional piety within individual experience, collective expression, and the recited Qur'ān to be a constant, mainstream, ongoing, and socially creative process. In this case, it rests on the Qur'ān itself in both theory and practice.

In Indonesia in the 1990s, affective dynamics within projects of learning and community-building were generative of increased or escalating Qur'ānic practice on individual and collective levels. Affect encompassed specific techniques as well as expansive goals within motivated projects of religious piety. Within such projects of ritual learning, the power of emotion potentially generated continued or escalating practice. The Qur'ān represents its own dynamics of transformation and amplifying engagement with itself by way of ongoing, affective encounter in vivid terms. To understand how this also occurred within lived experiences and a particular social system requires an understanding of emotion that carries motivational, directive "force" at both individual and social levels. Instead of highlighting the modes by which external forces act on the individual (such as with a view that would construe affect as a one-way mechanism of internalization), the perspective adopted here emphasizes how social phenomena also radiate out from the desire for self-cultivation and contribution to community—especially by way of voluntary and long-term projects of piety. Emotion in projects of learning and practice drew on both the domains of the individual and the social system.

The approach to affect in this study adapts the standard academic dichotomies within the analytical category "emotion." In contemporary analyses, the issues of characterizing emotions (often along two-dimensional lines, such as "public" and "private") have joined larger methodological and philosophical conversations. These tend to grapple with some form of the tension between thought and social structure, on the one hand, and feeling and embodied experience on the other. For example, Lutz and White list a few of the issues elicited in approaching emotions from an anthropological perspective in terms of the following polarities: materialism and idealism (are emotions biological or ideational?), positivism and relativism (are emotions universal or cross-culturally particular?), individual and private (are emotions "social" or "personal"?), and the tension over "rationality" among romantic and rationalist perspectives.[73] The approach to affect here, like much current theory, construes the concept of "emotion" at the outset to be a dimension of religious systems operative on both the levels of private experience and social structures; and, unlike in many contemporary approaches, emotion is posited to be separate from both cognition and embodiment.

The position an observer takes on the issues outlined by Lutz and White above often determines what will be considered to be "emotion" in any given analysis: cultural norms, social structures, discourses of and about emotion, or other, nonnormative emotional expression. This study describes processes of emotion, many of them self-conscious, within a Qur'ānic system. When feeling is described as religious or even distinctively "Qur'ānic," these are meant to be descriptors of an encompassing system rather than assertions of the essential character of particular feeling-states. One reason for this is that the attempt to develop emotionological vocabularies invites the exhausting problem of naming "types" of emotions. In addition to segmenting a continuous stream of experience into discrete labels, this approach often produces a situation in which descriptors (and questions of cross-cultural variation) come to eclipse the object of study itself. For example, sociologist Peggy Thoits has suggested a typology based on the following categories of types of experience: "feeling" (an experiential state), "emotion" (a type of feeling), "affect" (evaluated feelings, often identified in terms of such types), "mood" (a less intense state and less tied to an eliciting situation), and, finally, "sentiment" (which is socially constructed and socially meaningful).[74] Methodological lexicons, however, may distract study in the direction of defining classifying terms, taxonomies, or typologies for named emotions, labels that may then obscure the richness and variability of personal, historical, and social experience.[75]

The goal of this study of emotions and projects of religious piety is not to develop maps or models for particular emotions or types of feeling. Many who use language and discourse as primary analytical tools for analysis have deployed a "keyword" strategy; even if a typology was not the aim of analysis, it is often the result of such a discourse-centered approach. The theorists who apply this approach, however, adopt it in part because they are acutely aware of the potential for European-language "ethnotheories" of emotion to influence the ethnographic description of other emotional systems.[76] The focus on emotion terms that are embedded in what theorists have called "emotion talk" is understood to contextualize usage and thus overcome these problems.[77] The result, however, is often the deployment of a limited array of discretely labeled "feelings" as the basis of conceptual organization. Although textures of named emotions are known through the discourses about them (such as the cases of named feelings like *khushūʿ*, *ḥuzn*, and *rasa*), and this analysis is a primary means of accessing emotional systems in this study, I will tend to highlight named feelings insofar as they are creative or instrumental techniques relating to practice or to the degree that they are ideals that relate to a wider Qur'ānic system. In these cases, description of context conveys particularity in terms of both overall kinds of emotion as well as the named emotions themselves. I follow what has become a trend within the study of emotion and culture and deploy the general term "affect" (but not the hybrid "thought-feeling") for a wide range of affective phenomena.[78]

In the various domains of Indonesian Qur'ānic practices in the mid-1990s, distinctive "moods and motivations" as dimensions of affect cross-cut multiple levels of experience and discourse, blending with the psychology of individuals as well as with the structures of social systems. Affect emergent within changing social systems and experienced situationally and over time in engaging the recited Qur'ān was a principal mechanism for meeting goals of the escalation of Islamic piety. These religious "moods and motivations" were not merely an effect but also a cause of religious resurgence.

Many researchers who have advanced the study of personhood, emotion, and psychological anthropology since the 1960s have worked in Austronesian language areas and in Oceania, often highlighting issues of emotion.[79] It was Indonesianist Clifford Geertz who defined "religion" as a symbolic "cultural system" in terms of enduring "moods and motivations."[80] Geertz actually uses the phrase twice in his famous statement: "A *religion* is: (1) a system of symbols which acts to (2) establish powerful, pervasive, and long-lasting moods and motivations in men by (3) formulating conceptions of a general order of existence and (4) clothing these conceptions with such an aura of factuality that (5) the moods and motivations seem uniquely realistic."[81] In Geertz' formulation of "religion," an enduring "system of symbols" drives "long-lasting moods and motivations," which in turn seem to function as a process of internalization for that same system.[82] Geertz presents the term "mood" as largely self-explanatory. Drawing on the work of the psychologist Gilbert Ryle, Geertz defines motivation as "a passing tendency, a chronic inclination to perform certain sorts of acts and experience certain sorts of feeling in certain sorts of situations."[83] The difference between "moods" and "motivations" in religious systems, Geertz goes on to explain, is that "motivations are 'made meaningful' with reference to the ends toward which they are conceived to conduce, whereas moods are 'made meaningful' with reference to the conditions from which they are conceived to spring."[84]

Geertz uses temporal terms (such as "passing" and "long-lasting") with respect to affect and feeling in a religious system. Such diachronic persistence or change within the Geertzian semiotic system of "religion" derives from properties of signification and not affect. With ethnographic methodology based on what is understood to be observable, describable behavior, this theory of religion, like other aspects of the Geertzian concept of "cultural systems," is primarily meaning-based rather than experiential. Along with Victor Turner, Geertz is among the best-known theorists of "meaning" and religious practice. In studying rituals, both Geertz and Turner emphasize theatrical properties, whether to be read as a "text" or interpreted as "dramatization" of symbolic systems: although both analyze the experiential aspects of symbols in performance, for them, performance, above all, imparts meaning.[85]

Since the equipment of Geertz' theory is calibrated to retrieve the "systems of symbols" or meaning that underlie "religion," it yields answers to questions about "moods and motivation" in religious practice in terms of the larger systems that are the focus of interest. Geertz writes: "Motives are thus neither acts (that is, intentional behaviors) nor feelings, but liabilities to perform particular classes of act or have particular classes of feeling. And when we say that a man is religious, that is, motivated by religion, this is at least part—though only part—of what we mean."[86] Geertz here does not seem to be primarily interested in how religious motivations affect the propensity to practice religion per se but instead in how being religious may affect proclivities with respect to non-religious activity.[87] The approach taken here to explain religion in Indonesian context rearranges Geertz' symbolic picture into a different pattern: how do the moods and emotions of religious education drive the long-term motivations to ritual activity?

Reconsidering Geertz' "moods and motivations" in terms of religious life-worlds is a question especially well suited to the field of the history of religions, as indicated when Thomas Csordas writes:

> Geertz (1973) can posit a definition of religion, and symbolic anthropologists take up the notion that it is a system of symbols, articulated in a system of social relationships. For the psychological anthropologist, it is the next part of Geertz's

> definition which is of principal concern, that religion acts to establish long-standing moods and motivations. I submit that the theoretical power to get at these moods and motivations may be found among phenomenologists and historians of religion such as Otto ([1917] 1958), van der Leeuw (1938), and Eliade (1958). These theorists conceived of the sacred in terms of the same "otherness" defined by Durkheim. They differed, however, in regarding the otherness not as a function of society, but as a generic capacity of human nature.[88]

Although it is not spelled out here what aspects of the nonreductive understandings of religion as a sui generis category Csordas finds especially promising or which of the approaches to "otherness" that figures such as Otto, van der Leeuw, and Long and Eliade adapted from the phenomenological tradition would be possible to recuperate, Csordas' perspective does point to the importance of reconsidering the role of affect as foundational to religious lifeworlds. In fact, many approaches in cultural anthropology, studying religious systems as does Geertz, have posited feeling as the internalizing "force" of salience for other structures. Drawing on insights from both the history of religions and cultural anthropology, this analysis takes affect to be a dimension of religious lifeworlds that interacts with modes of action and thought as a semiautonomous third term.

I do not posit any specifically "religious emotions," nor do I wish to revive old romantic theory in the academic study of religion that asserts that "religion" is somehow essentially affective and authentic only when it is.[89] The field of the history of religions traces some of its deepest roots to a romantic movement seeking to understand such "religious experience," which is often identified with "affective experience." For some within this tradition (notably Schleiermacher and Otto), forms of emotion were seen even to be definitional of religion itself. In contrast, this study furthers a recognition that emotion works in learning projects as a generative mechanism on a number of levels of sociality. In addition, experience within religious systems includes much more than affect; some dynamics of engagement and repetition are carried forward by affective processes, however, and affect is a key to the recognition of achievement in projects of religious self-cultivation.

In the quarter-century since Clifford Geertz first offered his influential definition of "religion," few besides Csordas have considered the "moods and motivations" that he presented as the interface between "systems" and associated "realistic" (or religious) experiences of real people. Even those engaged in the study of ritual have rarely considered how "moods and motivations" may be experienced as "long-lasting," "powerful," and "pervasive." A possible response to this question is that the experiential dynamics of repeated practice, such as learning to perform ritual action more effectively, may themselves motivate more practice in a potentially self-sustaining system. Just as the system of the recited Qur'ān has recursive and self-referential properties, the affective experience of religious practice may impel actors toward further practice. The "moods and motivations" to engage projects of religious piety and to acquire ritual competence are located, in part, in the repetitive aspects of ritual and ritual's characteristics as a learning process. The repetition of ritual is potentially an ongoing development, building cumulatively in experience; qualities of this learning experience may pull subjects forward, potentially motivating long-term projects in the practice of religious piety.

A trend toward this kind of perspective in contemporary learning theory as well as in cultural anthropology draws inspiration from the work of the Soviet psychologist Vygotsky. Vygotsky's dialectical perspective highlights how social interaction shapes self-development. This work is becoming increasingly relevant to anthropologists who attempt to understand processually the mutual influence of selves and social systems as well as those who study learning and wish to highlight this activity and its contexualization.[90] These perspectives, typified by the work of Jean Lave, represent a rapprochement between the fields of psychology and anthropology and an important step beyond interactionist frameworks in sociological study. Their approach, as it is generally understood, relates person to social context developmentally, and often encompasses domains of affect and self-perception.[91] While the method of analysis I apply to the reading of the Qur'ān in Indonesia is hardly "neo-Vygotskian," it does locate affect within developmental processes, especially those that relate people and their self-understandings, affectively, to the Qur'ān as well as to socially specific structures of religious practice. In the case of Qur'ān recitation in modern Indonesia, an understanding of "religious practice" or "ritual piety" that encompasses not only isolated instances of performance but also the wider preparatory, educational, and repetitive aspects of activity illuminates the ongoing pull that may be sustained by the affective dynamics of practice.

The academic work of Lave and others suggests that "learning" encompasses all human activity, which would include the repetition of religious practice, formal and semiformal study, and even everyday "activity" not marked as "learning" per se. Blending dichotomies such as "formal" and "informal" education and the "learning curriculum" and the "teaching curriculum,"[92] Lave and her colleagues list four "premises" with respect to "learning" and its "social contexts":

> 1. Knowledge always undergoes construction and transformation in use; 2. Learning is an integral aspect of activity in and with the world at all times. That learning occurs is not problematic; 3. What is learned is always complexly

> problematic; 4. Acquisition of knowledge is not a simple matter of taking in knowledge; rather, things assumed to be natural categories, such as "bodies of knowledge," "learners," and "cultural transmission," require reconceptualization as cultural, social products.[93]

Lave remarks that viewing "learning-in-practice" in a "seamless way" does not require that "indeterminacy and open-endedness" be viewed as "infinite or random." Rather, "understanding" (which may be practical competence or "craftwork") may be a "partial and open-ended process while at the same time there is a structure (variously conceived) to action in the world."[94]

Lave defines "learning" as "changing understanding in practice."[95] She writes:

> It is difficult, when looking at everyday activity . . . to avoid the conclusion that learning is ubiquitous in ongoing activity, though often unrecognized as such. Situated activity always involves changes in knowledge and action . . . and "changes in knowledge and action" are central to what we mean by "learning." . . . We have come to the conclusion . . . that there is no such thing as "learning" *sui generis*, but only changing participation in the culturally designed settings of everyday life. Or, to put it the other way around, participation in everyday life may be thought of as a process of changing understanding in practice, that is, as learning.[96]

Lave and her colleagues thus make a strong claim: all action is essentially some form of developmental learning, and people change over time with respect to repeated activity. Ritual activity is such a dynamic process for the practitioner in terms of his or her competence and self-understanding as an actor. A person will change over time not only with respect to the Message of the Qur'ān, for example, but also with respect to his or her own ability to read it and, more globally, in reference to social structures and who one sees oneself to be.

Such learning processes cross-cut both individual experience and shared social system. For example, in the case of Qur'ān memorization in Indonesia, social norms determined a subjectivity of ongoing practice prescriptively, while in practice the continual nature of the task itself was additionally determined by the constant repetition required in the presence of others to preserve accurately the Qur'ān in memory. In the case of learning to read the Qur'ān, Indonesian strategies of affect drew on public evaluations in order to shape specific types of learning processes and to create self-consciously particular kinds of learners. With the performative model of expressive recitation, new pedagogies interacted with the psychology of religious piety, effecting change in an overall affective and religious system. And, finally, in Indonesian Qur'ān recitation competitions, a social system articulated standards of practice that were the basis of individual and collective projects of motivating religious piety.

Building on the centrality of affect to sustaining piety, as recognized and applied by Indonesians themselves, this study views long-term dynamics of religious practice to be fundamentally a learning process. One inspiration for this idea comes from the work of John Dewey, a thinker who brought together the fields of psychology, phenomenology, religion, aesthetics, and education and learning in his prolific work.[97] Dewey shows his interest in how to conceptualize the expansive properties of human behavior, such as activities of learning and the production of art, for example, when he writes about the ever-changing, "experimental" nature of action. His logic, similar to the argument made here about the system of the recited Qur'ān through escalating and intensifying projects of feeling and learning in Indonesia, is that practice is a "self-funded" means as well as an objective that leads toward more practice. In later work, Dewey considered time-bound processes in another way, focusing on "instrumental" processes of critical thinking and problem solving; this is similar to the way in which emotions will be shown to be self-conscious techniques of improvement and self-making in processes of pious engagement.

In *Art as Experience*, Dewey considers how a relation of inner and outer realities draws persons forward into productive or creative activity. Although emotion is not elaborated a great deal in the theory, he sees the process as emotional in nature, writing, "I have spoken of the esthetic quality that rounds out an experience into completeness and unity as emotional," adding, "The reference may cause difficulty." The difficulty, he explains, is in misrecognizing the changing qualities of emotions as a part of the process—not to take feeling to be named states but rather to be fluid, changing patterns of flux and flow. He writes, "All emotions are qualifications of a drama and they change as that drama develops."[98] "Impulsion" is Dewey's term for the impetus driving the ongoing process that he describes in *Art as Experience*. He examines the process in terms of mechanisms of "propulsion," or the "combustion" of the creative impulse.[99] He compares this to the original act of the Creator, and he further describes it in religious language, citing another American phenomenological "radical empiricist": "What William James wrote about religious experience might well have been written about the antecedents and acts of expression."[100]

In his overall conceptualization, Dewey collapses a creative process and a learning process into a single model of "growth," described in terms of the way an organism develops. Culminating points of ending and completion become "funded" into being new beginnings in a cumulative process. Dewey suggests that confronting sequential tensions or challenges is integral to the process of realizing a coalescing relationship between self and "environment." This continual "impulsion" to expand beyond boundaries and constraints is constitutive of self-understanding since, as in learning, encountering challenge within developmental processes shapes understandings of world and of self.[101] The difference to Dewey between this creative dynamic and the educational process, in Bertram Morris' words, is that while art processes potentially have a finish or a final endpoint, education is always open-ended. Morris quotes Dewey: "There is nothing to which education is subordinate save more education."[102] Dewey thus offers a model of processes of expansion through learning within committed domains. Rather than use language of religion evocatively or metaphorically, as does Dewey in *Art as Experience*, this work recognizes these dynamics within actual religious acts themselves.

Projects of piety and ritual practice, as human activity, naturally comprise such processes of learning, although religious enactments and education may not always be an explicit goal of a religious movement as in Qur'ānic Indonesia. In particular, acquiring ritual competence enhances expansive, cumulative, and open-ended qualities of practice, orienting the practitioner affectively with respect to the continuous nature of practice itself. An interaction of affective registers within these regimens propels religious projects of learning and practice. These dynamics of feeling, especially within motivated projects of learning, are potentially generative of practice.

In the ongoing and escalating projects of the recited Qur'ān in Indonesia, practitioners sought self-consciously to "fund" their own and others' religious projects. Learning and repetition within social contexts reveal the affective elements of sustaining and escalating piety within this Islamic system of religious revitalization. Expansive dynamics of "feedback," often overlooked in the study of ritual and repetition, informed this dynamic, and experiences, perceptions, and affect in turn informed individual and collective practice, changing how ritual actors thought of themselves and their activity over time. Such "feedback," for example, may occur among individual and system, as with the shared standards and situations that inform individuals' motivation. "Feedback" may also comprise an experiential sense of "orthopraxy" or the coalescence of perceived ideals and realities of practice, both of which are generated within the learning context. Such dynamics in Indonesian Qur'ānic practice delivered affective force, impelling ongoing practice, and determined understandings of the self as ongoing practitioner.

Self-understanding emerges as a combination of cognitive, practical, and affective dynamics within the cumulative learning dynamics of ritual. In particular, in the Indonesian Qur'ānic system of education and revitalization, subjectivities of engagement formed through affect in ritual rehearsal, especially through modes of aesthetics and the social and developmental assessment of qualities such as personal ability and performative "orthopraxy." Also combining affective and social dimensions of experience in a theoretical work, sociologist Jack Katz theorizes "the essential place of aesthetics in all behaviors, however mundane or esoteric," and thus considers a universalized "aestheticized subject" as an extension of his insight that humans both "do" and are "done by" their emotions. He writes that emotions produce an aesthetic system, since the self is known indirectly through others by way of their assessments.[103] Although theorists of ritual, unlike Katz, have not often recognized the changing state of the practitioner in relation to knowledge and activity, there are important exceptions, such as Williams and Boyd in *Ritual, Art, and Knowledge* and Humphrey and Laidlaw in *The Archetypal Actons of Ritual*. Humphrey and Laidlaw address one aspect of this self-consciousness when they explain that "ritualized action . . . presents an arena in which one individual may experience and 'work on' the self in a variety of ways."[104] They elaborate, "Just as concepts of the self do not spring fully fledged from life or from sacred books, but must be learned, so also in ritual action it must be the case that agents' encounters with the acts which are ready to be performed can change how they think of themselves." They emphasize the aspect of self-assessment and self-knowing in ritual, continuing, "in religions . . . which exhort people to *measure* themselves against ideals it [this change in self] is all the more likely."[105]

In each of the chapters to follow, affect and learning are shown to propel shared projects of Qur'ānic engagement and also to determine self-understandings as ongoing practitioners. Emotion emergent in ongoing practice and learning resonated with more expansive affective patterns outside of contexts of education and performance, thereby motivating continued practice. In Qur'ānic Indonesia, affect took the form of attention to the recited Qur'ān within the project of its preservation in memory; this extended to emotional strategies of managing that very ability socially in order to remain a memorizer. Sentiment conveyed both by the "learning curriculum" and the "teaching curriculum" of Arabic reading manipulated feeling to encode specific emotions into the activity of vocalizing the Qur'ān by way of apprehending the sound and shape of its language. In these regimens, self-understandings were a tool to solve problems in practice, reconstituting the self in terms of sentimental systems of learning; affective senses such as "tradition" and "modern" determined understandings of motivated self and motivating system through specific pedagogical strategies. Norms of Qur'ānic performance articulated an aesthetic and affective sense of "having it right" through systems of learning in which the dynamics of affect determined a specific technique and a compelling pull to escalating practice. Affect was also a self-conscious goal of the project of competing in the recited Qur'ān. In Indonesia, modes of hierarchizing experience among the many goal registers that were conveyed by tournaments privileged a self-conscious quality of "*motivasi*" (motivation) itself. In Indonesia in the 1900s, affect shaped Muslims' subjectivities as ongoing practitioners of the recited Qur'ān. Practitioners were self-conscious about the modulation of their own and others' affect in order to achieve competence as well as to solve problems (such as "being able to" read beautifully) in lived situations. Often, the problems relating to ongoing practice were articulated in relation to expansive ideals that were in turn affective as well (such as sensing one is "getting it right" or the project of "motivating" others to join in). Within these processes of ongoing engagement, affect transformed individuals, even as affective systems themselves underwent change, escalating engagement with the recited Qur'ān on individual and social levels.

The affective contours of self-conscious projects of acquiring, perfecting, and sustaining abilities related to reading the Qur'ān on individual and collective levels formed a widespread system of continuous motivated involvement in Indonesia in the 1990s. Under the conditions described, religious practice—while maybe not always making perfect—may generate more practice. Perfection—as both a perception and a project of learning and performance—was making practice through the new subjectivities of practicing Muslims, especially through individual and collective modes of feeling.

CHAPTER 2

MEMORIZING

Attentive Modes of Preserving the Qur'ān

Prolonged engagement with the Qur'ān effects long-term transformation of its readers over time, socially and individually. This is presented as self-evident in the Qur'ān, and Muslims also recognize this transformation to extend directly from the project of preserving the Qur'ān in memory. Those who memorize the Qur'ān are recognized to be its "preservers" (*ḥāfiẓ*, pl. *ḥuffāẓ*), known for a specific social persona that derives from an ability to recite the Qur'ān without the aid of a text. The ongoing practice of committing and maintaining the Qur'ān in memory requires that memorizers negotiate affectively the expectations for the social role and responsibilities of one who "carries" the Qur'ān in memory for the community. At the same time, they undertake the continual management of the technical challenges of safeguarding that memory on a daily basis. The confluence of social, cognitive, and emotional challenges facing Qur'ān memorizers necessitates continual balancing of tasks, norms, and the self-understanding that comes with achievement. Memorizing is thus a process of ongoing remaking of the self through a specifically Qur'ānic involvement grounded in both the text and its social contexts.

Ongoing care of memory among Qur'ān memorizers in Indonesia created a distinct and consistent subjectivity in terms of the ongoing nature of practice. A proficient Qur'ān reciter reads the Qur'ān differently than a novice, although the two are clearly related developmentally. All practicing Muslims must memorize enough of the Qur'ān in order to fulfill the obligation of canonical worship (*ṣalāt*, requiring memorization of the opening *sūrah*, al-Fātiḥah, and also a few other short *sūrahs*). In the beginner's ability are the seeds of ritual expertise for those who wish to develop it. Although the Qur'ān does not change, the *ḥāfiẓ* reciting a section as a part of the rehearsal of the entire text each night during Ramadan (a traditional practice) is not doing the same thing as a child who struggles to read through a passage for the first time; likewise, the self-understanding of the memorizer and the beginning pupil differs. The social understanding of the practitioners is also not identical; commitment to complete memorization of the Qur'ān brings with it the need for attention to normative expectations as well as the kind of practical needs for attention to the text that determine comportment in social situations.

The memorization of the Qur'ān brings along with it an expected comportment with the Qur'ān as well as with others. Cognitively and socially, memorizers continually observe the role of "preserver" with little leeway for mistakes. The textual and social domains are interrelated domains of risk, and the same challenges and tensions arise again and again, in historical communities as well as for each memorizer over time. For example, at one contest for religious boarding school students (over seven hundred attended), a contestant in memorization could not identify the verse provided by the judges. As the contestant became increasingly confused in front of the crowd, some of the children began to laugh and clap. Of course, it is patently unacceptable ever to laugh when the Qur'ān is being recited, as the entire crowd of children was admonished in no uncertain terms with a stern rebuke by a contest leader right after the episode. Kids, however—excited to be on a trip far from home with their friends at a special event, late at night, in the big city—will be kids. As a general rule, to present oneself before a group of people claiming to know the Qur'ān implicates patterns of expected comportment for the memorizer even more than for the audience. If these expectations are broken—if the memorizer makes some kind of mistake, for example—the ramifications may be serious. This is all the more the case if the mistake is not merely textual, but judged to be moral as well.

The expected social comportment of the memorizer is based on the maintenance of his or her cognitive ability as well as care of the moral self. Memorizers have taken both the Qur'ān and the self as their object and must maintain each relationally. In order to maintain both the social role as well as the "preserved" Qur'ān, memorizers apply affective strategies in each domain, in situations of both cognitive and interpersonal problem-solving. The ongoing management of affect that this task requires makes and remakes the memorizer as a continuous practitioner. The combination of social norms deriving from patterns of the text and the Message in the Qur'ān itself, the maintenance of this expertise, and the negotiation of interpersonal interactions as a part of the project of memory and becoming or remaining a "memorizer" generates through affective dynamics the subjectivities of Qur'ān memorizers as ongoing practitioners.

Memorizing the Qur'ān is especially challenging owing to the unique style and structure of the Qur'ān. The demanding cognitive and affective tasks of memorizing contribute to the development of a distinctive subjectivity of a memorizer as an ongoing practitioner. The Qur'ān conveys its Message in a structure and style that continually shift and refract in human thought and memory. Evidence of the difficulty for memorizers in holding Qur'ānic structure in memory is the frequency with which variants of a particular *ḥadīth* is cited, in Indonesia and elsewhere. The account reports that the Prophet Muḥammad stated that memorizing the Qur'ān is more difficult than tethering a camel that is trying to run away. This report is related in variants such as "Guard this Qur'ān, for, by He who has the soul of Muḥammad in His hand, it is easier for it to escape from the mind than for a camel to escape" (Bukhārī and Muslim) and, through another *isnād* ("support" for transmission): "The possessing of the Qur'ān is like a tied up camel. If one is fastened tight to it, then one can hold it fast, but if one loosens it, then it will go" (Bukhārī and Muslim).[1] Qur'ānic statements in fact suggest their own design to demand continual attentive "reminding" *(dhikr)* in order for universal meanings and particular expressions to remain firmly anchored in memory. Although this is suggested by the Qur'ān to be an "easy" task for those whose hearts are open, unique stylistic features of the recited Qur'ān also ensure that maintaining the ability to recite from memory will be a lifelong process of highly focused engagement.

In Islamic traditions, the memorization of the Qur'ān is a special religious duty incumbent upon Muslims who bear a responsibility to their communities as "preservers" of revelation. Because the memorizer carries *(ḥamala)* the Qur'ān in memory, he or she is a special kind of person, a "preserver," who performs a religious obligation on behalf of this community. "Preserving" *(taḥfīẓ)* the Qur'ān as a memorizer *(ḥāfiẓ/ḥāfiẓah)* comes under the Islamic legal classification of *farḍ kifāyah*, or a collective religious duty. Another example of *farḍ kifāyah* is *qaḍā'*, or serving as religious judge *(qāḍī')*. Unlike an individual duty *(farḍ 'ayn)* such as *zakāt* (legal almsgiving), which is required of all Muslims provided basic conditions are met, not every Muslim is required to carry out complete memorization of the Qur'ān. Instead, in *farḍ kifāyah*, the community as a whole is charged to see that at least some individuals are undertaking the preservation of the Qur'ān at all times. The norms of comportment *(adab*, pl. *ādāb)* incumbent upon memorizers not only reflect the history and status of their social and religious roles, but they also support directly the practice of continually maintaining the ability to recite from memory through specific given standards. This involvement is necessarily collective and affective because of the communal dimensions of moral responsibility as well as the more practical reason that memorizers must work together to make certain that no error enters into transmission.

Memorization of the Qur'ān forms the fundamental basis of Muslim learning and is traditionally the prerequisite for further study in the Islamic religious sciences. The process of Qur'ān memorization provides both a specific and an idealized model of "traditional" education, established by structures of textual transmission, orality, aurality, and memory. The social role of the educated person *('ālim)* begins with the memorization of the Qur'ān. This has shaped patterns of Muslim schooling, from basic "Qur'ānic schools" (Ar. *kuttāb;* Ind. *pesantren*) to religious colleges (Ar. *madrasas*). In traditional *kuttāb* (schools dedicated to elementary learning, such as Qur'ān reading and memorization) and *madrasas* (historically, institutions of higher education such as those for legal study), aural transmission and memorization was the dominant mode of schooling; this began with the memorization of the Qur'ān by the age of seven or eight at primary school *(kuttāb)* and continued with memorization of short but comprehensive introductory works in areas such as jurisprudence or Arabic grammar.[2] This pattern has continued in Indonesia. In Indonesia, regional institutions and networks, in turn, have reflexively shaped the methods by which Muslims have learned and practiced memorizing the Qur'ān.[3]

In Indonesia, the *kiai* (learned religious teachers) who taught memorization were seen to embody the faculty of memory that is idealized in traditional Islamic education.[4] One such *kiai* who had studied for years in the Middle East had his own *pesantren* exclusively for Qur'ān memorization in Makassar, where young boys would be sent to memorize the Qur'ān before beginning their formal schooling. This conforms to a typical institutional pattern present in Indonesia since at least the nineteenth century, whereby religious scholars returning from the Middle East founded schools, some of them fairly large *pesantren* (boarding schools). There are several such *pesantren* in South Sulawesi and many more on Java and elsewhere across Muslim Indonesia that correspond to the same pattern; many of these institutions feature a specialization, "*takhassus*," in memorization. Families who sent their children to study with *kiai* at these schools could be confident that instruction in Qur'ānic memorization would form part of the basic curriculum.[5] Teachers at these institutions were traditionally not paid in money, but received services and gifts from students and their families, especially when a child "completed" *(tammat)* the memorized Qur'ān.

The special respect afforded the *ḥāfiẓ* throughout the Islamic world was enhanced in Indonesia by the fact that Qur'ān memorization has not historically been a widespread aspect of children's education. Since it was relatively rare for a scholar to have had the opportunity to study the Qur'ān in Cairo or the Arabian peninsula, "traditional" *kiai* with this background and who taught memorization were afforded special prestige.[6] The most-respected teachers among the generation of older *kiai* active in South Sulawesi in the 1990s had generally studied in the Middle East, first having memorized the Qur'ān there. These *kiai* would usually teach in varied contexts of schooling. One common pattern was to serve as the head of a rural *pesantren*. Another pattern, for *kiai* in urban areas who were not themselves at the head of an institution in the country, was to instruct at a "modern" *pesantren* during the day, while also having young people come to their private homes at dawn and in the evening for ongoing memorization study (and, in addition, during the afternoon, children would also come by for semiformal study of basic reading). For example, at the *pesantren* Mahadul Hadiths (also known as Pesantren Biru) in Bone across the peninsula from Makassar, there was a set memorization curriculum taught by the local *kiai*. At Pesantren Biru, each of about four hundred children was to learn all of "Juz' 'Amma" (the last thirtieth of the Qur'ān) and lengthy *sūrahs* like 18 al-Kahf, along with shorter ones such as 67 al-Mulk. In addition, in mornings and evenings outside of more formal schooling, students would come to this same *kiai*'s home, where his semiformal program in memorization was called Taqsimul Huffaz and comprised the entire Qur'ān. Some students lived in the *kiai*'s home and did household chores in exchange for their board. In order to work with *kiai* such as this one, students were first tested for "fluency" *(faṣāḥah)* of reading (if they failed, they usually did not get a second chance), and then they would begin to memorize, *juz'* by *juz'* (one thirtieth of the Qur'ān at a time).

In the 1980s, accompanying the resurgence in Qur'ānic practices overall in Indonesia, there was a movement in Islamic higher education that followed the model of the prestigious Islamic universities (notably al-Azhar in Cairo) explicitly in emphasizing memorization. There was also an effort to enhance memorizational aptitude among university students in the field of Islamic law, for example, at national Islamic universities, or IAINs. Other Islamic colleges had special faculty for voluntary programs in memorization. In addition, the 1970s and 1980s saw the establishment of special Qur'ān colleges (such as PTIQ and IIQ in Jakarta, and STAI in Makassar) that adopted the model of Cairo's al-Azhar and featured memorization (as well as recitation, along with basic subjects like *ḥadīth* study, Arabic grammar, and Islamic law and theology) as part of the curriculum. The heightened profile of memorization among girls and women especially in the 1980s and 1990s was encouraged by these new institutions as well as by the impact of the competition system. There was a steady flow of young men and women Qur'ān memorizers and teachers between the old and newer institutions in Indonesia in the 1990s, with students from the small country *pesantren* coming to the more urban colleges to study in preparation to teach, and then cycling back from the big *pesantren* centers and colleges in city areas to teach in rural schools, often in their hometowns. The network was compact in part because the number of memorizers was still relatively small. Unlike the overlapping programs to promote melodic recitation, the state (and LPTQ) appeared uninvolved in memorizational networks.

One of the traditional institutional roles of the (male) Qur'ān memorizer in Indonesia is as a mosque imam, or prayer leader. This may represent year-round employment or it may be in the form of more limited service during the month of Ramadan (when, over the course of the month's *tarāwīḥ* prayers, the entire Qur'ān is recited, necessitating that the imam must have committed large portions of the text to memory). At the home of a prominent *kiai* just before Ramadan began, for example, I spent an afternoon hearing the phone ring off the hook as requests came in from various parts of the province of South Sulawesi, inviting his memorization students to spend the holy month in their respective districts as imams. An increasing awareness of the memorizer as a potential performer, whether in the mosque or at a tournament, was inspiring many memorizers to study melodic forms of recitation in the 1990s, in the words of one young imam, "so that people will want to come and listen to you [lead prayer]." Many competitive memorizers were also beginning to study *lagu* (melodic modes), even though this was not a judging area for *tahfiz* (memorization) events. This trend was partially attributable to the fact that coaches who traveled to lead the top training sessions for regional teams of reciters were experts in melodic recitation; naturally, this is what they would tend to teach mixed classes of competition reciters and memorizers. Top memorizers would be coached in these sessions, for example, to modulate their *murattal lagu* with the "answer" to each "*soal*," or "question," that judges pose in competition. Other male and female memorizers, who were neither imams nor competitors, wished to improve their *tajwīd* and *lagu* in keeping with more general, and inflating, aesthetic standards for the recited Qur'ān.

The subjectivity of a memorizer is doubly made through the mechanisms of affect that he or she applies in interaction with the Qur'ān and with others. Affective strategies of preserving the Qur'ān in memory were connected to the structure and style of the Qur'ān as well as to social expectations. These combined in Indonesian memorizational practice to produce a subjectivity of Qur'ān memorization as one of continuous engagement. These techniques of social and cognitive "emotion management" for Qur'ān memorization do not pertain most directly to the meanings of the Qur'ān. They derive instead from social and experiential problems and tensions arising from aspects of ritual rehearsal and repetition, based on cognitive, affective, and social features of the memorized Qur'ān. The first kind of problems memorizers had to solve related to the repetition of the text itself; they relate to the affective techniques Indonesian memorizers applied in order to retain cognitively the material in the Qur'ān, whose structure and style demands unique modes of attention. A second area of tension pertains to social selves and specifically the need for self-conscious management of self and feeling in order to maintain the social relationships that make possible the sustained and concentrated practice of preserving the Qur'ān in memory and thus remaining in the role of a "memorizer." A moralized Qur'ānic system of cultivated practice, including norms of comportment based on the Qur'ān itself, establishes patterns of problems that need to be solved socially, cognitively, and personally. The cultivated subjectivities of memorizers emerged from the emotion work necessary to solve these problems and to maintain their competence in relation both to practice and to interaction.

Remaining a memorizer, just like the very first steps in beginning to memorize a part of the text of the Qur'ān, is difficult work and a serious responsibility. The ongoing practice of committing and maintaining the Qur'ān within memory requires that memorizers meet the expectation of social role and religious responsibility for one who "carries" the Qur'ān in memory for the community. At the same time, memorizers must also undertake the continual management of the technical and interpersonal challenges of safeguarding that memory within groups of memorizers and in relation to others on a daily basis. The confluence of social, cognitive, and affective challenges that face Qur'ān memorizers necessitates continual balancing of tasks, norms, as well as the self-understanding that comes with achievement. Domains of social and ethical norms, maintenance of practice, negotiation of interpersonal dynamics based on practice, and features of the repeated Qur'ān itself generate a subjectivity of an ongoing practitioner. Affect is self-consciously a part of this ongoing effort, building in all of these domains upon features of preserving text in personal memory and in the social self.

What Is a (Ritual) Emotion?

Muslim communities recognize Qur'ān memorizers for a social persona that extends from their ability to recite the Qur'ān without the aid of a text. Maintaining this ability cognitively requires constant engagement with the affecting syntax and structure of the Qur'ān as well as the application of strategies of "emotion management" for rehearsal and retention. The required rigor of repetition extending from the Qur'ān ensures a transformation of the memorizer. Under the influence of the technical and practical demands of memorization, one will necessarily be changed by the ongoing project of carrying the Qur'ān in memory, and this transformation is based on a combination of cognitive, emotional, and social experiences and obligations. Activity in the institutions in which the developmental process of memorization occurs elaborates these patterns, and less formal social networks that are based on the requirement to rehearse memorized material further reinforce and sustain them. Emotion management of social interactions coupled with the affective "attention" that the Qur'ān continually demands generate a subjectivity recognized for the capability to meet demands and responsibilities of ongoing ritual work. This comportment, not coincidentally, meets expectations widely shared for Qur'ān memorizers who have encountered the same kinds of problems and tensions across the Muslim-majority and Muslim-minority worlds since the earliest times of Islam.

In the contemporary human sciences, affect is often theorized as a one-way internalizing "force" of social structures or as a kind of explanation for the experiential salience of shared meanings that are otherwise accessed through rhetoric. Affect is also often treated as a sort of body sensation that is shaped socially as it is performed, aestheticized, or intellectualized. It is usually a category used to explain ideation in the mind or sensation in the body with the primary question being either how are shared structures significant for individuals, on the one hand, or, on the other hand, how personal experience relates to social worlds. If emotion is instead seen to be a dimension that potentially operates autonomously from both socially determined cognition and embodied states, another kind of picture may emerge, however. Qur'ān memorizers in Indonesia, for example, theorized affect as instrumental techniques that correlate experience with the social self. Emotion was individual and social, bonded with theory and practice through the engagement with the Qur'ān as a stable term. In praxis and metapraxis (discussions of practice), memorizers synthesized issues such as "private versus public" and "mind versus body," just as they are also now coming to be blended in contemporary academic theory.

A response to the general methodological problem of reconciling "private" experience to "culturally constituting" social structures has been emerging in recent cultural anthropology. Naomi Quinn and Claudia Strauss present the issue to be the following: "It is time for us to confront the contradiction in this definition of culture as meaningful, symbolic, signifying, conceptual, ideational, but not to anyone in particular, that has encumbered the analysis, and required circumlocutions in the analytic language of so many anthropologists. It is time to say that culture is both public and individual, both in the world and people's heads."[7] Scholars such as Quinn and Strauss working in the field of psychological anthropology are here addressing the problem of an overall lack of theory for internalization that would take both experience and sociality into account. Strauss sums up the emerging recognition of the individual in cultural anthropology in the following way: "Rather, social action is the result of a process by which public events are turned into private representations and acted on, thereby creating new public events, and we need a better understanding of how this happens."[8]

Many of the "classical" problems in emotion theory in the human sciences also relate to the question of apprehending the site at which religious structures exert a real presence: a human being. Whether expressed as a "self," "person," "role," "subjectivity," or "identity," the categorical label the theorist chooses to ascribe to an individual often exposes his or her own operative theory of cultural systems.[9] Concern, often Marxian in orientation, is often expressed about the culture-bound presuppositions that accompany psychologizing another as an "individual" in the study of cultural systems, especially in contexts in which the idea of the autonomous "individual" is supposedly not elaborated as emphatically as it is in Western ethnotheories.[10] Preferred in recent decades, especially by those sympathetic to such criticism, has been a sociological framework like Foucault's or Bourdieu's in which, often, no individuals appear at all. Whether the emphasis is on overall "systems" or the experiences of individuals within such systems, if a "culture" cannot cry (or if crying is not a behavior "culture" produces directly by "constituting" it), then the question arises of who or what should be said to "have" the experience—and how? In order to highlight processes that span multiple domains of experience and sociality, I prefer simply to deploy the term "individual," using "subjectivity" to denote a self-labeling process that is a component of self-understanding.

Another reason for seeking robust and general categories such as these is that the question of accessibility of emotions remains a stumbling block in the human sciences, often stuck in the "either-or" dichotomies such as "mind and body" and "inner and outer" without affording alternate terrain. For example, in *How Emotions Work*, Jack Katz addresses this issue with new theory, outlining these kinds of problems while also echoing longstanding phenomenological approaches: "The prevailing folk and scientific cultures for considering our identities doggedly refuse to acknowledge that there is no point of separation between what is 'outside' and what is 'inside,' no definable limit to the penetration of self into world and world into self, no place where one's identity neatly ends and the social environment obdurately begins."[11] The public-private split in the study of emotion and social systems to which Katz refers is closely related to the mind-body problem. This is because shared social meanings tend to be construed in academic "emotion theory" in terms of cognition, language, and "discourse," whereas selves are studied terms of interior and embodied experience (even though there is no evidence that thinking is a more public activity than feeling).

The literature coming from two general perspectives in cultural theory of emotion, social constructionism on the one hand and embodiment theory on the other, tend to loop back on one another in a way that suggests that theorists may actually all be addressing the same problem, framed alternately either as the sociality or the personalization of emotions. These approaches are far more nuanced than a schematic overview allows and many of them actually take up these issues explicitly as their focus of analysis. Nevertheless, when viewed historically, neither of these general theoretical approaches, originating from two different starting points on the "mind-body" axis (body sensation/cognition), has taken seriously enough the proposition that "emotion" may be an autonomous domain of perception (after Sartre's definition) that may be seen to transcend such dichotomies from the outset.

For convenience, it has now become somewhat common to identify the roots of the standard academic approaches to emotion in the human sciences with the respective views of two foundational figures in the field of the history of religions, Emile Durkheim *(Elementary Forms of the Religious Life)* and William James (author of *Varieties of Religious Experience*), on emotion.[12] When traced along a developmental trajectory of theoretical formulations, these orientations feed back into one another. Social systems of sentiment, usually seen in terms of language and "discourse," lead to the problem of experience and internalization, whereas emotions viewed as embodiment lead back to the problem of public expression. This circularity suggests that contemporary discussions of emotion in the human sciences may have been orbiting around the actual phenomenon of emotion itself, whose categorical autonomy remains relatively underrecognized. A synthesis of embodied (personal) and cognitive (social) approaches—not as oppositional but as pointing to a third term—reveals how aspects of emotion may blend into other spheres of experience, activity, and social systems, as well as their potentially generative power for ongoing religious projects of piety, such as voluntary Qur'ānic engagement.

Many theories in cultural anthropology and related fields, including an "ethnotheory" of emotions dominant in the field of psychology (which posits "primary" and "secondary" emotions), begin with the "body" and its sensation as the basis for understanding emotion. For example, William James' answer to the question that titles his essay "What Is an Emotion?" is that emotion is an awareness of a physiological response, or, in his words, emotion is a "perception of a visceral disturbance."[13] Specifically: "Our natural way of thinking about these standard emotions is that the mental perception of some fact excites the mental affection called the emotion, and that this latter state of mind gives rise to the bodily expression. My thesis on the contrary is that *the bodily changes follow directly the* PERCEPTION *of the exciting fact and that our feeling of the same changes as they occur* IS *the emotion*."[14] Emotion here is not exactly an embodied state but an epiphenomenal recognition of a sensory experience. One does not cry because one feels sad or wants to feel sad, for example, but in James' formulation one feels sad because one is aware of crying. James' contemporaries criticized his theory of emotion, and contemporary theorists also criticize James for neglecting the cognitive aspects of emotions, leading to what is referred to as the "two layers model," which Lutz and White compare to Freudians' primary and secondary processes.[15]

Many contemporary theorists working in this area approach "affect" from the standpoint of "embodiment," implying that "emotion" is a type of physical sensation; although recognized to be attenuated by structures of sociality, the approach focuses primarily on individuals' perceptive sensation. Such contemporary phenomenological studies relating to feeling and experience often draw on Merleau-Ponty's work on the body.[16] The study of "embodiment" in current social theory has come to support "experience-near" methodologies as well as a great deal of literature on questions of pain and healing. These studies of feeling and healing often open up critical questions in the analysis of experience and expression, such as how to interpret patients' descriptions of inner states, because attempting to understand suffering selves leads immediately to questions of access and expression.[17] Although this orientation is distinct in many ways from the theoretical concept of "the body" that views it a site of signification or symbolic manipulation,[18] when "embodiment" is understood in terms of emotion, the ground nevertheless shifts to questions of signification. Studies of healing in cultural anthropology especially often frame this question in terms of aesthetics and performance. For example, in *Body and Emotion*, Desjarlais makes an identification of emotion and a cultural "aesthetic system," a move that allows him to use standard ethnographical methods of cultural interpretation that also function as a study of embodied emotion.[19] Thus, even if some kinds of embodied "experience" (such as pain) can be universalized or essentialized to permit "understanding," the anthropologist's question then becomes the interpretation of social signals about such experienced conditions.

These considerations resonate with some of the earliest questions posed in the study of emotions in this academic tradition, such as Darwin's writings on expression and other understandings of emotions' "signal functions." Investigation of these questions in psychology, for example, was advanced by Ekman's famous study of facial expressions, and cultural anthropologists such as Richard Schechner have considered these issues in terms of theatrical performance.[20] An "embodiment" approach to emotions, sometimes a reaction to cognitivist perspectives, thus doubles back to questions about the communication of experience and social understandings of emotion that are conveyed especially through language (and sometimes music). Beginning with the "body," sociality thus becomes the problem. Understanding emotions in terms of social meanings typifies the perspective of Durkheim as well as later "social constructionists."

Durkheim's sociological formulation of religion and social systems in *Elementary Forms of the Religious Life* includes a consideration of mourning observances in Australian cultures, claiming that "mourning is not the spontaneous expression of individual emotions," but rather it is a ritual convention and expectation enforced by the group. Elsewhere Durkheim presents affect ("effervescence") as the engine of social change, but he presents ritual affect here to be as a form of control of individual feeling.[21] This view readily implies a distinction of (genuine) inner and (spurious) outer emotion, a persistent issue now known as the "sincerity problem" in the study of emotion. In addition to supporting a pervasive bias in Western ethnotheories of emotion (that "private" emotion is authentic whereas "public" is fake) that stresses emotion in terms of public meanings, Durkheim's theory also anticipates the later "social constructionist" view of emotion in significant respects. Anthropologist Michelle Rosaldo illustrates a typical contemporary social constructionist description of emotion when she states that emotions may be approached as "self-concerning, partly physical responses that are at the same time aspects of a moral or ideological attitude; emotions are both feelings and cognitive constitutions, linking person, action, and sociological milieu."[22] As emotions are aspects of cultural systems, it follows in this perspective that analysis should relate the person primarily to social structure rather than to "naturally" responsive internal states.

A birfurcation of "inner" and "outer" emotional selves has actually come to be rejected by most social constructionists. M. Rosaldo points out that generalizations about "outer" and "inner" selves can lead to harmful cultural relativizing on the one hand and inappropriate universalizing on the other.[23] In stating, as does Rosaldo, that "private selves are not distinct from social personas,"[24] social constructionist approaches to emotion in effect treat the "inner" as subordinate to the "outer" dimension, tending to collapse the two since, as Rosaldo proposes, "innerness" is shaped by "culturally laden sociality."[25] Anthropologists working from the social constructionist position are often cognitivist in approach, sharing her assumption that emotions are "embodied thoughts" and often preferring to label emotion "thought-feeling." Since feeling and thinking are both instituted "culturally," they may be approached with the same methodology, which is to consider key lexical words and "discourses" of the languages of "emotion talk."[26]

In what is called the "strong thesis" of social constructionism, emotions (including physical sensation) are effects of society and culture even as they structure the social world. The "weak thesis" of social constructionism applies various theoretical strategies to allow for some nonconstituted "natural emotions."[27] Even proponents of attenuated positions such as "commonsense naturalism," however, still tend to have more interest in cultural systems than in felt experience.[28] The issue of the limits of social constructionism questions how much nonmediated embodied sensation can be understood or ascribed to actors within social systems. An approach based in sociality here leads back to Jamesian questions of felt experience.

This "mind-body" circularity around the study of emotions in the human sciences may have an alternative. Such an orientation would allow a fuller picture of thought, embodiment, and affect than do approaches that are concerned with which of the first two categories constitutes the third. An example of this theoretical shift is Jack Katz' study *How Emotions Work*. Katz writes that he synthesizes three separate strains of investigation into one methodological approach to emotion in his book. He describes the first as the "Freudian exercise of double interpretation but with the phenomenological twist that both meanings must be grounded in evidence of the subject's own doubly resonant experience." By this he means considering what is "sensually" perceived by actors as well as meanings "manifest" to others. The second strain is from the "sociological" tradition, or the question of "how emotional expressions are shaped in anticipation of how they will be perceived," citing the work of George Herbert Mead. The last field of study on which he draws pertains to the "embodiment of conduct," an emerging field of study.[29] He draws the following conclusion:

> We do not "present a self" by some means or in some time and place that is separate from "the embodiment of our conduct," in turn separate from developing our "construction of meanings" of the situation. . . . Our selves are best summarized as prisms, not as looking glasses. Any given action is the result of a person's integration of three simultaneously sustained processes. A moment's doings in social life entail maneuvering in detailed ways to make recognizable sense of one's situated behavior, even while one senses how the current situation fits into one's ongoing life, and even as the metaphoric vehicle of one's conduct is being transformed, often seemingly beyond one's control.[30]

One of Katz' main points, echoed by an earlier thinker, Dewey, is that emotions solve problems and are expressive, aesthetic, and performative of self.

The insight that emotions are not merely reactive but instead a site of creative agency or problem-solving is not new, especially in the field of sociology. The concept of "management" in its functionalist or instrumentalist form may be seen to originate in the interactionist tradition and especially the work of Erving Goffman. Goffman includes emotions as a part of the fields of interactions of lived experience, writing, "I want to stress that these emotions function as moves, and fit so precisely into the logic of the ritual game that it would be difficult to understand them without it."[31] Goffman's model remains influential in the current form of theory of "emotion management" but is often attenuated. For example, in an article surveying multiple dimensions of the sociology of affect, Steven Gordon expands the idea of the "management of sentiment" (referring to Goffman's work) to include a more complex relationship between experience and expression in both "public" and "private" contexts.[32]

Two more recent works highlighting "emotion management" indicate a nuanced understanding of affect that is transactional but not, however, identical to tactics of "rational choice." Like Katz' work, they point to the possibilities of "double-anchored" alignment between interior perception and shared levels of feeling in religious systems. These are the sociological work of Arlie Hochschild on modern American experiences of work and family, and Unni Wikan's medical-anthropological work on Balinese culture. Hochschild, a sociologist who coined the term "emotion management," takes both the "micro" and "macro" levels of analysis into account in her work,[33] as she demonstrates the application of "feeling rules" and the economy of "emotion work" in social situations.[34] Wikan uses a generalized term "affect" for "thought-feeling" and reveals the relationship of management of emotions in social situations to internal states, especially the "emotion work" undertaken by Balinese people to maintain the outward impression and felt experience of a pleasant and pleasing emotional state.[35] Both Hochschild's and Wikan's work highlight possibilities of emotional agency within social structure, indicating ways in which actors take emotions as a site for self-transformation and how emotions are a mode of continuity and change in social systems.

Being a *ḥāfiẓ* is a dynamic process that brings ideals of social role together with the realities of daily, disciplined practice in the situational "management" of affective attention. This attention relates to cognitive, emotional, and moral situations. Working from Katz' phenomenological, sociological, and psychological model along with the insights of Thomas Csordas, Corinne Kratz, and Jonathan Z. Smith that ritual is a form of "attention" that is potentially transformative of self and community, stratified levels of experience ("inner and outer," "mind and body," "public and private") can be combined in terms of a larger process of attending to the recited Qur'ān. The task of memorizing is highly personal in engagement with the text, while the contextual role and practice are social; the feedback between these domains produces the unique subjectivity of the practitioner. Subjectivity is described in this case as an effect of an interactive framework on the levels of groups and individuals having reciprocal impact through moral, cognitive, and especially affective modes. In the case of affect and the continual transformation of Indonesian Qur'ān memorizers as ongoing practitioners, social and cognitive registers of "private" and "public" projects relate to emotional problem-solving within a ritual system that is grounded in an experienced and embodied text.

The Qur'ān could be seen to carry its own internal affective properties, and affective strategies for its internalization forge relationships to text and within social contexts. Here, the recited Qur'ān is a "prism" for affective tensions and opportunities—technical challenges and social, moral norms—that occupy these affective modes of attention; these may or may not be focuses of awareness or "erased" in the automatic habituation of behavior. These Qur'ānic processes of attention have made and remade memorizers with a subjectivity understood in terms of the ongoing nature of their continual work. This was as much the case for Indonesian memorizers in the 1990s as it was for Muslims in the distant past.

Adab: A "Technology of the Community"

While on the one hand the Qur'ān is not experienced as a social product, neither, on the other hand, have the "technologies" for its memorization come ready-made. The interaction of individual practice and social models shapes memorizers' subjectivities, as also do the prescribed norms for the conduct for one who has achieved the status of a *ḥāfiẓ*. Although Qur'ān memorization seems like a lonely and solitary pursuit (and at times it must be), it is simultaneously a highly social activity. A person is required to interact with others in order to memorize the Qur'ān not only to guard against errors in transmission, but also as a component of fulfilling the communal duty of discharging legal *farḍ kifāyah*. Memorizing, although it is a practice cultivated by individuals through effortful, ongoing work, is not merely a process of reflexive impact on the individual in the form of an instrumental "technology of the self," nor is it primarily a question of a unidirectional (and possibly unreflective) reproduction of social structure. Memorizing is, ideally, adopting a named, social self and a named comportment along with the "preservation" of the text for the sake of religious community. Memorizing is thus a "technology of the community" and one that requires continual emotion management and affective attention in order to maintain the activity's characteristic subjectivity of engagement.

Strategies of affect, whether viewed within the text of the Qur'ān itself or under the social conditions of Qur'ānic interactions, reinforce memorizers' self-understandings and social roles through the attentive management of unanticipated tensions. This is a different, although potentially complementary, understanding of the relationship of affect to moral self from the strain of European-language philosophy that identifies sentiment with moral sensibility (as in the work of Locke, Smith, Hume, and, recently, Nussbaum). Expectations of comportment related to Qur'ān memorization produce the standards, challenges, and goals of continuous engagement. Just as memorizers apply strategies of repetition for the sake of ongoing maintenance of memory, emotional strategies are also applied within particular institutions and social settings in accord with the needs of practice as well as overarching social expectations. The key Islamic idea of "*adab*" (normative comportment) captures the reciprocity of experienced subjectivity and the embracing social norms contained within the system of Qur'ān memorization. This idea conveys Qur'ānic practice to be the moral standard for conduct and explains how, for memorizers, Qur'ānic practice is the actual test of a moral self, constituted in Qur'ānic terms.

The complex intertwining of personal and collective levels of structure and experience in this system requires a robust analytic framework that can model processes of feedback, variance, and change over time. The weak psychology of a popular academic model like Foucault's "technology of the self" tends to attribute a homogeneity to actors that captures neither the variability of individuals' thoughts, feeling, and experiences over time nor the diversity of their experiences overall. Technical and social aspects of Qur'ān memorization are inseparable; together, they form a pattern of affective subjectivity defined in terms of ongoing practice. For this reason, transformation of a person into a memorizer is not best explained in terms of Foucault's approach, which views the self as constituting itself as a subject within social systems.[36] In order for a framework like Foucault's to be applied to a system such as Islamic revitalization in Indonesia, "technologies of the self" must be enhanced with the recognition that they are also "technologies of the community." This is because, in Foucault's conceptualization, "technologies" appear to be ready-made disciplines individuals take on, often relating to some kind of interiorized monologue (such as Christian confession). The feedback between goals of community-building and self-cultivation that is natural to religious systems (such as Christian "charity," Buddhist "merit," Islamic *da'wah*) is not captured well by the model. Even in Sufi theories of self-making, for example, which could be seen in terms of the "technology" of the "path," the ultimate goal of annihilation of the self in realizing Divine Unity (*fanā'*) is balanced with a higher goal: return to the plurality of the created world in order to reside there on a new perceptive level *(baqā')*, an ideal that often includes ideals of social engagement and commitment.

Similarly, an Islamic concept of conditioned comportment through educational practice, Ibn Khaldūn's *malakah*, is not the most helpful model for the process of Qur'ān memorization. As discussed in his famous *Muqaddimah*, it pertains to applied competence within a particular domain of activity in contrast to abstract theoretical "understanding."[37] Like Bourdieu's "habitus," the concept is best described not as knowledge but as a kind of practical, habituated "know-how"; and, in the sociological theory of Ibn Khaldūn, it is acquired purposively. As a one-way process of transmission by which norms become a part of the self, as well as the mechanism by which norms of society are produced and reproduced, *malakah* is a neutral tool, the description of an idealized process for an individual as well as the perpetuation of social systems. It is not really a final goal or a way of moral and social being in the world, nor is it actually a response to tensions formed by experience in real, morally ambivalent lifeworlds. In the Muslim tradition, this is *adab*.[38]

Adab is a property of moral comportment associated primarily with the quality of being "well-educated" or learned. This key concept is a focus of important European-language analyses of Islamic cultures and societies,[39] especially in the subfield of Islamic studies that focuses on the transmission of knowledge, since it is strongly associated with ideals of education in the Islamic religious tradition. The term "*adab*" has a wide range of meanings, but all of them express some aspect of the quality of being "cultivated" and thus convey a sense of normative conduct appropriate to particular persons or specific situations. In his study of the "charismatic role . . . for the concept of knowledge in Muslim society," Franz Rosenthal shows the centrality of *adab* in the Qur'ān and also in Sufi, Shī'ī, and philosophical traditions. He writes that, in classical Islamic usage, "*'ilm*" (knowledge) and "*adab*" are closely linked (as also are *'ilm* and *'amal* [actions]). Comparing *'ilm* and *adab*, Rosenthal explains, "*adab* is clearly the wider term, as it includes matters of ethics, morals, behavior, custom, in addition to those of learning."[40] By the time that formal treatises on "*adab*" were composed, many vocations such as the judge *(qāḍī')* and memorizer *(ḥāfiẓ)* had their own codes of "*adab*," originating in *ḥadīth* and other authoritative materials. This flexible concept was foundational for Sufis, as shown in the many Sufi manuals of *adab* that were in circulation by the twelfth and thirteenth centuries. In the larger Islamic tradition (including Indonesia), "*adab*" is sometimes even a general term for "literature." The concept is also strongly elaborated in Muslim tradition specifically in relation to Qur'ān reading.[41]

In the system of Indonesian Qur'ān recitational education, "*adab*" may have any or all of the meanings above, but the term is associated especially with the memorizer and his or her comportment with the Qur'ān. *Adab* is a fluid concept that embraces the risks, rewards, and ambivalences around being a person who "carries" knowledge personally and socially, indicating the kinds of emotional challenges that span interior and interactive affective work. The framework of *adab* in general, and specifically as it applies to Qur'ān memorization, encompasses the interactions of prescribed norms, processes of practice, and conduct in lived social situations that shape the subjectivity of the memorizer as continuous practitioner. In Indonesia and elsewhere, the term often conveyed a direct and concrete meaning (in part owing to contest usage) of bodily comportment with the Qur'ān, translating transcendent ideals into the smallest details of actual practice. One *kiai* who coached *adab* for contestants described it as "things like walking respectfully and holding the Qur'ān properly," while another defined it, winkingly, as "getting the opening and the closing right, and remembering always to take off your shoes."

The "classical" literature on the *adab* of learning in general and for "carrying" the Qur'ān in specific provides the framework from which Indonesian patterns are direct historical extensions as well as their immediate models. Tracing the historical development of Indonesian material on the subject is not as significant for understanding contemporary experience as is understanding how *adab* is a model that Indonesians and other Muslims turn to in present experience. In memorization, the maintenance of the memorized Qur'ān and of a related social role require continual practice, and such ongoing Qur'ānic practice is identical with social responsibility. *Adab* material proliferates around Qur'ānically based and community-instantiated problems and tensions, especially when moral responsibility to the community may be understood to set the memorizer at odds with the competing expectations of the community itself. It comprises the kinds of affective tensions and ambivalences in subjectivities and social roles that memorizers must "manage" along with their cognitive ability. The classical *adab* literature of reading and studying the Qur'ān, especially "holding" it in memory, outlines the social opportunities and challenges facing the *ḥāfiẓ* as well as how they are resolved by the standard of reading the text itself.

Material included under the heading "*adab*" was compiled and systematized in the context of institutions of formal and semiformal education. These included especially the legal colleges known as *madrasas*.[42] This world of learning in the formative period was shaped by *ḥadīth* collection, transmission, and study, especially in relation to the field of jurisprudence *(fiqh)*. In *Knowledge Triumphant*, Franz Rosenthal surveys "books and chapters on knowledge" found in early Muslim scholars' works, which tend to emphasize matters relating to *ḥadīth* collection and transmission. Some books on the transmission of knowledge include a separate "book of *adab*."[43] *Adab* literature conveys a variety of practical information, from how to ask questions of a teacher to the permissibility of taking academic advice from a scholar who commits evil acts. It also includes the correct ways to offer instruction, such as the importance of saying "I don't know" when one does not, in fact, know an answer. Consistent with the vocation of a *ḥadīth* scholar, there is also critical concern for the power and potential of the faculty of memory, the moral character of one who transmits revealed knowledge, as well as detailed description of the hardships he or she must overcome in order to become a truly learned person.[44]

For example, a writer in the classical period concerned with education, Abū'l-Ḥilāl al-Ḥasan al-'Askarī, in his work *Al-ḥathth 'alā ṭalab al-'ilm wal'l-ijtihād,* enumerates six things that a scholar needs. They are, as presented by Rosenthal: "a penetrating mind, much time, ability, hard work, a skillful teacher, and desire *(shahwah)*." According to al-'Askarī, the ideal search for knowledge must be unselfish and insatiable, and he cites well-known *ḥadīth* reports about the value of travel in search of knowledge. He also includes detailed accounts of how noted scholars such as Abū Ḥanifa would study day and night (Abū Ḥanifa is said to have claimed that the only means to acquire knowledge is "lamp oil").[45] He also expands on issues relevant to learning practice that would have been familiar from earlier tradition, mentioning, for example, which foods harm the memory, while also discussing inherited tendencies for memory. The *adab* of the legal scholar and Qur'ān preserver overlap in this idealized tradition of understandings of knowledge, just as they overlap in practice as well.

Material on the *adab* of the memorization of the Qur'ān begins with the earliest Muslim experience of its preservation; it applies to the kinds of tensions and challenges a memorizer faces in any historical period or geographic region. Historically, the *adab* of Qur'ān memorization is based in the practice of the earliest Islamic Community, and especially the practice of the Prophet, indicated by a commonly cited *ḥadīth* account, "The best of you is one who has learnt the Qur'ān and has taught it" (al-Bukhārī, Ibn Mājah, al-Dārimī). Islamic historiography records that memorization of the Qur'ān was encouraged since the time of the Prophet. The early reciters of the Qur'ān were known as *qāri*'s, or "readers," and they were charged with an important function in the propagation of Islam in its earliest years.[46] Islamic historiographical accounts report that the Prophet dispatched Muslims to teach the Qur'ān even before the Hijrah and that the Prophet singled out some memorizers to teach the Qur'ān to others.[47]

Names of the earliest Qur'ān memorizers are recorded meticulously in Islamic tradition as critical links in the transmission of revelation from the

Prophet Muḥammad to the present time. Islamic historiographical accounts relate the names of Companions who reviewed the entire Qur'ān with the Prophet before his death. The Prophet's wives, for example, played a special role in the preservation of the Qur'ān, and several devoted themselves especially to the task of memorization as a part of their unique role in the Community.[48] In the reports of early battles, historiographical materials make special mention of the names of persons who had been lost to war who knew some or all of the Qur'ān by heart; the Community's loss of these persons was said to be part of the original impetus to collect and compile the Qur'ān. The later sources from the formative period that pertain to Qur'ān reading and memorization are compilations of such previous accounts, especially from *ḥadīth* material that was being compiled and written down by this point as sources for jurisprudence. Naturally, the themes of the most-circulated material also reflect the concerns and conditions of their own time.

The material on the *adab* of Qur'ānic teaching, learning, and recitation demonstrates ambivalences and problems in how Qur'ān preservers relate to power, people, and ultimately the text itself. Some of these issues reflect the tension between the developing tradition of piety (nascent "Sufism" as well as *ḥadīth*-focused "*sharī'a*-mindedness") and a social and political mainstream, including the power structures supported and represented by religious scholars with more worldly tendencies.[49] Rosenthal sums up such tensions as they are commonly expressed in the *adab* literature:

> Reflections on the material rewards of successful efforts to acquire knowledge and to achieve the rank and status of a scholar generally made these points: 1. The efforts are difficult and involve many hardships, humiliations, and deprivations. 2. They must be made regardless of any hope for material rewards. 3. They lead, however, to material rewards in the form of prestige which brings with it a position of high regard in society and a certain measure of affluence. But 4. Knowledge by itself is a much more valuable possession than any material gain that may come to the scholar.[50]

Along with the idealized role of the memorizer there potentially comes an idealized ambivalence about the social role itself, extending from its very basis in the Qur'ān. Historically, this tension intensified in exchanges between those with pious commitments and other established religious authorities. The former, turning to models like Ḥasan of Baṣra (d. 728), claimed legitimacy by criticizing the alleged corruption of scholars who served the state and other interests; the paradigm for this conflict is the historical event of the *miḥna* (inquisition) over the nature of the Qur'ān (833–847). Among the Sufi-minded, after the death of al-Ḥallāj (d. 922), an emerging tradition of esoteric piety, although growing in popularity in an expanding Muslim world, was also on the defensive, exacerbated by local political tensions and rivalries.

Ambivalences about the public alliances of Qur'ān readers echo a greater concern among Muslim scholars, Sufis, and others, who deplored what they saw to be generally inappropriate conduct among the learned, and especially the exploitation of knowledge for the sake of power, prestige, money, and vain or self-serving scholarly or public recognition. The literature on these issues ranges from the problem of hypocrisy to the danger of outright corruption. The theme of moral decay among the learned appears fairly early in the tradition, related to political critique and developing alongside the rise of the movement in Islamic piety that was known by the third or fourth Islamic century as "Sufism" *(taṣawwuf)*. According to Rosenthal, criticism of the so-called corrupt scholar *(al-ʿālim al-fāsiq)* contains many statements attributed to the Prophet ʿIsā' (Jesus), a Prophet who is exemplary for his sincerity and his criticism of the establishment, and who is said to figure largely in Sufi traditions of early ascetic piety.[51] Statements that condemn the alleged moral decrepitude of those with religious knowledge present these conditions as a decline in the perceived purity of the early Community as represented by the *sunnah*. For example, Dhū'l Nūn al-Misrī (d. 859), later accepted as an early Sufi, while also a "*sharīʿa*-minded" *ḥadīth* traditionist (arrested, like Aḥmad b. Ḥanbal, in the famous *miḥna*, or "trial," over the nature of the Qur'ān), wrote:

> There was a time when a person of knowledge *(min ahl al-ʿilm)* by virtue of his knowledge acquired an increased hatred for this world and became more ready to renounce it. Today, a man's knowledge instills in him an increased love for this world, and he becomes more ready to seek after (material prosperity). There was a time when a man spent his property on the acquisition of knowledge. Today, he acquires property through his knowledge. There was a time when a man of knowledge *(ṣāḥib al-ʿilm)* could be observed to grow, both inwardly and outwardly. Today, many men of knowledge can be observed to grow in corruption in both respects.[52]

Rosenthal writes that such an ambivalent, or outright pessimistic, depiction of the contemporary scholar's world was expressed by many social critics along with famous ascetics like Dhū'l Nūn.

Responsibility for supporting the moral order as a person of religious knowledge, especially as a "bearer" of the Qur'ān, entails negotiating relations with those who lay claim to power and patronage within the social order. According to *adab* literature, this necessitates an extra effort to avoid moral compromise in multiple domains. Although the memorizer provides standards of conduct for the community, he or she ideally must not rely on others for support, specifically in order to maintain his or her moral autonomy and integrity. For example, a statement attributed to the foundational figure emblematic of ascetic piety, Ḥasan of Baṣra, adds valences of *tawakkul* (reliance on God, sometimes the first "station" in articulations of the Sufi Path) to this basic idea: "I swear by God, besides the Qur'ān there is no sufficiency, and after [the deprivation of] the Qur'ān there is no poverty [worse]."[53] The idea that the scholar or person with religious knowledge cannot, or should not, be "bought" (especially in the context of pious critiques of political establishments and the opportunities they endow) admonishes Qur'ān readers always to be focused on religion *(dīn)* independent of world-directed interests *(dunīa)*.

Piety, social critique, and emergent Sufism all dovetail in the idealized commitment to "preserve" the Qur'ān. The ideal for the memorizer is to rely exclusively on God and the Qur'ān, depicted as the only real power or riches that exist. Such piety, it is implied in authoritative statements, protects the "preserver" of knowledge from the potentially corrupting influence of patronage. This is achieved for the sake of the Qur'ān, through the Qur'ān, and, finally, the Qur'ān itself is depicted as the ultimate judge of character held to this transcendent standard.

Scholars and those who "hold" the Qur'ān, in both the past and the present, may or may not negotiate directly their relations to structures of political power, but all face in some way the daily, practical problem of securing a livelihoood. A key issue treated in the *adab* literature of the Qur'ān is remuneration, or taking a fee for Qur'ānic practice. *Ḥadīth* reports on this point, cited by the pious in the formative period, underscore strongly that the Qur'ān is to be cherished for its own sake and should not be deployed for worldly gain. Al-Nawawī (d. 1278), summarizing previous works, takes up the subject specifically as it relates to Qur'ān readers in his text *Al-tibyān fī adab ḥamalat al-Qur'ān* (The Explanation of the *Adab* for Bearing the Qur'ān), explaining, "The most important thing for a transmitter of the Qur'ān to guard against is being occupied with the book as a way of life such that it becomes a means of life." He cites accounts that the Prophet said, "Recite the Qur'ān but do not eat by it nor demand riches from it," and "Recite the Qur'ān before a group of people arrives who will slander it by demanding a reward for reciting."[54] Nevertheless, people certainly did and still do earn their living from knowing the Qur'ān, which was no doubt the reason for the lengthy discussion that follows in al-Nawawī's text. Al-Nawawī summarizes the differing positions on this disputed point, which range from prohibitions against ever accepting any fee for reading to the permissibility of taking money as long as it is not an initial condition for performing the reading (related on the authority of Ḥasan of Baṣra), and finally he notes that the schools of jurisprudence following Mālik and al-Shāfiʿī allow it even under those circumstances.[55]

As "preservers," those who carry the Qur'ān not only should be above moral reproach and scrupulous in every transaction, but they also have a responsibility to contribute to the greater ethical order of society. Moral responsibility to the community is often illustrated in the literature through representations of the reciter's unending commitment, often portrayed as practice continuing both night and day: Qur'ān reading by night and constructive moral action by day. Not only a metaphor, this phrase also reflects the documented practice of the Prophet himself,[56] leading to binding practical directives in the form of *sunnah*. An example of the valuation of never-ending, day-and-night practice of the Qur'ān preserver and the affective comportment that accompanies it is the well-known statement attributed to the Companion and Qur'ān reader Ibn Masʿūd:

> Ibn Masʿūd said: "The holder of the Qur'ān should realize [the value of] his nighttime when people are asleep, of his daytime when people commit excesses, of his grief when people are joyful, of his weeping when people laugh, of his silence when people are engaged in vain talk, and of his humility when people have a haughty deportment. The holder of the Qur'ān should be gentle and soft-minded; he should not be harsh, or quarrelsome, not one who shouts much, nor one who makes strong noises in markets, not a man of hasty temper who gets angry quickly."[57]

The night-day opposition echoes throughout the literature.[58] It resonates with Sufi-oriented as well as normative piety, traditions that overlap historically in Qur'ānic commitments. It is reflected in actual practice in modern Indonesia, where the most well-respected *kiai* in Makassar and his family would stay up all night, for example, every night during the month of Ramadan, reading the Qur'ān straight through.

In addition to maintaining a direct relationship with the Qur'ān, the *ḥāfiẓ* has special responsibilities to the community that involve social interaction, as indicated in the well-known statement repeated by many transmitters, including al-Fuḍayl b. ʿIyāḍ (d. 802), an early Sufi figure famous for his piety, stating, "A man bearing the Qur'ān is [in effect] bearing the standard of Islam," and thus should not engage in compromising activities or associate with compromised persons, or make "unlawful amusement" or be around those who do so, or be unmindful or his duties or associate with unmindful people, and, finally, "should not utter nonsense to one who utters nonsense."[59] The Qur'ān reader is a moral exemplar, defined in terms of the kinds of people with whom he or she associates and interacts, and these associations overlap domains of devotional piety as well as action in the world.

The means for achieving this state as well as the ultimate criterion for its evaluation is the Qur'ān itself expressed in terms of the process of repeated practice. Those who "hold" the Qur'ān do so, ideally, by an intimate knowledge and active engagement of the actual text in their hearts. There is, for example, a *ḥadīth* tradition transmitted by Bukhārī to the effect that one cannot judge piety by outward appearance, and the ultimate test of inner virtue is found specifically in reading the Qur'ān: "There will be such people among you that when you compare your prayers with theirs, your fasts with theirs, your good deeds with theirs, you will consider yours to be very inferior. [However] they will read the Qur'ān, yet it will not sink deeper than their throats." A transformation is implied to accompany the continuous Qur'ānic practice that allows the Qur'ān to "sink in past the throat" and into the heart. In this system, the process begins with the Qur'ān becoming embodied in human memory and subsequently working through other faculties of understanding. Indonesian Qur'ānic discourse similarly often articulated a close relation between "*menghafal*" (memorizing, from the same Arabic root as "*ḥafiẓ*") and "*menghayati*" (internalizing, with a root meaning "heart" in Malay and Bahasa Indonesia).

The ideal means for a memorizer to avoid hypocrisy is to live the Qur'ān in his or her actions, that is, to be transformed tangibly by practice and to be palpably present with the meanings of the Qur'ān. In order for this to occur, not only the intentions but also the attention of the Qur'ān memorizer when practicing is crucial. Authoritative statements on the *adab* of memorization in the classical tradition express concern about unmindful or unreflective study that would not allow the meanings of the Qur'ān to enter the lived experience of the reader. There are numerous statements attributed to the Prophet and others to the effect that if reading the Qur'ān does not make one avoid what it prohibits, then it has not really been read at all.[60] There are other disapproving statements about reading too rapidly so that reflection on the meanings of the Qur'ān cannot take place. The Companion Ibn Mas'ūd is said to have made the statement, "Certainly one of you reads the Qur'ān from beginning to end [so thoroughly that] not a single letter of it is dropped out of his reading, whereas to act in accordance with it is dropped out."[61] The best of recitation and study, then, can obscure a fundamental lack of "comprehension" of Qur'ānic content because the reader has not allowed himself or herself to be transformed by the repeated activity of reading.[62]

Spiritually and psychologically, the memorizer faces a heavier burden than do other pious people owing to the combination of social and individual obligations placed on him or her by virtue of Qur'ānic knowledge. The opportunity of holding religious knowledge carries with it risks for the impious, and these risks are high. Such hypocrisy is often related to the reader who pretends that he or she reads the Qur'ān only for pleasing God but who really seeks worldly reward, as echoed in the following statement of the Prophet, transmitted in the name of the great pietist Aḥmad b. Ḥanbal, "Most of the ostentatious people of this community [i.e., Muslims] will be its Qur'ān-readers." As the Companion and transmitter of traditions Anas b. Mālik allegedly stated, anything less risks backfiring on the Qur'ān reader, and it is the very act of reading that provides the test: "It often happens that a man recites the Qur'ān, and the Qur'ān curses him."[63] The kind of hypocrisy that is depicted in terms of the Qur'ān "cursing" its own reader is sometimes portrayed in the gravest terms, analogous to apostasy, as with the statement of the ascetic al-Dārānī (d. ca. 838): "Guards of Hell will hasten to the holders of the Qur'ān who disobey God more than to the worshipers of idols, since they disobey God after holding the Qur'ān."[64]

The literature expresses pious apprehension of the Qur'ān reader's responsibility in terms of this world as well as the next, as in a statement al-Ghazzālī quotes from Ibn al-Ramāḥ, "I am ashamed of knowing the Qur'ān by heart, for I am told that people concerned with the Qur'ān will be asked [by God] concerning that of which the prophets will be asked on the Day of Resurrection."[65] This heavy burden, like that which Prophets bear, comes not only from ethical obligations with respect to moral order, but also because of the responsibility placed on the reciter not to forget or to backslide in his or her practical ability. For example, Abū Dāūd and al-Tirmīdhī transmit statements of the Prophet such as "I will reveal the hearts of my community and I will display the sins of my community until the end of time. I do not know a sin greater than a person who forgets a *surah* or a verse from the Qur'ān" and "Whoever reads the Qur'ān and forgets it will meet God on the day of resurrection and will be totally cut off from any reward."[66] The literature shows that one who "holds" the Qur'ān and takes on the social role of the *ḥāfiẓ* maintains a relationship to the Qur'ān and to community, with ultimate risks and rewards.

Idealized *adab* connects Qur'ānic comportment to moral and ethical ideals on both individual and collective levels, defining standards for behavior and for interpersonal interaction. This *adab* must be negotiated continually in terms of pious self-understanding, as well as the practical needs of maintaining ability. The norms and expectations of the continuous practice of maintaining the Qur'ān thus engender tensions on both textual and contextual levels. Although prescriptive, stated *adab* norms do not necessarily determine all of the consistency of patterned experience and behavior for memorizers over space and time. The direct, everyday experience of Qur'ānic engagement constantly reinforces these patterns based on the requirements of the ongoing task. Everyday practice naturally corresponds to idealized norms, because the same problems arise over and over with the same solutions sought again and again. The ongoing, repeated ritual "work" of the Qur'ān memorizer begins first and foremost with responsibility to be attentive to the text itself, which conveys its own affective tensions and challenges.

Holding Patterns of Fluency

The reason Muslims recognize for the difficulty of maintaining the Qur'ān in memory, expressed in the famous *ḥadīth* about the difficulty in tying a camel, is not just the unreliability of human memory but also the structural aspects of the Qur'ān, which memorizers know will challenge even the best capacity for memory. Memorizers of the Qur'ān continually must guard their knowledge of the Qur'ān "by heart" so that it will not slip away from them. This involves ongoing attention to the expression of Qur'ānic language, as well as application of affective techniques to manage memory itself. Awareness gained through repetition over time enhances, rather than diminishes, such demands of affective attention.

Along with fulfilling a moral and social role, in Indonesia a memorizer is expected to have mastered a Qur'ānic practical competence called "*faṣāḥah*," here denoting smooth reading without any stops or mistakes. "*Faṣāḥah*" is a key term in traditions of Arabic rhetorical expression. In pious and doctrinal discussions of the "inimitability" *(i'jāz)* of the Qur'ān, the incomparable "eloquence" of the Qur'ān, termed "*faṣāḥah*" (also *balāghah*), is evidence of its revelatory nature.[67] In the Arabic-speaking world, the adjective "*faṣīḥ*" indicates (literary) "eloquence" in religious and nonreligious expression, including its "purity" and clarity of pronunciation (related to the word "*fuṣḥa*," denoting the Arabic language itself). In reciting the Qur'ān, the term denotes fluent vocalization with correct articulation of each letter, following the rules of *tajwīd*. When introducing the idea to a group of contest judges, for example, one Indonesian *kiai* defined "*faṣāḥah*" as "pronouncing a word correctly and with facility" *(mengucapkan kalimat benar serta muda)*. He went on to outline the three main categories of fluent speech: words (Ar. *kalīmah*), phrases or sentences (Ar. *jumlah/kalām*), and the flow of speech overall (Ar. *mutakallim*).

Faṣāḥah is associated with memorizing in Indonesia especially through its connotations of comprehension, rapid reading, and knowledge of the criteria for sectioning that depend on the meanings of the Qur'ān. Memorizers are expected to have mastered the ability to begin and end the relatively long passages they rehearse without pausing for a breath (in contrast to slower, melodic *mujawwad* styles, for example) and also to know how to pause at the end of syntactical sections (which do not always correspond to *āyah* sectioning). Although there are points in the Qur'ān at which it is required or impermissible to pause (as well as gradations in between), these do not occur with enough frequency to determine when every pause will occur, nor will the ends of *āyah*s always occur at the ends of grammatical sentences. Such concerns come under the technical heading of "*balāghah*" ("eloquence," usually associated with rhetoric) but are seen as a part of *faṣāḥah* more generally in Indonesia. Here is an example given by a *kiai* in Indonesia to a group of provincial recitation coaches: the verb "he did" *(fa'ala)* may be separated from the object of the action (known as the "*maf'ūl*," the passive participle of the verb "to do"); in contrast, the verb "he said" *(qāla)* should not be separated from the utterance itself (the "*maqūl*," as in 12 Yūsuf 65 and 36 Yā Sīn 52, to use examples from commonly read *sūrahs*). This kind of example is among numerous *mushkillāt*, or "difficulties," enumerated in handbooks and classical sources; recitation coaches in Indonesia who had not memorized the Qur'ān often expressed amazement during my fieldwork at how difficult it is to move from slow melodic "readings" in the *mujawwad* style to a more rapid rehearsal of the text in accordance with these rules.[68] Reciters and others study and memorize isolated instances of such points and special cases, but the memorizer is expected to understand the generative grammatical principles underlying them in order that his or her rapid recitation be truly "fluent" *(fasih, lancar)* in both exceptional and nonexceptional cases.

In Indonesia, it was memorizers more than other types of Qur'ān readers (such as *qāri*'s) who were most often characterized as being *faṣīḥ* (an adjectival form of "*faṣāḥah*," Ind. *lancar*) in reading the Arabic Qur'ān. Indonesian memorizers of the Qur'ān often had schooling in *pesantren*, in *madrasas*, or in the Arab world, and thus had formal education in the Arabic language (that *qāri*'s may not have). The rapidity with which memorizers tended to rehearse without faltering as well as the length of portions of the Qur'ān that they recited smoothly from memory are also aspects of Indonesian understandings of *kefasihan*, or "fluency." In Indonesia, however, Qur'ān memorizers also tended to have the least developed *tajwīd* in comparison to reciters (*qāri*'s). This is because memorizers had most often studied in rural *pesantren* under the strong influence of local pronunciation styles (whereas, in contrast, *qāri*'s struggled to replicate the vocalization of Arab reciters heard in contests, broadcasts, and recordings). Thus, while in Arab-speaking regions *faṣāḥah* pertains to the technical aspects of sound articulation, in Indonesia (where this is also the case), *faṣāḥah* is more deeply associated with the religious knowledge and aptitude of memorizers, shading into ideas of comprehension, even though they may be faulted for their vernacularized styles.

The Qur'ān, understood by Muslims to be unique and inimitable in its expression, requires unique strategies of attention to preserve in memory. The fluent maintenance of the text requires that memorizers continually solve textual and cognitive problems automatically. This does not occur, however, through automatic habit that "disappears" in perception with increasing competence, but more significantly through a continuous hyperawareness and attention. Jack Katz explains: "Each of our effective actions requires that we disattend to the body as we act, focusing away from the point at which our body intersects with the world."[69] In the case of religious learning and ritual rehearsal, however, Merleau-Ponty's "effacement" of the body may work in reverse: a kind of hyperawareness may be sought at "expert" levels (as with, for example, Qur'ān memorization), while automaticity is a goal at the beginning stages when practitioners attempt merely to habitualize the rules for activity as such (as in the case of basic reading). Just as the social ideals of the *adab* of being a memorizer require continual vigilance in moral comportment in ambivalent circumstances, the unique structure and style of the text that Muslims recognize also demand continual awareness and affective interaction with the tensions of Qur'ānic poetics, structure, and style.

Psychologists, especially those interested in the acquisition of literacy, have studied closely Qur'ān memorization and similar competencies in Morocco and elsewhere. These studies show that explanatory frameworks such as "episodic" and "semantic" memory cannot be applied straightforwardly to this case without some modification. Claudia Strauss' recognition that the memory task required for Qur'ān memorization is "episodic" (not only a "semantic" acquisition of "meaningful prose," as previous researchers claimed) must be emphasized. Her survey of studies of the psychology of memory and "chanting" in her article "Beyond 'Formal' and 'Informal' Education" draws on research in Morocco to suggest that "chanting" is a special case of memory acquisition, even a distinct mode of cognition.[70] Strauss identifies the cognitive aspects of memorizers' performance with the musical aspect of "chant," noting that in some theories song structures and language structures are "mediated by different brain structures," and concluding: "Material learned by chanting is cognitively processed as songs are—and recalled in the same effortless way that songs can be. This could be the physiological basis of the preference of chanting to facilitate rote memorization in so many cultures."[71] The "musical" aspects of recitation cannot fully explain the special kind of ritual attention the memorizer must apply, however.[72] When recited from memory, in fact, the Qur'ān would seem to be an exceptional case within any general model of "chant." This is not only because melody is not fixed; it is also owing to the nonsequential properties of the text that Muslim scholarship has long recognized to be part of the Qur'ān's unique and miraculous "inimitability."

Rhythmic features of the recited Qur'ān make its mnemonic features seemingly natural to consider from the frame of "chant"; the Qur'ān is certainly "chanted" rhythmically in recitation with a regular structure of pitch variation (most simply, alternating two pitches and ending sectioned phrases on the lower of the two). However, the fact that the Qur'ān is chanted or always has some musical qualities in accordance with *tajwīd* does not alter the Qur'ān's actual structure and syntax (on which *tajwīd* builds). Aspects of the chanted text itself often disrupt the kind of automaticity usually associated with "chant" practice rather than supporting it; the reason for this is that Qur'ānic rhetoric breaks patterns even as it establishes them. A "singsong" vocalization established by the rules of *tajwīd* does not overcome the features of Qur'ānic syntax that induce affective states of heightened attention, including disorientation through irregular patterns, as in ruptured speech (an example is the dialogue of the confused sleepers in in the "Story of the Cave" in 18 al-Kahf, a *sūrah* with a theme, in fact, of the limits of knowledge and coherence).[73] The problems memorizers themselves identify as the most challenging are not those of maintaining a continuous flow in textual recall—which would be the "chanter's" problem—but involve the way in which nonlinear structure actively tricks memory to jump nonlinearly from one location in the Qur'ān to another. In this way, the dynamics of Qur'ānic speech ensure the kind of visceral attention that the text also demands for itself semantically in its own discussions of affective engagement with the Qur'ān.

Nonlinear syntax and structure of the Qur'ān's "episodes" frustrate automatic recall and require continuous attention. Carried away by rhythm and pattern, reciting or chanting with a flow from memory may actually produce a mistake rather than a correct rendition, as when the text's own patterns are broken, whether by semantic ruptures (*iltifāt*, see below) or by other characteristic irregular structures. Qur'ānic structure and style "improvises" structurally on semantic themes (even as melody is improvised in its vocalization), and its own rhetorical style may actually frustrate automaticity, demanding disciplined practices of attention. This occurs even as the recited text persuasively addresses its listeners to "ponder," "reflect," and listen and to react to the recited Message. Memorizers encounter and address these internal challenges of the recited Qur'ān through ritual repetition and rehearsal. Stylistic and rhetorical features of the recited Qur'ān induce affective modes of attention through patterned variance, while memorizers say they also require specific affective techniques to retain for the same reason.

Academic studies of ritual that acknowledge it to be potentially dynamic have tended to look for such dynamism in diachronic change, usually overlooking the possibility that dynamism may also inhere in rituals' inherent patterns. What Abdel Haleem has termed the "dynamic style"of the Qur'ān (including the combination of regular and irregular patterning of the text that is a focus of Islamic traditions of the study of Qur'ānic expression) is more immediate to the daily project of rehearsing of the Qur'ān than is pondering the discursive meaning of the text. This project requires continual attention on the part of the memorizer, in the course of each reading as well as in repetition over time. As the Indonesian case demonstrates, these practices of ongoing attention may be independent of apprehending the semantic meanings of the text and may intensify over time for the practitioner.

The growing criticism of the hermeneutical approach in the study of human action (of which Geertz' and Turner's perspectives on ritual are usually taken to be emblematic) in fields across the human sciences echoes views that have been expressed for some time among Islamicists, musicologists, and historians of religion who study ritual.[74] For example, J. Frits Staal, adopting a formalist stance in "The Meaninglessness of Ritual," emphasized ritual's "intrinsic value" as action over and above its signification, writing, "Ritual is pure activity. . . . Ritual has no meaning, goal, or aim."[75] Historian of religions Jonathan Z. Smith has also affirmed what he calls the "Reformation" perspective that rituals are "empty," not intending to denigrate rituals (as had early Protestant critics), but rather to highlight what really happens in ritual itself rather than in its extraritual referents.[76] The strength this approach and others like it that recognize ritual as "activity" is that they do not treat ritual merely as a mode of signification, the vehicle of cognition, categorization, or communication, but instead they take ritual to be a class of action and a site for experience.[77] Staal suggests that this type of "scientific," "syntactical" approach to Vedic ritual ought to be generalized as an approach in religious studies, a move that would abrogate the damaging and "erroneous assumption about ritual," namely, "that it consists in symbolic activities which refer to something else."[78]

Other approaches in the academic study of religion resistant to a search for overarching "meanings" have emphasized rituals' capacity to induce heightened "attention"; Smith defines ritual primarily as a "means of paying attention" or of "marking interest."[79] Others, such as Humphrey and Laidlaw, have attempted to describe the experience embodied in ritual activity from a phenomenological viewpoint. Thomas Csordas has studied embodiment and expression in ritual, also outlining "somatic modes of attention."[80] The questions raised by this literature resonate with long-standing questions about "meaning" in Muslim rituals posed by Islamicists, such as John Bowen's work on *ṣalāt* (canonical worship) in Indonesia,[81] and they also overlap the foundational problem of the "referentialty" of music in relevant fields.[82]

Some of the power of rituals derives, at least in part, from their very structures, independent of any other influences or elaborations. Ritual structure is dynamic to the degree that its "rules" include and allow for complexity and tension within structured pattern. These aspects pertain to an experience of structure that is experientially prior to performance and the reception of discursive meaning in actual engagement. As Stanley Tambiah observes, rituals are performed and experienced on many levels and along many axes; they are conduits for many types of meaning; among these, the structure of a ritual itself may compel attention.[83] Tambiah cites Roman Jakobson in connection to an alternative "definition" of ritual meaning, formulated in terms of "*pattern recognition* and *configurational awareness.*"[84] Tambiah writes of ritual: "Controlled modulation" in ritual creates "recognizable patterns and unanticipated tension and outcomes."[85] "Unanticipated tension" is an affective state and one that is critical to the experiential engagement of memorizing the Qur'ān.

Qur'ān recitation, the "rehearsal" or "following" *(tilāwah)* of the Speech of God, is a case of a ritual being structured not *around* a text, but also *as* the text. Such repeated ritual structure, even apart from the exercise of performative or improvisational agency, is not necessarily static. When Jonathan Z. Smith writes, "Ritual gains force where incongruity is perceived and thought about,"[86] and when Theodore Jennings describes similar tensions in an influential article "On Ritual Knowledge," they refer to ritual practitioners' awareness of the difference between enacted ritual ideals and everyday realities. The perception of apparent incongruity within the unchanging recited Qur'ān, however, is a critical component of its affective potential prior to human elaborations such as melody or "extra-Qur'ānic" systems. If Smith is correct to identify ritual as primarily a "means of paying attention" or of "marking interest," then the heightened awareness induced by ruptures in the Qur'ān's syntactical patterns are a fundamental dimension of the recited Qur'ān's affective "force." These dynamics also require the ongoing attention of those who hold it in memory. For a memorizer recounting a section of the Qur'ān, unexpected patterns in syntax maintain an affective state of attention that is a crucial dimension of orthoprax reading. This is determined by aspects of that single reading as well as the cumulative effects and expectations that derive from having read the entire Qur'ān many times over time.

Margaret Drewal, who writes on ritual and improvisational performance, observes that there are two types of ritual repetition: repetition *in* ritual and repetition *of* ritual.[87] Both types of repetition are fundamental to the establishment of expectations of well-formedness for the recitation of the Qur'ān, and neither may be completely separated from the other in Qur'ānic context. Repetition of the Qur'ān does not, emphatically, alter the Qur'ān (as Drewal shows human improvisation might alter the patterns of other ritual system over time); instead, the Qur'ān is rendered fresh and immediate in each orthoprax "following" *(tilāwah)* of its unchanging internal dynamics.[88] In both its syntax and the Qur'ān's overall structure, patterned variance is an aspect of what professional reciters call the affecting power of the inherent "music" of the Qur'ān and the distinctive modes of attention it demands. According to Nelson, professional reciters in Egypt would discuss this internal "music" as the structure on which they improvised and performed with personal technical artistry. In a Qur'ānic system, this internal "music" is recognized to carry its own affective properties. A kind of "improvisation" may thus be woven into ritual structure itself, and the power of surprise need not always come from the creativity of human actors. Ritual may itself be a structurally dynamic, generative grammar for affective attention, even prior to the exercise of performative human agency.

The expressive power of the syntax of the Qur'ān also invokes states through its manipulation of expectations of rhetorical well-formedness. Moments of syntactic rupture, when the Qur'ān's poetical and expressive patterns are shattered and can no longer be anticipated, may be a constitutive aspect of the emotive power and experience of its recitation. In theories in a number of academic fields, including musicology, there has been in the past a shared tendency to locate the potential affecting power of expression in the breakage or suspension of established expectation. Like Walter Benjamin's "principle of interruption," moments of syntactic rupture in Qur'ānic expression establish states of acute perceptivity and visceral awareness.[89] The Qur'ān claims its affecting presence as both "rule" and experience, and then manifests this presence through, for example, its manipulation of its "voices" and linguistic registers. The Qur'ān's rupture of expectation set by its own repetitions as a "horizon" opens up a space of potential "shock," as in Benjamin's famous description, or space for the redeployment or redoubling of semantic meaning and aesthetic sensibility. Qur'ānic "voices" that characteristically shift in deictic category and perspective as well as in narrative, "hymnic," and other modes of speech, break established rhetorical patterns and expectations; they shock, challenge, and make Qur'ān recitation not only an aesthetic performance but also a lived emotional engagement with the revealed Message. In addition, as readers render the "voices" of the Qur'ān within their own, their embodied experience merges with the meanings of the speech of God in a unique religious subjectivity of participation in revelation.[90]

These features are recognized as a unique aspect of Qur'anic language and poetics, captured in a well-known contemporary statement by Sayyid Hossein Nasr, explaining that the Qur'ān's language is like natural language that has been "crushed by the power of the Divine Word," "as if human language were scattered into a thousand fragments like a wave scattered into drops against the rocks of the sea."[91] The most prominent of these aspects for the sound of Qur'ān recitation are rhyme (both end rhyme and internal rhyme), assonance, and rhythm.[92] These are perceptible even for those without extra-Qur'ānic familiarity with the Arabic language. Although some of the syllabic rhythmic patterns of the Qur'ān can be apprehended according to the classical Arabic meters, these meters, as Nelson writes, are not as representative of Qur'ānic style "as are the Qur'ān's abrupt and progressive shifts in rhythmic patterns and length of line, as well as its shifts between regular and irregular patterns."[93] The field of rhetorical study of the Qur'ān specifies, labels, and emphasizes such features, in reference to the idea of *i'jāz* (inimitability). These aspects of the Qur'ān's gripping poetics, when heard, experienced, and embodied in memory, interact with the affective aspects of the artistry of the recited Qur'ān, especially in cases when they underscore the "sense" of meaning.

Influenced by the Islamic sciences of the study of the rhetoric and poetics of the Qur'ān as well as by the work of Roman Jakobson, Michael Sells defines "sound figures" in the Qur'ān as "extended acoustical patterns that take on semantic, emotive associations or 'charges.'"[94] Jakobson developed approaches for the analysis of affective aspects of syntax and sound,[95] holding that emotion potentially intersects all aspects of linguistic structures. In "Linguistics and Poetics," Jakobson enumerates the functions of verbal communication, which include referential, poetic, and phatic, in addition to emotive, conative, and metalingual functions.[96] Jakobson's approach contrasts with that of others who implied that "expressive phenomena" are outside the scope of linguistic analysis. In *Approaching the Qur'ān: The Early Revelations*, Sells applies a related approach in rich detail to selected shorter, Meccan *sūrahs*, accompanied by a sound recording, providing rich analysis of their linguistic and expressive qualities.

As can be studied readily by English speakers using Sells' materials, each *sūrah* and each section of a *sūrah* has its own mood and affective style, determined by both semantics and syntax. The shorter, Meccan *sūrahs* tend to have especially distinctive affective moods, deriving from the combination of their imagery and linguistic features. For example, contrast the despair and hope of 103 al-'Aṣr (beginning "Truly, humanity is in loss"), the jubilation of 110 al-Naṣr ("When the help of God comes, and the victory"), the righteous anger of 111 al-Masad ("Perish the hands of Abū Lahab! And may *he* perish!"), and the reverent proclamation of 112 al-Ikhlāṣ (which opens, "Say: He is the One

God"). The Qur'ān complements lexical content with its expressive syntax, such as in the phrasing of *āyahs* and their length and rhythm, especially in the "early revelations" of Mecca.[97]

There is an enormous amount of material in the Qur'ān to memorize and then to be rehearsed continually so that the patterns that shift continually in experience and memory do not, like the camel in the *ḥadīth* account, slip away. Memorizers often follow the recommendation to repeat the entire Qur'ān once every week, one-seventh of the text each day. Daily repetition of the Qur'ān from memory is a principal act of Muslim piety and required to conduct canonical prayer, or *ṣalāt*. It also represents more than that for memorizers, however, because the structure and style of the Qur'ān necessitate intensive and continual maintenance. Features of Qur'ānic rhetoric and poetics render it a compelling kaleidoscope—always familiar, but always shifting to reveal new connections and new aspects—which guarantees that it will be a significant challenge to preserve in memory. Most of the Qur'ān is not structured narratively, nor is it organized topically (although this is a standard arrangement of much Qur'ānic exegesis) or according to the chronology of its revelation to the Prophet Muḥammad; on the contrary, much of the material at the beginning of the Qur'ān is accepted to have been among the last revealed to the Prophet, whereas the short *sūrahs* at the end of the Qur'ān are among the first said to have been sent down. The principle and experience of overall Qur'ānic coherence comes through the continual repetition and rehearsal of the sound and feeling of the entire recited text itself.

In the Qur'ān, material addressing the changing conditions of the early Muslim Community, sacred history, discourses on divinity, faith, eschatology, and moral, ethical, and legal injunctions are set into an exquisite mosaic at any one point of which the material seems familiar, and yet its juxtaposition within a given context continually suggests new dimensions to be recognized.[98] Narratives, for example, are related again and again, providing a backdrop of familiarity, yet in each instance they are presented with subtle changes that call to attention a new aspect or theme of the narrative that grabs the reciter's and audience's attention. The same could be said for formulaic expressions and even stylistic modes more generally. For these reasons, the kinds of structured, visual "arts of memory" deployed mnemonically in other traditions are continually undermined in the case of memorizing the Qur'ān.[99]

Repetition of regular and irregular Qur'ānic structure over time requires memorizers to rehearse in a special mode of attention. A straightforward example, one discussed by memorizers themselves, is the narrative mode, which can cause one easily to jump from one place to another in the Qur'ān when reciting from memory. There is not a systematic treatment of narrative in the

Qur'ān (with exceptions such as 12 Yūsuf, the entire *sūrah* being the "most beautiful" story of the Prophet Joseph, and the example of various accounts in *sūrahs* such as 11 Hūd and 18 al-Kahf).[100] There are segmented narrative passages regarding various Prophets interspersed throughout the Qur'ān, with these narrative units referencing others through association and repetition of image, phrase, and rhythm. Narrative accounts of Prophets often appear in sequences within the Qur'ān, usually preserving an ordering of accounts within the series; each cluster of accounts usually has a distinctive rhetorical pattern that one particular episode in the series may then break.

The example Indonesian memorizers gave most often regarding the difficulty of retaining the narrative mode are accounts of the Prophet Mūsā (Moses), which comprise about five hundred of the approximately 6,500 verses of the Qur'ān, almost one-tenth of the Book, with this material often placed in proximity to material about the difficulties that the Prophet Muḥammad faced within his own community. The structural characteristics and sheer amount of material make it difficult to remember any one account of Mūsā through multiple repetitions of the entire text, especially with respect to stylistic phrases or concepts that may trigger other passages. As in this example, the Qur'ān generates rhetorical impact in dispersed narrative accounts through variation on pattern, each particular account conveying a distinct mood or emphasis, depending on its rhetorical style and its juxtapositional relation to other elements of the *sūrah*.

Beyond structural characteristics such as the kaleidoscopic narrative accounts that can defy mnemonics, there are also famously tricky passages that have been highlighted for centuries by memorizers that come under the technical heading of "difficulties" *(mushkillāt)*. The problem of skipping mistakenly to the wrong place comes not just with relatively lengthy passages such as many narrative accounts, but also with sentences, phrases, and even individual words. Passages or phrases that are repeated with a slight variation are among the most difficult for the memorizer.[101] Such variations may appear at the beginning, middle, or end of an *āyah*. They are enumerated in classical sources as well as in Indonesian handbooks devoted to these special cases, and memorizers commit such handbooks to memory along with the Qur'ān itself. Such popular handbooks studied by memorizers list *āyahs* that closely resemble one another with slight variance, and this is the kind of issue most often discussed by memorizers as a challenge to over come.

A straightforward example serves as an introduction to more complex cases.[102] First, consider the beginnings of the verses 4 al-Nisā' 135 and 5 al-Mā'idah 8. The first is in *juz'* 5, whereas the second is in *juz'* 6, meaning that if a memorizer repeats one *juz'* a day (repeating the Qur'ān over the course of a month, for example), these passages will be rehearsed on separate days. In these verses, two prepositional phrases are transposed, thus permuting the order of the final three words of the *āyahs*:

> *Yā'ayyuhā alladhīna āmanū kūnū qawwāmīn bi-l-qisṭi shuhadā' liLlāhi*
> O you who believe! Be steadfast for justice as witnesses to God
> (4 al-Nisā' 135)

> *Yā'ayyuhā alladhīna āmanū kūnū qawwāmīn liLlāhi shuhadā' bi-l-qisṭi*
> O you who believe! Be steadfast to God as witnesses for justice
> (5 al-Mā'idah 8)

The potential reversal is straightforward, and these are the only two *āyahs* in this class. The memorizer may readily commit this single instance of inversion to memory as a unique case.

Another pair of *ayahs*, a well-known example of this phenomenon, shows how grammatical expectation may further challenge the memorizer. The following two verses, from different *sūrahs* of the Qur'ān, both contain a form of the verb "to promise." In both verses, the verb carries two objects (something is promised to someone), but the order of the objects is reversed in each case respectively. The meaning of each phrase is the same, and the syntax of each is as natural as the other in *fuṣḥā* (standard) Arabic. Both verses are a retorts uttered by the unbelievers against the validity of the Message. Compare (the English interpretation conveys the sense of the ordering of the words in question in each case):

> *Laqad wu'idnā naḥnu wabā'unā hādhā min qablu in hādha illā asāṭīnu alawwalīn*
> To us and to our forefathers this has been promised before! Truly, this is nothing but the old stories of the ancients!
> (23 al-Mu'minūn 83)

> *Laqad wu'idnā hādha naḥnu wābā'unā min qablu in hadhā illā asāṭīnu alawwalīn*
> This has been promised to us and to our forefathers before! Truly, this is nothing but the old stories of the ancients!
> (27 al-Naml 68)

In the two verses given above, the memorizer who has studied this case will know that the ordering can only be one of two permutations. Another, more complex example is 2 al-Baqarah 136 (and the beginning of verse 137) and 3 Al 'Imrān 84 (and the beginning of 85). Compare:

> [136:] Say [*qālū*, plural imperative] (O Muslims): We believe in Allah and that which is revealed unto us [*'ilainā*, preposition with suffix] and that which was revealed unto [*ilā*, preposition] Abraham, and Ishmael, and Isaac, and Jacob, and the tribes, and that which Moses and Jesus received, and that which the Prophets received *[wamā ūtī an-nabiyina]* from their Lord. We make no distinction between any of them, and unto Him we have surrendered (in Islam). [137:] So if they believe in the like of which you believe, then they are rightly guided *[fa'in āmanū bimithli mā 'amantum bihi faqad ihtadā]*.
>
> (2 al-Baqarah 136–137)

> [84:] Say [*qul*, singular imperative] (O Muḥammad): We believe in Allah and that which was revealed unto us [*'alainā*, a slightly different preposition than above] and that which was revealed unto [*'alā*, a slightly different preposition than above] Abraham, and Ishmail, and Isaac, and Jacob, and the tribes, and that which Moses and Jesus and the Prophets *[wan-nabiyina]* received from their Lord. We make no distinction between any of them, and unto Him we have surrendered (in Islam). [85:] And whoever seeks as a religion other than Islam it will not be accepted from him *[waman yabtaghī ghair al-islāmi ilkh]*.
>
> (3 Al 'Imrān 84–85)

Here, an inattentive memorizer might mistakenly skip at related points from one *āyah* to the other, located elsewhere in the Qur'ān. Or, the memorizer may simply substitute the preposition from one verse into the other. In the examples above, however, one may still systematically memorize the two cases to try to prevent this from occurring.

The scope of problems the memorizer encounters with multiple repetitions and variants is much greater than the cases above would suggest, however. Consider the phrase "gardens underneath which rivers flow" *(jannātin tajrī min taḥtihā al-ānhāru)*, which is commonly cited as an example of why memorizing the Qur'ān is so difficult. It is found interspersed within the Qur'ān twenty-eight times with some variation, including the vocalization of declensional case endings.[103] Even if the phrase is exactly the same, the variants in case endings may be very difficult to master for nonnative speakers of Arabic who have not internalized advanced Arabic syntax to the degree that it flows automatically in speech. Added to this, there are at least six more close variants of the phrase "Gardens underneath which rivers flow," each with slightly different wordings (such as "Gardens *of Eden* underneath which rivers flow," which occurs three times), as well as additional related phrases.

The possibilities for error in a case like this are many. In addition, since the phrase "gardens underneath which rivers flow" is almost always embedded in a description of the conditions of the hereafter, each of which has its own distinctive style and phrasing, the expression may trigger an associated phrase that does not belong. For example, it is often followed with the phrase "and they shall abide there [forever]" *(khālidīna fīhā ['ābadan]),* but not always. Habitual familiarity with the phrase can thus cause mistakes rather than correct reading. For example, consider, 71 Nūḥ 12, which (unlike the verses considered above, which describe Heaven) refers to the life of this world: "He will bestow on you gardens and bestow on you rivers." For the memorizer unheeding of context, the word "gardens" may automatically trigger the rest of the phrase "under which rivers flow." A memorizer may come to one of these phrases and use it as a spurious transition point, skipping to another section of the Qur'ān that also contains the same phrase.

The cognitive challenges facing the Qur'ān memorizer arise from both syntactic and structural aspects of the Qur'ān. Complementing the challenges of Qur'ānic structure are those of poetics and style. The unique syntax of Qur'ānic style makes it difficult to apply internalized principles of grammatical consistency as a mnemonic technique, even in coherent registers such as narrative. Syntactically as well as structurally, the Qur'ān refracts in memory, breaking linear patterns with affective impact even as they are established. In the Qur'ānic sciences, the technical term for this kind of rupture in syntactical pattern is "*iltifāt*" (a literal meaning of the term is to "turn" or "turn one's face toward").[104] Abdel Haleem defines "*iltifāt*" as "a sudden shift in the pronoun of the speaker or the person spoken about." In addition to shifts in deictic category (person), the phenomenon is related in analysis to the Qur'ān's changes in verb tense, changes in number (between singular, dual, and plural), changes in case marker, and other features.[105] Al-Zarkashī (d. 1391) defined *iltifāt* as "the change of speech from one mode to another, for the sake of freshness and variety for the listener, to renew his interest, and to keep his mind from boredom and frustration, through having one mode continuously in his ear."[106] It is thus defined in classical sources as a destabilizing "principle of interruption" within the Qur'ān's own poetics, understood to be for the sake of maintaining the attention of the listener. A straightforward example given by Abdel Haleem is *āyah* 4 of the opening *sūrah*, the Fātiḥah (the second sentence to follow), in which there is a shift from praise in the third person to the second person: "Praise belongs to Allāh, the Lord of All Being, the Most Benificent, the Most Merciful, the Master of the Day of Judgment. You alone we serve, You alone we ask for help."[107] *Iltifāt* are a key aspect of Qur'ānic style that demand a continual technology of attention for the memorizer.

Consider, for example, the rhetorical questions (which undercut complacency and underscore content) and imperatives (which confront the reader) in the passage 68 al-Qalam 34–47. Whether or not the meanings are fully apprehended, the reciter must nevertheless be prepared for grammatical register shifts as well as other aspects of *iltifāt* (such as switches from singular to plural):

> 34: Truly, the Righteous [will] have Gardens of Joy with their Lord.
> 35: Shall We treat the Muslims as the wrongdoers?
> 36: What is the matter with you [plural]? How do you judge?
> 37–39: Or do you have a Book with which you learn, that through it you shall have whatever you choose? Or do you have covenants with Us, that extend to the Day of Judgment, that you shall have whatever you demand?
> 40: Ask them, which of them has such certainty!
> 41: Or do they have "partners" [in divinity]? Then let them bring on their "partners" if they are truthful!
> 42–43: Their eyes will be cast down; ignominy will cover them. They were called to bow down while they were still unimpaired [before it was too late].
> 44–45: Then leave Me [God] alone with those who reject this Message; We will deal with them in increments, from directions of which they are not [even] aware. I will take a long time with them; truly, My design is great.
> 46–47: Or do you [plural] ask them for a reward [for teaching them], so that they will carry a heavy debt? Or so that they can grasp [grope] at the Unseen, or so that they can write it [the Unseen] down?
> 48: So you [singular] be patient for the Command of your Lord. Do not be like the Companion of the Fish [Yūnus, Jonah] when he called out, distressed.

In this passage, rhetorical questions alternate with persuasive challenges. There is a switch from plural to singular address (*āyah* 48), and God's voice also changes from the first person plural (*āyah*s 37 to 39) to the first person singular (*āyah* 44). These dynamic aspects break consistency in the pattern of rhetorical questions. In addition, because the use of the first person singular for God's statements occurs relatively rarely in the Qur'ān, its appearance in the example above seizes attention and also makes the passage both especially evocative and also especially difficult to remember.

Since the ritual of Qur'ān recitation is the embodied voicing of the Qur'ān, the "syntax" of the Qur'ān may be taken as a key determinant of the structure of recitational performance and thereby its aesthetic, cognitive, and emotional effect as well as the challenges that the memorizer faces. The recited Qur'ān establishes and intensifies rhetorical and ritual patterns through its repetitions of itself and within itself. The continual repetition of the Qur'ān in part and whole gives rise to its own expectations socially and experientially. An overall sense of Qur'ānic style is built up in the reader through repeated vocalization and listening. Expectations of "well-formedness" come from ritual repetitions themselves, beginning with the repetitions in syntax and semantics within the recited Qur'ān. These expectations are often interrupted or underscored within moments of the Qur'ān, with emotive effect. Throughout the Qur'ān and within each performance, these expectations are ruptured and elaborated on in ways that manipulate the very expectations that were established by prior repetitions.

The experienced affect of reading the Qur'ān includes the heightened awareness or embodied attention produced by repetitions within the Qur'ān and repetitions of the recited Qur'ān. These may be elaborated by discursive meaning, and they are also the basis of further affective techniques that the Qur'ān memorizer cultivates in order to preserve structure and style in memory. Like the tensions described in *adab* literature that determine the social role of the "holder" of the Qur'ān through moral vigilance, the actual work of rehearsing the Qurān in lived situations conveys textual tensions and "difficulties." In remaining attentive to these textual challenges in lived social contexts, thus managing them cognitively as well as emotionally, the memorizer establishes his or her own unique subjectivity as an ongoing practitioner.

Managing to Memorize

The challenge for the memorizer is not simply to memorize the Qur'ān once but continuously to maintain the Qur'ān. At one *kiai*'s house in Makassar, students would arrive at dawn to stand outside, entering in ones and twos in order to recite for the *kiai*. (Beginning students went directly upstairs to work with the *kiai*'s sons.) As each entered, the *shaikh* remarked on who had "*tammat*" (memorized the entire Qur'ān) and who had not. It was a quiet, stately, relaxed procession that lasted for an hour or two, with the *kiai* sometimes moving outside for a cigarette (still listening), sounding a high little noise to alert a mistake (other *kiai* would rap on a table as an alarm) and with the students kissing the *kiai*'s hand as they came and went. When asked whether students returned to repeat with them over the years, the *kiai* whom I interviewed reported that there are some who do, but many also do not. The maintenance of the ability to recite the Qur'ān from memory necessitates not only a consistent moral and social comportment forged by expectations of *adab* but the active continuation of required textual practice in social context. Memorizers have their subjectivity doubly determined by the real needs of practice and its maintenance as well as by the ideals of social role and expected aptitude. Both aspects require affective and interactional strategies to meet the continuous cognitive and affective challenges of attention in memorizing the Qur'ān.

New memorization student requesting permission to become the *kiai*'s student at a dawn practice, Makassar

The idea that memorizational ability "runs in the family" was sometimes heard in Indonesia (although I never heard a *ḥāfiẓ* say it). Whether hereditary or not, the need for daily repetition of memorized material necessitates that small groups of memorizers will cluster around the practice for continual repetition and in order to guard against mistakes. Among the most obvious and available networks for these groups are family relationships. Women who were at the center of such close-knit memorizational groups tended to memorize too. Just as memorizing implicates a social role and memorizers form necessary social bonds as a part of the practice of memorizing, they must also manage their interactions with others in order continuously to safeguard both their memories and their committed time for concentrated and continuous practice. The demands made by attentive practice itself require that the memorizer have a unique location within social settings and interactions, and this enhances and continually reinforces the subjectivity of the memorizer as continuous practitioner.

In Arabic, the lexical root for "memory" and "intelligence" is the same *(dh-k-r)*, also related to general connotations of "strength." In Sufi-oriented traditions, drawing on a Qur'ānic basis (for example, 18 al-Kahf 24 and 33 al-Aḥzāb 41), "*dhikr*" is a key individual and communal practice of "remembrance" (often through recitation of the Names of God, as suggested in 7 al-A'rāf 180, or active internalization of the statement "witnessing" faith, the *shahāda*), a mode of attention that leads to transformation of self through habituated practice and the cultivation of related embodied states. In addition, classical writings on learning, continuing the tradition of oral transmission of the Qur'ān and *ḥadīth*, assert the superiority of memorized knowledge. For example, Abū'l-Ḥilāl al-Ḥasan al-'Askarī, treating this subject in the writings on schooling and education studied by Rosenthal, claims that memorized knowledge is the most difficult to acquire but that this is "the kind of knowledge that swims with you when your ship sinks."[108] In Qur'ān recitation, the very faculty of memory is critical for a memorizer's understanding of self and his or her own capacity to memorize.

The concern of *ḥadīth* transmitters for strong and accurate memory is evident in canonical collections such as Bukhārī's, and part of his "Book of Knowledge" treats explicitly the subject of good memories. According to Jonathan Berkey, biographical dictionaries *(ṭabaqāt)* from the formative period of Islam include frequent mention of the scholars who were known especially for their impressive memories (including *ḥadīth* compilers) as well as those whose memories were not considered reliable.[109] An illustration of the significance (and instrumentality) of the faculty of memory to the scholar is the popularity of a story related about one of the greatest scholars of all time, al-Ghazzālī, who was rebuked by robbers after they had stolen all his books from him, "How can you claim to have the knowledge of their contents when by dispossessing you of them we dispossessed you of their contents and deprived you of their knowledge?" According to the story, al-Ghazzālī then went back home to Tus to spend three years memorizing all his notes, just so he would never be afraid of losing his books again.[110]

Indonesian students (and especially Qur'ān memorizers) were self-conscious about the faculty of memory itself as well as the speed with which they could absorb memorized knowledge. This topic and the related self-assessments often came up in casual conversation with memorizers. Indonesian students would often remark, for example, on how many "pages" they could commit to memory in a day or even an hour. With increasing systematization of memorization pedagogy as well as the growing popularity of memorization in Indonesia, it was common to hear calculations of the period of time it would take for a hypothetical memorizer to reach the "*target*" of complete Qur'ān memorization. Such measurements, when compared with a real subject's actual capacity for memory (or sheer stamina), impact self-understanding. In addition, achievement required social interaction for accurate rehearsal and transmission, as memorizers (often teachers and students) rehearsed together. This reinforced a distinct social role by group identification as well as differentiation of individuals' aptitudes within the group; the maintenance of the Qur'ān also determined a social persona in interaction with those who were not memorizing.

Instructional systems for memorizing in Indonesia were built on and used the terminology of traditional Islamic pedagogical techniques. Teaching circles (*ḥalqahs*) have been the primary setting for instruction since the "classical" period, and students in such groups are expected to repeat constantly with the *shaikh* or other authority in order to make sure that what has been memorized one day does not erode the next. In the traditional systems of legal colleges, teaching assistants *(mustamlī, mufīd, mu'īd)* served as drill instructors and intermediaries. Another aid to teaching was the practice known as *mudhākara* (a verb built on the same root as *dhikr*, denoting "mutually reminding"), which is a sort of quiz that students would put to one another and instructors put to students. For *ḥadīth* scholars, this activity could sometimes reach the level of semipublic competitions.[111] George Makdisi quotes eleventh-century scholar al-Khāṭīb al-Baghdādī's advice on how students ought to quiz one another after leaving class, "The only thing that does away with knowledge is forgetfulness and forsaking *mudhākara*."[112]

The methods of memorization taught by various Indonesian *kiai* showed little variation across Indonesia and also resonate with long-standing Islamic patterns. There was common emphasis on reading the entire Qur'ān through multiple times (forty being a usual number) before actually beginning to memorize. Many *kiai* described a similar method as their personalized regimen, which one referred to as his "ladder method." This was a process of memorization page by page, undertaken in the following manner: reading the entire page through a specified number of times (usually four), then memorizing the *āyah* at the top of the page, then that *āyah* plus the next, and then the first two plus the third, and so on. I also heard of other methods, such as memorizing by the stops and starts in the text ("but if you ever lose your place, you're totally lost," one reader commented). Cassette recordings were seldom featured as a part of memorization study in Indonesia (perhaps because students with access to a set of all thirty *juz'* were rare in the area where I researched, and the older *kiai* whom I interviewed, although they did not object to the idea, had no use for them). I also met individuals who had exceptional memories as well as their own methods, such as one champion *qāri'* who described reading a page several times and memorizing it "by his tongue." Almost everyone (with only the exception of one *kiai* I interviewed, who disagreed) stated that knowing the meaning of the Arabic text aids memorization. Drs. K. H. Muhaimin Zen's popular handbook for memorization, for example, highlights the method of studying the semantic contexts in which *āyahs* that resemble each other are located in order to differentiate among them, and this was also the method that the author emphasized in an interview.

The process of memorizing in Indonesia in the 1990s almost always involved three aspects, whether undertaken in formal or informal schooling, or in "traditional" or "modern" settings: reading through the *muṣḥaf* (written text of the Qur'ān) a specified number of times, actively memorizing alone and rehearsing with a teacher, and, finally, repeating the memorized material for the teacher and also with others in a form of "peer learning."[113] A description of the ideal process of memorization study in an Indonesian *pesantren* context as given by a memorization instructor is the following:

> (1) In memorizing, the students first read the *ayat* that are to be memorized several times looking at the *mushaf*, and then repeat them without looking at the *mushaf* until they are truly in memory. The special *mushaf* that is used is the "Bahriyah," often called the "*mushaf pojok*" (because every "*pojok*" [corner] at the end of a page is exactly at the end of an *ayah*), which has on each page fifteen lines, and one *juz*' takes up twenty pages *(pojok)*.
>
> (2) In rehearsal *[setoran atau talaqqi]*, the student reads his or her memorized material in front of the *kyai* or the "*badal*" *(asisten kyai)*, which is the formal limit *[ukuran formal batas]* for the student's memorization work. In a *pesantren* especially devoted to memorization *[khusus tahfidh]*, a student is required to perform rehearsal twice a day, whereas for those that do not specialize in memorization it is only once a day or a few times a week.
>
> (3) In repetition *[takrir]*, students repeat the material that has already been rehearsed *[sudah disetorkan]*. With *takrir*, the student reads ten or five pages from the material he has already rehearsed, in front of the *kyai* or the *badal*. However, apart from this the student must also repeat his material *(takrir)* alone following a schedule and without further restrictions *[jadwal dan batas yang bebas]*.
>
> (4) Study together *[mudarasah atau sima'an]*, working in groups with other students on a routine basis *[secara rutin]* to repeat all of the memorized material or a few *juz*'. When one person is reciting, the others listen, or all recite following in turns, page by page or *ayah* by *ayah*.[114]

This description contains the basic components of memorization, such as the use of a special *muṣḥaf* (often in bound separate booklets, each containing one *juz*'). In even more systematized approaches, such as the official guides distributed for Qur'ān colleges, the number of times one should read an *āyah* in order to memorize it may be specified, and a daily amount or overall "*target*" is often also fixed. (For example, two pages a day for memorization plus twenty for daily repetition calculates as 576 pages, or all thirty *juz'*, in approximately one year; divide the numbers by two for a two-year plan.)

The techniques applied for memorization were both cognitive and emotional. In Indonesia, some teachers addressed explicitly potential feeling-states related to the project of memorizing the Qur'ān (such as desire, inadequacy, discouragement, and complacency) while they also articulated specific affective techniques to manage and maximize memory. These techniques shaped an ongoing affective engagement with the Qur'ān. Examples of such techniques are included in a modern manual for memorization by Drs. K. H. Muhaimin Zen, *Tata Cara/Problematika Menghafal al-Qur'an dan Petunjuk-petunjuknya* (which translates roughly as "The Proper Ways and the Problems of Memorizing the Qur'ān and Guidance in These Issues"), which was first published in 1985. At the time of research, it was out of print although very much in demand, since it was seemingly the only complete handbook of its kind in Indonesia (and thus extremely popular). It treats affective aspects of memorization as technical points along with other material; it also lists *āyahs* that resemble one another and methods for familiarization and repetition of the text. The advice it gives to students reflects a widespread Islamic genre of manuals and instructional advice for learners. An example of this literature is Ibn Khaldūn's lengthy section of the *Muqaddima* pertaining to the "Methods of Instruction," in which at one point Ibn Khaldūn even addresses students and their challenges to learn in the direct voice of a coach.[115] Today, there are many contemporary Arabic-language memorization handbooks similar to Zen's modern Indonesian manual.

Almost two-thirds of Zen's handbook is a listing of tricky passages to which the memorizer must devote special attention, expected in a standard memorization handbook of textual "difficulties." The author also devotes at least one section of the book to the personal challenges memorizers may face. Here, the work links memory management to the management of emotional states, especially in its instruction on how to manage affectively social interactions with those who are not memorizers. After a general introduction to the treatment of memorization in *ḥadīth* reports and other materials, Zen opens chapter 3 of *Tata Cara* with the rationale for his focus on four specific "problems that are encountered and their solutions" *(problem yang dihadapi dan penyelesaiannya)*:

> Just as the present author has done in his search for *data* on the significance of [men and women] memorizers *(hafidz & hafidzah)* [in the Islamic tradition], he has also undertaken interviews with many memorizers *(penghafal)* of Al Qur-an,

starting with those who have utterly failed *(gagal total)* and up to those who have succeeded, as well as memorization teachers *(guru-guru penghafal)* for Al Qur-an, from the level of junior instructor *(ustadz yunior)* up to the *senior* level, and not only those who teach in *pesantren* but also those in postsecondary education. In addition to this, a questionnaire was also sent to numerous institutions devoted to instruction in memorization as well as to many individual memorizers *(hafidz & hafidzah)*. The results of this survey indicate that 98 percent have the same problems, whereas the remaining 2 percent are out of the ordinary. From out of the 98 percent, the problems that are experienced *(dirasakan)* are as follows:

1. *Ayahs* once memorized are forgotten all over again *(Ayat-ayat yang sudah dihafal lupa lagi)*
2. The great number of *āyahs* that resemble each other but are not the same *(Banyaknya ayat-ayat yang serupa tetapi tidak sama)*
3. Psychological disturbances *(Gangguan-gangguan kejiwaan)*
4. Disturbances in the surroundings *(Gangguan-gangguan lingkungan)* [116]

The author addresses each of these types of problems in order. He begins with the problem of forgetting what has been memorized, starting with the need for the memorizer simply to accept the inevitable fact that he or she will tend to forget what he or she knows.

Zen lists four reasons for forgetting material: having a weak impression of it to start *(kesan yang lemah)*, lack of practice or application *(karena tidak dipakai)*, mixing things up *(percampuran)*, and finally, unconscious "repression" or suppression *(represi atau penekanan tanpa disadari)*. With the psychologization of these issues, Zen injects self-consciousness and awareness of levels of interpersonal interaction into the theory and practice of the affective management of memory. For instance, he introduces "mixing things up" with examples such as a story about an American professor of fishery science who was promoted to become the chancellor of a major university and, upon trying to remember everyone's name, found that with each student he met he forgot the name of a species of fish. Examples of the categories of "repression and suppression" of memory due to emotional conflict include forgetting a disturbing dream. Zen further compares the high probability of having a dentist appointment slip one's mind with the slim likelihood of forgetting about a future planned encounter with an interesting, attractive person.[117]

In the section on "optimistic and pessimistic memory" *(ingatan yang optimis dan pesimis)*, Zen presents his advice for memorizers in terms of principles of emotion management. After providing various examples of the facility with which pleasant experiences are remembered and negative ones forgotten (presented as a normal tendency here, not as a problem such as "repression" or "suppression"), he suggests that this tendency be deployed as a technique for memorization, as a sort of emotionally associative "art of memory":

> Looking at the examples above, it would seem that experiences that are colored *(diwarnai)* with feeling *(perasaan)* (not just pleasant ones but also ones that are unpleasant) are more easily recalled than neutral *(netral)* ones. Because of this, we must always try to associate *(menghubungankan)* the material we are studying with something we like.
>
> For example, the name of a hotel is easier to recall if it is associated with a fun vacation we once enjoyed there. Sometimes we have difficulty studying something until we master *(menguasai)* the material by picturing an image that holds meaning for us, and then we feel good about it. That can help us to remember the material better.[118]

Zen concludes the section with a verse attributed to the great legal scholar al-Shāfiʿī about how God gives the faculty of memory to those who do good deeds. Classical Islamic sources on education, addressing students centuries ago who were confronting precisely the same problems as were Zen's students in modern Indonesia, include information on things that aid the memory, such as honey, toothpicks, and eating twenty-one raisins per day as well as the avoidance of foods (such as coriander, eggplant, and bitter apples) that allegedly damage the capacity for retention.[119] Standard *ḥadīth* collections such as Bukhārī's include prayers to aid memory, which continue to be useful to students.[120] In the Indonesian case, instead of these practices, emotion was highlighted as the primary memorizational technique.

The following section, on "psychological disturbances," seems to be Zen's own contribution to understanding the psychological and emotional states of the memorizer. Zen's analysis here blends actual problems, "emotional management," and interactive issues, such as a feeling of isolation that may accompany "difficulties" in memorization:

> Usually, the "problem" is this: in the morning the *ayat* have been memorized until they flow *(dihafal dengan lancar)* like the waters of a fast-moving river, but once that's over then it's time to move on to do something else. But by the time the afternoon comes along, there's no trace of it [what has been memorized] left *(sudah tidak membekas lagi)*. Even if you try right away to rehearse it *(ditasmikkan/diperdengarkan)* with an *instruktur*, you find you can't picture even one of the *ayat*. A problem like this is not encountered by just a single person, but [in fact at one time or another] virtually all of the memorizers of the Qur'ān experience it.[121]

Zen then offers his students encouragement by reminding them of a "feeling-rule" taken directly from the Qur'ān:

> If you happen to have a *problem* like this, you must not feel discouraged *(cemas)* and lose hope *(putus asa)*. You're not alone, and in fact you've got a lot of company *(kawan)* in this. You must not lose interest *(bosan-bosan)* or give up *(putus asa)*. Hopelessness is forbidden by religion, as God proclaims [as it says in the Qur'ān].[122]

Zen provides emotional encouragement by normalizing feelings of frustration. He also cites the verse 12 Yūsuf 87: "Never give up hope of Allah's soothing mercy," which is the voice of the Prophet Ya'qūb (Jacob), when he refuses to give up on his sons, the Prophet Yūsuf (Joseph) and his brother. (The idea that losing hope is a "sin" was commonly used by recitational coaches in other Qur'ānic contexts as well.) Turning next to the problem of laziness, Zen explains that it comes from the devil and then offers a helpful incentive to combat it: "As someone in the process of memorizing the Qur'ān, you will someday be a person of status." Laziness, he continues, will only keep you from really memorizing the Qur'ān and also inhibit "success" *(kesuksesan)* in pursuing your "*karir.*"

Immediately following this, Zen provides additional practical advice for how to overcome the problem of discouragement (and the associated feelings described) through another, more subtle practical and emotional technique. The trick he suggests demonstrates the way that Indonesian memorizers apply self-conscious affective strategies to solve their cognitive problems. Zen writes that the way to overcome the problem of *āyah*s disappearing from memory is to repeat everything you have memorized so far before you rehearse any new material with the instructor. This way, he writes, you will *feel* the sense of having achieved a fixed memorization with the old material associated with what you are memorizing for the very first time (a loose translation of "*tentu anda akan* merasakan *hasil hafalan anda dengan mantap di banding dengan menghafal yang pertama*").[123] This is not merely a case of repeating in order to keep the old material fresh. It represents a sophisticated technique that deploys the perception of competence arising from having already memorized material previously as an emotional boost or point of leverage on the problem of competence and confidence with new material. It is a combination of emotional management and cognitive technique.

Zen's manual develops an established tradition in classical literature on learning, providing it with affective emphasis. For comparison, consider George Makdisi's summary of an influential medieval text also treating the daily practice of memorizing:

> The best time for memorizing one's lesson is early dawn; and the best of places are second-story rooms rather than the ground floor, or any place far from distraction. It is not advisable to study in places of vegetation, or on river banks, not on the highways, for in these places something is always taking place that is bound to distract his attention. Furthermore, it is best to study on an empty rather than a full stomach; but extreme hunger should be avoided as an impediment to study. One must also manage one's diet, avoiding heavy foods. . . . Every now and then one must give one's mind a rest so that the work of assimilation may be accomplished, and the mind allowed to relax in preparation for fresh effort.[124]

Zen's perspective is consistent with this classical tradition but highlights the management of mood and space rather than physical condition. For example, at the conclusion of his own discussion of appropriate places to study, Zen suggests that the best place is a mosque or a place of worship *(mushalla)*. His criteria are not only those of concentration, however, but also of the emotional state of the memorizer:

> But [in the mosque] you may start to feel affected by the atmosphere [*merasa jemu*, lit. "get tired of it"] because there it is always so formal and serious all the time *(selalu formil dan serius setiap saat)*, whereas you want to feel more relaxed *(anda termasuk orang yang santai)*, so you may just look for a place outside, like in a garden under broad trees in the shade.[125]

Most of Zen's advice for creating the optimal context for memorizing concerns how to manage affectively the inevitable social interactions that will arise as the memorizer balances multiple obligations and expectations. These exchanges constitute the subjectivity of the memorizer as an ongoing practitioner through the memorizer's "emotion work" of resolving affective ambivalences arising around the expectations of social role and needs of required practice.

Zen begins discussion with how a space *(ruangan)* may be prepared for the activity of memorization, treating the ordinary challenges that any memorizer is practically guaranteed to encounter each and every day. For example, he warns against memorizing in a place for everyday activities, like a bedroom, because of the problem of wanting to lie down and take a nap or the natural tendency to waste time on "little unnecessary tasks" *(hal-hal kecil yang tidak perlu)*.[126] His specifications include good light, good temperature and ventilation, a good chair with a straight back that's not too soft, and a table that is the proper height. Not far down the list, however, with the idea of attention ("don't let your thoughts wander anywhere"), other people begin to appear. For example, in describing a "quiet location," he writes, "Some kinds of sounds, especially the voices of people talking, can disturb *konsentrasi*." The last task he mentions is to minimize interruptions, and specifically those coming from a friend who wants to ask a question or who may just feel like chatting with you.[127]

Even before discussing the preparation of such a room *(kamar)* for memorization, Zen devotes much discussion to how to balance the demands of memorizing with social obligations. First, there is the problem of the memorizer's formal social duties, introduced with the practical point that the study space ought not to be near the guest room, kitchen, or front door:

> The result of that would be that, should an acquaintance *(kawan)* of yours just happen suddenly to drop in as a guest, and just suppose even more this is a person whom you would like to treat well *(segani),* then it is not possible for you to postpone visiting with that guest or to avoid seeing him or her, even though you are under the pressure *(dituntut)* of limited time and the amount of material that you must *target*. But if you select a place that is not near the guest room, the kitchen, or the front door, then you can avoid guests who stop by, by asking a member of your family to tell every visitor who wants to see you that you can meet with them later after you are finished memorizing for such-and-such many hours, for example.[128]

Managing one relationship (the guest) implicates not only conflicting demands around that particular visit, but the required strategy may additionally involve an even wider circle of social relationships: namely, the family members who are enrolled in the project of protecting the memorizer's ongoing and concentrated effort with the Qur'ān. One family member's task of memorizing thus potentially implicates not only his or her personal relationships, but an entire household may engage in emotion work around socializing with outsiders in an ongoing way because of the presence of a Qur'ān memorizer among them.

Second, Zen mentions another kind of "disturbance" that potentially involves more complex interpersonal tensions. Continuing from the ideas above, Zen acknowledges that just being in proximity to others may potentially bring on an implicit social obligation:

> The space should not be close to a place where people "hang out" *(tempat bersendagurau),* the television, or the telephone. The reason is that your concentration will be disturbed. You will feel left out *(terkucil)* whenever your friends

> are having a good time joking around *(ramai-ramai bercanda),* but you are all by yourself reading [*berkomat-kamit,* lit. "reading silently with the lips moving"] while you memorize. A situation like this invites your friends to feel unfriendly *(mengundang sikap sinis)* toward you.[129]

This passage represents a problem of emotion management around social interaction, but now with respect to an informal situation (unlike a guest's social call above). Once again, Zen's concern is not only the feelings of the memorizer but "managing the feelings of others," especially in terms of the potential damage to social relationships within the memorizer's own peer group. In the end, the one who may feel cynical is not just the memorizer (who could begin to resent not having fun) but, more significantly, the memorizer's friends who feel slighted that the memorizer does not participate in their activity.

Finally, with the issue of the telephone, Zen suggests that conflicting responsibilities bring on interpersonal, affective, as well as moral tensions. While the phone ringing may seem like a minor annoyance, given the attentive demands of the task of memorizing the Qur'ān, such distraction may pose a serious obstacle. Zen expresses the problem of phone calls in terms of a moral tension. He presents the telephone as a moral obligation that affects the economy of social feeling inside and outside the home, in addition to hindering cognitive goals and generating a conflicting "responsibility." He explains the *adab* of the telephone for the memorizer as follows.

> The place for memorizing must not be near the location of the phone. If you select a room in which to memorize that is close to the telephone, you will bear a moral responsibility *(menanggung beban moral).* If the phone rings and you do not pick it up, you will feel bad *(perasaan anda kurang enak),* because maybe it was for you. And if you do answer it and it just so happens that it was not for you, then you also feel a responsibility, and that is the responsibility to take a message or to get someone else to come to the phone. And supposing that you do not forward the message or call the person—you are a person who has accepted an obligation [*amanat,* lit. "trusteeship"] and it is incumbent upon you *(wajib)* that you forward the message, but if you do get up to call someone to the phone or to carry out your obligation *(menyampaikan amanat tersebut),* the result will be that your time will be used up *(tersita)* for that and your concentration will be broken *(bubar).*[130]

The way to solve the problem of the telephone is decisively to remove oneself from the location of the phone whenever memorizing. The memorizer is thus, in an ongoing and intensive way, constituted as "someone who should not be near the phone" (just as he is unavailable to guests and invisible to friends). All of these preemptive strategies to manage potential affective situations shape the subjectivity of the memorizer—not only through socially recognized status or engagement with the text but also by way of the practical demands of emotional *adab* with respect to text and social context.

Rehearsal, Repetition, Retention: Ongoing Will and Work

The subjectivity of the memorizer is made through his or her continual affective attention to memory and its preservation of the Qur'ān. Just as specific affective techniques are applied to text and memory, the memorizer must also apply complementary strategies in order to manage ability in everyday situations through emotional modes as an *adab* for the memorized Qur'ān. Worlds of "management," textual and contextual, private and public, are interconnected through the demanding will and the work to maintain Qur'ānic memory and also to maintain a Qur'ānic social self. These dimensions, combined, compose the "technology of the community" that sustains the social role of the memorizer and makes possible the memorizer's ongoing contribution to religious community.

The *adab* of being or becoming a *ḥāfiẓ* determined self-presentations, modes of interaction, and self-assessments with affective implications for memorizers, which in turn reinforced the ongoing risks and rewards of the role. One *kiai*, for example, would introduce family members as they walked in the door at dinnertime in terms of how much of the Qur'ān they had memorized (five out of seven sons had memorized the entire Qur'ān, and the two others had completed an impressive amount). When narrating how he himself had memorized in Arabia, he also described himself relationally, in comparison to how rapidly his brother had memorized. At a point early on in the narration of the account, the *kiai*'s son picked up the familiar family narrative about his uncle: the uncle disappeared into a private room one day and nobody saw him come out for the next six months except to eat and relieve himself. And then one day (the *kiai* here picked up the story about his brother again), he came out and said to the *kiai*, listen to what I've memorized. And the *kiai* said, how much? How much did you memorize? How many *juz'*? His brother answered, all thirty *juz'*, the whole Qur'ān. And, according to the story, he recited the whole Qur'ān from memory right on the spot, right then and there. The telling and retelling of this story as a narrative of family identity underscores the significance of the ability to remember as part of memorizers' subjectivity and how that is shaped by both feeling and interaction.

Wonder at the perseverance and abilities of the memorizer reverberates around the person of the *ḥāfiẓ* (f. *ḥāfiẓah*), especially in Indonesia. In conversations about memorization, some Indonesians wished to establish to a foreigner the very fact that a person could be capable of accomplishing the task at all. For example, I had a long conversation with an instructor at a *pesantren* in South Sulawesi who had formerly attended the IIQ Qur'ān college in Jakarta. Persistently she asked whether I thought that people in America, like my own future students, would ever really believe me if I were to tell them that someone was capable of memorizing the entire Qur'ān. One international champion reciter spoke humbly of his profound admiration for the achievement of memorizers. He took it for granted that his newborn son had inherited a great voice for Qur'ānic performance (the baby's virtuosic crying was seen to be ample evidence of his destiny), but he repeatedly expressed his profound wish that his child would someday be able to memorize the Qur'ān. For Indonesian memorizers themselves, especially students at religious colleges who had memorization as one of their requirements for graduation, comparing one's abilities with those of others as well as to authoritative ideals gave rise to a complex of feelings.

Although "completing" *(tammat)* a reading of the Qur'ān without the aid of the text marks one as a memorizer, recitation from memory is not a one-time achievement. The accepted practice of reciting the entire Qur'ān in one session is itself a metaphor for the subjectivity of the practicing *ḥāfiẓ*. Once the whole Qur'ān is read through *(khatm)*, one does not simply end. Neither does one finish the Qur'ān, say a prayer, and end there. Instead, one finishes the Qur'ān, recites a prayer, and then recites the entire first *sūrah* (al-Fātiḥah), continuing uninterrupted into the second *sūrah* (al-Baqarah), and reciting that until the end of the fifth *āyah* (the word "*mufliḥūn*," meaning "those who prosper"). Whether or not the memorizer was actually seeking out personal or religious self-cultivation when first beginning the project of memorizing, once the process has begun, his or her disciplined practice is defined and necessitated by "technologies of the community" and the responsibility never to forget what he or she is now charged to "preserve" and to repeat. A social responsibility as well as a mode of attention, memorizing is, ideally, a perpetual cycle that draws those committed to it into a subjectivity of continuous practice.

In the project of memorizing the Qur'ān, simply maintaining ability is work, often "emotion work." Through continuous textual effort the experience and subjectivity of the memorizer is continually remade in social situations. A dialectic between individual practice and social obligation forges a memorizer's subjectivity around practice that cuts through multiple levels of experience, time, and space with the consistency of the ideals of *adab*. The subjectivity of Indonesian Qur'ān memorizers formed distinct patterns for the very same reasons that the techniques and institutions for memorization have demonstrated such similarity across time and over space; Muslims have negotiated the same challenges with the Qur'ān generation after generation, relying on continued traditions of education while looking to the same Prophetic model in present experience. Social norms (such as *adab*), the challenge of the task itself, and the ongoing emotional negotiation that becoming (and remaining) a *ḥāfiẓ* requires shape a shared affective framework. Emergent understandings of self consistent with Qur'ānic models arise out of the affective processes involved in the ongoing task of memorization.

Both the social risks and textual risks of this project are ongoing, and both kinds of risk are affective. One *kiai* narrated an account of serving at a contest in Qur'ān memorization "up in the country" for a group of *pesantren* children. He initially served there as a judge along with another, local *kiai*. At one point, the host *kiai* made a mistake while he was correcting one of the contestants' errors, and the embarrassed local *kiai* could not continue after that. The *kiai* narrating the account said that after that point he had to judge the rest of the contest all by himself, sitting for long stretches, having to be alert every single moment for the smallest of mistakes, and the contest still went on for days and days. The *kiai* went on to relate the burdens of working such contests as well as the obligation to go all the way out to the main mosque five times a day to lead prayers as its imam, a responsibility that becomes more weighty with advancing age. The *kiai* pointed out that, just like with the contest in the country, there was just no one else who can do it. As he was saying this, a family member remarked softly to me, just out of the *kiai*'s earshot, that his health was actually failing, and it was having been a *ḥāfiẓ* all these years that had worn him out. His wife made the same remark many times during my visits. This individual passed away within two months of these conversations, and Muslims all across South Sulawesi were heard to remark at the time that he was one of three of a great generation of respected *kiai*s, politically active in the province during the 1950s, all of whom God had made *marḥūm* (deceased) within months of one another in the late spring of 1997. I once asked this *kiai*, whose funeral was observed in the last week of my stay, what was really, actually required to memorize the Qur'ān. He did not respond in terms of applying special tricks or techniques; having a certain gender, teacher, or family lineage; or possessing an inborn virtue or ability. "All you need," he answered, "is the will and the work" *(kemauan dan kerajinan)*. The Qur'ān memorizer's ongoing, attentive effort is consistent over space and time; it is based in affective patterns of the recited Qur'ān, expected norms of moral feeling for readers, as well as the emotional demands of daily repetition with respect to text and social context.

CHAPTER 3
READING
Affective ABCs of Learning

The project of acquiring the ability to voice the Qur'ān in Indonesia drew Muslims into a large-scale Islamic movement that was both educational and practice-centered. A social understanding of Qur'ānic learning was emerging in Indonesia in the 1990s that combined two basic types of learning systems for basic vocalization of the Qur'ān. These two systems, which could be seen to be in tension, were in fact increasingly coming to be used in combination. An overall synthesis was developing in terms of the "senses" that each evoked, labeled "traditional" and "modern." In learning, teaching strategies infused multiple aspects of reading practice with affect, using feeling as a strategy of competence. This was achieved by coding self-consciously parts of the process, even the letters on the page, with emotional valences, even as affective selves were recognized in the overall process of learning. A "learning identity" of Qur'ānic reading in Indonesia, when combined with the affective dynamics of piety, changing social systems, and the recited Qur'ān itself, became a subjectivity of an ongoing or lifelong learner who would continually develop the process of acquiring competence.

In learning to read the Qur'ān, the system to be mastered is named "*tajwīd*," a term that most often refers to the system of rules for correct vocalization. Reading the Qur'ān aloud according to the rules of *tajwīd* is the first kind of formal religious instruction that most Indonesian Muslims receive. The ability to vocalize the Arabic of the Qur'ān properly is also the basis of other Qur'ānic practical abilities (such as reciting from memory or reciting in advanced melodic modes). *Tajwīd* is an aspect of the more general field of "*qirā'āt*" (readings), and it along with exegesis and other fields of learning form the classical "Qur'ānic sciences." *Tajwīd* marks the distinction between the sacred speech of the Qur'ān and ordinary Arabic, since many of its rules are not applied to Arabic speech and song (such as extension of the duration of vowels and the assimilation of certain consonantal forms). In Indonesia, however, it was not unusual to hear all Arabic vocalized with *tajwīd* rules, from *ḥadīths* to prayers. The goal of apprehending and mastering the rules of *tajwīd* includes the ability to read without errors, to make appropriate choices in sectioning, and to do all of this smoothly and fluently.

A first, and ongoing, goal in learning to read the Qur'ān in Indonesia was to be able to vocalize Arabic phonemes without any trace of the characteristics of local languages in pronunciation. Native speakers of Indonesian languages concentrate on certain sounds in particular: for instance, pronouncing correctly the Arabic "*fā*" (not "*pā*") and "*thā*" (not "*sā*"). Many learn to erase some nasalization tendencies (such as on pharyngeal "*'ayn*" or, especially in the region where I worked, nasalizing an open "*ā*"), while also attempting to nasalize other sounds (such as applying what is known as "*ghunna*" to the consonants "*nūn*" and "*mīm*"). *Tajwīd* also requires mastery of the many notations in the Qur'ānic text, especially those that indicate permissible, preferred, and prohibited "pauses and starts" in sectioning. With every breath, the reciter must also make choices about his or her sectioning of a passage that may or may not have corresponding textual notations for guidance. Reciters learn to exercise the flexibility built into orthopraxy, making necessary choices in phrasing where options exist. The stipulated optionality of the system of *tajwīd* makes orthoprax reading of the Qur'ān the continual application of impeccable judgment as well as good habits.

To meet the challenge of exercising the choices in vocalization (such as stops and starts) according to the rules of *tajwīd,* a truly proficient practitioner would, ideally, possess some knowledge of the meaning of the Arabic text. Basic instruction does not emphasize comprehension, however, focusing instead on technical competence in vocalization. What is emphasized is *apprehension,* which James Baker (in his discussion of reading Arabic-language texts in the eastern Indonesian archipelago) defines as "an activity, inherent in the practice of communicating—and thus also in reading—in which one confronts and takes hold of what there is to know and remember."[1] Although it is no substitute for direct knowledge of Arabic, apprehension often doubled as a kind of comprehension for Indonesians, implied by the robust usage of the Indonesian term "*faham*" for Qur'ānic understanding. This is not merely comprehending "meaning" but sometimes realizing a profoundly meaningful "sense" based on the experiential qualities of apprehending the symbols on the page.

Despite the many statements by Islamicists and historians of religion on the centrality of oral-aural dimensions of scripture as well as the shift away from semantic meanings as a stand-alone framework for understanding religious activity, this point remains much misunderstood, even by Indonesianists working in Muslim contexts.[2] A "miracle" of the Qur'ān that is traditionally undisputed among Muslims is its effect on people in both an immediate sense and over time. An example is the claim that a lack of knowledge of the Arabic language does not hinder appreciation or affective apprehension of the Qur'ān. A story attributed to the great *ḥadīth* traditionist Aḥmad b. Ḥanbal, for example, evokes the piety of Qur'ānic practice under these conditions: "I saw the Almighty in a dream and asked, 'O Lord, what is the best way to manage to be near you?' He replied: 'My Word, O Aḥmad.' I inquired, 'With understanding or without understanding?' He said, 'With or without understanding.'"[3] Accounts of non-Muslims hearing the recitation of the Qur'ān and becoming affected by the force of the performance, and consequently embracing Islam, begin with some of the first figures in Islamic history; similar accounts have continued to be immensely popular throughout the Islamic world. Stories of people who do not comprehend Arabic but whose experiences nevertheless confirm the universal power of the Qur'ān's speech affirm to believers that the Qur'ān transcends particular human language. In addition, these accounts convey the idea that those speaking any and all languages may accept and validate the universality of the Qur'ān.

Older women meeting in study groups in Makassar often related that they would sometimes read a difficult passage in the Qur'ān, study its Indonesian interpretation, but still not be able to realize the meaning fully. They only came to understand completely, they reported, after they had read the Arabic out loud multiple times, a process through which they eventually came to "comprehend" *(faham)* its meaning directly. This practice is consistent with normative understandings of Qur'ān reading in the Islamic tradition (such as al-Ghazzālī's writings on the subject) and Sufi-influenced theories of diverse modes of experiencing knowledge, and it also shows the degree to which the act of reading itself, apart from the discursive content of what is read, may determine emotional states and self-understanding. It was perhaps a direct result of the low level of discursive comprehension of the recited Qur'ān in such contexts that practical aspects of apprehension were emphasized so strongly, and thus the hyperawareness of language, self, and learning, and feelings arising in projects of learning were enhanced all the more.

In the mid-1990s, Indonesians were learning to read the Qur'ān through two primary pedagogical systems. Neither was a part of the national schooling system; public school education at the primary level typically included just one hour of religious instruction per week, in which time only a small part of the curriculum was devoted to the study of the Qur'ān and Qur'ān recitation.

In Islamic learning environments, however, pedagogies for basic reading are the mainstay of teaching and learning. In Indonesia, two kinds of pedagogies, labeled "traditional" and "modern" by participants, were identified by their specific techniques as well as their general affective "senses." Evaluations of these learning systems were not merely "symbolic," but also functioned as modes of affective memory that determined what from the past would be salient in the present moment as well as how practitioners imagined possibilities for the future.

Contrasting qualities of "speed" versus "depth" were the key operative assessments for the two types of teaching methods. The "modern" mode was dominated by a highly successful new method to teach children to read, known as "Iqra'," which was valued for being more rapid *(lebih cepat)*. This curriculum, which coincidentally shares a name with other global Muslim curricula, was developed near Yogyakarta (a major educational and cultural center in central Java); the materials were first published and distributed in the early 1990s.[4] By 1997, the Iqra' method had spread throughout the archipelago, along with the proliferation of "Qur'ānic kindergartens" (Taman Pendidikan Anak-anak, or "TPA"). In this period, many Muslims (especially in urban centers) were engaged in a grassroots educational movement, taking the initiative to teach recitation in their homes with the Iqra' materials. At the same time, formal TPA programs with uniform schedules and uniformed dress were springing up in mosques under the confederation of an official umbrella organization, and with support usually procured locally by those who initiated the programs. In rural areas, the Iqra' method was spreading rapidly, encouraged through the efforts of Muslim college students completing their social service by serving as teachers in rural areas (through the required program of applied study, Kulia Kerja Nyata, or KKN). The widespread popularity that the Iqra' method enjoyed in this period was in part attributable to a general acceptance of the claim that with Iqra' children could acquire the ability to read faster than they would following the "traditional" method of instruction.

The "traditional" method was known as "Baghdadi" in all places in which I worked.[5] This method also had its supporters, who advocated its continued use on a number of grounds. Some of the claims about the superiority of the "traditional" method cited its alleged technical effectiveness, but the most widespread endorsement on behalf of the Baghdadi method was that it was more "deep" *(lebih dalam)* than the Iqra' method. The quality of "depth" often referenced a technique of sounding out the names of the letters and the vowel markings for each word in a chanted formula (in a vernacular language) before vocalizing complete words in Qur'ānic Arabic. The perceived "depth" of the method involved more than a conception of rigor, perception of proximity through native language, or nostalgic or pious attachment, however. The qualitative assessment of pedagogical efficacy was also often a statement about the interpersonal and affective dimensions of the method's learning context. Together, the two methods, Iqra' and Baghdadi, synthesized in both affect and application a complete, although ambivalent, educative system that embraced multiple dimensions of learners' self-understanding with respect to practice, social relations, and religious ideals.

Many anthropological studies of the Muslim world touch on systems of Islamic schooling, and some take it as a primary frame of analysis. These works build on a subfield in Islamic studies that has focused especially on "traditional" educational institutions (*madrasas*, *kuttāb*). In addition, the branch of anthropology that focuses on cross-cultural questions of literacy has drawn much data from Islamic educational contexts.[6] In general, there has been a tendency within contemporary anthropological work to treat the practices of "traditional education" as somewhat opaque.[7] They are often characterized as facets of a precolonial institution that is of interest insofar as it contrasts with features of the colonial, postcolonial, or "modern" systems that have replaced it. Because the stated concerns of these investigations often pertain to the power of texts and institutions (rather than the situational transactions of learning), in anthropological analyses of Muslim education, it is often sufficient to say that students learn "by rote" without examining what that entails situationally in terms of personal or social experience. For example, in *Colonising Egypt*, Timothy Mitchell engages the issue of "the authority of writing." He briefly contrasts the Qur'ān school in Egypt to colonial education, likening "village schools" to trade or vocational education and writing that the role and function of "the village school teacher . . . was not to 'educate' . . . but to provide at proper moments the written and spoken word of the Qur'ān."[8] In contrast, the discussion below focuses on describing affective associations, ambivalences, and patterned emotional textures that enveloped experiences of Qur'ānic education in Indonesia during the time of my research.

Feelings about learning and who is a learner, and the use of learning to forge local and translocal community were self-conscious projects in Indonesia. Brinkley Messick, who has elsewhere considered the question of acquiring literacy and learning "by rote," considers the study of texts in Muslim Yemen in his work *The Calligraphic State*. His work refers briefly to Qur'ān schools, and Messick's description of schooling does include affective dimensions: specifically, how some informants said that they hated going to school. Since his study concerns the perpetuation of orality and textuality, however, the author's primary concern is with the transmission of non-Qur'ānic legal material rather than such experiential patterns.[9] When Messick considers oral-aural and recitational pedagogy, however, he cites two standard instructional

Studying reading with the Baghdadi method in Bone, South Sulawesi

Students at the Iqra' center in Kotagede, Central Java

poems that Yemenis were known to have memorized.[10] Naturally, given the close historical contact between the Yemeni Hadramaut and Indonesia (as well as consistent patterns of education that extend throughout the Muslim world), these poems are also standard in Southeast Asia. Such instructional poems take the form of rhymed couplets, named for the number of verses they contain, such as "*ālfiyyah*" for a thousand or "*arba'ūn*" for forty.[11] (Among the better-known in the Islamic world, including both Yemen and Indonesia, is Ibn Mālik's "Thousand," a text on Arabic grammar.) Messick mentions the poems in a discussion of mnemonic techniques and explains them in terms of their function of ensuring the accessibility and greater retention of the original texts from which they are derived, whose authority and transmission are his principal concern. In Indonesia, these very texts were also recognized to be a system of feeling.

In Indonesia, Muslims expressed strong sentiments about such learning systems, including the poems Messick cites. In the course of fieldwork, my presence and questions among religious educators frequently provoked discussion of personal memories of methods of basic Qur'ānic instruction, which often took on a nostalgic tone. In the course of conversation among modernist religious leaders from islands throughout the eastern archipelago (meeting to discuss the organization of education in Islamic universities), for example, two educators reminisced that the sole method of Arabic language instruction in their childhoods was to memorize Ibn Mālik's verses that give the rules of Arabic grammar. The subsequent test of student proficiency in Arabic was not the application of the principles conveyed in the abstract list of points, but instead the mastery of the poem itself, line by line. The two men laughed warmly about learning and repeating the poem, delighting in shared experience spanning far-removed space while also reaching far back in time to boyhood. What seemed to matter most in the moment of their exchange was not the poem, Arabic grammar, or comparative systems of Islamic education, but instead the unifying, leveling effect of their congruent memory. Similarly, throughout the analysis below, the focus is not the content of Arabic-language education (even when presenting material on curriculum strategies), but instead the affective textures that these strategies explicitly or implicitly impart to learners themselves.

Like Wittgenstein's idea of "depth" or Eliade's "nostalgia" that colors religious lifeworlds, this "sense" of tradition is always experienced in the present. It mediates relationships and situations even as it restructures perceptions of the fixed past and the open future.[12] What is emphasized here, however, is not the formal pattern to which practices correspond (the degree to which they are or are not "traditional" by some objective measure) but the "senses" of process and experience that they produce in the present. Such feeling in and about learning systems built on the emotional microstrategies and personalized experiences and memories of activity itself, creating ongoing learners focused on continual effort.

Competence in Qur'ānic reading was no longer a fixed quantity measured in *tammat* (completion), but in Indonesia in the 1990s it was coming to represent a system of open-ended curriculum in which all Muslims were increasingly seen potentially to participate. Popular programs of reading education in Indonesia construed the fundamentals of practice as a long-term project. Readers came to be energetic learners through the modes of affect that were deployed in relation to orthography, registers of pronunciation that also labeled individual identities, and the affective textures of pedagogies developed for children that refracted on learners of all ages. Individualized understandings of selves that were based on patterned affective valences of learning had become a widespread and shared learning identity, as Indonesian Muslims came to forge meaningful relationships not just to other practitioners, teachers, and students, but also to the ongoing process of learning itself. Feelings about new, synthetic systems and the strategies of affect emergent in actual practice focused practitioners' subjectivities on learning and even relearning how to learn. Relationships formed through the activity of learning were no longer defined as primarily teacher to student but as practitioner to process, coded and evaluated affectively. New ways of conceptualizing reading as a layered, cumulative development and emotional experiences of self and system restructured basic competence in Qur'ānic vocalization from being a fixed accomplishment to being an ongoing pursuit.

Sentimental Identities of Learning

Because Indonesia is not an Arabic-speaking area, Indonesian Muslims must learn the Arabic alphabet and pronunciation of its letters as the first stages in the process of acquiring competence in Qur'ānic reading. Arabic represents a system of orthography and phonemes that, despite whatever exposure Southeast Asian Muslims may have had since early childhood, is nevertheless a significant challenge to apprehend. Since the Arabic letters are not commonly seen outside of religious contexts,[13] the method of Qur'ānic learning in Indonesian can encode both the visual shape and the sound-shape of the letters with strong affective association. Affective properties of sonic and visual aspects of reading were self-consciously cultivated in Indonesian pedagogy, and some teaching methods resonated with old, influential techniques of relating the impression of Arabic letters with affective states. With the aural aspect (that is, the production and assessment of sound in terms of dialect, accent, and "orthoprax" Arabic), the process of learning additionally indexed learners' identities with respect to the registers of social systems. Ongoing practice reinforced these aspects of language and affect, which, even when knowledge of reading was understood to be "complete," were continually open to evaluation and improvement according to the perceptions of others. New identities of learning and feeling thus emerged both about and within systems for the ritual practice of reading the Qur'ān in Indonesia, in terms of both the "teaching curriculum" and the "learning curriculum."

Most influential theories of ritual take ritual "knowledge" to be information about external realities that are somehow encoded by a ritual. Rituals are often assumed to reference larger social, political, symbolic, or cosmological realities, and the study of ritual has often functioned as an avenue for access to these wider contexts. Many of the treatments of ritual in the history of religions emphasize symbolism, particularly rituals' connection to myths or to other symbolic representations of power. A ritual is presumed to be, following Clifford Geertz' famous phrase, a model of and for something other than itself. Along with the debate about diachronic change in ritual,[14] a classic question in ritual studies has been ritual's "noetic function," that is, the capacity of a ritual to impart knowledge about more encompassing systems. For example, Theodore Jennings writes in an influential article, "The performance of ritual . . . teaches one not only how to conduct the ritual itself, but how to conduct oneself outside of the ritual space,"[15] and it is this latter connection that Jennings discusses at length in his piece "On Ritual Knowledge," especially in connection to historical changes in rituals over time. Although Jennings shows concern for ritual action (in addition to "extraritual meaning"), he nevertheless dispenses with the "learned" qualities of ritual at the outset as the trivial case.[16]

With the exception of analytical frameworks drawing on a theatrical analogy for performance, the study of ritual has often overlooked the impact of processual and developmental aspects of rehearsal or repetition.[17] Theorists of ritual have tended to construe ritual learning as a one-time affair, as if once a ritual has been performed successfully, it is mastered and concluded (perhaps then to be repeated "archetypally"). Learning, or what Lave and her colleagues term "changes in knowledge in action,"[18] is often treated in terms of a single performance in the study of religious ritual rather than change over time. This is in part due to a lingering emphasis on the paradigm of initiation rites in the theory of ritual,[19] in which learning is presented as a form of structured information transfer. Initiatory rituals, the basis for much theorization of ritual, are not the best models for understanding the long-term effects of ongoing, repeated, voluntary practices. Many approaches to ritual, including those with an implicit liturgical model, downplay the possibilities of religious enactments to effect change, concerned instead with the preservation of information being conveyed or how ritual reflects changes in the wider conveying structures themselves.

It is not surprising, then, that theories of ritual (or voluntary religious enactments) have not tended to focus on how a ritual is learned, and few have in fact highlighted the fact that rituals are learned at all.[20] The study of religion and education (or "ritual knowledge") has been concerned primarily with the question of what information is transmitted through a religious practice or its discourse or symbolism, rather than how rituals themselves are learned. To the degree that ritual activity and learning are considered together, theorists have tended to consider what (nonritual) knowledge is being transmitted in or by rituals: what could be called the "hidden" (or revealed/hierophonic) curriculum, symbolism, or agenda of religious practice. Pedagogy, or the learning of ritual, if recognized, has tended to be subordinated to the function of expressing or transmitting such knowledge.[21]

Ongoing religious practice, however, may generate a developmental "learning identity" because of its nature as ongoing activity owing to the fact that competence is acquired cumulatively. Jean Lave is among those who developed the concept of "learning identities," claiming that learning is an activity that forges subjectivity in direct relationship to activity. Lave also explores how people come to be accepted into "communities of learning" or how a person comes to be accepted as a part of a community of practice over time. Her approach shifts the focus, she writes, "from individual as learner to learning as participating in the social world, and from the concept of cognitive process to the more encompassing view of social activity," including "the sustained character of developmental cycles of communities of practice."[22] In a later work, *Understanding Practice*, part of Lave's collaborative project is to "contextualize" learning so that formal and informal settings for education may be viewed as sites of social production and as processes of generating such "learning identities."[23] The situated activity of learning to read the Qur'ān, especially through the relations established developmentally to self, to others, and to practice itself by way of affective strategies, created new "synthetic" subjectivties in Indonesia. Creating these "learning identities" was sometimes the first step in what was imagined to be a communal project of developing a revitalized Indonesian Muslim community of Qur'ānic engagement.

Some abilities to recite the Qur'ān were acquired in Indonesia through what Lave has termed "legitimate peripheral participation," which is an informal kind of mimetic learning. Many religious practices, such as canonical prayer, were transmitted in this way; most Indonesian Muslims, for example, first learn the Fātiḥah, the opening *sūrah* of the Qur'ān, through this sort of informal education. This mode of learning also characterizes non-Qur'ānic Arabic recitational systems (such as the Barzanji), in distinction to the Qur'ān. Although it was widely recognized in Indonesia that children "pick up" the Qur'ān through continuous exposure (there were even words for this, such as "*gelandangan*" in Javanese), formal Qur'ānic pedagogy will duplicate such a process of emulation, and necessarily so. When it comes to Qur'ānic learning, abilities acquired by unstructured imitation were not actually considered to be "legitimate" with respect to the social understandings of the transmission of religious knowledge; formal systems, whether redundant or not, were also required for authoritative knowledge transfer.

Even if a child had, for example, successfully memorized a short *sūrah* to be used in prayer (such as the first *sūrah*, al-Fātiḥah, required for canonical prayer) by imitating others, this child was still expected to "learn" that *sūrah* from a teacher, using a written text. One reason for this is the ontological status of the Qur'ān as revelation, shown in the strong distinction made in Indonesia between the "Language of the Qur'ān" (Bahasa Al-Quran) and the natural language, Arabic. Another reason for this redundancy is that the generative rules of *tajwīd* are not abstractly evident from a single "reading"; a child who has learned one *sūrah* cannot internalize and unerringly transfer to other readings the principles of pronunciation. For this, a system must be taught. Indonesian theory and practice thus marked a clear separation between "teaching" and "learning" curricula, providing possibilities to develop affective "senses" of self and system through cultivated awareness of the minute details of vocalizing the letters on the page.

In modern Indonesia, self-conscious strategies to develop an affective relationship with letters and sounds in learning to read the Qur'ān informed the experience of recitation as well as self-understanding of the reader as learner. Such affective valences of the recited Qur'ān arose out of more than an aesthetic appreciation of performance. The emotional coding of Qur'ānic visual symbols occurred more meaningfully to readers through the contextualized process of learning to vocalize them, which provided grounds for further emergent feeling in and around the recited Qur'ān. In learning to read, transmitted along with the symbols of the very letters themselves are affective valences (resonating with a long-standing tradition of piety in the Islamic tradition that codes the letters of the alphabet with associative meaning). This also included assessment of linguistic registers identified by labels such as "vernacular," "Indonesian," and/or "Islamic." In Indonesia in the 1990s, each of the two principal methods in use for teaching basic Qur'ān reading propagated distinctive affective valences and "learning identities," and an affective synthesis emerged that held the two in synthetic, productive tension. This new system altered practitioners' relationship to the very process of Qur'ānic reading itself.

Three primary affective dimensions of reading activity arose through the processes of basic Qur'ānic learning. First, identities were implicated affectively in the discourse of teaching and evaluation; this was not merely referential but a rich strategy of affective communication and internalization based on speech registers that were deployed in pedagogy. Second, the activity of acquiring fluent "literacy" encoded affective associations into reading practice that could then be carried forward into other domains of competence. In the course of learning, students developed direct linkages between affective states and linguistic registers of speech (including different "native" languages and Qur'ānic Arabic) as well as with the sound and visual shape of the Qur'ānic language itself. These nascent associations may be observed within actual learning contexts and teaching practices, revealing how concepts and experiences are actually formed in relation to practice. Third, contextualized self-understandings relating to the activity of learning to read the Qur'ān fostered in Indonesia in the 1990s widespread "learning identities" described by practitioners in terms of a self-conscious relationship to an ongoing process.

Tajwīd: Apprehending a System

Tajwīd is a classic "Qur'ānic science," part of the "science of readings," and it is treated in detail in foundational writings such as al-Suyūtī's *Itqān fī 'Ulūm al-Qur'ān*. *Tajwīd* is often defined by some variant of the phrase "giving each sound its correct weight and measure." *Tajwīd* determines the distinctive sound of the recited Qur'ān, since many of the rules and guidelines of *tajwīd* are not applied in spoken Arabic (whether colloquial or standard *fuṣḥa*). Although *tajwīd* comprises a set of formalized rules (and is almost always presented that way), as Kristina Nelson has argued, *tajwīd* is better conceptualized in terms of the qualities of sound that it produces.[24] In a classical statement quoted by Denny, Ibn al-Jazarī, the great expert on recitation, elaborates the rules of recitation in terms of actual sound production:

> *Tajwīd* is not slurring of the tongue, nor hollowing of the mouth [so as to make deep tones], nor twisting of the jaw, nor quavering of the voice, nor lengthening of the doubled consonants, nor cutting short the lengthened vowels, nor buzzing the nasals, nor slurring the *r*'s. Recitation *[qirā'ah]* shuns these impressions, and the hearts and ears reject them. On the contrary: gentle, sweet, pleasant, fluent recitation—that we point to and present as of the utmost importance in what

> we say; with no inaccuracy, nor affectation, nor manneredness, nor extravagance, and no straying from the natural hallmarks of the Arabs, and the speech of the truly eloquent and pure with respect to the "Readings" and accepted performance.[25]

A sound-centered perspective also explains how Indonesians themselves actually teach and learn *tajwīd,* whether for the beginner or at advanced levels, in which instruction often takes the form of referencing the (recorded) recitations of others, usually Egyptian *qāri*'s.

The treatment to follow presents the aspects of the *tajwīd* system that the beginning student of recitation first faces, especially those that pose a challenge for nonnative speakers of Arabic (and highlighting the problems that native speakers of Indonesian languages in particular characteristically encounter).[26] This presentation from the "learner's point of view" is far from a complete treatment of *tajwīd*, although it does cover many of the basics. As is also the case in beginning instruction in Indonesia, the language I use to describe *tajwīd* will be nontechnical, attempting to render clearly what are the primary features of orthoprax vocalization that the student first encounters and may continue to grapple with for a lifetime as a learner.[27]

In learning *tajwīd* or acquiring competence in basic Qur'ān recitation, Indonesian learners developed personal affective relationships to the very process of reading: With increasing mastery, increased awareness of the process itself and not automaticity was the goal. Automaticity and fluency were the objective of the beginner seeking minimal competence, but the more advanced the level of reading skill, the more sophisticated were the "rules" of which experts were expected to be vigilantly aware. Formalization of the rules of *tajwīd* may be seen as a solution to the historical problem of standardizing style and sound in recitation with respect to the great linguistic and geographical diversity of the Islamic world. The rules of *tajwīd* expressly provide clear guidelines, assuring a uniformity and consistency of pronunciation of Divine Speech. Since the rules do not derive directly from aspects of classical or colloquial speech, being a native speaker of Arabic—of any register or dialect—does not guarantee proficiency in the practice of *tajwīd*. The orthoprax vocalization of the Qur'ān is an acquired ability for any Muslim, a competence that inevitably requires some degree of explicit study. The rules of *tajwīd* were learned at first not as complicated schemes but as embodied habit, and Indonesian teaching strategies emphasized their personalization and internalization.

Indonesian Muslims, like most Muslims, face the challenge of learning how to pronounce the sounds of Arabic when learning to vocalize the Qur'ān. Taken from a beginning handbook, here are two instances of common types of errors that can distort meaning, both found in the opening *sūrah*, the Fātiḥah (recited seventeen times a day by practicing Muslims); these words appear in the first and last *āyahs*, respectively:

al-ḥamd: "all praise" (is often mispronounced as)
al-hamd: "to put out a fire"

ḍāllīn: "those who go astray" (is often mispronounced as)
dāllīn: "those who follow the right path"[28]

Meaning may also be altered in any reading by careless vowel mispronunciation, common on verbs. Even when pronunciation renders a word intelligibly and correctly, the rules of *tajwīd* stipulate further scrupulous attention to the technicalities of sound production.

One of the first elements of learning to read the Qur'ān aloud is to study the *makhārij*, or "points of articulation" of letters. They are identified in classical terminology by the part of the mouth in which they originate, such as "*lisānī*" (tongue) letters (i.e., *qāf, kāf, jīm, shīn, yā, lām, nūn, rā, fā*) and "*shafawī*" (lip) letters *(bā, mīm, wāw)*, as opposed to "*ḥalq*" ("throat," or guttural) letters (*'ayn, ḥā, ghayn, khā*, and the "*hamzah*" glottal stop), which are articulated back in the throat.[29] Indonesians would memorize and practice pronouncing these letters according to this system of classification. The systemization of phonemes in *tajwīd* contains far more information about Arabic sounds than is included in this basic typology, however. For example, the letters of the alphabet are also grouped according to classes of "attributes" *(ṣifāt)* that determine degrees of sound assimilation. These include qualities such as elevation *(isti'lā')*, depression *(istifāl)*, softness *(tarqīq)*, and heaviness *(tafkhīm)*. These attributes may be classified as necessary or conditional, depending on whether or not they are influenced by a given vowel *(ḥarakah)* combination. Each letter has at least five essential *(lāzim)* or basic *(aṣlī)* attributes, each expressed as one of a pair of opposites (such as *shadīdah*/strong or *rikhwah*/soft); in addition, there are also ten (sometimes said to be seven) secondary but essential attributes that are not arranged in pairs of opposites, and a letter may have one or two of these ten attributes (such as the *ṣāfirah*/sibilant or "whistling" letters, which comprise *ṣ, s*, and *z*).

There are three primary types of rules pertaining to pronunciation, and they all influence the sound quality, phrasing, and rhythm of recitation: (1) rules for the pronunciation of consonants, especially the letter "*nūn*" (which is sounded on the endings of most indefinite nouns in all three declensions); (2) rules for the vocalization of vowels, especially in terms of their relative length (whether extended through *madd* or shortened through *qaṣr*); and (3) rules governing pauses and abbreviations (which are a shortening of a terminal vowel), including an important class of rules for determining the "pause and beginning" at points in reading *(al-waqf wa al-ibtidā')*.[30]

A first principle is that consonants with the same point of articulation assimilate, or blend together. Two types of letters are classified with respect to this process: fourteen "solar" or "sun" *(shamsī)* letters, and the remaining fourteen "moon" *(qamarī)* letters. "Sun" letters blend. For example, as in spoken Arabic, *al-rasūl* (the Prophet), is pronounced as *ar-rasūl*, because *rā* is a blending "sun" letter. In *tajwīd*, other kinds of consonantal assimilations (and partial assimilations) also occur, which are not heard in ordinary spoken Arabic. This practice does not come naturally to those unaccustomed to hearing the Qur'ān, and even mistakes in failing to assimilate the *l (lām)* of the definite article *(al-)* on nouns beginning with a "sun" letter can be heard by intermediate students who are nonnative speakers of Arabic.[31]

Unique to Qur'ānic pronunciation are rules for particular letters (such as *mīm* and especially *nūn*). There are special conventions for nasalized pronunciation (*ghunna*, Ind. *sengau*) of *mīm* and *nūn* when they are doubled in a word or if doubling happens between two words *(mushaddad)*. There is also a class of rules related to changes that these letters undergo based on adjacent consonants. For example, *mīm* and *nūn* do not get clear pronunciation *(iẓhār)* in the following situations: full assimilation (*idghām*, as in the examples of assimilations given above), suppressed pronunciation (*ikhfā'*, when the sound is influenced by letters with similar points of articulation), and change or conversion (*qalb* or *iqlāb*, for *nūn* only). As an example of the latter case, "*minbar*" ("pulpit," and in Indonesia, a place to perform public recitation) would be pronounced as "*mimbar*" in the Qur'ān since the *nūn* is converted to a *mīm* by the following *bā*. (*Iqlāb* is marked in the text with a *mīm* symbol, and some other assimilations are also marked.)

Consonantal assimilation (*idghām*, with the letter "*nūn*"), the first case given above, receives a great deal of attention by the beginning student, in part because it appears so frequently. (Indefinite case endings usually carry a terminal *nūn [tanwīn]*, denoted below in superscript, which is not written as an explicit letter in the text.) An example of this type of assimilation is the pronunciation of "*an-lā*" (that no), which is voiced as "*al-lā*," as in the testimony of faith (*shahādah*, the first "Pillar" of Islam) and heard frequently in the *ādhān* (call to prayer):[32]

ashhadu	<u>*an-lā*</u> [pronounced <u>*al-lā*</u>]	*illāha*	*illā*	*Āllāh*
I testify	<u>that there is no</u>	god	except	God

In another example from the *shahādah*, the final nasal of the (indefinite accusative) case ending on the name of the Prophet is also assimilated:

wa	*Muḥammad*^{an} *rasūl* [pronounced *Muḥammadarrasūl*]	*-ilLāh*
and	Muḥammad is the Messenger	of God

The *nūn* may further assimilate in ways that are not heard in spoken Arabic.

Besides consonants, a second major area of beginning *tajwīd* study pertains to vowels. Vowels are classified according to their duration, in terms of a basic unit or weight (called "*madd aṣlī*" or "*madd ṭabi'ī*") of one short vowel (a long vowel counts as two basic units, "movements," or beats, called "*ḥarakāt*"). Vowel sounds adapt according to the preceding consonant, and vowel sounds also assimilate under other conditions. Related to this are important rules about the duration of vowels. There are three vowels in Arabic (*a*, *i*, and *u*, in long and short forms), and adjacent consonants affect not only their sound shape (as occurs in standard spoken *fuṣḥa* Arabic) but, in Qur'ān recitation, also their duration. The example below illustrates how vowels before doubled consonants (two consonants together) are shortened:

ashhadu	*al-lā* [see above]	*illāha*	*illā Āllāh* [pronounced *illalLāh*]
I testify	that there is no	god	except God

The relative weight of consonants and nouns is critical to the recited Qur'ān and provides its rhythm.

Elongation of vowels is called "*madd*." It occurs when a long vowel (*maddah* letter) and a "condition of *madd*" (such as a glottal stop or *hamzah*) appear together. Mistakes with *madd* account for many common errors among beginners as well as among more advanced students who may allow their technical artistry in melodic modes to interfere with the proper duration of vowel sounds. There are five kinds of extended *madd* (*madd farī'*).[33] One type occurs when a long vowel is followed by the glottal stop called "*hamzah*" and is subsequently lengthened, usually by a degree of three to one if it occurs within a word and a degree of two to one if it appears between two words. For example, the word "*al-malā'ikatu*" (angels) is pronounced with an extended *ā*, counted with three beats of measure: *al-ma-la*^{1}*-a*^{2}*-a*^{3}*-'i-ka-tu*. Another rule is that a long vowel before a certain rare class of modified doubled consonants is lengthened, such as "*ḍāllīn*" (with *lāms* doubled from an original form, *ḍālilīn*, "astray"), which is the penultimate word of the Fātiḥah. In this case, the *ā* of "*ḍāllīn*" (those who go astray) is pronounced drawn out with five "original" or "fundamental" (*aṣlī*) weights of measure (*ḥarakāt*): *ḍa*^{1}*-a*^{2}*-a*^{3}*-a*^{4}*-a*^{5}*-ll-i*^{1}*-i*^{2}*-n*.

Another type of rule relating to vowel durations is the pausal abbreviation on words occurring at the end of phrasings. Depending on sectioning, these may occur at the marked ends of *āyahs*, but this is not always the case (as in *āyahs* that are too long to recite in one breath). With such pauses, the final element is unvoiced *(sākin)* whether it be a case of *tanwīn* (a nasalized ending on indefinite nouns, as in "*Muḥammadan*," above, which would be pronounced as "*Muḥammada*"), a declensional or conjugational vowel (*i'rāb*, which could also include final short vowels on pronomial suffixes), or a *tā marbuṭa*, pronounced "*t*" (as in "*al-malā'ikatu*," which would be pronounced as "*al-malā'ika*"). Because pausal abbreviation may leave out grammatical cues to meaning, it is advised that after a pausal abbreviation the reciter repeat the final word of the previous phrase (which, now being the first and not the last word to be voiced, would not be in pausal form). There are also rules that pertain to giving the dropped terminal vowel *(ḥarakah)* some indication by a subtle prolongation or by making the shape of the vowel with the lips but not voicing it.

A third class of rules, one that receives a great deal of attention, pertains to stops and starts *(al-waqf wa-l-ibtidā')*, which only occur at the end of a complete word. Kinds of stops are grouped according to the reasons for the stop: "forced" *(iḍtirārī)*, which is an unplanned stop, such as coughing; "informative" *(ikhtibārī)*, which would be a stop made in order to explain in teaching; and "voluntary" *(ikhtiyārī)*, which comprises almost all of the stops that reciters actually make.[34] Stops are classified in terms of their desirability and appropriateness with respect to meaning: "perfect" *(al-waqf at-tām)*, such as at the end of an *āyah* when there is no connection in meaning to the one that follows; "sufficient" *(al-waqf al-kāfī)*, which occurs at the end of a verse in which the sense of meaning continues in the following verse; "good" *(al-waqf al-ḥasan)*, which occurs in the middle of an *āyah* when a phrase is complete, but there is still a meaningful relation to the remainder of the verse; and bad or "ugly" *(al-waqf al-qabīḥ)*. An example of the last is 4 al-Nisā' 43, at which there is a marking for an impermissible stop. This is because reciting only the beginning part of the *āyah*, "Do not approach *ṣalāh* [prayer]," and stopping there without completing the phrase with what follows ("when your mind is not clear") would seriously distort meaning (possibly conveying the absurd idea that one should never pray).

With sectioning, the reciter constantly exercises choice. The rules in fact stipulate choice. There are seven most general forms of stop, such as the *lāzim* stop (marked "*mīm*"), where a stop must be made or else meaning would be distorted. There are also places, as in the example above, where it is impermissible to stop (marked "*lā*," meaning "no" [stop]). In between are at least five levels of preference (such as "permissible to continue, but stopping is better [*jā'iz*, *jīm* symbol]" or "permissible to stop, but it would be better to continue [*murakhkhaṣ*, *ṣād* symbol]"). Other passages are designated as "embracing" *(mu'āniqah)*, in which there is one sense of meaning if a stop is made but another if reading is continuous, and both are allowed.[35]

In traditional instruction, students first learn the letters and then begin to recite with their *shaikh*, having their errors corrected as they occur in practice. Later, they may study *tajwīd* more systematically. In Indonesia, the presentation of more advanced material thus often first emerges through direct reading practice, called "*tadarus*," with a teacher. Even with the "systematic" Iqra' materials, for example, the special booklet published by Iqra' that gives the formal rules of *tajwīd*, titled *Tajwid Praktis*, is not used by many instructors at the local level as a part of the program; the basic information given in the first standard six booklets is understood to be adequate to put the student on the level of "proficiency." Curriculum is thus implicit and practice-driven, even in formal and semiformal education. Because of a redundancy in the systematicity of the formal science of *tajwīd* and the actual practice of reading from the Qur'ān correctly, only advanced expertise is usually called "*tajwid*" in Indonesia. Experts have, supposedly, studied the "rules" formally in contrast to beginners, who follow them in practice without the more specialized knowledge of the theoretical system of *tajwid*.

The distinction drawn between the "teaching curriculum" and the "learning curriculum" for Qur'ān reading in Indonesia reveals the role of affect in apprehending systems from the learner's point of view. One coach at an intensive session for corporate reciters, for example, introduced technical material from the field of advanced *tajwīd* study one afternoon: the classification of attributes of letters *(ṣifāt al-ḥurūf)*. He wrote out the names of the attributes on the whiteboard, demonstrating standard mnemonic formulae in Arabic for remembering all of the letters within each class. The students diligently copied the information into their notebooks. When the lesson was completed, the coach acknowledged that the material was just the same as that which would have been imparted by study by listening to cassettes of reciters. He remarked that the information was all useless anyway unless it contributed to good habits in actual reciting, for which what one really needs to have is a "practiced tongue" *(lidah terlatih)*.[36]

At one point in the session, this coach turned away from the board and asked the group a rhetorical question: "So, what's the use *(manfaat)* of all this?" He then continued, stating, "It's *ilmuttajwid*," the "science of *tajwid*." The systematic treatment was valued as "*ilmu*" (knowledge), and its redundancy did not reduce its significance as such; it must eventually be mastered cognitively as well as in practice if one is fully to "understand." This "understanding," as he said to the group, requires feeling: "*Tajwid* is written out *(tertulis)*. *Tajwid* is quantified *(terhitung)*. But you will never be able to see it *(tak bisa dilihat)*. *It is at its basis a feeling (rasa)*. So try, work, every day. Try to add a little bit more to it every day. Everything can always be improved" (emphasis added). This particular coach was hardly lax about his students' *tajwīd;* he was the most meticulous and demanding of any I encountered. He had in fact taken first prize in the international recitation competition in Riyadh, Saudi Arabia. He would urge all of his students to read all the time, especially aspiring national competitors (with constant instruction such as, "Go and read this fifty times every night before you go to sleep"). He also recognized, however, that *tajwīd* is not just an abstract theory or set of rules as systematized by a "teaching curriculum" but a practice to be perfected only through learning and to be fully internalized through applied strategies of feeling.

Indonesian systems for mastering *tajwīd* were not only understood in terms of "rules," but more salient for learners' practice was their own situational competence and the affect conveyed through contexts of pedagogy. Contrasting systems of learning *tajwīd* were themselves understood as coherent processes, labeled affectively in both theory and practice. In learning to read, a self-understanding as practitioner emerged through the continuous process of developing sensibility by an encounter with the letters on the page; this was an ongoing negotiation of feeling as well as a developing cognitive mastery.[37] The process of learning to perceive and to vocalize Qur'ānic Arabic thus took the form of a self-conscious cultivation of affective states in both theory and practice.

Feeling Registers and Alphabetic Association

Qur'ānic sound production and orthography reference learners' identities in processes of study and thereby forge an affective relation to practice, especially within educative contexts. For Indonesians and other nonnative Arabic speakers, recognizing the Arabic letters and vocalizing them correctly, and particularly pronouncing them correctly at the standard tempo of recitation, are a challenge. Much elementary recitation training in Indonesia represents an attempt to erase traces of spoken languages—not just Bahasa Indonesia, but also other Indonesian languages such as Javanese, Acehnese, Ambonese, Buginese, and Makassarese—that influence the pronunciation of Arabic phonemes. While these local accents may index various qualities (valuations like "educated" or "unschooled," "country" or "cosmopolitan"), the entire spectrum of local pronunciations provided an overall system in which all Indonesians could share performatively. Often pedagogical strategies deployed these shared associations expressly in order to alter how people felt about their location within the process of learning to read and, by extension, the actual sounds that they produced. These were "registers" both of sound and of self, used to internalize enduring "learning identities" of practice through feeling strategies relating both to self and to system.

Registers of speech and identity that emerged in Indonesian instruction for Qur'ān reading coded affect and a sense of identity through the situated practice of learning.[38] Linguistic "register" may be defined as "a coherent complex of linguistic features linked to a situation of use."[39] Judith Irvine explains that the concept of "linguistic register" developed within a movement in British linguistics that sought to study language use in context: "register" (variety according to use) stands in opposition to "dialect" (variety according to users). Irvine suggests that "varieties according to use" have an affective dimension that "organizes some of their linguistic characteristics."[40] In Irvine's work, application of the theory of registers allows her to focus on the ways in which "feelings are conventionalized" in a Senegalese community according to varying modes and through aspects of performance expressing emotion as well as representing social rank. Irvine's analysis treats registers that are adopted by multiple speakers in order to express their sentiments and their social and cultural identities.[41] Here, I consider such registers as they were deployed and evaluated by Indonesians within Qur'ānic teaching and learning practices.

Many "traditional" teachers and *kiai* still had their recitation marked by traces of local languages, a phenomenon frequently noted in public discussions of recitation among students and teachers in other contexts. Many "non-traditional" instructors imitated vernacular pronunciation as a part of their pedagogy, both for entertainment and subtle (and not-so-subtle) criticism and evaluation. During classes, one would commonly hear stock demonstrations of a range of vernacularly influenced pronunciations: "The Acehnese are like this, the Javanese like this, people from Kalimantan sound like this. . . ." The examples thus given represented regional identity like an idealized New Order pageant of "unity in diversity" in pronunciation styles. The practice of imitation offered the appreciative appeal of recognizing the characteristics of different regional teams. These performances were understood to inject "interest" (humor) into Qur'ānic pedagogy, and they also played the widespread game of identifying pan-Indonesian regional characteristics. Attempts to identify the origins of characteristic pronunciations were often accompanied by mimicry of the speech patterns of others, a practice common in Indonesia in nonreligious contexts as well. People payed close attention to patterns of Qur'ānic vocal inflection and imitated them not as a form of mockery (as might be the case elsewhere), but as a kind of vocal "participation" in the speech act of the initial interlocutor. In learning, it also effected a form of confidence: students may anticipate that their own problems could be overcome by recognizing the problems of others. Implicit was the suggestion that the overall "unity" of Indonesian languages imagined together might overcome the "diversity" of local pronunciation difficulties. For example, Javanese can nasalize *ng* especially well, while Mandar speakers have a knack for *khā* that others do not, and so forth.

The pedagogical strategy of playing with regionalized registers and localized senses of self was based on a technique that relies on the mastery of multiple speech registers as a form of humor and thus more effective teaching. The paradigm for this kind of practice is the popular Islamic preacher (examples are K. H. Imaduddin and K. H. Zainuddin M.Z.) whose humor relies heavily on improvising on various speech registers, voices, and vocal styles. Among such Muslim Indonesian preachers' techniques was to play discursive content off against the form of a variety of performance genres. For example, a preacher would imitate the cadence of a *dangdut* pop song while his semantic content commented (usually disapprovingly) on the genre of the songs themselves. This was very funny. This kind of practice is an example of what Indonesians meant by instruction undertaken in an "interesting" way, and it no doubt contributed to the tendency of Qur'ān teachers to use registers and roles in a similarly humorous way in order to "pull" the interest of students. In formal instruction, for example, teachers would sometimes continue to use *murattal* pitch variation, while switching from reading the Qur'ān to intoning its Indonesian translation in order to explicate a point.

A book treating the work of the preacher K. H. Zainuddin M.Z. explains the educative paradigm of his sometimes comedic approach. The following passage gives the overall rationale for such strategies, while also employing rhythm, assonance, and formulae similar to those a preacher might use:[42]

> In his *dakwah,* K. H. Zainuddin M.Z. often uses a *huamanistis (kemanusiaan)* approach, which means that in his *dakwah* he more often touches people rather than offends them *(menyentuh/menyinggung),* welcomes them rather than ridicules them *(mengajak/mengejek),* embraces them rather than punches them *(merangkul/memukul)*; his examples pinch but they do not hurt *(ibarat mencubit/terasa sakit).* This approach is really derived from the method *(metode)* used by the Prophet SAW when he would perform *dakwah.* . . .
>
> The material of his *dakwah* is offered with a sincere *(ikhlas)* heart. K. H. Zainuddin M.Z. holds the principle that something straight from the heart will, God-willing, reach the heart, and *dakwah* that is honest and sincere *(tulus ikhlas)* will easily be accepted by the religious community *(umat).*[43]

Good-natured play on speech patterns among those in the world of "*qari profesional*" in their teaching as well as in lighter moments has grounding in the assumption that an entertaining, amusing performance (and even sometimes poking a little fun) is part of meaningful communication, religious solidarity, and effective pedagogy.

Qāri's would often play on multiple registers and identities among themselves. Before a coaching session for a national team from South Sulawesi, for example, a group of recitation competitors was relaxing, waiting for the coach who had just been flown in from Jakarta to appear. After imitating the cadence of a devotional text with nonsense syllables, one young reciter offered a send-up of a stereotypical old *kiai* by pinching his spectacles on his nostrils and demanding that the whole class do the same, because this was the only sure way to effect *ghunna* (nasalization) in pronunciation. The idea that the group of reciters from South Sulawesi would teach and learn like back-country *kiai* in front of the champion guest coach from the capital made the moment seem especially funny. This kind of joking is not only the stuff of schoolkids but was part and parcel of sophisticated strategies for Qur'ānic teaching and learning in Indonesia.

Qāri's constantly used multiple registers of speech and identity for amusement, irony, and effective instruction. Once a contest judge, for example, climbed up on the stage in a quiet moment during a competition when everyone (the contestants and sponsors) had left the hall except for a group of old friends. She solemnly delivered a bogus "*program*" for the remainder of the evening, imitating the formal oration of the "*pembukaan*" opening of a public event *(acara)*, with its distinctive vocal style and comportment *("Ibu-ibu bapak-bapak yang saya hormati . . .")*. In another example of self-consciousness with respect to multiple registers and roles, when a champion was coaching a pair of girls for a public school recitation program, he did a hilarious rendition of the standard, softly gendered, and earnest "*puitisisasi*" and "*tarjamahan*" (translation) of the meaning of the verse in Indonesian, providing the proper paradigmatic model for performance but also with awareness that his high, breathy voice and anguished expression could be seen as amusingly tongue-in-cheek. The country *pesantren* teacher, the bureaucratic New Order officiator, the revolutionary/reformist orator, the plaintive voice of expressive piety, the hilarious preacher—the same people, some of them *qāri*'s, performed these registers and roles in public situations and in moments of privacy, playfulness, and pedagogy.[44]

In trying to impart new habits with respect to Qur'ānic orthopraxy (rather than the more general religious values preachers convey), the registers of applied recitation pedagogy could sometimes "pinch (but not hurt)." Identities were affectively evaluated through the stereotyping performances of the registers of others' speech and recitation. A speaker delivering a formal address that opened an Islamic event, for example, pronounced every Arabic-derived word with exaggerated articulation. He tickled the audience, and he also conveyed the message that the tone of the entire event could be more self-consciously Islamic than it was, as his *tajwīd* style contrasted with the standard inflection of Arabic-Islamic words in everyday Indonesian speech. At the same time, overly affected orthopraxy indexed through Arabic pronunciation could be subtly criticized in some Qur'ānic contexts (as "*tiru-tiru*," or trying too hard), as when one coach demonstrated amusingly the grossly hypercorrected pronunciation style that was said to please competition judges (especially those from Java) at the national level.

Pedagogical mimicry brought to bear ambivalences about multiple and hybrid Qur'ānic subjectivities. An example is a training session held for college students who were about to teach Qur'ān reading in outlying schools as a part of their social service requirement. During the session, the coach mimicked local styles of pronunciation to the side-splitting laughter of the hundreds of students in attendance, some of whom may have laughed out of fond recognition of the styles of their own relatives and teachers in their own *kampong* (hometown). Heterogeneity allowed for self-recognition and possibly even shame as the contrast referenced the qualities of older styles of education. Ambivalence was also marked in a Barzanji-reading contest that valorized "localness" while at the same time it had "*tajwid*" as a judging criterion; participants enjoyed identifying participants on stage by their area of origin through their pronunciation styles, while at the same time they also imitated playfully overly extended and rolled *r*'s and nasalized open vowels.

In the course of Qur'ānic education, students establish a relation with the written text that is determined not merely by their own literacy or the ability to recite, but also by the registers in which they were introduced to the experience of reading aloud. In Indonesia, language and linguistic registers were often indexed according to their perceived primordiality, leading to affectively charged associations based on the degree to which language was perceived as being "natural." The "natural" language in this system is one's native language—which, for many Indonesians, was not Bahasa Indonesia (the national language). Qur'ānic instructors found parallels between the pronunciation of Arabic and vernaculars that were particularly "natural" to a student, thereby forging a more intimate relationship between the student and the vocalization of the Qur'ān.

For example, in one class a reciter from the island of Java was mispronouncing the Qur'ānic formula that concludes recitation, "*Ṣadaqa-lLāhu-l-*

ʿ*aẓīm*" (Thus Almighty God has spoken truly). She sounded the initial *ṣ* (the Arabic letter "*ṣād*") as "*sh*," a common conversion for speakers of Indonesian languages to make. In this case, the teacher was trying to get her to change the *sh* to a simple *s* sound—presumably later he would "thicken" the sound to a *ṣād*—by having her pronounce the Indonesian word "*saya*" (the first-person singular pronoun) repeatedly. This she did again and again. Then he had her try the formula once more. She pronounced it successfully. Later, however, she concluded another passage of recitation by once again making the old mistake, mispronouncing the first word, "*shadaqa*." The teacher, a native of Sulawesi, asked her if she was from Java (everyone, including him, knew that she was). She said yes. He then had her pronounce a Javanese phrase, "*Ara iso*," which means (with irony that certainly was not lost on this teacher) "It is not possible." She did not have trouble with the formula again. After, the master teacher explained that his pedagogical method was to find something in the native language *(bahasa daerah)* that fits *(cocok)* with the Arabic sound, and that is what does the trick. These associations of Arabic phonemes with particularly "native" registers of speech in Indonesia created both cognitive and affective relations between Qur'ānic readers and their own ability to voice sound.

Qur'ānic reading pedagogies revealed the Indonesian perception that underlying one's "native" language is a prelinguistic ability to produce primordial sounds; Arabic phonemes were often indexed with respect to this imagined prelinguistic, precultural power to vocalize. Qur'ānic Arabic, with sounds unfamiliar within everyday speech, was suggested by some teaching strategies to be found within a forgotten stratum underneath all natural languages and formal linguistic systems, even those acquired very early in one's life. Arabic sounds, this pedagogical tactic implies, were present before one's own native language. For example, on another occasion I heard a teacher use everyday examples that emphasized the primordial quality of Arabic phonemes, linking them to everyday, domestic, and nonlinguistic human sounds. I believe that he did this in order to help prevent them from being affectively exoticized and thus engaged through an unnatural mode that would lead to them being overemphasized (or even mispronounced) in recitation. The letter "ʿ*ayn*" for example, was said to be just the sound a baby makes as it is being fed—the most natural sound in the world, the teacher emphasized. By comparison, in an American university, the phoneme "ʿ*ayn*" was introduced as "the sound of a camel braying"; although an example given in classical texts, this was not a sound of students' lived world. *Sh* or *shīn*, according to the Indonesian teacher, was just the sound one uses to shoo a cat from the kitchen.[45] You are already making this sound every day without even realizing it, he said. Such primordialism in teaching was a tool to influence practice instrumentally. An implicit message was that Qur'ānic sounds are primordial, found in one's first language or to be recalled from the first sounds encountered in domestic space before one acquired any language at all.

Multiple mechanisms in the Indonesian system of learning Arabic reading coded the perception of "Qur'ānic" letters affectively for the learner and identified them with internal states and even with the human body itself. This latter conception is a long-standing tradition in Islamic systems and was strategically deployed in Indonesian curricula. Two basic forms of the self-conscious strategy of attaching emotional valences to the practice of reading were operative in Indonesia, one "classical" and one modern. The first was an affective mechanism of bringing perceptions of letters into accord with internal states, a kind of technique that is also explicit in many Sufi practices of "*ḥurūfī*" (alphabetic) piety, which elaborate on the orthography of the Qur'ān experientially.[46] Just as Sufi-oriented descriptions of reading practice correlate the processual cultivation of internal affective states, bodies, and the technical process of reading, modern Indonesian Qur'ān-reading pedagogies also attempted to forge a similar connection that was explicitly intended to cultivate an affective relationship to the activity of reading (and, thus, to the very experience of the Qur'ān itself).

Comparing an exposition by a classical Muslim scholar with a children's book from the modern period suggests a homology and a continuity of affective process in this area that is distinctive to Muslim religious systems of reading. Both kinds of influence, classical and modern, exerted force in contemporary Indonesia. In both cases, Arabic letters become intentionally saturated with qualities of intimacy, comfort, and ease. I begin with a description of affective reading from the classical tradition that relates "internal" to "external" states; this material, influenced by Sufi thought, has been widely influential in many types of Islamic systems of thought and practice and is well known and well studied in Indonesia.

The great scholar Abū Ḥāmid al-Ghazzālī (d. 1111) employs the categories of "internal" and "external" in his description of proper recitation, given in the eighth book of his compendium *Iḥyā' 'Ulūm al-Dīn* (Revivification of the Religious Sciences). In al-Ghazzālī's treatise on recitation, which also considers the controversial issue of *samā'* (spiritual "audition"), the two sets of "tasks" incumbent upon the reciter (the External Rules of Recitation and the Mental Tasks of Recitation) prescribe parallel dimensions of affective and technical activity.[47] Al-Ghazzālī juxtaposes the categories of formal, technical rules on the one hand and cultivated experience expression on the other. This discussion is typical of his project in the *Iḥyā' 'Ulūm al-Dīn* overall, which is to represent interiorized models of normative piety. His ideational bifurcation of "inner" and "outer" experience and their implied synthesis in practice demonstrate the ideal, intimate relation of types of feeling in the practical performance of recitation. This kind of logic reemerged in modern Indonesian pedagogies that imparted feeling-states by way of coding the symbolism of reading and the very letters of the Qur'ān with embodied affect.

Al-Ghazzālī's External Rules are ten.[48] The first rule concerns the condition of the reciter; he or she should be in a state of purity and should assume a vigilant posture. The second and third rules provide an acceptable range of options for the amount of reading to be done (such as the division of the text into sections of five, ten, or all thirty parts, or *ājzā'*). The fourth task concerns the orthography of the Qur'ān. The fifth task is that the reciter read the Qur'ān with *tartīl;* al-Ghazzālī writes that it is better to read one *sūrah* slowly than to "babble" the entire text. The sixth rule is to weep; al-Ghazzālī notes that weeping is praised in the Qur'ān and writes that both reciter and listener weep as an effect of the content of the Qur'ān, especially its threats and warnings.[49] The seventh and eighth rules concern the prostrations to be performed at various moments of the recited Qur'ān (marked in the written text) as well as the proper prostrations to be made before and after recitation (including formulas to recite). With the ninth rule, al-Ghazzālī's External Rules take on a more subjective quality. The ninth rule calls on the reciter to read the text aloud yet without ostentation and without disturbing others. The tenth task is to read beautifully and with control; al-Ghazzālī writes that the rewards for remembrance of God through beautiful recitation are great, unless the reciter engages the art as an "affectation." Notice that in al-Ghazzālī's "external" system, objective and quantitative instructions elide into subjective and qualitative instructions.

After the External Tasks of recitation, al-Ghazzālī's *Iḥyā' 'Ulūm al-Dīn* turns to the ten Mental Tasks incumbent upon the reciter.[50] The first mental task instructs the reciter to "magnify the Divine Speech"; to do this, the reciter considers the attributes of God. The second mental task is the "magnification of the speaker" in the Qur'ān; once the reciter has magnified the Divine Speech, he or she amplifies the Speech within himself or herself, in preparation for imparting the Speech of God to listeners. The third mental task is the abandonment of the "inner utterances of the soul"; this is an instruction to the reciter to pay attention and to follow the Qur'ān closely, recognizing that each letter of the written text is an affective topos to be explored. The fourth mental task is to ponder the recited verse, to listen to it *(samā')*, and to read slowly. The fifth mental task is understanding. The sixth mental task is to remove all obstacles to achieving this understanding; here, al-Ghazzālī warns the reciter of the four "veils" of obstruction that Satan uses to lead the reciter astray: mispronunciation, dogmatic convictions, pride, and unreflective reliance on *tafsīr* (exegesis). The seventh mental task is for the reciter to render the teachings specific; the reciter must understand that the entire Qur'ān is intended for him or her individually. The eighth mental task is for the reciter to feel emotionally the Qur'ān; he or she is to be affected by the meanings of the verses rather than simply to narrate them. The ninth mental task is for the reciter to rise into a state in which the speech of recitation is not from the reciter but actually from God; al-Ghazzālī explains that there are three grades of recitation: reading at God, reading such that God hears, and reading such that God's Speech is present in the words. The tenth mental task is for the reciter to abandon not only pride but more completely the sense of personal agency and power.

The juxtaposition of al-Ghazzālī's "external" and "mental" tasks and their interconnection within the text of the *Iḥyā'* show that specific technical practices are ideally not distinct from an affective encounter with the recited Qur'ān. With the "third mental task," which is to pay attention to the Qur'ān and to abandon the inner utterances of the soul, al-Ghazzālī alludes to a complex potential relationship between the perceived forms of the Arabic letters and the affective experience of one who engages the text:

> In the Qur'ān is present that with which the soul can have warm relations if the reciter is fit for it. How can it seek an intimate connection with the thought of anything other than the Qur'ān, seeking that the reciter is in a pleasant place and a place relieved of cares, and one who is relived of cares in a pleasant place does not think of another place? It is said that in the Qur'ān are to be found fields, gardens, closets, brides, brocades, meadows, and *khans*. All *mīms* are the fields of the Qur'ān. All *rās* are the gardens; all *hās* are its closets; all *sūrahs* starting with the glorification of God are its brides, all *sūrahs* starting with the letters "*ḥā mīm*" are its brocades, all the *sūrahs* in which laws, stories, etc., are expounded are its meadows, and all other parts of it are its *khans*. When the Qur'ān-reader enters into the fields of the Qur'ān, plucks different types of fruits from its gardens, enters into its closets, views the brides, wears the brocades, is relieved of cares, and dwells in the *khans*, and then all these absorb him wholly and keep him from things other than these; consequently his mind cannot be inattentive, nor can his thought be separated.[51]

Here, al-Ghazzālī infuses letters with affective qualities, associating them with visual imagery and with a feeling-state of absorbed "attention" and comfortable "friendly relations."

Al-Ghazzālī is also here describing an actual technique, not merely an idealized consciousness. In contemporary pedagogy, whether a student is told in Indonesian that a symbol is an Indonesian "*bandera di atas*" (flag [flying] on top) of a letter or an Arabic *waṣlah*, a "dead letter" (Ind. *huruf mati*) or a *sukūn* (Ar.) influences the degree of affective ease or "closeness" students may feel about the Arabic letters themselves. This also echoes a fascination with orthography that seems to permeate many Southern Asian religious systems.[52] The Arabic script has different names in different regions of the archipelago, each locality with a unique relationship to Arabic writing,[53] determined in part by the differing processes of having it conform to local languages or orthographic systems. This visual conformity is not often taken for granted, since, when Indonesian languages such as the translocal Muslim language of Malay (Melayu) are written in Arabic script, without vowel markings (as they have been historically), they require special skill to apprehend. The classic example is the Malay-Indonesian phrase "*Kumbang di-kembang datang kambing kumbang terbang*," which means "A bee sat on a flower; along came a goat and the bee flew away." It is unintelligible if written in Arabic letters without vowel markings (as Arabic and Malay often are), since "bee" *(kumbang)*, "flower" *(kembang)*, and "goat" *(kambing)* would all be written exactly the same.

Modern Indonesian reading pedagogy also deployed the visual and associative properties of language strategically. In contemporary Indonesia, feeling about the Qur'ān, its language, and its letters was often promoted in educational programs through song. A fast-growing genre of "alphabet songs," composed especially for children, introduced students to Arabic pronunciation with catchy melodies and instrumentation borrowed from *dangdut* popular music. These songs accustomed children to the sounds of Arabic in familiar, inviting ways even before they began to read. They evoke a consistent set of feelings and moods, rendering affect an intentional dimension of the curriculum and thus the learning experience. At the same time that students learned to pronounce the phonemes of Qur'ānic Arabic, such instructional activities provided lasting patterns of emotional engagement with the material of study. An example is the *dangdut* hit "Kamus Arab" (Arabic Dictionary) by Effi Naviri, which has an intense and compelling pop groove. It starts with a standard improvised "*ya lail*" opening and proceeds to equate parts of the body in Indonesian and Arabic ("eye" for "eye": "*mata*" is "'*ayn*"; "nose" for "nose": "*hidung*" is "*ānf*"; and so on). It is the title song of the cassette, which also includes a karaoke version of "Kamus Arab," along with other songs in the genre. These include "Belajar Baca Alquran," a pop song with lyrics describing the effects of reading the Qur'ān "sincerely" *(sungguhan)* on the hearts of pious practitioners. On television, the most popular video in this genre at the time of research was "Dua Puluh Lima Nabi," a *dangdut* hit about Prophets named in the Qur'ān; the singers, young girls in bright green head scarves, danced in a loose formation and held up their fingers every time the count came around again in the chorus.

This modern Indonesian genre of song, which takes the form of juvenile ensemble pop singing (often heard on television and radio), could be termed the "*anak-anak shaleh*" (pious children) type. Such children's singing punctuated the soundscape of Indonesian broadcast. *Anak-anak shaleh* songs had topics such as God, respecting parents, prayer, the Islamic greeting *(Assalamu alaikum)*, and the blessings of the month of Ramadan and the merits of fasting in it. They were big studio productions, whereas within Qur'ān kindergartens (where almost every lesson has a theme song attached), in contrast, tunes tended to be well-known melodies such as the Indonesian "Happy Birthday" (Panjang Umurnya) with adapted lyrics. An example is the famous European tune "Topi Saya Bundar" (My Hat Is Round), which was also sung in language classes for Bahasa Indonesia in the United States to learn the syntax of negation *(bukan* versus *tidak)*. In Indonesia, children sang another version of the song in Indonesian to affirm religious commitment: "My religion is Islam / Islam is my religion / If it is not Islam / It is not my religion." In other contexts, students were taught simple Arabic songs so that they would become accustomed to articulating the sounds of the language. Such methods index correct ritual speech, establishing contrasts with the vernacular languages (and vernacularized pronunciations of Arabic), making linguistic fields of style, register, and sound "meaningful" and enjoyable in several dimensions.

Modern Arabic "alphabet songs" in Indonesia were infused with the affective ideals of Qur'ānic "motivation" *(motivasi)*, an adaptation of the classical ideals of engagement al-Ghazzālī discusses. The recitation of the letters of the alphabet in order to drill their pronunciation was certainly not new (it makes up the fundamentals of the Baghdadi method). In Indonesia, however, the Arabic alphabet itself also became a principal means of transmitting *motivasi* as a part of the movement in Qur'ānic reading practice in the 1990s. A person credited in Makassar with the origination of one of the alphabet songs that was popular nationally explained the genesis of a version taught at IAIN Alauddin in Makassar. In 1990, the account went, the LPTQ had a conference to determine why teaching the reading of the Qur'ān was not working. There were two sides in the conversation: one blamed it all on the students, and the other blamed the problem on the teachers. The narrator stated that he had been in the second group, holding that if something was not working with teaching Qur'ān reading in the villages, then the problem naturally had to be that teachers were not motivating their students enough. So, he said, he came up with a song, and a student at IAIN Alauddin came up with the tune. The pattern goes like this, and it works through all the letters of the Arabic alphabet:[54]

<u>b</u>a <u>b</u>i <u>b</u>u <u>b</u>af   <u>b</u>au <u>b</u>an   <u>b</u>ani <u>b</u>a<u>b</u>na   min al-mu<u>b</u>ni   ma<u>b</u>īb$^{a[n/m]}$ <u>b</u>ani<u>b</u>$^{a[n]}$

<u>t</u>a <u>t</u>i <u>t</u>u <u>t</u>af   <u>t</u>au <u>t</u>an   <u>t</u>ani <u>t</u>a<u>t</u>na   min al-mu<u>t</u>ni   ma<u>t</u>īt^{an} <u>t</u>ani<u>t</u>$^{a[n]}$

And so now, the story continued, university students go out to the villages and teach with the Iqra' method and also use this alphabet song. It was implied by this educator that the success of the Iqra' program in South Sulawesi's rural areas might even be due in large part to the success of this alphabet song: "Everyone likes to sing, and everyone likes to hear singing—you know, just about everyone sings when they're taking a bath."

I observed approximately eight hundred Islamic university students over two sessions on two separate days (each lasting approximately one and one-half hours) practicing this very alphabet song, and others, in preparation for the upcoming weeks of social service (KKN). The song was understood by the group to be the "signature trait" *(ciri khas)* of their school's teaching method (and, further, the song also enjoyed national popularity). In the first session, after a discussion of the problem of poor pronunciation in the villages, the professor leading the session introduced the idea that the way to "motivate" people to improve their reading was through *"qasida"* (denoting "song"). He then launched into the alphabet song (which was not due to be taught until the following session). First the men's side sang it, then the women's side sang it (it was suggested we should have a competition), and then we all sang the alphabet song some more, and after that we started to sing it all over again with Arabic letters chosen randomly by the leader, interspersed with his energetic commentary about the song's effectiveness in inducing *motivasi*. This seemed to be borne out by the session itself: interest in the alphabet song never flagged, and the whole episode burst with the escalating enthusiasm of a pep rally, generated, it seemed, by the motivating power of the alphabet song when sung in unison. While it would be difficult to find any other activity that could have been chosen besides an "alphabet song" that is Qur'ān-related and could still incite such groupwide emotional enthusiasm, other materials treating the Arabic alphabet in Indonesia demonstrated a similar strategy of the self-conscious cultivation of "motivating" affective valences with respect to Arabic letters in more restrained and disciplined modes.

The actual letters of Arabic orthography are a site at which to infuse affective texture self-consciously into the process of Qur'ānic reading. The following example of this process in modern Indonesia is visual, not aural, coming from a popular Arabic alphabet coloring book for children. The notes for parents given in the foreword introduce the book's strategy:

> This book directs and encourages your children to study while they play *(learning by doing)* in a mode that is *aktif, kreatif,* and *produktif* so that your children will not be bored *(bosan)* while studying it. In addition, the advantage *(kelebihan)* of this book is that it accustoms your child to practice with sensitivity *(kepekaan)* and to associate *(mengasosiasikan)* forms that are all around in the environment with the shapes of the letters of the Qur'ān. With this method of the association of forms, it is hoped that the child will more quickly and easily get to feel close and intimate *(akrab)* with the letters of the Qur'ān.[55]

The Dewey-like emphasis of the passage is nothing new in contemporary Qur'ānic pedagogy. The attempt to locate affect in Arabic letters and thereby foster an emotional relationship to the act of reading is also not new, and in

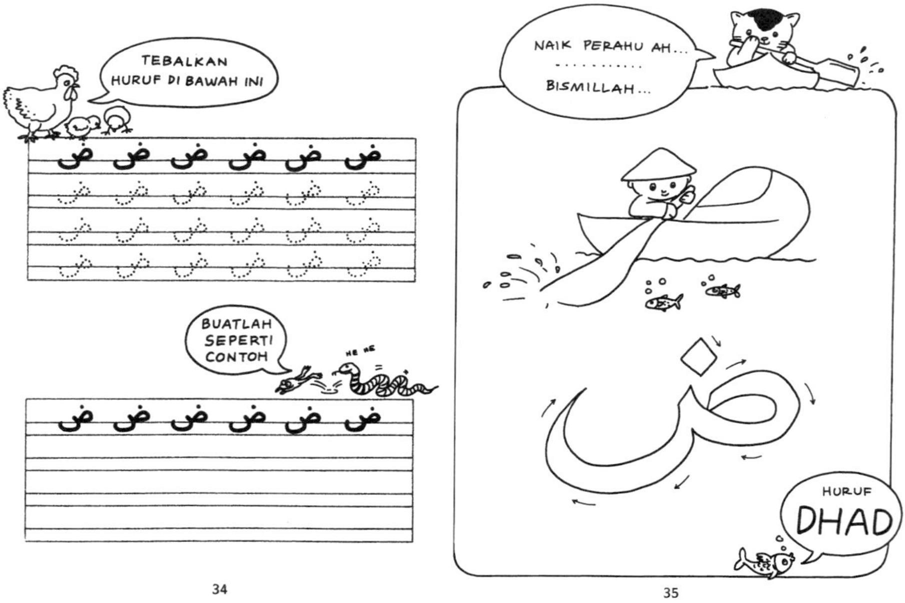

An alphabet book making letters "friendly," *Belajar Mudah Huruf Al-Qur'an* by Hendi Indyawan, design by Andi Y A. The caption reads, "Going by boat, ah . . . [say] Bismillah," while cartoon animals encourage tracing and rendering the letter "*ḍād*" after the example. (Reproduced with permission from Penerbit Mizan)

fact it resonates with long-established traditions of piety extending back almost a millennium. The esoteric tradition of *ḥurūfī* piety, for example, features prominently representations of the Arabic letters as human bodies (as in prayer and so on). Similarly, the pictures in the Indonesian book play symbolically with the letter shapes, which not only represent but actually embody the letter for the learner. Some of these animations are animals: *dāl*'s open mouth is introduced with characters who alert, "Help! It's a crocodile"; *jīm* is a snake laying an egg; and *bā*'s broad horns form the head of a water buffalo. Indigenous images, like distinctive boats and fruit, are common. Unlike much romanized alphabet imagery, the shapes are imagined whenever possible within the space of the human body itself: *khā* خ is "somebody dancing around" *(orang sedang berjoget)*; *dhāl* ذ is a boy sitting *(sujūd)* during his prayers, whereas *wāw* و is "just your own fist if you look at it from the side," and *sīn* س is a pair of shorts (implying an absent body) hung to the right of an oblong tablecloth that drips over the clothesline under a smiling sun. Cute, energetic characters animate each picture, encouraging kids to color and inserting a voice of interaction into the text by addressing the child directly and emphasizing active engagement.

In these examples and more generally in Qur'ānic curricula in modern Indonesia, Arabic sounds and letters were imagined within pedagogical representations as kinetic processes of feeling and doing, not primarily as static abstractions. In basic materials teaching alphabetic recognition, this was certainly the case when the letters themselves were presented as undergoing a process, as with imagining principles of change in sound and visual shape.

The final example is a song about a visual process. A cassette tape produced for use along with the Iqra' method presents various songs identified with the lessons of the numbered booklets of the curriculum, emphasizing the main "rule" of the unit. There is, for example, a *madd* song ("Tanda Panjang"), as well as separate songs for each of the assimilation rules (a ballad for the *tajwīd* rule of "conversion" of the *nūn;* "Iqlab," for example, is a lilting duet). The production values for these recordings are highly professional. One of the songs, "Huruf Sambung" (Connecting Letters, corresponding to the second booklet), is about the shapes of Arabic letters according to whether their position is initial, medial, or terminal in a word. In this case, not only is a "motivating" activity and experience of song associated with the letters, but the letters are identified with parts of the body, anthropomorphized, and presented in terms of undergoing processes (translated here with an effort to convey the mood of the music):

Come on, let's all study how to connect the
letters!

There are some that don't change and some that do		
ba, *ta*, *tsa*, their form stays the same	ـبـتـثـ	ب ت ث
ja, *ha*, *kha*, they lose their tails	ـجـحـخـ	ج ح خ
sa, *sya*, *sha*, *dha*, their bellies disappear	ـسـشـصـضـ	س ش ص ض
'*a* and *gha*, their feet go away	ـعـغـ	ع غ
and in the middle their mouths close up tight		
The letter "*kaf*" takes on a whole different shape	ـكـ	ك
The letter "*mim*," its foot changes	ـمـ	م
The letter "*ha*" turns into a pair of glasses	ـهـ	ه
The letter "*ya*," its head comes right off.[56]	ـيـ	ي

The letters are bodies in motion, and the song medium injects an emotional quality into the process of learning while students recognize letters in their variant forms. The mechanism relates cognitive perception to emotional state, with the explicit purpose of coding reading with affective resonances that will not only facilitate learning but also "motivate." The emotional qualities are to be carried forward in time, in order to build what the cassette liner (as well as other related materials from Iqra') touts as the "Qur'ānic generation" (a term possibly derived and modified from the writings of the Egyptian Islamist Sayyid Qutb).

Within processes and projects of learning, registers of speech in pedagogy encoded affect and indexed practice with respect to social identity; these models and registers thus came to influence the self-understandings of practitioners. This occurred through teaching strategies that referenced pronunciation styles, teaching methods that rendered Arabic "natural" or primordial, and other strategies to create self-conscious relations to letters and learning. In Indonesia, two principal systems for teaching reading were promoted as the basis of these systems, and their implementation changed readers' relationships to the recited Qur'ān as well as their understandings of themselves as learners in relation to the process of continuing to learn to read.

"Traditional" Methods: "Deeper" Learning

At the time of research, there were two primary methods for teaching elementary Qur'ān recitation in Indonesia: one labeled "traditional" and one called "modern." The "traditional" system in Indonesia was known as "Baghdadi," and the most popular "modern" system was "Iqra'." "Modern" teaching methods began to gain popularity in the late 1980s and had become remarkably widespread by the mid-1990s. The goal in the following discussion is not to endorse either method, but instead to describe each and to compare them, with respect to the salient affective descriptions of comparative "depth" *(lebih dalam)* versus "speed" *(lebih cepat)* that Indonesians gave. In practice, these methods were increasingly being deployed in combination in Indonesia in the 1990s, altering Indonesian Muslims' sense of the ongoing processes of perfecting reading overall.

The technical differences between the two methods are not as great as were the different associations that clustered around them. The key practical contrast is that with the "traditional" method, students learned the names of letters along with their sound qualities and "spelled out" words with the named letters according to set formulae before vocalizing them. With the "modern" method, students vocalized the letters without first going through the process of parsing the word by spelling. The primary difference Indonesians emphasized between the methods was precisely the practice of "spelling out" *(ejaan)* within the traditional method, which was judged by many to be too time-consuming. But the Baghdadi method was "deeper," its proponents said; sometimes it was characterized in terms of a greater quality of *faham* (comprehension or apprehension). These evaluations emerged from overall assessments of learning contexts as well as from the actual experiential senses established through practices such as spelling and vocalizing letters. The two methods represented different affective relationships to authority and to the process of reading, as well as differing conceptions of self as learner.

Underlying the Baghdadi method was a distinctive understanding of the teacher-student relationship, often valued either positively or negatively by mature Indonesians who could relate their own sentimental memories of early Baghdadi experiences. In traditions of Muslim education across space and over time, a personal model of instruction has dominated; historically, this model has been especially significant for the practice and study of *ḥadīth* transmission as well as other systems of knowledge transfer (such as Sufi orders). Jonathan Berkey, in his study of institutions of learning in Mamluk Egypt, explains the overall "importance of the personal, as opposed to the institutional, connection," writing, "An education was judged not on *loci* but on *personae.*"[57] Although much Muslim knowledge (such as *ḥadīth* material) was preserved in books, a student did not simply read these texts but "heard" them from a living person—the most authoritative means of transmission. In a medieval treatise on educational institutions studied by Berkey, Ibn Jamā'a (a fourteenth-century scholar and jurist), for example, writes that valid knowledge comes only from a real person and not from books; persons who tried to base their education on the written word were guilty of "one of the most scandalous of acts."[58]

Similarly, Berkey quotes a scholar who said: "Whoever does not take his learning *('ilm)* from the mouths of men is like he who learns courage without ever facing battle."[59] Learning thus implies a dynamic and meaningful relationship with those who transmit religious knowledge.

In contemporary Indonesian systems of learning to read the Qur'ān, in spite of the proliferation of pedagogical techniques and technologies, one must study with an authoritative human source. The personal relationship with a teacher is an essential dimension of the educational process in the "traditional" mode especially. A student's self-consciousness and identity as a reciter derives not merely from the material learned, but also from interactions with the teacher. The classical and contemporary *adab* of the teacher-student relationship places significant obligations on the student; Berkey cites al-Zarnūjī, for example, in a treatise on education widely read and copied in the Middle Ages, writing, "Flattery *(al-tamalluq)* is blameworthy except in the quest for knowledge. In order to learn from them, flattery of one's professor and associates is inevitable."[60] Respect for one's teacher is unconditionally incumbent upon every student. For instance, Berkey documents that Ibn Jamā'a, in his treatise *Tadhkirāt al-sāmi'*, advises students to manage the emotional exchange of this relationship through careful displays of respect and tact:

> If the shaikh began to recite something the student had already memorized, the student should listen attentively, and try to convey his great joy at hearing the recitation, as if for the first time. If asked if he had memorized the text, the student should not simply say "yes," which would imply he no longer needs his teacher's instruction on the point, nor should he say "no," for that would be untrue; he should instead respond by saying "I prefer to hear it from the shaikh," or "[I memorized it] long ago," or "from you it is more correct," or with some such delicate phrase to extricate the shaikh from potential embarrassment. Again, if the shaikh made an error, the student should not point it out, but should gently give him an opportunity to correct the mistake, for example by repeating the error himself in the shaikh's presence; if the teacher persisted in his error, the confused student should simply take the question to another shaikh.[61]

Among former students in Indonesia, the discipline and personal relationship to the *shaikh* was often what was vividly recalled about "traditional" Qur'ānic education with the Baghdadi method.

Similar relations between students and their *shaikhs* persisted in contemporary educational environments in Indonesia, such as at a coaching session for a national contest. For example, when a young memorizer of the Qur'ān was reviewing with the great national coach K. H. M. Sayyid Abdullah in the months before the MTQ, drilling the melodic modes he might use in the upcoming competition, Ustaz Abdullah noticed right away that the student was "*sengau*," or had a tendency to nasalize open vowels. The *shaikh* and the student worked on the pronomial suffix "*hā*" for twenty minutes or more. The *shaikh* finally asked the boy about his memorization teacher—was he from a rural part of the province? When he affirmed this, Ustaz Abdullah instructed the child to go back to the village and tell his teacher, "Ustaz Abdullah told me that I am *sengau*, and may I please be corrected?" Ustaz Abdullah commented to the group, "Because of course you know it's the *teacher*." The presence of the teacher is basic to understanding how the student learns Qur'ānic material at any level.

The focus of the "traditional" Baghdadi method is in gaining the ability to read the last thirtieth of the Qur'ān, "Juz' 'Amma,"[62] an achievement traditionally seen as the attainment of minimal Qur'ānic proficiency (associated with the rite of passage known as "Khatm al-Qur'ān," or the "sealing" of the Qur'ān). The primer used throughout Indonesia was called *Qā'ida Baghdadiyya ma' juz' 'amma*. It shares its format with the basic reading books used throughout the Islamic world, including Arabic-speaking countries such as Egypt. The book begins with the alphabet in sequence (followed by a *salām* formula, as is also found in the sectioned breaks in texts of devotional readings), and subsequent sections present the alphabet with each letter carrying patterned vowel markings in the same order (e.g., *ba bi bu, ta ti tu,* and so forth; this would be followed in the next section with b^{an} b^{in} b^{un}, t^{an} t^{in} t^{un}). Short combinations of the form consonant-vowel-consonant are then followed by increasingly complex patterns, which are applied to the series of letters of the alphabet. In later sections, letters that have similar visual forms (such as *ḥā*, *jīm*, and *khā*) are juxtaposed, followed by sentences that include conjugated verbs running through deictic categories, and, subsequently, even more complicated phrases are presented. The balance of the book is the last thirtieth of the Qur'ān in reverse order, from the last *sūrah* to the seventy-eighth ("Juz' 'Amma," sometimes called the "*Qur'ān kecil*," or the "little Qur'ān," as opposed to the entire text, the "*Qur'ān besar*").

What people remembered about this method, and what distinguished it most vividly from the "modern" method, is the spelling procedure based on visual identification. In the application of the spelling formula, the *fatḥa (a)* and *kesra (i)* vowel markings *(ḥarakāt)* are recognized to be the "same" marks, distinguished by whether they appear "on top" or "below" a consonant, respectively, whereas the *ḍumma (u,* the unique shape that only appears above letters) is vocalized in the aural formula as a "dummified" letter. The formula, in English translation, would be pronounced in the following way (here based on the letter named "*nūn*"):

> *nūn* [given a mark] on top, "*na*";
> *nūn* [given a mark] below, "*ni*";
> *nūn* [given a] *ḍumma*, "*nu*"—"*na, ni, nu*"

The formula is recited in local languages (although it was occasionally applied in Bahasa Indonesia). Thus, a student from South Sulawesi might study in Bugis: "*Alif di'asanna* [on top] '*a*'; *alif dirawanna* [below] '*i*'; *alif didepanna* '*u*'—'*a*,' '*i*,' '*u*.'" To underscore the significance of the visualization of the letters in the formula, when I asked for a translation, "*ḍumma*" was said repeatedly to mean "not *depan*" ("in front of" in Bahasa Indonesia). It took me a little time to figure out that the verb "*depanna*" meant "given a *ḍumma*." I have heard variants of this formula in Makassarese, Madurese, Javanese, and other languages. My questions about the method prompted numerous group discussions, marked by older persons' nostalgia. In one conversation in Bone that began with my research questions, an elderly *kiai* from a family who had studied in the Arabian peninsula, a female college student, a pious rector of a major Islamic university with modernist commitments, a journalist from the big city, and a few others all laughed and joked, sharing and comparing their experiences in learning with this method in diverse settings and in various Indonesian languages.

As people loved to relate and to imitate, the Arabic spelling was often chanted, sometimes in a simple singsong and sometimes using a *lagu* with more melodic properties. As the student begins to read complete words, the formula is applied to each letter in sequence. Thus, "*al-ḥamdu*," the first word after the Bismillah in the opening *sūrah* (al-Fātiḥah, a *sūrah* that is sometimes called the "Alhamdu"), is read, in translation:

> *ālif; lām* dead letter [*huruf mati*, no vowel]—"*al*"
> *ḥā* [given a *fatḥa*] on top; *mīm* dead letter; *dāl* [given a] *ḍumma*—"*al-ḥamdu*"

Even when a student reaches the level of reading reasonably fluently from the text, any mistake prompts the requisite spelling of the word, letter by letter. It is this cantillated, formulaic spelling that adults remembered, and the close association with the letters in the vernacular language is considered to be a process that is "deep" *(dalam)* with intimate "understanding" *(faham)*.

In actual Baghdadi sessions, students would sit in rows behind wooden stands, holding either their "*Qur'ān kecil*" (primer) or their "*Qur'ān besar*" (*muṣḥaf*) and chant in a cacophony.[63] They usually would have swept up the space and performed other chores in the teacher's home before the lesson began. Often a whole family would teach the students who came ("You can always tell how many students are inside on any given day by the number of shoes out front," one grandmother, teacher, and memorizer's wife remarked). One student at a time would be called to the front for audition with the teacher, who might simply listen, or he or she might correct mistakes, offer suggestions, or recite for the student to listen and repeat. At a "traditional" setting for Qur'ānic instruction in the home of a family of Qur'ān memorizers in Makassar, lessons were conducted in the Bugis language; it was said that parents sent their children there expressly for this vernacular instruction. It was reported that this method of instruction was no longer welcome in some mosques, but it was still to be found in some homes (although much home-based instruction for neighborhood children had recently switched over to the Iqra' materials). The "traditional" Baghdadi method was associated with a form of education in which the student has a direct relation with the *shaikh*; when students read for the teacher, it was one-on-one and not done as a group.

In the Baghdadi method, a system of rewards and punishment was understood by adults to instantiate the value of discipline and also to reinforce efficacious recitation; students were given sweets to help their recitation and were said to be struck or otherwise disciplined if they were forgetful or disruptive. Many mothers who sent their children to the traditional settings mentioned this system of incentives and punishments as a deciding factor in their choice of this form of Qur'ānic education, and they would reminisce sentimentally about their own childhood experiences. The "deep" and "comprehensive" spelling method combined with the distinctive learning context was what parents valued, overlaying this with nostalgic memories of their own personal experience. Many would say that this method was "*lebih dalam*" (deeper) or "*lebih faham*" (literally, more "comprehensive"), indicating both affect and efficacy. Enhancing this sense of the "traditional" method in Indonesia in the 1990s was the "modern," which built on and modified these powerful affective structures in an idealized process of continuous, lifelong learning.

"Modern" Methods: "Faster" Learning

The study of reading begins, in both the "traditional" and "modern" methods, with learning the Arabic alphabet. Both methods then drill students on basic combinations of letters and words. The principal technical difference between the two methods is whether or not students practice "spelling out" by naming the letters. In addition, "modern" methods of instruction highlight systematic aspects of the rules of *tajwīd* (such as consonantal assimilation, although this occurs only at the advanced level as the curriculum's capstone), whereas the "traditional" method tends to rely on the teacher to intervene at the appropriate times to correct pronunciation errors. These and other "characteristics" *(sifat)* of the Iqra' method are enumerated in a teacher's guide for Iqra' as the following:

1. immediate reading: without spelling out; it is not necessary to introduce the names of the letters. There is no memorization of the Arabic letters *(huruf hijaiyah)*
2. CBSA (*Cara Belajar Santri Aktif*, "Students Study Actively"): the students are the ones who study, without guidance
3. *privat:* the students work directly with the teacher
   listening skill: practicing hearing the sounds of the letters and words
   oral drill: oral practice, pronouncing what has been heard
   reading drill: reading the letters that are heard and pronouncing them
4. *modul:* the students study according to their [level of] ability
5. *asistensi:* the *senior* students become assistants helping to teach (overcoming a shortage of teachers)
6. *praktis:* the *teori* of the science of *tajwid* is taught only after the students are able to read the Qur'ān
7. *sistematis:* taught in stages *(secara bertahap)*
8. *variatif:* the six books of Iqra' have differently colored covers
9. *komunikatif:* in the Iqra' books there are directive signals *(rambu petunjuk)* that are friendly *(akrab)* and easy to understand
10. *fleksibel:* appropriate for all ages; from kindergarten, elementary school, junior high, high school, up to adults[64]

In affective association, the difference between the Baghdadi and Iqra' methods is not just between valuations of the concepts of "tradition" and "modern" but is more profoundly recognized in the emotional process through which the student learns: Baghdadi is characterized as "slow" or "boring" (by its detractors) or, alternatively, as "deep" and "comprehensive" (by its supporters).

The kinds of merits perceived by proponents of the Iqra' method are introduced by the "Opening Song" ("Lagu Pembuka") for the method that children themselves are taught to sing about their own learning process:[65]

there are six books for Iqra'	*buku Iqra' ada enam*
small, light, and colorful	*kecil tipis warna-warni*

simple, easy, practice-based, systematic	*sederhana, mudah, praktis, sistematis*
just right for children and for grown-ups	*cocok untuk anak maupun lansia*
clear explanation, reading right away	*jelas petunjuknya, langsung bacanya*
active drills, careful pronunciation	*aktif latihannya, simak ucapannya*
they sort out how to articulate the long and the short [vowels]	*bedakan makhrajnya dan panjang pendeknya*
in so little time, they yield great results	*singkat waktunya, bagus hasilnya*

The six books demonstrate a structure similar to the beginning of the Baghdadi primer in terms of their drills, but they insert additionally the names of the *tajwīd* principles being presented. They often include notation at the top of a page corresponding to the particular process that is being introduced (such as the assimilation of vowels or consonants). On every page, direct address to the student assumes the voice of an instructor within the text: "Be careful!" "Go slow here!" "Repeat this again," all injecting a virtual interaction into the materials and thereby potentially modifying the direct role of the teacher in the classroom.

Besides the lack of the spelling-out practice and the emphasis on "*sistematis*" presentation, the principal arguments given for the merits of Iqra' are its speed and efficiency as well as the progressive benefits of the learning environment itself. Underlying these arguments is a vision that extends beyond mere educational curriculum to what might be called a religious revolution of sorts. The materials, along with the vision, were developed by Team Tadarus "AMM" in Yogyakarta, central Java. The story of Iqra' as told by Team Tadarus "AMM" began in 1953, with the establishment of a group known as "PPKS,"[66] which had used the Baghdadi method to teach recitation. In 1973, instruction was systematized within the main Kotagede teaching mosque near Yogyakarta, with the introduction of "administrative materials" (*sarana administrasi*) such as report cards and progress forms. In 1973, Bapak As'ad Humam, the originator of the Iqra' method, began to hold discussions in his home on the difficulties encountered in teaching basic reading, and a "team" was formed to overcome these obstacles. Within ten months, it was determined that the problem was that the teachers themselves did not know how to recite well, and the first step in addressing this situation was, naturally, to hold a contest (Lomba Tartil Membaca 5 Surat Pendek), in which three hundred persons participated.[67] At the event, it is reported that Bapak As'ad Humam addressed the crowd with the following historic words, thus beginning a national movement in Qur'ān reading study: "You are all 'AMM' (Angkatan Muda Masjid dan Mushalla, the 'Youth Generation of Mosques and Places of Worship'). Because of this, after you are able to read *(membaca)* the Qur'ān, it is imperative that you enliven *(menghidupkan)* the recitation of children and all together undertake a movement *(gerakan)* of MAJLIS TA'LIM DAN TADARUS AL QUR'AN in this place of worship minimally once a week."[68]

When other local mosques started to follow the lead set in Kotagede, they were welcomed into the AMM movement. The story of Iqra' continues:

> Conditions continued to develop quickly along these lines, and at last the Organizing Team (Team Pembinaan) came officially to be known as the "*Team Tadarus* 'AMM'" Yogyakarta, whose focus at the time was on activities to motivate *(memotivasikan)* in every mosque and place of worship the realization of assemblies for recitation *(jamaah tadarus)* for little children that would all follow the same structure of activities *(pola kegiatan)* led by the youth movement (of men and women). . . .
>
> In their advancement *(kiprahnya)*, in addition to establishing the youth assemblies led by young people, Team Tadarus "AMM" also studied as a team the recitation of children from a historical perspective. *The Team hoped, by establishing the youth movement, that later they would become pioneers* (pionir) *and that they would be able to make flourish* (menghidupsuburkan) *the recitation of children in their own communities.*[69]

The group's subsequent reported findings were that understanding and engagement of the Qur'ān were lacking overall, that evening practice in the mosques was weak, that religious practice was losing out in competition with new entertainment-oriented activities (such as watching television) overall, and, finally, that the *metodologi* of teaching only to read "Juz' 'Amma" was "incomplete."

After "experimentation" with various formats for afternoon Qur'ānic kindergartens, a system developed that began to be emulated in other parts of Java, such as Gresik and Semarang. In 1988, the organization received recognition from the provincial Ministry of Religious Affairs, at approximately the same time that the Iqra' books were first becoming available (they were distributed nationally in 1992). The associated schooling system was known as "TKA" (Taman Kanak-kanak Al-Quran) and "TPA," for children under five and of elementary-school age, respectively. Eventually, the system came under the auspices of the BKPRMI (Badan Komunikasi Pemuda Remaja Masjid Indonesia, "Organizing Body for the Youth Groups of Indonesian Mosques," formerly BKPMI), which coordinated the movement in accord with its *da'wah* effort. Other organizations (such as Nahdlatul Ulama, NU) also endorsed the activities, and promotion continued along multiple channels, as with the live mass recitation by 1,500 children broadcast nationally as a part of the national MTQ contest in Yogyakarta in 1991.[70]

Whereas the government of Malaysia has adopted the Iqra' method, in Indonesia in the late 1990s the BKPRMI has remained the semiofficial organizing body of the national system, and promotion by way of the Ministry of Religious Affairs and the LPTQ was loosely structured. The BKPRMI trained teachers for TPA instruction using the Iqra' materials, especially at the main center in Jakarta, and it promoted other activities as well. For example, in April of 1997, at Masjid "Al-Markaz," on the suggestion of the central leadership, hundreds of TPA students in Makassar participated in a huge mock-Hajj event at the mosque. Prominent locations in Mecca were simulated on the grounds; the students, dressed in *iḥrām*, performed *wuqūf* in the courtyard, *sa'y* in the corridors, and circumambulated a replica of the Ka'bah in front of the mosque's principal building. (Hajj simulation, controversial even in the time of the tenth-century Sufi figure al-Ḥallāj, has been known in Indonesia for a long time, including in South Sulawesi.) Promotion of the Iqra' method itself (and, ideally, local TPA programs) also occurred by way of college students, such as those from IAIN campuses who went to the countryside to introduce Iqra' and teach Qur'ān recitation. In literature about TPA, complicated flow charts diagram the ideal structural relations among levels of organization and influence, demonstrating how the imagination of process and system was replacing the "traditional" model of authority with a new idealization of a comprehensive educative network.

In 1997, Team Tadarus "AMM" was continuing to develop a curriculum for children and youth for Qur'ānic instruction as well as for other aspects of basic Muslim education.[71] The stated goal of the overall program (for both its materials and institutional organization) was to inspire the "Qur'ānic Generation," defined as "a generation that loves the Qur'ān, is committed to the Qur'ān, and makes the recited Qur'ān daily practice and takes the Qur'ān to be the outlook on everyday life."[72] The basic objectives of the program were to instruct students in reading, proper worship, the memorization of short *sūrah*s and prayers, and to impart basic writing skills. The classroom environment is the focus of attention in much of the literature about the program, and the ideal interactive and engaging atmosphere is laid out by careful guidelines and lesson plans that set up both structured and unstructured class time. The instructional method is known as "reading, storytelling, and singing" (BCN, "Baca,

Ceritera, Nyanyi"). Students change out of the cream-colored TPA uniforms into lavish robes for graduation ceremonies *(wisuda)*, a tradition also said to have begun in Yogyakarta.[73] At the higher levels, a curriculum was being developed for basic Qur'ān comprehension as well as more advanced recitation and *tajwīd* study, along with *ḥadīth* and other basics of Islamic learning. In most places, however, only the basic six books were being used, whether in mosque programs affiliated with the BKPRMI (such as at the program at Makassar's Al-Markaz mosque, which began in 1996) or in informal instruction in homes.

The objective of the new curricula was students' practical involvement and affective engagement. This led to synthesis rather than opposition to other systems on both technical and experiential levels. Just as "motivational" affect overlaid preestablished affective patterns in pedagogy, the "modern" system subsumed rather than replaced "traditional" structures of Qur'ānic education.

Contoh Rapor

DATA PRESTASI SANTRI TPA

Semester : _____ Tahun : _________

Nama Santri : .... No. Induk : .... Kelas : ....

No.	Materi Pelajaran	Nilai	
I	**Materi Pokok**	Kefasihan	
1	IQRO' sampai dengan jilid		
	atau tadarus Al-Qur'an s.d. juz		
II	**Materi Penunjang**	Jumlah Hafalan	Kefasihan
1	Hafalan Bacaan Sholat		
2	Hafalan Surat-surat Pendek		
3	Hafalan Do'a Sehari-hari		
4	Hafalan Ayat-ayat Pilihan		
5	Menulis Huruf-huruf Al-Qur'an		
6	Ibadah Praktis		
7			
8			
III	**Lain-lain**		
1	Presensi		
2	Ketertiban		
3			

Mengetahui
Wali Santri. Direktur. Wali Kelas

(______________) (______________) (______________)

Aslinya kertas manila berukuran setengah folio

Contoh Rapor

DATA PRESTASI SANTRI TPAL

Semester : _____ Tahun : _________

Nama Santri : .... No. Induk : .... Kelas : ....

No.	Materi Pelajaran	Nilai	
I	**Materi Pokok**		
1	Tadarus Al-Qur'an sampai dengan juz ..... (Khatam Al-Qur'an .... kali)		
2	Dasar-dasar Ulumul Qur'an		
		Jumlah Hafalan	Kefasihan
3	Hafalan Bacaan Sholat		
4	Hafalan Surat-surat Pendek		
5	Hafalan Do'a Sehari-hari		
6	Hafalan Ayat-ayat Pilihan		
7	Menulis Huruf Al-Qur'an		
8	Kaifiyah Wudlu dan Sholat		
II	**Materi Penunjang**		
1	Ilmu Tajwid		
2	Bacaan Murottal		
3	Terjemah Materi Hafalan		
4	Hadits		
5	Mahfudzot		
6	Bahasa Arab		
7			
III	**Lain-lain**		
1	Presensi		
2	Ketertiban		
3			

Mengetahui
Wali Santri. Direktur. Wali Kelas

(______________) (______________) (______________)

Standard photocopied report form for TPA students, prepared by Team Tadarus "AMM," distributed for widespread duplication and use in Qur'ān kindergarten (TPA) programs

This process of synthesis was seeming to take on a life of its own apart from institutional guidelines. For example, the methodology of Iqra' explicitly encourages students to begin reading the Qur'ān with the second *sūrah* (Sūrah al-Baqarah, rather than "Juz' 'Amma"), as stated on the back of booklet 6. The first reason given for this pertains to students' feelings with respect to the Qur'ān and their own ability. Superimposed on the image of Bapak As'ad Humam, the full jacket copy reads:

> Why, after finishing book 6 of Iqra', go straight to reading from the first *juz'* and not "Juz' 'Amma"? . . . (1) it gives confidence, and it feels natural to students, because they can really read the Qur'ān; (2) in reciting, it is *sunna* to read from *juz'* 1 until finishing; (3) pronunication in "Juz' 'Amma" is harder, compared to the earlier *juz'*; (4) because many students have already memorized the short *sūrahs* they do not pay attention to the writing *(tulisan)* in "Juz' 'Amma," to the point that they can make errors with every prayer; (5) in any case, the *sūrahs* from "Juz' 'Amma" are best as *(dijadikan)* material for memorization review *(menyimakkan)* by a knowledgeable teacher; (6) this system supports the awareness that "Juz' 'Amma" is the Qur'ān, and there is not the impression that "following" [*turutan*, meaning emulating others as a mode of learning] the short *sūrahs* of "Juz' 'Amma" is or is not or is not yet the Qur'ān.[74]

This passage shows a committed rationale for a certain curricular trajectory based on awareness of students' process and perception. The program's trajectory thus continues with 2 al-Baqarah, the first *sūrah* of the Qur'ān after its "opening," the Fātiḥah.

There nevertheless appeared in 1993 a book of "Juz' 'Amma," the last *sūrahs* of the Qur'ān (which are early "Meccan revelations"), bound together with the Iqra' materials, a project initiated and officially sponsored by the Ministry of Religious Affairs with the cooperation of Team Tadarus "AMM." I was surprised. When I asked about this, expert curriculum developers smiled as if to say, "Yes, but you know that's what people want to use." This kind of adaptive, synthetic process of curriculum application was also evident in transitional educational contexts, such as in homes where Baghdadi had traditionally been taught, but the host family had no strong objection to changing over to the Iqra' method. In these situations, a combination of both methods was frequently used. Often students began learning by using Iqra' exercises; after they completed the Iqra' sequence, they started over again, learning the very same material using Baghdadi techniques. The original developers of the Iqra' program in Kotagede, Java, seemed surprised to learn that this was occurring in Sulawesi in 1997.

In South Sulawesi, it was not difficult to see how this was happening, however. At an orientation meeting in Makassar for students preparing to do their social service by teaching with the Iqra' materials in the countryside, students were coached on how to approach prospective pupils in the mosque in a way that would not cause divisiveness in the community, and especially to avoid conflict or offense with local Qur'ān teachers who might employ "traditional" teaching styles. College students were instructed to be very sensitive to the feelings and the status of the local teacher whose knowledge and authority they could be perceived to undermine as a function of their work; this could also be one reason for the adaptive use of multiple systems.

Affective evaluations of the two methods, Iqra' and Baghdadi, overlapped rather than competed directly. For adults and educators, "traditional" and "modern" were moods as well as normative descriptors, not necessarily defined in terms of a clear distinction between the two terms. They often worked by continuity, not by contrast. As with new acquaintances' joy to discover "traditional" education to have been a shared experience (no matter what they would recommend for their own children), these characterizations built on lived memories and not just the maintenance of historical precedents. Indonesians rehearsed and recounted again and again the minutia of education—how they received sweets if they learned their lessons well or how they were expected to sweep up before class by their *shaikhs*. Through a sharing of mutual experience, they forged connections that later allowed them to feel blended and possibly ambivalent nostalgia, discomfort, or other affective qualities associated with their own memory. These personal contrasts were the basis for given intellectual comparisons of the feelings such methods were supposedly to produce in children: motivation on the one hand and the sense of a meaningful apprehension *(faham)* on the other. The adults who made these assessments based them, naturally, on their own memories of the experience of learning to read, which over time had become saturated with emotional qualities such as nostalgia or perhaps energetic enthusiasm for Islamic education, usually both. The overall affective synthesis recast education not as normatively "traditional" or "modern" but as a system in which everyone was seen to share in a uniform process.

Indonesians did, however, also assess the relative efficacy of teaching methods on the basis of the actual abilities students developed under different educational regimens. For example, one master coach insisted that the "traditional" teaching method was superior on the grounds that students were well prepared for smooth reading in his classes when they had been trained under the Baghdadi system. Usually, however, the methods were compared on the basis of the feelings that they evoked even when evaluating teaching and learning practice. Learning to read by "spelling out" Arabic letters in Bahasa Bugis, one vernacular language, for example, contrasts vividly with learning an "alphabet song" sung in Bahasa Indonesia and set to contemporary *dangdut* melodies like those heard on the radio and seen on television.

Adults made choices about the kinds of education their children would receive on the basis of such sentimental associations. Through these choices, they did not reproduce static distinctions between "traditional" and "modern" but forged a new affective landscape for Qur'ānic learning that included both dimensions vividly. In this synthesis, idealized process took precedence. The main focus of the Iqra'-Baghdadi discussion was the imagined emotional experience or "learning identity" of children. With Iqra', children were said to be more "motivated" because the method is "applied" or "participatory" *(praktek)*, featuring activities such as singing. Likewise, the "depth" of Baghdadi related to a recognition of the maintenance of a "traditional" affective bond between teacher and student and a proximity to language that comes "naturally." While ambivalent in distinguishing between the two systems, for many, the ideal was to combine the best of both and thus become "*maksimal*"—and, it was hoped, lifelong—learners.

Synthetic Processes of Education and Example

Widespread change in Indonesia in the 1990s restructured Qur'ānic affect and identities of learning around Arabic ritual speech according to emergent social and religious ideals.[75] Like studies that view "sentiment" in terms of social processes and evaluations, the site of this widespread change could be seen as the practice of individuals, and its effect was felt within personal learning processes. In situations of learning, Indonesian Muslims modified the affective base of practice, creating new identities of sentiment and learning to match religious ideals.

After mastering *tajwīd* and fluent reading (according to whatever standard may be in effect), Indonesian students may have continued their study of the recited Qur'ān in one of three principal directions. First, they may have learned how to comprehend the meaning of the Arabic text; clearly a primary component of *pesantren* curriculum (whether "traditional" or "modern"), this was the direction that the developers of the Iqra' materials were pursuing for advanced curricula at the time of fieldwork. A second avenue for the development of Qur'ānic practice after learning to read was to begin the project of memorizing the Qur'ān. A third potential project was to improve the aesthetic dimensions of recitation, to begin to study the melodic modes, or "*lagu*," associated with recitation.

Many who sought projects of piety related to Qur'ānic practice pursued the third path, the aesthetic potentials of recitation, and would begin to study *lagu*, the melodic modes associated with *mujawwad* styles of recitation. They would adopt programs of practice that extended from the fundamentals of programs of perfecting Qur'ānic reading. This activity necessarily built on the technical and affective experience initially developed in the process of first learning to read the Qur'ān. With the heightened sensitivity to sound quality and sectioning associated with *mujawwad* reading (and, in Indonesia, awareness of competition standards), *tajwīd* would reemerge in advanced training out of the domain of automatic knowledge to become once again a rigorous focus of study. A more advanced level of technical competence requires increased, not diminished, self-conscious awareness of the fundamental elements of reading aloud. It also necessitates scrupulous attention to rules of *tajwīd* that may have only limited application in the reading of the Qur'ān, in order not to overlook carelessly an exceptional case. In his coaching at the national level, K. H. M. Sayyid Abdullah would say, "In Indonesia today, *tajwid* is our real challenge. Even the mice in Indonesia all know *lagu* by now. What we need to do is to strive to develop our *tajwid*." Whether with international competitors or kindergartners, the act of improving reading was increasingly being seen to be an ongoing pursuit, underscored by the recasting of ritual practice as a process of learning and by self-conscious manipulation of affective registers within programs of study and performance.

Part of this affective change in the realm of Qur'ān reading rested on the contrast between the two learning methods that carried the assessments "traditional" and "modern." These are not merely descriptors of systems but affective evaluations that influence understandings of self and mediate relations with others. These evaluations were held ambivalently, sometimes compatibly, but they were not necessarily in diametrical opposition in discourse, application, or felt experience. The contrast between "traditional" and "modern" was an affective assessment of the relationship of the student to self, to practice, and to others, grounded simultaneously in memories of past experience, nostalgia persisting in the present, and idealizations about the future.

There was ambivalence even among the most pious mothers about a process—learning—having come to dominate the domain of religious practice where the authority of more structured, intimate, and hierarchical relationships had once ruled supreme. One afternoon a group of mothers who were practicing Qur'ān recitation exchanged stories about their own children's religious comportment. One, who led TPA instruction in her home, said that her seven-year-old son had recently informed her that it was un-Islamic for a woman like her ever to cut her hair. She said that she explained to him that it is perfectly Islamic to get a haircut (in fact, in Muslim Southeast Asia, haircutting ceremonies for infants are common, accompanied at times by the recitation of a text recounting the Prophet Muḥammad's own "shaving," or *bercukuran*), and, she said, what does it matter anyway if one always has it covered up, and besides, it's just too hot and uncomfortable to do anything else. The mothers all shook their heads, asking one another, how do children come up with these things? All then agreed that it was the influence of TPA, praise God. Then they shook their heads once again before praising TPA for its success in instilling piety in the young generation. While ambivalent about the results, the women themselves were nevertheless adopting the same means.

The very activity in which the women were taking part as they shared stories about their children demonstrates that changes in basic religious education in the form of reading the Qur'ān was not something that was happening only, or even primarily, with children. The mothers were meeting expressly to do the same thing that their children were doing in TPA, learning to read the Qur'ān. At the end of fieldwork, the women were planning a formal *wisuda* graduation ceremony for themselves and designing the robes for the event. The women with whom I spent time used no study materials except the Qur'ān. However, just before the end of fieldwork, the reciter here called Ny. Nurhayati distributed a *tajwīd* book among a group of women who studied with her, commenting that she was getting tired of correcting so many mistakes. Many older women in Indonesia were returning to the study of Qur'ān recitation, at times bringing along their children and grandchildren, all the while attempting to improve their religious knowledge in order to have a more efficacious practice of piety. They were creating the very sense of what it meant to acquire Islamic knowledge and self-consciously transmitting that understanding as an example to their children.

"The older you get, the harder you study" *(Makin tua, makin belajar)*, Ny. Nurhayati once remarked, after singing in an interview a little song about how old people supposedly cannot assimilate new information. She was referring to the bursting halls of women meeting to improve their Qur'ān recitation. On the subject of her own tireless teaching, Ny. Nurhayati said of the Qur'ān: "Affirmed—studied—read aloud—memorized," adding, "this knowledge must be given to others, it's a responsibility *(amanat)*." She said that the women were coming to her sessions for worship and knowledge *(ibadah dan ilmu)*, adding, "I have to value their desire [to learn]."[76] In relearning to read, the women were studying what they had once learned as children. Noting that women were also starting to meet for the purposes of memorizing, studying *tafsīr* (Qur'ān exegesis), and holding *diskusi*, Ny. Nurhayati remarked that when the women met on Sundays, they only studied *tajwīd* together and did nothing else. She explained the emphasis on practice and the rediscovery of learning identity in the following way:

> When they [the women] study *tajwid*, they start to become aware that what they learned long ago was all wrong *(mereka sadari bahwa pelajaran yang mereka pelajari dulu salah)*. They see that if they are wrong in reading just a letter, then they are wrong in the very basics, that they are going to have to start over from the very beginning *(mulai dari dasar)*. It's a case of admitting having been wrong *(ada pengakuan salah)*, a realization that it can be possible to be wrong in this way at all. [The women think:] "And if we are wrong in reading just this one letter, then we must be wrong with the whole meaning," and so they start with the very basics all over again.

If the "fundamentals," what is taken for granted, are something that needs relearning, then how much more of what is taken for granted about Islam also needs to be relearned? In this sense, returning to the study of Qur'ān recitation is paradoxically a first step in a continuous process not only in perfecting reading habits, but also in reconstituting the self as a lifelong learner.

When I asked some of the women why they were starting to study recitation again, there were a number of answers; one characteristic response related to the religious education of their own children, for which many seemed to feel primarily responsible. When I first heard this answer, I presumed that the women were telling me that they wanted to know how to recite so that they could impart this knowledge to their own children in the home. While this could have been the case, this is not what they emphasized in their conversations; instead, they described a situation in which everybody was now going to a teacher. One woman, for example, who said she was studying recitation because she had "loved the sound of it since childhood," explained her practice in terms of the impact her study was having on her children. She did not teach them *tajwīd* herself, but instead she strove to set an example of learning for them.

Kids these days just aren't like they used to be, she began: they say "*tidak*" (no) and they look at what their parents do, and you have to be studying hard yourself in order to get them to study at all. Other women affirmed, it used to be that parents could say, "Go, recite the Qur'ān, go and study," and the children would do as they were told. But today the children talk back with their questions. They ask, "Why should *I* study recitation—or do my homework—if *you* don't?" Several women described a shared strategy: to remind their children that Mother also goes to a Qur'ān teacher to study, and at the same time Mother is also working a full-time job to bring home money for the family, and, on top of that, it's Mother who is doing all of the household chores without any outside help—and so if Mother can manage to practice her reading, then they can, too. Acutely aware of what works emotionally and what does not with their own children, they recognized that they needed to put a more effective model of incentive into play. In this model, everyone's "identity" was as a learner or a student; the primary affective relationship was to a process and not necessarily to an authoritative person such as a *shaikh*—or even a mother. Everyone was a potential participant as well as a practitioner, and everyone potentially had a relationship to the same ongoing process. To inspire their children, adults did not present completed mastery, but instead they actively modeled the process and feeling of engaged, ongoing Qur'ānic learning.

CHAPTER 4

EXPRESSION

Emotional Projects of Performance and Pedagogy

In Indonesia in the 1990s, rapid change was taking place in perceptions of ideal Qur'ānic practice. This change occurred largely through acceptance of melody types heard in performances of the recited Qur'ān in Egypt. The received Egyptian model of performance in its perceived qualities conformed to Islamic expectations for expansive Qur'ānic "orthopraxy," that is, what Indonesians understood as the right way to perform or practice the recited Qur'ān. These idealized perceptions and expectations were based in a conception of the inimitable Qur'ān, the Speech of God, and were also socially and situationally produced and affirmed in projects of teaching and learning. Virtuosic models for aesthetic performance became increasingly associated with orthoprax reading in Indonesia, and Indonesian pedagogical strategies were aimed at rendering these virtuosic ideals attainable in ordinary practice. The combined effect of projects of learning was changing the overall system of the recited Qur'ān in Indonesia, causing practitioners in ongoing projects of piety and ritual practice to follow new expansive norms of orthopraxy.

Projects of religious learning in Muslim Indonesia in the 1990s impelled dynamics of escalating engagement with the *mujawwad* style of reading. Unlike the affective ideal of a "steady state" that has been described for other kinds of "musical" systems in Indonesia,[1] the combination of aesthetic, educative, and religious practice related to Qur'ān recitation in this period had dynamic emotional modulation as a goal and a strategy. In Indonesia in the 1990s, new norms of performance that were adapted from recorded virtuosic performances conveyed idealized affective norms of beauty (including the use of melody), improvisation, and feeling; these were increasingly accepted as the "correct" mode of practice to which every pious practitioner could aspire. The process by which Indonesian Muslims embraced these as religiously orthoprax and pedagogically expedient brought about overall change in expectations for the performance of Qur'ānic reading. A widespread escalation of engagement was a result.

"Melodic" recitation (*mujawwad*, usually called "*tilāwah*" in Indonesia) is a musically sophisticated form of vocalizing the Qur'ān with a slow tempo, ornamentation, and the application of melodic modes known as *maqām* (pl. *maqāmāt*) or *naghm*.[2] In Indonesia, they were known as *lagu*. This type of recitation differs from the style known as *murattal* (or *tadarus* in Indonesia), which is usually a semiregular variation on four or five pitches. The *mujawwad* style of affecting, aesthetic performance by skilled readers is where some observers have sought to investigate the "emotion" of the recited Qur'ān. For example, Kristina Nelson analyzes such performances in terms of what she calls the "ideal recitation,"[3] which emphasizes emotive exchange between performer and audience. Although aspects of the recited Qur'ān potentially generate immediate emotive and visceral response, the "ecstatic" model for Arab music as developed by Ali Jihad Racy and others is not the best framework for the Indonesian system.[4] One reason is that Indonesians themselves did not apply it. Rarely did audiences respond with the kinds of appreciative outbursts common in Egypt; instead, they would sit quietly, sometimes talking among themselves or possibly humming along after the performer to try to capture the melodic cadence of the phrase. In Indonesia, virtuosic Qur'ānic performances were most likely to be received as "*kurikulum*," since popular focus was not on appreciating the performances of others as a spectator but instead on developing Qur'ānic potential in long-term projects of piety that may transform affectively individuals and groups. This pattern is consistent with Muslim systems of moralized aesthetics, including Sufism, as well as the Islamic legal injunction to recite the Qur'ān "beautifully."

Ordinary Indonesian practitioners of the recited Qur'ān in the 1990s increasingly sought ways to grasp intelligibly and to formalize fluid and spontaneous aspects of virtuoso performance in the *mujawwad* style. Situational ideals of realistic curriculum and competence were effortfully matched with the more expansive ideals that were based on Indonesians' reception of what Nelson has termed the "ideal recitation" from Egypt. These ideals, in Indonesian context, combined with expanding expectations for realizing the Qur'ānic requirements of improvisation, affect, and aesthetics. With the standardization and availability of more technically elaborate models of practice (such as recordings of the recitations of the great Egyptian *shaikhs*), Indonesian Muslims sought to acquire increased capability *(kemampuan)* with the Qur'ān by being "able to" *(mampu)* recite with *lagu* (standard improvised melody types). The system of melodic recitation and the pedagogy Indonesians developed to teach it drew people compellingly into sustained projects of piety. One reason for this powerful draw was that improvisation and affect were explicitly part of the performative system that was adopted in projects of learning. Pious anticipation of stipulated beauty, spontaneity, and emotion open a space of potential that practitioners sought to fill with their own experience, drawing them more deeply into technical and experiential "horizons" of performance.

In projects of learning, the recited Qur'ān is the object and method of learning as well as the standard for evaluation and achievement. When expressive aspects of the recited Qur'ān (such as improvisation with a complex modal system or the realization of idealized emotional experience) are understood to occupy the domain of revelation, proximate models and techniques that are historically specific blend with the system of the recited Qur'ān and its "inimitability" in both perception and performance. In Indonesia in the 1990s, "orthopraxy" emergent in received models and teaching strategies for *mujawwad* reading pushed the standard for individual achievement and collective evaluation of religious practice toward what was, paradoxically, a seemingly attainable standard of a virtuoso. Mastery occupied the domain of revelation through open-ended projects of perfecting beauty and feeling, and practitioners who took their own competence as an object increasingly evaluated their own Qur'ānic piety with respect to these goals and ideals.

Competence tends to be imagined as a discrete property ascribed to individuals rather than a continuous process. However, many Indonesians who set out to become someone "able to" recite the Qur'ān found that the open-endedness of aesthetic systematizations emergent in particular goals guaranteed that their project would be an ongoing pursuit of the feeling that one has at least, or at last, gotten it "right." This idea was suggested in a conversation I had with Drs. H. Burhanuddin, imam of Masjid "Al-Markaz." Drs. H. Burhanuddin was a native of the Mandar region of Sulawesi, a champion Qur'ān reader who had taken first place in the international competition held in Saudi Arabia in the early 1980s. We would often discuss the widespread revitalization movement in Qur'ānic practices that was occurring in Indonesia in the 1990s. One day, I asked him the principal question I had brought to fieldwork: Why were Indonesian Muslims of all ages and from diverse social locations developing so energetically their abilities to read the Qur'ān aloud?

Although H. Burhanuddin usually led classes for aspiring competition reciters and only occasionally taught in the popular women's circles, I posed to him versions of the same questions I had been asking participants in the groups. Why were so many women in Makassar studying Qur'ān recitation so intensively, I asked? Why were they exerting strenuous efforts to learn how to do something that they had supposedly already mastered long ago? Why, in a single afternoon, were dozens of women gathering at Al-Markaz and other locations in the city of Makassar in order to study how to recite the Qur'ān on the model of the great Arab virtuosos? Why were these mothers and grandmothers learning to recite the Qur'ān with the styles used by professional *qārī*'s from Egypt, abandoning their own *lagu*—which, by their own accounts, carried powerful and meaningful emotional valences for them? What dynamics of inspiration were driving this system?

In response to my questions about the resurgence in Qur'ānic practice in general and the local women's mosque movement in specific, Drs. H. Burhanuddin and I discussed many of the changes that Indonesia had seen in previous decades in Qur'ānic education for children and adults, including the influence of Qur'ān recitation competitions and competition standards. After half an hour or so of this conversation, however, it seemed as if he was less than satisfied with explaining religious subjectivities as if they were solely determined by social structures. Finally, Drs. H. Burhanuddin leaned forward. He enunciated carefully so that he could be heard over the monsoon rains that were drumming on the metal roof, and he slowly explained: there is an "inner power" *(kekuasaan batin)* that comes from the Qur'ān, and a profound feeling within the heart comes along with it. This is a feeling, he said, of being "more *khushū*'" (a Qur'ānic term important to Sufis as well as contemporary revivalists, interpreted here as "earnestly pious").[5] He restated this several times. When one recites in a way that one knows is not correct, he continued, or when one has to question whether a *lagu* is right or not *(betul atau masih salah)*, a sense of "*ibadah*" (worship or pious practice) is missing. So when the women study, he concluded, they no longer need to question themselves. They can be certain, he said: they can *feel* that they have gotten it right.

Expert in his knowledge about the local and national institutional structures in Indonesia that supported the recited Qur'ān, Drs. H. Burhanuddin framed his explanation of a movement in religious revitalization in terms of religious affect. Although he was a figure known nationally for his virtuosic skill and master teaching, his statement did not focus on the development of particular categories of technical expertise. Instead, he named feeling states as the object and methods of Qur'ānic piety. Across the spectrum of age, gender, and class, in the energetic system of Qur'ānic practice and education in the 1990s, affect was a goal, a strategy, and a mechanism for groups and individuals within projects of learning and practice. As H. Burhanuddin described it, it also comprised a pious confirmation: it's right when you *feel* that you got it right. Drs. H. Burhanuddin's statement suggested that, in Indonesia in the

1990s, affective modes that both formed and informed a shared, pious goal of the sense of orthopraxy circulated with increasing power through multiple levels of a movement of acquiring competence and intensifying Qur'ānic learning and practice.

In addition to representing a normative evaluation, H. Burhanuddin's response to the question about the energy of the women's groups implied that "orthopraxy" is a situational perception and assessment and, more meaningfully, an affective state that emerges developmentally in processes of learning. In Indonesia in the 1990s, orthopraxy, competence, or "getting it right" was an experiential and evaluative pivot point around which systems of adapting standards, variable trajectories of learning and feeling, collective interests, and changing social circumstances revolved. A stable ground under rapidly changing individual and collective circumstances of Islamic religious revitalization in Indonesia was the acquisition of an affective sense of having the ability *(kemampuan)* to do what others could do and the accompanying pursuit of the feeling of getting it right. These feelings comprised "moods" cultivated and experienced in practice as well as self-conscious "motivations" for oneself and others within a social system.

Three aspects converged in the world of Qur'ānic recitational practice in Indonesia in the 1990s to produce an escalation of orthopraxy, facilitated by self-conscious pedagogies and social strategies of promotion. They were, first, the perception of qualities of "closedness" of the system of Qur'ān reading, based on the doctrine of *i'jāz*, the expectation of the well-formedness of practice, and the tendency to imagine competence as a fixed and stable property. Thus, the system of Qur'ānic practice first offered to memorizers, readers, and reciters a sense of a fixed horizon, supported by the dynamics of repetition, which produced overall cumulative expectations of fixity and closure. Second, the "openness" of normative musicalized standards such as "beauty," "feeling," and "improvisation" afforded the development of both formalization and expansion in projects of teaching and learning.[6] Properties of flexibility stipulated within the system combined with the affective aspects of learning to generate an expansive quality as reciters attempted actually to achieve receding horizons of "competence" and "orthopraxy." Third, an interplay of these two dimensions sustained ordinary Indonesians' practice in melodic recitation and also supported escalating engagement in many cases. In multiple domains of practice, there was a generative system in effect, based on the internal dynamics of the recited Qur'ān and amplified and enhanced by the institutions and discourses of a particular social system. Efforts to align expansive ideas with actual practice were the mechanism of inspiration for a widespread movement of Qur'ānic revitalization.

Inspiring Ritual Pedagogy

The inherent openness of Qur'ānic practice produces ever-expanding expectations for conventions that systems of pedagogy then formalize for the learner. The demanding flexibility of the learning process, combined with the improvisational and aesthetic norms and ideals of the recited Qur'ān, support the development of graded standards for progressive competence. Such situational ideals are the very standards that structure the learning process itself, and they emerge developmentally.[7] They are part of the recited Qur'ān, while they are simultaneously based on authoritative norms, and they always have social components. They comprise aspects of practice such as affect *(rasa)*, the recognition and development of individual "style," and established patterns of improvisation. They form the basis of situated "orthopraxy" in terms of performance, pedagogy, and evaluation in real situations. This orthopraxy doubles as musicalized competence. With the affective recognition that these ideals realized in situations of learning also correspond to the expansive domain of "revelation," they operate as what others have called an affective "lure" or "propulsion" to continued practice.

The question for ordinary practitioners first engaging the *mujawwad* system of recitation in Indonesia was, how does one know when it is right or wrong? What is an interesting *variasi* (variation) in an unfamiliar and improvised musical system, what, on the contrary, sounds bad, and what is just plain wrong or a mistake? How does one know that one has gotten beauty "right"? The more that flexible criteria such as "beauty" and "feeling" were adopted as foundations of orthopraxy within the ritual system of the recited Qur'ān, the more that the open question of what is "right" impacted self-understandings as well as the structures of practice. Received norms from Egyptian performance were grafted onto the expectation of the inimitable Qur'ān. This produced regimens of teaching and learning that deepened the recognition of potential for religious mastery, as well as the means and desire to attain it, among Indonesian Muslims.

In the case of the recited Qur'ān in Indonesia in the 1990s, the combination of aesthetic, musical, and religious practice suggests how an experiential constellation of "orthopraxy" may be dynamic, generative of enhanced practice, and a cause of change in religious systems. Islamic traditions have often been characterized in the field of Islamic studies in terms of a relative emphasis on "orthopraxy" over matters of "orthodoxy."[8] More generally, scholars of religion have emphasized the "orthoprax" aspects of ritual action as a criterion for comparison of religious enactments. This is a perceived fixity that fosters overall expectations and a tendency especially to perceive practice as closed, "archetypal," or well-formed both in an absolutely idealized form as well as in each particular performance or stage of learning. Practitioners of the recited Qur'ān apprehend a sense of "stipulatedness" or orthopraxy through repetition; it develops over time in interaction with progressive transformation of ability and self. Practice continually modifies expectations of the possibility of closure. "Orthopraxy" is not merely an imposed measure or a horizon to which practitioners aspire in developing competence, however; the recited Qur'ān itself, in stipulating its own affecting ideals, continually opens up new horizons of this perception in experience over time.

In a typological theorization of ritual, Humphrey and Laidlaw identify a concern for correctness with qualities of increased "ritualization" overall. The distinction they draw in *The Archetypal Actions of Ritual* between categories such as "liturgy-centered" and "performance-centered" ritual action, however, collapses in the case of the recitation of the Qur'ān. On the one hand, *mujawwad* reading is clearly a spontaneous "performance"; on the other hand, the ritual "works" when it is "gotten right" according to stipulated, "liturgical" standards.[9] Unlike the case of musical performance, practitioners share the conviction that they could "get it wrong."[10] This is because in religious enactments, practitioners align ideals and realities of ritual, assessing these qualities relationally. When they are perceived to have coalesced, there emerges a situational sense of having "gotten it right," recognized as developmental "competence." The social recognition of such an alignment propels the practitioner onto a new level of achievement and possibility, as ritual repetition, learning, and perfection continue to transform both the self and the system itself over time.

Clifford Geertz explained ritual as the site at which "symbolic forms" exert their powerful influence to render into reality the experience of an "imagined world" through the internalizing force of "moods and motivations." Affect within ritual, according to him, aligns levels of "lived" and "imagined" worlds, and effects transformation in self and system. In Geertz' explanation, rituals are the context of this alignment through the mechanism of "moods and motivations":

> [It is] in ritual—that is, consecrated behavior—that this conviction that religious conceptions are veridical and that religious directives are sound is somehow generated. It is in some sort of ceremonial form—even if that form be hardly more than the recitation of a myth, the consultation of an oracle, or the decoration of a grave—that the *moods and motivations* which sacred symbols induce in men *and the general conceptions of the order of existence* which they formulate for men *meet and reinforce one another.* In a ritual, the world as lived and

the world as imagined, fused under the agency of a single set of symbolic forms, turn out to be the same world.[11]

Geertz does not specify exactly what psychological functions emotions perform in his "cultural system" of religion, although he does identify them with his key concept of "ethos."[12] Other theories, however, suggest ways in which the "reinforcing" alignment of moods and motivations and "general conceptions," to use Geertz' words, are actually "somehow generated."

Multiple approaches in the study of ritual share a recognition that rituals in some way align ideals and realities, bond parts and wholes, orient maps and territories, and homologize universals and particulars. Jonathan Z. Smith writes that ritual renders a relation of how things "ought to be" in opposition to how things "are."[13] When Geertz states that the "world as lived" and the "world as imagined" become one and the same in ritual, it is not the case, however, that symbols perform this magic all on their own. An interaction between levels of affect within ritual activity performs the transformation Geertz describes over time and propels forward continuing or escalating engagement with religious structures. Feedback between the levels of ideals and realities may produce intensifying "force" within projects of religious piety; their dynamic overlap may generate continued or intensifying voluntary practice. Practitioners of voluntary piety seek to manifest expansive, affective ideals within their activity, leading them to rehearse and to perfect. This repeated rehearsal has an indeterminate quality, and with increased ability there open up new "horizons" of possibility that could be rendered palpable in performance.

Jonathan Z. Smith writes that ritual is "work"; practices of ongoing religious piety are a "project." Through repetition and rehearsal, not just a single performance, ideals and realities are progressively matched. In projects of Qur'ānic piety in the 1990s, "practice" was not unreflective activity performed as if by habit but was pursued in an effortful and self-conscious way in order to perfect and to realize and recognize perfection. For the recited Qur'ān in Indonesia, in contrast to a static understanding of ritual repetition in time and over time, tensions between perceived ideals and self-understandings of ability dynamically opened up continual vistas of potential competence in continuous processes.

Theodore Jennings writes that structural ritual change over time is motivated by a shared (he claims, universal) tendency to try to improve ritual, to create elements that are more "fitting" (his term), in order to realize "the presence of something like coherence and correspondence tests of adequacy."[14] This "fit" of ritual elements depends on nonritual systems of coherence in Jennings' theory, since he assumes that an external referent is the primary standard to which ritual learning is held.[15] The argument being made here, in contrast, is that perceptions of how things "ought to be" may be a perception of practice that emerges from within practice itself, and is not necessarily derived entirely from the representation of an external order. The "fit," or resonating correspondence between particular realities and encompassing ideals, is a perceptive feeling about a doing, evaluated in language of competence and piety.

A two-tier model of ritual ideals and realities should be attentuated in order to encompass a notion of intermediate, situational ideals that the practitioner strives to achieve as a part of a cumulative process in acquiring ritual competence. This dimension, enforced by ritual repetition, explains the compelling qualities of projects of learning and the modes by which Indonesians accepted and adapted received ideals of feeling and beauty in Qur'ānic performance. Situational ideals are the potentially attainable possibilities directed toward an absolute "ideal," emergent in learning and often identical with applied pedagogical strategies and techniques. They are constituted socially, blending into embodied experience to the degree that they are instantiated in action and performance. They also reference the expansive ideals of a ritual and may share in this ontology. Qur'ānic abilities, for example, are both open and closed: expecting to acquire a stable "competency," the learner continually encounters unanticipated challenges to manage or to overcome. The cumulative situational ideals of ritual practices such as these explain how the expectation, perception, and sense of orthopraxy may generate experiences with affective and directional force, and thereby inspire ongoing practice.

A key component of ritual learning, especially in projects of voluntary religious enactments, is a quality of situational orthopraxy that references expansive ideals while it is simultaneously rendered palpable in lived realities. This quality influences self-understandings in terms of evaluations of potential and "competence." In pedagogy, propaedeutic, proximate, or intermediate strategies and techniques emerge as seemingly attainable ideals of competence that then guide the practitioner's developing mastery. Such situational ideals are understood to be social and cultural products, but in the performance of the recited Qur'ān, they also become a part of the encounter with revelation, energizing the sense of piety and the desire to improve. Indonesian Muslims associated the expansive ideals of revealed Divine Speech with aesthetic and musical aspects of a received system of performance. Specifically, the concept of the "inimitable" Qur'ān (the doctrine of *i'jāz*) interacted with idealized performances; Indonesian reciters attempted to access the improvisational and affective aspects of this virtuosic system within formalized pedagogy in order to realize them in personal and individual practice. The affective modes of changing competence combined with the apprehension of attainable goals within a fluid system generated cycles of escalating engagement. Competence, realized through situational ideals, is the intermediate level of the attainment of orthopraxy, when practitioners attempt to make ideals and realities coalesce.

A model of ritual orthopraxy, doubling as "competence" in the case of the recited Qur'ān, captures key aspects of ritual learning in terms of ultimate ideals understood to be transcendent, the variable realities of actors' abilities and self-evaluations, and, finally, the mediating, proximate, or situational ideals that are emergent within pedagogy and learning processes. Competence may be viewed as an intermediate tier of ritual evaluation, a level at which practitioners' ability and self-understanding intersect with religious goals on the one hand and situational ideals of practice on the other. Competence is a category that varies across groups of individuals as well as over time. The models and stages of ritual competence both share in a perception of expansive orthopraxy and also represent the developmental, situational ideals of ritual learning. With ritual repetition of the recited Qur'ān, the acquisition of competence continually renders new self-understandings that are measured against the goals of piety. The more ritual skill the individual achieves, the more a religious system may be internalized in terms of its ideals, embodied competence, and self-understanding as a pious practitioner.

How does the observer access competence, the ideals the practitioner attempts to achieve realistically in a particular situation, from the "learner's point of view"? Because the "stipulated" aspects of Qur'ānic practice include improvisational choices and fluid aesthetic standards, and are further determined under changing social conditions, an understanding of ritual "rules" alone will not provide an adequate concept of "competence." In addition, positing structural "maps" as learners' "territory" effaces their actual learning trajectories. Anthropologist Dorothy Holland comments on a similar problem in social theory, pointing out that "if expertise, salience, and identification co-develop in an interrelated process . . . then our descriptions of cultural content—by implication—become even more complicated than we had thought." Expert knowledge ("as rules and maxims or gestalts"), she writes, "may falsely impart a homogeneity of expertise, salience, and identification, as well as a homogeneity of content."[16] Overly idealized or universalized portrayals of competence or orthopraxy flatten the progressive nature of developing ability, risking an overemphasis on what Holland calls "expert's culture." In addition, competencies are not acquired in the same way nor are they understood in the same way by everyone.

A concept of "musical competence" developed by ethnomusicologist and Indonesianist Benjamin Brinner suggests a direction for conceptualizing situational ideals of ritual orthopraxy for the case of the recited Qur'ān in contemporary Indonesia. In a formulation deriving from Brinner, competence may be understood to be "individualized mastery of the array of interrelated skills and knowledge" that are required by a "tradition or community." Like orthopraxy, it is "acquired and developed in response to and in accordance with" the demands of "general and specific" social and cultural conditions. This conceptualization, as Brinner points out, allows for "ideal and actual competencies, stressing norms and constraints without precluding individual differences and socially or culturally instituted distinctions."[17] Recognizing that "competence" changes over time for the individual, while it also reflects the diversity of practice within a community, Brinner observes: "While we need to elicit communal ideals, we must also assess particular individuals' knowledge, remaining alert to variant learning progressions and recognizing that these ideals not only derive from individual articulation but influence them in turn."[18] For religious enactments like the recited Qur'ān, understandings of competence also influence conceptions of orthoprax ritual performance and self as religious practitioner. In a case in which a musical system is also a ritual one, when competence is like orthopraxy, "getting it right" in terms of technical skill or aesthetic evaluations takes on heavily weighted significance for such projects of piety. This may lead to an inflation of practice, especially in a case in which "competence" in projects of learning is evaluated in terms of the performances of virtuosos.

Pedagogical conventions—although they may be accepted as arbitrary (such as the rules for the number of melodic modes to be used in a Qur'ān recitation competition)—often function like definitive standards. These interact with the inherent openness of practice as well as the pious desire to have one's religious expression pleasing to oneself, to others, and especially to God. Ritual curriculum, therefore, may be doubly significant. Instrumentally, curriculum is expedient for learning, and its conventions are accepted as means to that end (with an implicit understanding that these means may be replaced with other, more effective ones). Psychologically, cumulative standards offer potential avenues to attain a sense of "correctness" at every stage of the progressive acquisition of competence. Along with these dynamics may come an understanding of self with respect to practice at each stage of continuous development, evaluated in terms of this potential. Ritual curriculum, always "stipulated" and at times seemingly arbitrary, fits fluid ideals into actual competence, creating a "lure" to increased practice.

An aspect of the escalating character of some religious practice derives from the directive force of thought and feeling related to this "stipulatedness," a concept that theorists Caroline Humphrey and James Laidlaw locate centrally within their theory of ritual. By this they mean that practitioners claim for ritual an ontological primacy as an "archetype" (in their formulation, this is analogous to a "natural kind" in philosophy and is not related to the meaning of the term "archetype" in the writings of Mircea Eliade and C. G. Jung). An "objectlike" experience of ritual is Humphrey and Laidlaw's "archetypal" quality. Practitioners take on actions that they themselves have not authored but that they "commit" to performing.[19] In the chapter of the book *The Archetypal Actions of Ritual* devoted to the idea of "getting it right," they emphasize variation in segments of ritual performance, variable learning trajectories, and the question of what is a "mistake" when one takes on the authority of performing "stipulated" ritual action from a "ritual stance." "In ritual you both are and are not the author of your acts."[20] They explain: "We have suggested that ritual action is, in a sense, like an object. This is not because people have a common idea of it, but because they do not. . . . Clearly rituals are not really objects, but an object-like existence is given to them by the fact that they are ontologically constituted beyond individual intentions."[21] Humphrey and Laidlaw recognize a developmental aspect to this process, "the result of the actor's progressively coming to have a mental picture of what the act is."[22] When they identify a tension between expectations of "closure" (their "archetypal quality") and the unconstrained nature of ritual practice, they have indicated a dynamic of some forms of pious enactments that makes them potentially self-sustaining in religious contexts.

For this developmental aspect, other ritual theorists apply the phenomenological idea of the "horizon,"[23] developed by thinkers such as Merleau-Ponty and others, and deployed by Ron Williams and James Boyd in their model of aestheticized ritual and repetition. Inspired by Sartre, Williams and Boyd explain in *Ritual, Art, and Knowledge* how aspects of ritual are potentially self-sustaining through luring, spiraling "horizons." Ritual action, they explain, is like a "spiral": familiar and definable, and yet at the same time never static. They describe "right repetition," implying something similar in meaning to the term "orthopraxy" as it is used here. They write that in order for ritual to have the property of "luring" practitioners into intensifying engagement, it would have to encompass qualities that allow it to be an expanding "horizon" rather than an "enclosure."[24] For Williams and Boyd, aestheticized ritual is inherently open-ended for the practitioner who returns time and again to the "same" ritual space to find ever-new opportunities there. The repetition of ritual, they claim, is a perpetual movement toward an expansive horizon, like an artistic "masterpiece" possessing the capacity to "lure" the practitioner into ever-intensifying engagement:

> Horizons have a double nature: compared to uncharted space, the horizon enters us; it provides stability and reference. At the same time, a horizon is a lure to

> exploration and continually recedes as we pursue it. These aspects provide a necessary addition to our hypotheses. If interacting with repeated rituals is like living with a masterpiece of art, then the ritual must be Janus-faced: *it would, on the one hand, have to instruct and pattern our behavior, acting like a stabilizing horizon, and on the other hand it would have to possess the power continually to lure us on and to recede from us, perhaps defeating inadequate or premature interpretations or understandings of itself.*[25]

"Stabilizing" horizons of increasingly engaging involvement with the recited Qur'ān in Indonesia were not only asymptotic, expansive aesethetic ideals of the kind suggested by Williams and Boyd. Palpable in actual experience, intermediate "horizons" were also the graded stages of learning stipulated within understandings of competence, pedagogy, and orthopraxy. These understandings and the associated "lure" to practice were affective.

Echoing the two-tier models of ritual ideals and realities, many theorists see emotion in similar structural terms. Humphrey and Laidlaw, for example, develop the idea of the "evocation of mood" in ritual enactments, writing, "The emotions involved in emergent moods are made quite specific, in that they are focused by the "union" of the subject with the object of his or her devotion."[26] Emotion theorist Jack Katz, while not considering religious enactments per se, also theorizes emotion in terms of bounded and expansive aspects. The question for Katz, as he frames it, is "What is the socially visible sense that a person is trying to make of the immediate situation of his action, and what is the current sense that the situation acquires within his awareness that his life reaches beyond the current situation?"[27]

Katz writes that emotions have both a "situation-responsive" and a "situation-transcendent" dimension (with a "double resonance" possible between them). Emotions are dialectal, Katz claims: they are "aesthetic" and expressive of self, and at the same time they encompass us even as we make them. Katz applies the phenomenological insight of persons simultaneously "making" and being "made by" their lived world to emotion theory in terms of his notion that we "do" or express emotions at the same time that they are experienced as forces that exert force onto experience, when we are "done by" them. Katz elaborates: "Our emotions are dialectical in nature, something we artfully produce and yet experience as forces that take us over independent of our will, because what we are reaching for through our emotion are sensual resources that operate as a foundation of our conduct only when they remain outside the foreground of our self-awareness."[28] Citing Freud, Katz writes that the correspondence between the two levels may hit a "double resonance" as the subject "attends both to the immediate situation and orients to transcendent dimensions of the moment's experience." He concludes that this alignment of dimensions within a situation is an experiential state: "The feeling, the sensuous reality of emotions, *is* this double resonance."[29] Such a "resonance" may be the religious recognition of competence, beauty, efficacy, orthopraxy, and experienced truth within religious systems.

Katz describes this dialectical experience of emotions in terms of their containment within a given social world, always apprehended by individual social actors. He writes: "Emotions do not *introduce* feelings and themes of transcendence into social action, they highlight them. . . . In a way, the understanding that emotions are in tension with reason, self-reflection, or thought exactly misrepresents what emotions are. Emotions are ways of turning back on the self, ways of reflexively amplifying and giving added resonance to the transcendent meanings of situated action."[30] As he explains it, affective "transcendence" is a kind of deepening of emotion already felt. Such expansive emotions are as social as the systems and interactions that propagate them and as personal as the projects to take them on as pious goals and standards. They are felt as evaluations, such as "beauty" or the "sense" of orthopraxy, in ways that may be stipulated and anticipated and also in ways that may never have been expected.

The alignment of two levels of ritual and emotion, transcendent and situational (as described by Katz), and their coalescence through practice and competence, is achieved and recognized through affective modes. People expect ritual to be complete, well-defined, and "closed," both in terms of a particular performance as well as with respect to long-term repeated practice. It is not only the case that they come to have a better "understanding" of the ritual "archetype" through engagement over time, but they perpetually confront the famous difference between ideal religious "map" and lived ritual "territory" through dynamics of repeated practice. The insights of Humphrey and Laidlaw and Williams and Boyd on ritual repetition show a two-tier model of actors discovering or applying "horizons" or "archetypes" in projects of progressive engagement. At the intermediate level of situational possibilities, learners' activity mediates the expectations of actual achievement and the possibilities of idealized practice, especially through emotion.

Recognizing that religious practice is engaged through recurrent, cumulative practice provides a way to explain why people keep performing rituals in general as well as an escalating engagement with the recited Qur'ān in Indonesia in specific. Dynamics of repeated action are potentially generative and potentially self-sustaining. Fixed parameters analogous to those of "curriculum" mark stages for self-understanding with respect to continuous processes of ritual activity. Just as in any other kind of learning, practitioners will tend to break down the process into available or attainable constituent parts. These represent not only stages of progressive competence but also measures of self. Qur'ānic reading changes subtly, gradually, but profoundly for the practitioner as he or she learns to practice it better and, as some Indonesian Muslims said, "to understand." The key to understanding the "impulsion" to increased engagement with ritual, to use Dewey's language, is to understand the progressive and developmental stages of overcoming the "obstacles" or achieving intermediate goals. In Qur'ānic Indonesia, the perception of recitational ideals was changing rapidly with the reception of the virtuosic possibilities of the Egyptian performance system. These ideals were then rendered by Indonesians into attainable qualities such as "style." The pedagogies that related ideals to realities had as their immediate goals expansive and affective ideals, rendering emotion as curriculum for performance as well as for the recognition of how to do it right. People were seeking out this feeling of competence and orthopraxy in order to inspire themselves and to inspire others in turn.

Orthoprax Musical Aesthetics

The internalization of concepts such as "*i'jāz*" may reference all aspects of Qur'ānic practice with respect to a vanishing point of perfect orthopraxy. The uniquely reflexive aspects of the recited Qur'ān underscore this tendency. For example, the Qur'ān offers prescriptions for its recitation even as it is recited (such as 75 al-Qiyāmah 16–19) as well as description of its immediate emotional impact (such as the visceral responses portrayed in 19 Maryam 58 and 39 al-Zumar 23). Statements attributed to the Prophet attest to the religious obligation to recite the Qur'ān aesthetically. These also function as prescriptions when the Qur'ān is read. Many "rules" for the recited Qur'ān in the most authoritative sources (*sunnah* and the recited Qur'ān itself) relate to aesthetic and improvisatory ideals. In addition, Muslim systems of Southern Asia have long developed the theory and practice of moralized aesthetics. The question for many pious practitioners of the recited Qur'ān in Indonesia in the 1990s became, how does one feel and improvise correctly?

Orthopraxy is a mode of evaluation based on shared norms, which may also be experienced as a feeling-state. The sense of Qur'ānic orthopraxy in Indonesia in this period included three components. First, there were ontological understandings about the Qur'ān, its language, and even "musical" properties as representing perfect and inimitable qualities of revelation. The system of associated ritual rules (which encompass fluidity, choice, "music," aesthetics, and affect) was often perceived to be normatively fixed and set, no matter how flexible these actual components of performance might be. Second, self-conscious evaluations of competence and ability that were emergent in ongoing practice included assessments of whether one has it "right," thereby relating orthopraxy to practice in real contexts of learning and performance. Third, there was a situational feeling of the personal "sense" of having it right in a given moment, an affective quality that was an inspiration for individuals to continue their projects of study. When the expectations of performance were for affect and aesthetics on the level of virtuosity, the intensity of projects to achieve these standards escalated, as did the effort to develop realistic and realizable pedagogical programs and frameworks.

Properties of the Qur'ān—theologically transcendent but always immanent when rendered in human voice—produce the expectation that there is a "right" way to recite with respect to affective qualities of performance. Most basic to this idea, and the evaluations it generates, are the Qur'ān's self-referential statements about its nature, its proper recitation, and ideal responses to its engagement. These combine with other authoritative aspects of tradition, such as *sunnah* (the practices of the first Muslims and more precisely the exemplary model of the Prophet) *ādāb* (also based on historical precedent), and especially *i'jāz*. Religious tradition, particularly the aspects influenced by esoteric piety (Sufism), further enhance the anticipation of a personal and immediate experience in accord with these norms. These authoritative sources propagate expectations in the lived present of a perfect, complete, and unique system of recitation. The processes by which pious Muslims attempt to learn and to apply such idealized formulations as in Indonesia in the 1990s led to an amplification of norms of orthopraxy as well as the energy to realize them.

Beauty, improvisation, and affect are all stipulated as necessary components of orthoprax vocalization; they could be seen to be legal requirements, as Kristina Nelson's survey of the literature suggests. For example, beauty is prescribed as an aspect of orthoprax vocalization, as conveyed by a *ḥadīth* account, "Beautify *(ḥassinū, zayyinū)* the Qur'ān with your voices." The Prophet himself is documented in numerous accounts to have been gifted with a beautiful voice and also to have appreciated the beautiful recitations of others. *Ḥadīth* reports such as "He is not one of us who does not sing *(taghannī)* the Qur'ān" and "God does not listen to anything as He listens to a Prophet sing *(taghannā bi)* the Qur'ān" are critical for those who develop the technical artistry of *mujawwad* recitation, as Nelson shows.[31] The more sophisticated the style of recitation, the more this kind of material is emphasized in theory as well as in practice. This information is also sufficient to carry the impact of injunction for pious Muslims who feel it is incumbent on them to emulate the practice of the Prophet in every possible respect. It is a basis for the pious development of melodic systems for reciting the Qur'ān. But how, asked pious Indonesians in the 1990s, is the required ideal of beauty for the recited Qur'ān to be achieved exactly, especially when the authoritative prescriptions in the Qur'ān and *sunnah* seem to emphasize fluid dimensions of performance such as improvisation and emotion?

In academic treatments of melodic practices in Islamic contexts, usually highlighted is the question of the legal "permissibility" of "musical" *(mūsīqī)* elements. Although Indonesians encountered many questions and challenges related to melodic structures and Qur'ān recitation in the 1990s, no one was ever heard expressing disapproval of "beautifying" the Qur'ān with voice. Furthermore, Muslims recognize that recitation of the Qur'ān, in conformity with *tajwīd*, will always have "melodic" qualities, since the voice of the reciter carries rhythm and (undetermined) pitch qualities that *tajwīd* establishes. In the Islamic tradition, legal scholars (with some exceptions, often Ḥanbalīs) have not articulated prohibitions against music per se. Instead, the debates among *'ulamā'* (religious scholars) have been concerned with the contexts, intentions, and experiences associated with practices of musical arts. When addressing the topic of the status of music in Islam, scholars such as Al-Faruqi, Nasr, and others explain that a conceptual hierarchy of practice places Qur'ān recitation at the apex and orients musical systems to a religiously appropriate ideal.[32]

One way that the concern over melody in Qur'ān recitation has been expressed historically is through what Kristina Nelson has termed the recitational "*samā'* polemic," which, like controversies in Islam over the practice of aesthetic "audition" *(samā')* more widely, highlights a tension between the cultivation of experiential perceptions related to "listening" *(samā')* on the one hand and the ideal of the absolute separation of transcendent revelation and human components on the other.[33] Qur'ānic and non-Qur'ānic *samā'*, like *dhikr,* is part of the array of Sufi spiritual obervances, and, like practices of *dhikr,* it has been a source of controversy. Many Sufi writings treat the idea and practice of *samā'*, often offering apologetic views regarding its origin in the *sunnah* of the Prophet or the benefits of the practice if observed in moderation. The theological resolution of this question for many with respect to the recited Qur'ān (such as al-Ghazzālī in Book 8 of the *Iḥyā' 'Ulūm al-Dīn*) has been to remove human agency from the conceptualization of Qur'ānic encounter. A practical and metapractical strategy identifies the affecting presence of the recited Qur'ān with the Qur'ān itself, effectively erasing the agency of human technical artistry. Subsequently, in practice, the reciter is to strive to diminish the aspects of performance that are not pure amplifications of the manifestation of an idealized presence. When this theory connects to practice, well-defined techniques of feeling and embodiment (like those of *dhikr*) may be applied specifically in order to manipulate feeling and experience in the service of this ideal.

According to Islamic tradition, "melodic" aspects of Qur'ān recitation may not be fixed in any one performance or in an overall system, so that God's Speech in the form of the revealed Qur'ān is not associated with human technical artistry. Improvisation is thus a legal requirement. Nevertheless, in Indonesia shared aesthetic frameworks, curricula for learning, as well as pious individuals' natural assessment of the "orthopraxy" of their own performances required norms of stylization. Such norms and standards for pedagogy and practice were not controversial in Indonesia in the 1990s; in fact, they were actively developed, promoted, and sought out by practitioners. The compelling pull to increased sophistication in styles was understood to represent a desirable and positive engagement with the Qur'ān. As the framework of competitions demonstrates, the process was seen to inspire others to accept the Qur'ān more intimately as well, either through appreciation of the beauty of others' performances or through personal engagement in an attempt to reproduce them.

Just as the controversy over music in Islam is not always a problem with the idea of music per se, but more often a concern over effects and intentions of "audition" *(samā')*, similarly, what was contested in Indonesia in the 1990s about melodic Qur'ān recitation was not "curriculum" or its fixity, but instead the piety and intention of the modes by which learning and practice of the recited Qur'ān were carried out. Although there was discussion of what kinds of *lagu* were permissible, the problem with which the recitation stars in Jakarta as well as the practitioners back at home were acutely concerned was not the status of music in Islam. Instead, religious tensions and ambiguities pertained to the experiential dimensions of practice, for example, how to understand questions such as "talent" or "mistake" when the model for ordinary practice was increasingly becoming that of the virtuoso. Persons who responded to new standards of "beautiful" Qur'ān recitation in Indonesia in the 1990s faced opportunities and challenges such as adapting long-standing practices, feelings, and perceptions to new evaluations within a system of ritual affect that was rapidly undergoing change.

Some aspects of the affective and performative system of the Indonesian recited Qur'ān do not change over time: for example, the Qur'ān, its claim of universal affecting experience, and the structure and style that comprises rhythms and cadences to be carried by the human voice. There are also, however, norms of Qur'ānic experience that have varied with social and historical conditions (for example, musical systems and patterned emotional responses such as weeping). Some norms of beauty, melodic practice, and emotion are thus fixed within the system of the recited Qur'ān (such as the case of "rules" contained reflexively within the Qur'ān itself), while other aspects are particularized over time and space (such as melodic practices as well as the specific application of general "feeling-rules" within social contexts). The lived realities of such cultural, affective, and musical systems evidence diachronic diversity (while, ideally, the ideals do not).

Apart from the influence of the competition system, the adoption of "Arabic" (and, more specifically, "Misri," or Egyptian) melodic modes was supported in Indonesia by the perception that they are more normatively "Qur'ānic" than others. New kinds of theorization accompanied the reception of the Arabic *lagu*, which were increasingly an aspect of orthopraxy in the recited Qur'ān in Indonesia in the 1990s. Partially because of the popularity of contests and in part also owing to the acceptance of the Egyptian-inspired model as ideal, competence in these seven musical modes had become the goal of intermediate and advanced-level recitational training in modern Indonesia.

The system of "Qur'ānic" *lagu* that was becoming widespread in the 1990s had developed over centuries from multiple and transregional branches of influence that converged to form the Indonesian system. It is difficult to demonstrate any of these branches to be a continuous line extending from the early Muslim Community (little historical data are available on the musical practices of the Arabs before the third Islamic century). The source *Kitāb al-Aghāni* (Book of Songs) by Abū al-Faraj al-Isfahānī, for example, dates back only to the tenth century. It is documented that practices of Qur'ān recitation developed into something resembling the *mujawwad* style around that time in the 'Abbāsid period, when reciters began to deploy the emerging modal system of art music (*maqām*, pl. *maqāmāt*). *Maqām* developed as a theory and a practice of music by way of a synthesis of Arabic and Persian forms. Intellectuals in this period analyzed the system, as in the writings of the great philosophers al-Farābī (d. 950) and Ibn Sīnā (d. 1037), and especially al-Kindī (d. 870), whose treatise on music was foundational. The system also received more esoteric formulations within cosmological frameworks (as in the thought of the Ikhwān al-Ṣafā' school, studied by Sayyid Hossein Nasr). Analyzed along with rhythmic cycles and developing concepts like the Greek idea of scale, mode was pictured in terms of the fretting board of the lute instrument, the *'ūd*.[34]

Diversity and flexibility characterize the Arabic modal system both diachronically and synchronically. The treatises of Ṣafī al-Dīn (d. 1294) formulated an analytical framework for the system that was followed for centuries, deploying musical characteristics in the identification of mode, such as initial and final pitch as well as, in some cases, melody types. As Philip Bohlman writes, however, not only are modes applied flexibly in practice, but the overall musical system itself is historically and geographically fluid, and thus difficult to formalize or classify in categorical terms. In the early nineteenth century, another system for analyzing scale (based on quarter-tones) became widespread in the Middle East, and its details were debated at the historic Cairo Congress on Arab Music in 1932. At this conference, the attempt was also made to codify all of the *maqāmāt* being used in Arab countries at the time. This effort, however, along with subsequent ones, faced the conceptual challenge of systematizing the diversity of the entire musical system as well as the technical problems of notation and standardization.[35] Studies of the use of modal systems in Qur'ān recitation specifically, in the Arabic-speaking world as well as Indonesia, also reflect diversity.[36]

The system of *mujawwad*-style Qur'ān recitation that developed in Indonesia in the 1990s was based on styles from Egypt, a pattern also found throughout the Islamic world. Contemporary Indonesian and Malaysian sources on recitation practice tersely group all of the Arab-derived *maqāmāt (lagu)* used in Qur'ān recitation into two principal types: "Misri" and "Makawi." *Misri lagu* are the *maqāmāt* that were introduced in the 1960s and after, denoting modes that were known and used in Egypt (Miṣr), whereas *Makawi lagu* are understood to comprise an older system from the Middle East, reportedly deriving from the recitational practices of Indonesian Hajjis and students who traveled to the Arabian peninsula (and Mecca, hence the term "Makawi") earlier in the century and before. In Indonesia, there have in fact been long-standing practices of reciting the Qur'ān with what were known as "*lagu Makawi*," understood to extend from the Middle East (primarily the Arabian peninsula, and specifically the Yemeni Hadramaut and the Holy Cities of the Hijaz); there were also indigenous Southeast Asian "*lagu daerah*" (local *lagu*).[37]

In Indonesia in the 1980s and 1990s, the older styles ("*lagu Makawi*" and local *lagu daerah)* were being replaced by a newly formalized system based on seven *lagu* that drew on the practices of great Egyptian reciters in the middle and later part of the century, and ultimately the classical system of Arabic musical modes *(lagu Misri)*. These seven standard *lagu* are named *bayati*, *soba*, *sika*, *hijaz*, *rast*, *jiharka*, and *nahawand*. While "melody" may not be fixed in recitation, trained Indonesian *qāri*'s did apply these melodic modes or melody types along with frameworks for structured modulation. In Indonesian Qur'ān recitation contests, proficiency in these well-ordered modal progressions as well as variations (*variasi*, improvisational patterns) within each of the seven competition *lagu* were fundamental judging criteria. In Indonesia, progressions of named modes were customarily composed in a loose arrangement *(aturan* or *susunan lagu)*. Reference was not made to instrumentation or other aspects of Arabic classical music (except the cassette recordings of vocal performances), even at the most advanced levels. Few teachers outside of special institutes in Jakarta (such as the Qur'ān colleges, IIQ, PTIQ, and special programs at the LBIQ) were aware of *Misri lagu* other than the seven standard modes.

Their reception, conceptualization, and application demonstrated a distinctively Southeast Asian pattern.

The seven *lagu* were becoming generally understood to be the proper, orthoprax modes for melodic recitation and were occasionally popularly conflated with the idea of the "seven readings," the basis of the idea of variant *qirā'āt*, which has nothing to do with pitch variation in the classical Qur'ānic sciences.[38] A phrase often heard in Indonesia regarding the system of Arabic *maqām* (musical "modes") in general and the seven melody types in specific was that they were "revealed in Arabia" *(turun* [or *diturunkan*] *di Arabia).* This phrase uses the same verb, "*turun*," that describes the event of the revelation of the Qur'ān (usually conjugated in Indonesian in the passive voice, "sent down," reflecting the transitive sense of the Arabic verb "*ānzala*"). Discussing this idea in connection to Arabic *maqām*, K. H. M. Sayyid Abdullah, the undisputed authority on recitation in Indonesia, mentioned an "excursus" *(maqalah)* called "The Qur'ān was revealed in Saudi Arabia (printed in Istanbul, and its recitation comes from Egypt)." Intrigued especially by this play on an old expression (Islamic books are elsewhere said to have been written in Arabia, printed in Cairo, and read in Baghdad), I asked whether I might ever find this "title" somewhere in print, in Indonesian or Arabic; this "*maqalah*" was said to be oral.

The boundary of orthopraxy in popular perception had surpassed (or, for many listeners, probably bypassed) a general conception of "Arabic *lagu*" in order to denote specifically the seven *lagu* standardized in Indonesia. For nonspecialists, such as the many thousands who have listened to a popular cassette series over a span of almost two decades, these seven melodic modes were often piously attributed to the original practice of the Prophet Muḥammad. "Arabic" *lagu* had become the high-water mark of orthopraxy in Indonesian recitation. In addition, Indonesian attitudes toward these "Arabic" aspects of the recited Qur'ān were being transformed in the 1990s with adoption of the seven "Egyptian *lagu*." The combination of Qur'ānic universality and regional particularity necessitated new kinds of musical and religious theorization along with the reception of Egyptian styles in Southeast Asia.

For the average Indonesian student of melodic recitation, the basic resource to study in order to apprehend the system of *lagu* for the recited Qur'ān was the recorded instruction of H. Muammar Z.A., whose series of eight cassette tapes, *Kunci Sukses M.T.Q.* (The Keys to Success in the MTQ), was immensely popular and influential. H. Muammar, a national champion reciter, was renowned internationally for his breath capacity (the longest in the world, it was said). H. Muammar Z.A.'s recitation was also heard in broadcast from minarets before daily prayer times. His instructional tapes were available in almost every cassette shop in Indonesia, whether Muslim-oriented or nonreligious. Since these were the only instructional recitation tapes distributed in most areas, and since this had been the case for almost twenty years, their impact was enormous by the mid-1990s. The first three tapes of the series introduce the basic *lagu* through "*tawshih*" (set learning pieces) that were first brought to Indonesia and Malaysia by Arab reciters in around the 1970s. Muammar teaches by alternating between the *tawshih* and progressive application of their melodic movements to a reading from the Qur'ān (so that, at the end of the third cassette in the series, the student has studied all of the *tawshih* as well as a set reading with modal progressions that may then be transferred to another reading from the Qur'ān). The additional five tapes develop further the idea of improvisational "*variasi*," answer questions, and coach on the psychological aspects of competing. H. Muammar was also featured on his own television show to teach recitation in 1996–1997, reproducing the same readings and melodic progressions heard on the instructional tapes.

On one of the instructional tapes the question is asked, "Do our *lahjah* [from Ar. "dialect," here denoting something like "accent" in Indonesian], style, and *lagu* have to be the same as those of Arabs? We are rich in *lagu*; can't we just use our own?" H. Muammar's answer begins with the standard phrase "The Qur'ān was revealed in Saudi Arabia." He then explains that the "*huruf hijaiyah*" (an old expression for the Arabic alphabet: "Hajji letters") are not "Arabic" letters ("Arabic" here inferring the spoken language in usage) when they are in the Qur'ān. Rather, they are "Bahasa al-Quran" (The Language of the Qur'ān), which is read in a special way, with the Qur'ān's special rules (meaning *tajwīd*). With this statement, H. Muammar implies a correspondence between the letters on the pages of the Qur'ān and the Arabic *lagu* he teaches, while at the same time he has distinguished the sacred "Qur'ānic language" from the natural language Arabic. Demonstrating how the Qur'ān changes even the names of the Arabic letters themselves when they are recited in the Qur'ān, H. Muammar provides examples of the extended vowel duration *(madd)* on "Yā Sīn," "Ḥā Mīm," and other combinations of named, paired letters (known as *muqaṭṭa'āt*) that open some *sūrahs* of the Qur'ān.

Second, still answering the question, H. Muammar cites the deployment of "Arabic" *lagu* as a legal requirement (as *sunnah*, derived not only by the Prophet's practice but also by his explicit stipulation). He reminds listeners of reports that the Prophet commanded Muslims to recite not only with beautiful *lagu* but with Arabic "melodies" (*laḥnu Arab*, using an Arabic term for "melody"). Third, he appeals to universalized aesthetic sensibilities, adding that to listen to anything other than Arabic *lagu* is simply "unpleasant" *(nggak enak)*. For example, he continues, there are regional *lagu (lagu daerah)* from

Sunda (West Java, his home province) that he says he knows well, but they are odd or "funny-sounding" *(lucu)*. He demonstrates after excusing himself first, immediately adding that his *tajwīd* was fine, but the *lagu* sounded like it was "playing around" *(kayaknya main-main)*; he points out that it did not resemble anything "Arabic" at all.

H. Muammar concludes his discussion by restating the key point that "the Qur'ān was revealed in Saudi Arabia," and so it must be given Arabic *lagu*, and to do anything else is aberrant or just "weird" *(ganjil)*.[39] On the one hand, the general public had come to escalate orthopraxy by restricting perceived "Qur'ānic" *lagu* to be the seven modes approved by the LPTQ for contests, replacing a less limited notion that the use of *tajwīd* alone is the marker between sacred and secular. On the other hand, among serious Indonesian students of melodic recitation, in practice anything "Arab" was unproblematically potentially Qur'ānic.[40] Indonesians were aware, as Muslims have been throughout the history of Islam, that the melodic principles applied in recitation show similarities to other musical structures, including popular music. I was once asked by a recitation coach whether I happened to know which came first, "pop" *lagu* ("*lagu*" is the word for a "song" more generally) or the Qur'ānic *lagu*. (He then answered his own question, surmising that all *lagu* must have come from the Prophet himself.) The question was actually a variant of one that was also asked early in Islamic history and in the development of melodic aspects of recitation, especially in connection with the high art music of the 'Abbāsid era.[41] In Indonesian context, some applications of "*lagu*" were known by experts from cassette tapes and were understood to relate to Egyptian popular music.[42]

Among advanced students, identification of "Arabic" and "Qur'ānic" blurred as an effect of teaching strategies that were borrowed from the Egyptian reciters themselves. Just as Indonesian children were often taught Arabic songs before learning to recite the Qur'ān in order to accustom them to vocalizing the sounds of Arabic, advanced reciters would study performances from the Arab world so that they could hone their skills in melodic practice. Top reciters (and also any who listened to H. Muammar's tapes) were encouraged to practice *variasi* that had been heard in *qasida* recordings, applying them to the (non-Qur'ānic) phrase "*ya lail.*" "*Layālī*" is a term for an improvisational vocal performance on the Arabic "*yā lailī, yā 'aynī*" (O my night, o my eye). Indonesian reciters practiced *ya lails* in order to improve breath capacity, since the vowels may be extended without the limitations of *tajwīd*. They would also apply the *variasi* heard on cassettes of Arab music directly to *āyahs* of the Qur'ān.

Nelson documents use of *qaṣīdah* for study of melodic components of recitation among professional reciters in Cairo, while in Indonesia in the 1990s reciters at all levels were instructed to listen avidly to these non-Qur'ānic performances in order to improve their *mujawwad* Qur'ān recitation.[43] The singing of the great women vocalists from the Arab world, such as Fairouz, Warda, and above all Umm Kulthūm (as well as men like 'Abd al-Wahhāb) were thus used as *kurikulum* on the same level as the recorded Qur'ānic performances of Arab *shaikhs*.[44] In a coaching session, one prominent national coach remarked that his "effort" *(ijtihad)* was to get the women in the group to recite in the style of Warda—suggesting what a shame it was that there were no Egyptian women reciters for them to listen to. Subtle ironies about gendered voices were not lost on this coach. He pointed out more than once that the great (male) reciters (in Egypt) derived some of their best styles from women singers; now, in Indonesia, the women must get away from just listening to the (male) reciters and get back to listening to women, he said.

As the standard for melodic reading of the Qur'ān in the *mujawwad* style increasingly became an orthoprax "Arabic" system in the period between the 1960s and the 1990s, the styles of Egyptian performers also became the *kurikulum* for ordinary Indonesian practice. Musical practices associated with these styles became invested with a prescriptive and even ontological reality in Indonesia. They became situational ideals that practitioners sought to attain and that they used to measure the development of competence as well as religious piety. The orthoprax "teaching curriculum" of "Arabic" *lagu* was rendered in terms of a "learning curriculum" of personalized "styles" derived from Egypt. From the "learner's point of view" within pious efforts to "get it right," Qur'ānic ideals became expansive and compelling to Indonesian reciters developing competence through a process of internalizing a received aesthetic and affective system.

These conditions developed under two key influences: paradigms of performance derived from Egypt and a process of pedagogical formalization that developed at home. Enthusiastic students seeking to adopt the styles of world-famous *qāri's* enhanced their ability to recite melodically by studying with teachers and by listening to recordings. Changing social and emotional systems that advanced these styles to the level of "orthopraxy" interacted with structures of religious piety, effectively making the personal realization of "situational ideals" in reciting the Qur'ān a process of escalating practice.

Specifying Style to Personalize Performance

Performance was curriculum in Qur'ānic Indonesia, where all forms of recitation practice were potentially participatory. In the 1990s, styles of Qur'ān recitation that were elsewhere in the Islamic world the restricted domain of persons with heightened ability and special training were coming to be viewed in Indonesia as available to all Muslims. The performer-audience model, in which a skilled reader induces heightened emotional states in listeners, was not operative in Indonesia in the same way that it was in Egypt, for example. In Indonesia, particularly under the influence of the competition system, skilled performances were likely to be understood to affect listeners in terms of their own long-term proclivities to emulate those very performances. Despite the unambiguous recognition that human technical artistry is not a part of revelation (coupled with the obvious cultural specificity of musical practice), in Indonesia a particular musical system had in fact come to be seen as authoritatively "Qur'ānic." Named Egyptian "styles" were developed in Indonesia as *gayas* (styles) to be modeled in learning and performance, rendering aspects of virtuosic "orthopraxy" personal and apparently attainable. Because these pedagogical structures reference an "ideal recitation," however, learning became for many ordinary practitioners an escalating project of religious engagement.

A combination of "orthoprax" expectations and the availability of contingent, situational ideals delivered motivational force to some long-term projects in the practice of religious piety. In the case of the recited Qur'ān, many norms of performance that may at first appear to be fixed are in actuality quite fluid: most "stipulated" rules for sectioning comprise a system of "preferences," for example, and melodic structures are required to be improvised. Because of the tension between this flexibility and the pious desire to affirm that one has "gotten it right" (based on the conviction there must be a "right way"), "orthoprax" criteria for learning and evaluation were actively pursued and energetically deployed. This process inspired pious projects to attempt to realize Qur'ānic perfection in open-ended improvisational, affective, and aesthetic practice. The pedagogical model of *mujawwad* performance in Indonesia in the 1990s was based on musical practices and performance "styles" derived from Egypt that had become the accepted standard of "melodic" recitation in Indonesia through several lines of influence.

The standard melodic modes (*bayati*, *rast*, *soba*, *hijaz*, *sika*, *jiharka*, and *nahawand*) were formalized by the pedagogical practices brought by the Egyptian reciters in their visits to Indonesia, especially in the 1960s and 1970s.[45] The LPTQ made these seven modes official for competition in 1977; it seems that this was when the schematization of the *lagu* according to their internal "levels" was put in place in Indonesia as well (Ind. *tingkat*, or registers, are a standard aspect of Arabic music theory and practice). The modes became widespread in Indonesia in the 1960s and 1970s through two principal developments. The first took the form of a series of reciters and teachers brought from Egypt to Indonesia to perform and to conduct classes, with the cooperation of the Egyptian Ministry of Religious Endowments. The *qāri*'s included the most famous reciters of the day, such as Sh. 'Abd al-Bāsiṭ 'Abd al-Ṣamad (whose performance in Makassar was so beautiful, said an eyewitness, it is known that somebody in the audience dropped dead on the spot).[46] The Egyptian *qāri*'s had their time divided among the various provinces during the month of Ramadan over a period of approximately twenty years. Most of the visits to South Sulawesi occurred in the 1970s, although Egyptian *qāri*'s continued to teach students at Mesjid Raya in the 1980s and early 1990s. It was reported during fieldwork, with heavy disappointment, that the last came to Makassar in approximately 1993 and that none had come since.

The second, related, impact of Egyptian recitation styles came by way of broadcast, especially programs that were relayed from Saudi Arabia via short-wave radio. Listening to these broadcasts (sneaking into the kitchen in the middle of the night to listen, as in one champion reciter's story), taping them, scrutinizing the recordings again and again became a national phenomenon among aspiring reciters. This, along with cassette traffic in the recordings of final rounds of Indonesian regional and national competitions, gave readers from remote areas the materials they needed to become national, even international, champions. K. H. M. Sayyid Abdullah joked that the voices of Indonesian reciters who listened to the radio in this period had even picked up the sound of the distortion from the short-wave broadcasts. In addition, with the melody types, ornamentation, and modal modulations of reciters on Arab sound recordings rapidly memorized, the *variasi* of these Qur'ānic performances captured on tape were then reproduced from memory by recitation teachers for advanced students, often evidencing an amazing musical memory in the process.

A typical question from a visiting national coach before he demonstrated was, for example: "Does anyone here know this *variasi* from Muṣṭafā Ismā'īl's recording of [Sūrah] al-Qaṣaṣ?"[47] An improvised melodic line from a cassette recording was here presumed to be memorized already, showing an expectation of musical memory analogous to photographic memory of a sentence on a page of text. At a five-day official meeting of the recitation contest judges of South Sulawesi, a reciter and coach who was a representative from the provincial LPTQ spoke at great length about the necessity of acquiring the most up-to-date recordings from Egypt: "Our *motivasi* is from Misir [Egypt]," he said, echoing the slogan of a premier national coach telling aspiring reciters always to "live with cassettes!" At the time of fieldwork, while techniques to introduce the *lagu* and their arrangements were becoming more widespread, for the most part students were still expected to familiarize themselves with variants of the modes through continual listening, especially at the advanced levels. Few teachers outside of special Qur'ān colleges taught *lagu* other than the seven standard, named *lagu*, however.

The reception and conceptualization of *maqāmāt* developed in a distinctively Southeast Asian pattern. When the Egyptian styles of Qur'ān recitation began to have influence in Indonesia, there was not a framework of Arabic art music in place to provide contextual continuity for their musical aspects. For example, H. Burhanuddin, an international champion from South Sulawesi, stated that before the official systematization *(aturan)* of *lagu* in 1977, his teacher taught simply by giving (unnamed) examples. Back then, he said, people "knew" *(tahu)* the *lagu* but did not have "knowledge" *(ilmu)* of them yet. Competitions disseminated a wider variety of *lagu*, but, according to him, even in the early years few knew their names. A retiree of the provincial Ministry of Religious Affairs, not a trained reciter, gave the impression that there had been a great breadth in melodic recitation styles before the 1970s ("No one really knew what notes to hit after the Basmalah [opening formula]," he said, implying a diversity of styles); he also reported that some of the names of *lagu* were in use at that time, although the actual "melodies" varied a great deal, and he said that they did not much resemble the *lagu* that were heard used with the same names in the mid-1990s. The issue of basic recognition of the standard *maqāmāt* and their improvisational *variasi* posed a challenge for many, including contest judges.

Working from a framework other than Arabic art music and theory, the identification of the recently introduced *maqāmāt* posed difficulties for Indonesians without prior experience in hearing them. These modes can be difficult even for those with some training if all the listener has studied are the set "*tawshih*" learning pieces. In improvised forms, the modes may be unrecognizable; this may emerge as a problem especially in contest judging. One teacher who initially learned autodidactically by listening to radio broadcasts (and went on to become an international champion reciter and an expert in melodic practices) could explain the perception of *lagu* at the transition point of familiarity. When asked about the problem of recognition ("How would someone know it was '*lagu hijaz*,' if he or she heard it?"), he explained that the *lagu* could be distinguished best by their "sound quality" (*bunyi*, selecting this term over possibilities such as "*nada*" [melodic pattern], "*gaya*" [style], and "*irama*" [rhythmic features]). He demonstrated an interval on two pitches, announcing, "You can already tell it's *hijaz*" (he also gave an example of a give-away interval for *soba*). (*Hijaz* is one of the more easily recognizable modes for the nonexpert, precisely because of its chromatic pitch intervals.) Asked whether it was actually pitch interval that he meant by "sound quality," he answered no, that would not always be reliable, because adding notes as *variasi* may alter the intervals of the basic pitch class. As if implying that each mode had its own special "tricks," he explained that he really meant that one had to listen for kinds of "sound" unique to each *lagu*. For example, he explained, there is a characteristic clippedness at the ends of *āyahs* with *madd ṭabi'ī* in *lagu soba*.

The *kurikulum* for acquiring advanced competence in *lagu* was actually a "style" *(gaya)*, specifically the "styles" of named Arab performers, mediated by pedagogy as well as the standards developed for competitions.[48] Teaching strategies based on competition standards and "styles" of famous reciters mediated the reception of the Egptian-derived system of melodic recitation. It cannot be overemphasized, however, that Egyptian "style" was a uniquely Indonesian perception; for example, the modulation requirements for competition (i.e., a fixed number of recognized *lagu* demonstrated within a set time) gave rise to a distinctive Indonesian structure. One international champion opened a coaching session with the statement, "We don't want *ḥaflah* recitation here, but what we want is recitation done in Egyptian style *(gaya)*," implying that the goal was not to produce free-form performances of long duration (as performed in the Arab world) but instead to apply aspects of Egyptian recitational technique within the framework already standard in Indonesia. The distinction was implicit when another international champion suggested that what Arabs liked so much about listening to Indonesian recitation (in addition to verification of the global universality of Islam) was the "well-orderedness" of the recitation *(susunan lagu)*. "Egyptian style" was the received norm, but it was modified in Indonesian context as an aspect of pedagogy. Actual performances were curriculum as "style" was standardized and personalized, rendering it a "situational ideal" emergent in learning processes. At advanced levels, the teaching materials for *lagu* took the form of recordings from Cairo, and terminology would at times be almost entirely references to the names of Egyptian reciters (some of whom may have been heard by students and many possibly not).

The single most influential Egyptian reciter at the time of research was Sh. Muṣṭafā Ismā'īl, but everyone had his or her own favorite.[49] Cassettes of Egyptian recitation were difficult for many Indonesian *qāri*'s to come by during the time of fieldwork. One national coach cautioned his advanced students to be very careful lending them to friends, and students would sometimes compare how many *biji* (units) of cassettes they had (usually it was only two or three, at the very most). Many students had none, but advanced pedagogy using the names of *shaikhs* from Cairo as terminology was nevertheless effective. Reciters from South Sulawesi would obtain the recordings when they went on Hajj or would ask a friend going to the Middle East to bring back recordings.

At Qur'ān training institutes (such as IIQ and PTIQ in Jakarta and STAI "Al-Furqān" in Makassar), students were customarily given tapes of Egyptian reciters that were perceived to correspond to their own emerging proclivities or tendencies (most basically, whether the voice was determined to be "high" or "low"). In one remarkable training session, K. H. M. Sayyid Abdullah helped a student to break down his personal style into constitutive components through interview and analysis: his makeup was found to be 60 percent "al-Bahtimī" and 40 percent "Muṣṭafā Ismā'īl," and the student was directed to continue to study the performances of each Egyptian *qāri'* according to that exact ratio. Even when teaching at a corporate training, a master coach would use the names of Egyptian reciters to characterize certain styles as well as to provide examples of *variasi* (cited from memory from recordings) that the students might want to try out in their upcoming contest.

Adopting a "style" was not a direct reception or imitation. Ideals were mediated through learning regimens that rendered the model personal. The system also highlighted aesthetic discipline and boundaries; these were the limits of control within the learning process that afforded potential achievement. H. Burhanuddin began an explanation of the use of cassettes in recitation teaching with the following statement: "Students can add one recording to another *(menggabungkan antara kaset dengan kaset yang lain)*. They can make up a new *variasi* by putting together what they hear, so they come up with a style that seems new, from the *kombinasi* of [what they have heard on] cassettes." When cassettes from Egypt provided material for constructing one's personal style, the limits set on this activity were not the boundaries of permissible expression but the danger that a performer could separate himself or herself from the watchful authority of a teacher. This guidance grounded the emulation of an expansive ideal in a personal relationship and disciplined regime.

H. Burhanuddin, for example, affirmed that the process of using recorded materials as the basis for innovation was "more *kreatif*" for aspiring reciters. Immediately, however, he added words of caution. Every student needs to be guided, and each student must be prepared before beginning to work with cassettes in this way. In his words: "Really, cassettes help a lot. It helps very much to have lots of cassettes, to collect them, it really does. But you also have to be careful. Sometimes the ear is only half as good as it hears, and you can't be sure whether you're making a mistake or not *(kadang-kadang kita ini telinga itu hanya setengah sepintar semendengar, kita tidak tahu persis kalau apa ada kesalahan atau apa)*." One champion narrated that he had first studied seriously with cassettes and by listening to broadcasts, but then when it came time to work with a teacher *(guru)*, he found out that there were many things about recitation that he did not know (most, presumably, related to advanced *tajwīd*), and aspects of his reading proved to be "shaky" *(tidak pas)*. At times, the knowledge of *lagu* was treated as analogous to esoteric knowledge, as when some stressed the necessity for students to start out slowly and carefully in order that beginners would not become overwhelmed and dangerously confused. (A common metaphor was that you should not start out learning to ride your motorcycle by going too fast, or else you may end up falling off and hurting yourself.) As with other kinds of religious projects for the development of knowledge, the student must have a guide.

Because they isolate the student from a teacher (and a group), recorded learning materials generated ambivalence among teachers, even those who had produced these very materials themselves. When asked whether he ever made recordings of the "*maqrā'*" he taught in class so that his students could study at home, H. Burhanuddin reported that they would often request that he do this, but that he did not oblige as a matter of principle. (H. Burhanuddin did in fact record a commercial instructional tape in 1982, about the same time as H. Muammar's was first produced in Jakarta; it quickly sold out and was never reproduced.) He was concerned that the students would take the recordings away and use them as a license to commit all kinds of errors *(salah-salah)*, for example, with stops and starts *(al-waqf wa-l-ibtidā')* and without even knowing it. He said twice: there must be a teacher *(guru)* who provides direction.[50]

A personal identification with the styles of named Egyptian *qāri*'s co-existed with hierarchical networks among Indonesian reciters. At one point, K. H. M. Sayyid Abdullah referred to the styles of the great Egyptian *qāri*'s as "*tariqas*" of reciting (using the word for Muslim Sufi brotherhoods), and he also referred to them as "*madhhabs*" (the term for schools of jurisprudence, and he reminded me that throughout the world there are four legal schools, but that in Indonesia we follow Shāfi'ī; he went on to comment that if one traveled the globe listening to recitation, one would find that most of the world followed the "*madhhab* of Mustafa Ismail"). K. H. M. Sayyid Abdullah also spoke of his own Indonesian "*silsilah*," the "chain [of transmission]" (a term for lineage, as in Sufi orders) of his students since the late 1960s and even earlier (there were hardly any champions who did not train with him at some point). Now, as he said, he was starting on the next link in the chain, the generation of "grandchildren." Indonesian reciters formed lasting and meaningful teacher-student relationships, and just one session together would mark a meaningful bond. After years of study, such ties could be intense and deeply affectionate. A coach once spoke with great deference of a champion reciter as having been his "teacher" since he was a child, but then later in the conversation he and this very champion reminisced about when they had met—which was long after both of their childhoods were over. When I inquired about the chronology, they clarified that before their first meeting the coach had been studying the recordings of the champion's readings that had been made during the final rounds of contests, and he only met him in person years later. Nevertheless, the coach had developed his style self-consciously as the champion's "student" long before they ever had direct association.

The style of H. Burhanuddin and other reciters in the "chain" of South Sulawesi's reciters was, as practically everyone in the area seemed quick to affirm, "straight from Egypt" *(langsung dari Misir)*. According to H. Burhanuddin himself, this was a way of saying that reciters from the area listened directly to Egyptian reciters (rather than, possibly, those from elsewhere in Indonesia, such as Jakarta) in order to come up with their own distinctive mixtures *(campuran)* and *variasi*. The straight-from-Egypt discourse was critical to the identity of reciters from the region especially in comparison with "styles" from other areas. Kāmil Yūsuf al-Bahtimī was said to be favored among South Sulawesi reciters, who were said to have "low" voices. During periods of competition preparation, provinces were scrutinized and compared in discussions among coaches and potential competitors in terms of their preparation (and the relative support available from provincial governments and other sources) for intensive training programs. These discussions sometimes identified regions with characteristic or representative styles. Sometimes they assigned provinces designations in terms of Egyptian reciters, acknowledging or imagining regional diversity through the terminology of *qāri*'s' names. For example, a reciter in South Sulawesi was told by a coach from Jakarta that he would be very popular as an invited performer in the capital precisely because his style (low in voice and "resembling [the Egyptian] al-Bahtimī") differed from what people were used to hearing there; he would be virtually bombarded by invitations to recite in homes and in public, he was told. (This reciter in fact went on to place third overall at the national competition a few months later.)[51] Such comparisons also had international dimensions: one international champion, for example, matched entire countries to *qāri*'s: Morocco was said to be the style of the Egyptian Manshawī, for example, because Moroccan reciters tended to start out high.

Along with the undisputed acceptance of the Egyptian model and the increasing formalization of practice in Indonesia on a national scale, the imagination of regional diversity and personal style in melodic Qur'ān recitation remained strong. For at least one reciter, the development of a unique regional "*kurikulum*" to teach advanced recitation, one that would emphasize the "signature traits" *(ciri khas)* of South Sulawesi but nevertheless still be applicable nationwide, was a priority at the time of my fieldwork. He suggested that South

Sulawesi did not need Jakarta for this project, that "we" could come up with our own curriculum and it could subsequently be adopted elsewhere, with one effect being that South Sulawesi's special style would come to be promoted on a national scale. His plan was, first, to get the regional style "set" (*tetap* or "fixed") and then to have several of the top reciters in South Sulawesi develop materials as a "team" before bringing a "corps" of students into the studio for a recording session. This is an excellent illustration of the initiative and enthusiasm Indonesians were showing for studying and teaching melodic recitation as well as typical aspects of its formalization for instruction in these years, including the expectation that there must be such a curriculum at all. This reciter compared his vision to the introduction of the Iqra' method for teaching basic Qur'ān reading; he was sure that there must already be such a curriculum in Jakarta, although he doubted there was any from the Middle East. Unless he meant the materials produced by the LBIQ, I had not encountered a curriculum produced in the capital along the lines he imagined.

With the recited Qur'ān in Indonesia, Egyptian styles had come to serve potentially as *kurikulum* for all, and the ideal of spontaneous, improvisatory expression was promoted as a practice of ordinary piety. In Indonesia in the 1990s, expanding evaluative criteria for *mujawwad* recitation pushed the boundaries of perceived orthopraxy outward in the directions of two poles simultaneously. On the one hand, there was movement toward an open, expressive ideal of spontaneity that has been strongly elaborated in the "classical" tradition and that was enhanced in Indonesia by the dominance of the influential paradigm of recitational performances from the Arabic-speaking world. On the other hand, as increasing numbers of Indonesians came to consider the ideal of the virtuoso to be potentially attainable, formalization by way of pedagogy strengthened the perception that there was in fact a "right" and "correct" process by which to learn to voice the beauty of the Qur'ān. This process was the guided adoption of the Egyptian virtuoso's model as an individual "style."

As formalized instruction came increasingly to imply possibilities of achievement, there arose a tendency for practice to become more homogeneous and uniform among those reciters without extraordinary innate ability. The more difficult the practice, the more closely the ordinary reciter tended to follow his or her instructional model. The result was not a "leveling" effect, however, with respect to the goals of learning. New orthoprax horizons for accomplished performance placed idealized uniformity in tension with the ideal of the expressive, improvisatory model of the truly gifted or proficient reciter. The tension between creative spontaneity and formalization of structures for improvisation and affect, both components of "style," amplified projects of personal and collective learning.

Formalizing Flexibility in Improvisation

Some standards for recitation that seem at the outset to be clear in ideal form become much more difficult to apprehend when engaged in actual activity. For example, to be "able to" read the Qur'ān means possessing the capability to produce the phonemes denoted on the page in accord with the rules of vocalization. But according to what standard of "Arabic phonemes"? And, how much of an influence of vernacular pronunciation should be permitted? When can it be said that one has "mastered" reading? When the whole Qur'ān is read through once? A part of it? What is expressive and "beautiful" and what is just a mistake? What is an impermissible "pop" melody and what melodies from cassette recordings from Egypt by singers such as Umm Kulthum should be studied and applied in recitation, just as the Egyptian *shaikh*s were said to do? People want to have the sense that they have "gotten it right"—not only in any single "reading," but on a more general level to become a competent "reader." In the absence of unambiguous authoritative criteria, there is a tendency to seek, even to create, such standards and conventions. In many cases in Qur'ānic Indonesia, these standards corresponded to the progressive, graded, and cumulative goals of pedagogy.

The concept of "style" was not enough alone for Indonesian learners to apprehend guidelines for improvisation and feeling in reciting the Qur'ān in the *mujawwad* style. The formalization of these concepts in curriculum induced further expansive ideals in practice. Pedagogical standards became situational ideals, and these newly introduced ideals in interaction with universalized expectations explain the escalation of this kind of Qur'ānic practice in Indonesia in the 1990s, especially the efforts to master systems of feeling and improvisation. Pedagogies naturally parcel a named skill or ability (such as being "able to read" or being "able to read with *lagu*") into graded and cumulative stages or units. This aspect of instruction affects how proficiency is imagined and experienced among learners, and it also determines a negotiated sense of final completion or mastery. Recitation standards that emerge out of pedagogical prototypes include "subjective" elements such as aesthetics, improvisation, and feeling, and these aspects affected the subjectivity of practitioners engaged in projects of self-cultivation related to reciting the Qur'ān especially powerfully. The standards appear fixed to the learner, first, because they are perceived to be "orthoprax" and, second, because they inform goals at each stage of the learning process. Although the expansive ideals of mastery and othopraxy seem fixed, for each practitioner they are in fact continually remade in performance, pedagogy, and evaluations of competence. In such a system, practice is generative of more practice as learners seek achievement, and pious goals contribute to the potential intensity of the project overall.

Situational ideals such as "style" impelled projects of learning to recite the Qur'ān melodically in Indonesia. The formalization of spontaneous performance as a model to be emulated and evaluated put in motion a process by which Indonesians attempted to gain the namable, graspable ability of reciting "with *lagu*." In undertaking such a project, however, many encountered a continually receding horizon. Formalized pedagogy enhanced ever-expanding possibilties for "getting it right," if not achievement. Systemization promised clear regimens and techniques and implied assured success, while at the same time the very standards of the system simultaneously encouraged improvisation, feeling, and idealized aesthetic evaluations of beauty. The Indonesian system thus valorized aesthetic fixity and improvisation at the same time. The promises of clear steps, stages, and standards implied attainability in a way that was potentially in tension with the affective and improvisational aspects of Egyptian-derived style, and this tension was productive of energetic systems of practice.

The modal system of classical Arabic *maqāmāt* applied in contemporary *mujawwad* Qur'ān recitation derives from a musical tradition of improvisational performance.[52] In order that human artistry is not associated with revelation, Qur'an readers are required by law to improvise melodically. In general, Middle Eastern musical practices have influenced comparative musicological frameworks for theorizing improvisation, especially in the pathbreaking work of Bruno Nettl on music in the Persian *radif*. Nettl explains improvisation and "composed" music as differing in "degree" but not in "essence." He shows that improvisation always includes qualities of spontaneity as well as a constraining "model" (such as rhythmic patterns). Even though listeners may not hear it as such, the musician has internalized this model and uses it as "building blocks" and as "points of reference" when playing or singing.[53]

Because of concerns about human artistry being associated with the Qur'ān through the fixity of writing, the *maqāmāt* for recitation are understood never to be written in any notational form.[54] This dimension of the Indonesian articulation of the *lagu* system further demonstrates the problem of fixing a fluid system within pedagogical conventions. One (rare) Indonesian instructional book on *lagu* explains the reason why "notes" (such as "*do, re, mi*") are not deployed in pedagogy:

> But [unlike "music"], it is another situation with *lagu* for *tilawatil Qur'an*, which cannot be studied with Western notation *(not-not)*, because the forms of the *lagu* have their own special characteristics *(ciri khas)*. In addition, the *lagu* of

> *tilawatil Qur'an* do not have musical instruments accompanying them. The exception to this is that, as needed, there are the *lagu* of the *qasida*, which have been simplified [for recitation study]. Also owing to the complexity *(kerumitan)* of the *variasi* and their [*hoyahnya*, possibly meaning "*āyahs*"], they are very difficult to study with notation.[55]

Some Indonesian manuals for Qur'ān recitation denote the rise and fall of the pitch variation with wavy lines, admittedly difficult to decipher (and I did not see the system ever actually in use) but reminiscent of the movement teachers often made with their hands to denote the rise and fall of pitch. As with other types of Qur'ānic practical instruction, learning methods for Qur'ānic *lagu* were oral (even instructional tapes were "guided" by the voice of a teacher). They deployed a method that ethnomusicologist Brinner has elsewhere called "directed emulation" to convey melody types that were never to be written in any notational form. (In general, very few published instructional materials were available at the time of research.)

The dynamics of group participation mediated a balance between the poles of creative spontaneity and patterned formalism in recitational pedagogy with *lagu*. In Indonesia, the fact of the participation of the group itself was an integral aspect of instruction. In all types of learning contexts, there was a marked tendency on the part of the students to follow audibly the student who was performing for the teacher, humming along softly with him or her (trailing perhaps a split second behind, but giving the overall impression of a sort of improvised ensemble performance). After the end of an *āyah*, there was usually a sounded trickle of little echoes, as students tried for themselves the cadences that they had just heard. Especially at the level at which *lagu* or patterns of basic improvisational *variasi* were first being introduced, students would tend to recite along with a teacher or student soloist (and also repeat after him or her). Teachers would occasionally adopt one student's performance as the study material: for example, especially at advanced levels, the whole class would be instructed to repeat (rather than spontaneously enact) the rendition of a particular student, underscoring peer learning and group participation. (On days when the teacher was absent, often one student would suddenly begin to act as the class leader, designating another student as the one to read in the role of a learner. The students would follow along as usual, occasionally pointing out a mistake or repeating a remark that they had remembered the teacher to have made previously.) Teachers of both genders also tended to alternate between their male and female students (classes were mixed, but men and women sat with their respective groups). If this gendering was self-conscious, as it often was, the instructor would sometimes use an aestheticized idea of gender difference to invoke the ideals of interest and engagement, pointing out that it was "boring" to hear voices of either men or women for an extended period of time (implicitly aestheticizing gender balance in sound).

The Indonesian system simultaneously aestheticized formalization and improvisation as it systematized performance as pedagogy. Whether application-focused or *lagu*-centric, all teaching systems included the development of creative expression and controlled feeling as a part of the standard curriculum. In pedagogy, once the basics of the *lagu* had been mastered either through systematic study of *tawshih* or, as was the case with some reciters, by grasping them through repeated listening to the improvised performances of others, the student was encouraged to develop "*variasi*," or improvisational techniques.[56] This is the case, for example, with H. Muammar's popular instructional cassettes, which teach the standard named *lagu* over three cassettes before moving on to examples of (paradoxically) set *variasi* and suggestions for arrangement of *lagu* for public "*acara*" performances. This system sets up a potential tension between formalization and spontaneity as ideals in recitation, as structured precision, patterned improvisation, and affective beauty—all prescribed by the tradition of Qur'ān recitation—coalesce in practice over time.

With the ideal of spontaneity, aesthetic ideas derived from the Egyptian system of performance come into play, emphasizing the "interest" that variation can provide for others, in harmony with the Qur'ānic idea that reciting for others "increases them in faith." At the top levels of instruction, the improvisatory ideal dominated concepts of well-ordered "arrangement," in part because these students had already mastered the formalized system and wished to develop the *variasi* that could make the difference in getting the attention of contest judges and increasing their scores. After a top national student had rendered an *āyah*, K. H. M. Sayyid Abdullah would, for example, customarily address the question to the entire group "Where was the beauty [in that]?" *(Di mana indahnya?)*. K. H. M. Sayyid Abdullah's overarching framework was the development of personal styles and individual potentials. This emphasis was evident in his habit of asking a reciter when he or she was at a transition point between two *lagus*, "Where would you like to take it next?" emphasizing the reader's personal taste and aesthetic judgment. Rarely did he criticize a student's *variasi* per se, but instead he encouraged good instances of *variasi* with his appreciative exclamations, imitating an Egyptian audience's response *("Ya Allah! Ya rabb! Ya gamil!")*, and would thus invite or guide the student to explore even further improvisational possibilities.

K. H. M. Sayyid Abdullah's criticisms were of inauthenticity or "affectation," such as "trying too hard" *(tiru-tiru)*, especially the tendency to go over the top in an overblown style in the opening and closing *āyahs* that, he claimed, marked Southeast Asians internationally. In training competitors, coaches like K. H. M. Sayyid Abdullah and others often addressed this problem. K. H. M. Sayyid Abdullah commented that at an international competition the Indonesians were often noticeable right away by their propensity to have overly dramatic openings and closings for readings, as well as overblown styles at the end of *āyahs*. After a few hours of coaching a special group, K. H. M. Sayyid Abdullah would comment on such a style heard in class as being: "*Meh-Meh-Meh*— ," and by then the students all knew to complete the word with him: "*MeLAYU!*" (here denoting "Southeast Asian" generally). He also articulated these expressive ideals of authenticity in the actual competition environment, as when he was interviewed on radio at the 1997 National Competition (MTQ). Here, he stressed the point that the choice and progression of *lagu* are always open during the final rounds. At other times while coaching, he emphasized an improvisatory ideal by pointing out that—although there is a vast field of melodic modes to be studied—"There is no book for *nagham (maqāmāt)*."

Indonesians without great aptitude, virtuosity, or ability to apprehend modal structures through listening to performances nevertheless attempted to achieve the technical artistry of experts. Since there was no established framework of related art music already in place, the mode of instruction for *lagu* determined the framework for their theorization, in a process that Andrew Weintraub has termed, for another Indonesian musical system, "theory through practice."[57] When the *lagu* were conceptualized in terms of the *tawshih* patterns of set drills, they were better understood in terms of "melody types" than the scalar pitch classes and musical "modes" of the *maqāmāt* in Arab music that reciters listening to cassettes of actual performances attempted to apprehend (although these recordings too were scanned for specific melody structures or "*variasi*," which were often then identified with the name of the performer and reproduced from memory).[58]

There were notable, although subtle, differences apparent among elementary teaching methods for *lagu* (in terms of, for example, their relative emphasis on reading naturally from the Qur'ān versus mastering an abstract melodic "*model*" or, additionally, contrasts between formalizing the "*model*" itself versus a more fluid process of familiarlization). All methods, however, shared the same objectives. First, students learned to apply melodic practices derived from Egyptian styles of recitation in a manner that conformed to the requirements of *tajwīd*. Second, this occurred along with the development of a style that was perceived to be beautiful, with improvised "*variasi*" on seven standard melodic modes. Third, pedagogy and performance corresponded to Indonesian expectations that included a loose compositional "arrangement" with respect to melodic structure *(aturan,* or *susunan lagu)*.

One significant contrast among teachers was the way in which they introduced the *lagu*: specifically, whether they preferred mastery of an overall system of *lagu* (by teaching the modes sequentially) or, alternatively, the developing students' ability to apply the *lagu* to the Qur'ān in a (predetermined) arrangement while reading by sight.[59] Master teachers, such as H. Burhanuddin, for example, would tell students that the very best way to learn *lagu* was always to listen to cassettes of expert performance and just "get the feel of it" *("menerima dalam rasa")*, but it was recognized that this would prove too difficult for most.

The primary systems used for basic recitation instruction, including private study at home with cassettes, relied on "*tawshih*" (Ar. "musical [or poetic] composition," pl. *tawāshiḥ*) to convey the basic patterns of the *maqāmāt*.[60] (They were also sometimes called "*qasida.*") Some of the *tawshih*, such as "Nur Nabi" for *lagu bayati*, are quite lengthy, while others are short.[61] Several of them are in praise of the Prophet and treat themes of mystical union of the type that a *munshid* would deploy in Egypt, while others such as "Arā Ṭairan" ("I saw a bird calling," for *soba*) are not explicitly religious.[62] The *tawshih* used in Indonesia and Malaysia for this purpose were exactly the same, having been introduced by the Egyptian teachers in previous decades.

The *lagu* were taught (and evaluated in competitions) according to an idealized "*tangga nada*," or a "ladder of melody." For advanced students, the named registers of a *lagu* were described in terms of "*soal*" and "*jawab*" (the "question" and the "answer"), alternating between them in their phrasing (as in Arabic classical music). Often, and within competitions, modes were conceptualized as progressing up through named "levels" *(tingkat)* of the registers, each higher than the next. This well-ordered progression is most apparent with *bayati*, the mode that begins and ends almost all melodic recitation in Indonesia (it is required as the opening and closing of competition readings). For *bayati*, the basic named levels are *qorar*, *nawa* (sometimes omitted), *jawab* (the answer), and *jawabul jawab* (the answer to the answer). Recitation with *bayati* follows this arrangement *(aturan* or *susunan lagu)*, ascending as each *lagu* is developed in consecutive phrasings. (Within each phrase, however, there is characteristically an internally descending melodic movement.) The conception of the "levels" of recitation derives from Arabic recitation (and musical practice), but the way in which they were conceptualized in Indonesia was distinctive. One knowledgeable international champion reciter suggested that the formalization of *tingkat* within a *maqām* was an entirely Indonesian introduction, made "by committee" (although there is evidence that it is also in use in Malaysia); before that, he added, the rendering of the mode was, as he said, "*bebas saja*," totally free.

Among Indonesian teachers, there were a variety of teaching methods.

One significant contrast among teachers was the progression they used to introduce the *lagu:* specifically, whether they preferred mastery of the overall system of *lagu* or, alternatively, the ability to apply the *lagu* to the Qur'ān in an arrangement while reading by sight. H. Burhanuddin's technique tended to the latter. He would provide a "*model*" ("*pola*" or paradigm) in the form of a set "*maqrā'*" ("reading [excerpt]") from the Qur'ān. The "*komposisi*" determined precisely *(persis)* which *lagu* correspond to which *āyahs*, and the pattern was not altered *(tidak robah-robah)* over the course of consecutive class sessions. After the passage had been "mastered" by the students, another reading was given that had the same *lagu* progression *(model)* as the previous one. He explained that the form of one reading is thus transposed to the other *(gaya model di sini ditransfer ke sini).* With this method, he continued, the students are "interested" (and not "bored"), they do not complain that the process is too difficult for them—and they are ready before too long. Having learned this way, it is then much easier for them to recognize the *lagu* elsewhere, to make new connections ("They see, ah, I can use this *lagu* here"), and to develop and apply *(menerapkan)* them on their own. He added, the theoretical level of terminology does not need to be made explicit in practice *(abstraknya tidak tampak)*; instead, it enters directly into feeling *(perasaan).* He said he found from experience that if the students use a *lagu* often, following this method, then they "memorize it automatically on their own" *(dengan sendrinya otomatis)*—"Oh, [I see] this is [really just *lagu*] *hijaz*, and it goes like this." Switching to another affective idea, he concluded, this way they *feel* like they have mastered it and like they really *got* it. It is a method aimed to cultivate competence—and confidence—within an improvisational system. (In this conversation, H. Burhanuddin emphasized continually the importance of students practicing reading the Qur'ān in order to become "fluent" *(lancar)* and to perfect their *tajwīd* daily, criticizing some for only practicing their *lagu* on fixed readings.)

In contrast to this pedagogical technique, some teachers on the national scene said that they did not favor a method based on set "readings" *(maqrā').* Some teachers preferred to teach instead in a "*lagu*-centric" way,[63] whether by way of *tawshih* or (as in the case of Dra. Hj. Maria Ulfah) by applying the *lagu* directly to various *āyahs* from the Qur'ān (with instruction still proceeding *lagu* by *lagu* over a period of time). H. Muammar's popular instructional cassettes actually synthesize such methods. They introduce the *lagu* one at a time by way of the standard *tawshih,* which are then applied to the first verses of Sūrah 55 al-Raḥmān, building up a composed "*maqrā'*" as each new *lagu* and consecutive verses are added on. After all seven *lagu* have been introduced, a model of the reading from Sūrah al-Raḥmān, demonstrating the *lagu* progression, is given straight through. Other teachers, when working with intermediate-level students, would suggest a given reading for the session and then allow students to recite according to the *lagu* progression of their own choosing (and also conforming to competition standards and conventions).

In general, *lagu* followed an "*aturan*" (order) and were taught according to an idealized *tangga nada*, or "ladder of melody," progressing uniformly through named "levels" *(tingkat)* of registers with a characteristic descending movement within each phrase. Egyptian *qāri*'s almost without exception begin in the lower registers and gradually ascend as the voice warms up, returning to the lower registers at the end of their performances; during the recitation, sudden shifts in registers often mark contrasts between phrases. In Indonesia, this arrangement was much more formalized, and this well-ordered progression was most apparent with *bayati*.[64] Ascending too quickly was a common mistake—often likened to (and pantomimed as) a helicopter bounding up suddenly in contrast to an airplane's gradual ascent. The modulation (transition) among *lagu* within a reading conforms to a loose "composition," or *susunan lagu* (sometimes called a "*komposisi*"): six *lagu* were required within ten minutes for a national competition reading.[65] Handbooks typically contained arrangements of appropriate readings for specific occasions, with *lagu* modulation (the *susunan lagu*, or arrangement) marked in the margins.[66]

The influence of formalized pedagogies (such as H. Muammar's instructional tapes) tended to homogenize recitation not only within South Sulawesi but across Indonesia, as students tried to apprehend the *right variasi* and to ask, what is a *variasi* and what is a mistake? The widespread use of the same materials and methods for instruction produces a felt aesthetic tension. For the ordinary reciter without extraordinary talent, the more difficult the practice, the more meticulously and faithfully reproduced is the pedagogical model. Even for top reciters, there was a tension between the loose arrangement of *lagu* or melodic progressions in the virtual performance frame of competition, on the one hand, and the ideal of the spontaneous, expressive reciter on the other. When judging the practice of music, being right or wrong is primarily an aesthetic consideration; with the recited Qur'ān, it is also a matter of ritual orthopraxy. The concept of *rasa* (feeling) was the technical basis of controlled spontaneity, beauty, and emotion in the Indonesian system, thereby expressing orthopraxy in terms of structured aesthetics, ideas of disciplined learning, musical sensibility, and changing emotional systems. Along with the musical system for Qur'ān recitation, the affective system was also undergoing change. Reciters' efforts to achieve these new affective ideals also generated new kinds of practitioners, who became increasingly engaged in realizing the model of the virtuoso in ordinary practice.

Rasa: Emotion as Curriculum

Emotion in the theory and practice of Qur'ān recitation is not left to the "internal" or remote reaches of individual experience but is explicitly prescribed as a normative response and as a technique. The anticipation of beauty, spontaneity, and emotion as situational ideals create a bounded space of affective potential that practitioners seek to fill with their own expansive experience, drawing them more deeply into technical and experiential systems of performance. As with standards for beauty and improvisation in classical and contemporary systems of the recited Qur'ān, emotion was stipulated for orthoprax recitation. In the 1990s, the Southern Asian framework of *rasa* in the system of *lagu* pedagogy for experience, technique, and evaluation of Qur'ān recitation emerged in distinctive ways, opening possibilities for escalating practice.

In the Indonesian system of Qur'ānic aesthetics, affective ideals described for "classical" Islamic tradition of performance that represented long-standing patterns of sadness and weeping had come to blend with the Southeast Asian idea of aesthetic, affective *rasa*. Recitation pedagogy in Indonesia deployed the culturally specific Southern Asian quality of *rasa* (from Sanskrit, meaning "essence," "taste," or "juice") as a formalized technique. *Rasa*, heavily theorized and elaborated in Southern Asian aesthetic systems, is not a single feeling type, but a category of sense, sensation, and sensibility.[67] It was understood to modulate improvisation and discipline its limits, and to provide affective sensitivity and aesthetic sensibility in performance. With *rasa* as a specific technique for projects of improving the recited Qur'ān according to new expectations of engagement, affect opened up new horizons for involvement in practice and it also necessitated emotional change along with the development of competence. *Rasa* allowed ideal and experienced affect to blend within specific techniques and styles of performance; specifically, it supported the development of a new affective system emphasizing both controlled artistry and expansive "motivation" and "interest."

Rasa, in the form of a new affective system of interested engagement in Indonesia in the 1990s, replaced older Islamic affective ideals for recitation that had doubled as specific emotional techniques. Kristina Nelson shows that, within the recited Qur'ān as well as in *ḥadīth* accounts and writings in the genre of *adab al-tilāwah*, there is an emphasis on one emotional quality in particular: *ḥuzn*, which may be loosely understood as an overwhelming sense of sadness and awe. Although the historical connections are not developed in Nelson's study, the grounding for this ideal is ascetic movements in the Islamic tradition and especially the model of early figures (such as Ḥasan of Baṣra) known as the "weepers," who are significant in Sufi lineages as well as in the history of

Islamic pietism. This tradition of piety, drawing on statements in the Qur'ān and *ḥadīth* materials that emphasize especially reflection on inevitable judgment, rendered crying and sadness a normative aspect of Qur'ānic practice.

Ḥuzn is simultaneously a response to the presence of the Qur'ān, an expression of the meaning of the Message and a self-conscious technique for this purpose, as well as an experience to be valued for its intrinsic power to transform religious selves. In her book *The Art of Reciting the Qur'ān*, Kristina Nelson writes that the concept of *ḥuzn* "embraces all of the qualities of the ideal recitation," adding that *ḥuzn* may be taken as a "key" to understanding the significance of the "total experience of recitation."[68] Nelson explains that "sorrow," "grief," and "plaintive" (words often used to interpret *ḥuzn*) do not convey the full sense of the concept. Since it is not possible to derive a single-word English definition of *ḥuzn* for Qur'ān recitation, Nelson offers an interpretation: "*Ḥuzn* is the awareness of the human state *vis-à-vis* the creator. With *ḥuzn* one knows true humility, awe of the divine, human frailty and mortality. This awareness, and the emotion it stirs on the part of the reciter, is communicated through the reciter's voice and artistry, heightening the listeners' sensitivity and awareness and moving them to tears."[69] Nelson writes that this is related to an idea of fear and apprehension also bound to the act of weeping, captured by the term "*khushū'*."[70]

As in the Qur'ān itself (in which Prophets and others are depicted fainting and weeping when encountering the power of the recited Qur'ān), there are *ḥadīth* accounts in which the Prophet Muḥammad prescribes crying as integral to the recited Qur'ān: "Recite the Qur'ān with sorrow *(ḥuzn)*. Verily the best reciter is he who when he recites the Qur'ān stimulates grief *(yataḥazzanu)*." And "Recite the Qur'ān with sorrow *(ḥuzn)* for verily it was revealed with sorrow *(ḥuzn)*."[71] Later authorities, especially Sufis, elaborate this reaction as normative and desirable even in its more extreme forms. For example, al-Ghazzālī describes effects of the recited Qur'ān to be weeping, swooning, and even dying (which all signify "listening" *[samā']* or "following" *[tilāwah]* the truth of its verses).[72] Sufis especially have recommended Qur'ānic *ḥuzn* as a technique of self-cultivation, such as Abū Ṭālib al-Makkī (d. 966), as expressed in a statement of al-Ghazzālī "Should he [one reciting the Qur'ān] not feel grief and weep as do those with purified souls, he should weep for his lack of grief and tears because this is the greatest of all misfortunes."[73] The rationale for the self-conscious incitement of *ḥuzn*, in addition to it being the *sunnah* of the Prophet, is moral and spiritual development that comes with the contemplation of impending Judgment.

Ḥuzn is not only an affective reaction and a religious quality to cultivate in classical Islamic systems. Statements such as those above establish Qur'ānic expectations for how to feel or to make others feel, and imply also how to translate this into a practical technique. Besides being a moral state and a felt emotion, *ḥuzn* is also an aesthetic, vocal quality and practical standard expected of the performer. Nelson shows that discussions of recitation draw a close connection between "*taghannā*" (a technique, reciting melodically) and "*taḥazzana*" (an act, feeling *ḥuzn*).[74] *Ḥuzn* may thus be, literally, embodied in practical techniques of vocal performance. In addition to being a technical quality imparted by the performer, *ḥuzn* is also a reaction to Qur'ānic beauty and intensity. Listeners are moved to tears by the spiritual audition of the performance of the recited Qur'ān.

Given *ḥuzn*'s significance as both feeling and technique, it should come as no surprise that literature on *tilāwah* often includes instruction on the intentional and self-conscious invocation of the feeling of *ḥuzn*. This is a practice termed "*taḥzīn*." A reciter's practice of *taḥzīn* ideally both induces sincere *ḥuzn* in the self and "causes *ḥuzn*" *(taḥzīn)* in listeners.[75] Statements cited by Nelson relate the importance of self-conscious *taḥzīn*, and some suggest that if the Qur'ān reciter or audience does not weep naturally and without effort, they should attempt to incite sorrow and weeping in themselves: "Read the Qur'ān and weep. If you do not weep spontaneously, make yourself weep" (Ibn Mājah) and "Verily this Qur'ān was sent down with *ḥuzn* and grief so when you recite it weep, and if you do not weep then feign weeping *(tabākaw)*" (al-Suyūṭī).[76]

The idea of *taḥzīn* leads to what some emotion theorists call the "sincerity problem" in the study of performative and affective systems. *Taḥzīn* is in tension with key Islamic ideals of truthfulness *(ṣidq)* and sincerity *(ikhlāṣ)*, strongly elaborated in systematic Sufi-oriented writings such as those of al-Ghazzālī. This very question of "sincere" and "insincere" emotion is highlighted in Muslim traditions in connection to *ḥuzn*, demonstrating the perceived significance of this palpable, verifiable, and replicable emotional experience. In particular, religious scholars warn against the danger of hypocrisy in the strategic use of *ḥuzn* in recitation. This warning connects to a more widespread concern in Sufi traditions about the states achieved in practices of esoteric piety, especially *samā'*. As an illustration, al-Qurtubī (d. 940) writes, "Let him be on guard against showing with his tongue what is not in his heart."[77] The practice of *taḥzīn* seems paradoxical: one "feigns" *ḥuzn*, an emotion that should never be false.

Al-Ghazzālī once again resolves an apparent contradiction in his discussion of *taḥzīn*, in this case by applying a characteristically Islamic evaluation of intentions (there is a well-known *ḥadīth* stating that "actions are known by their intentions"). He draws a distinction between affectation of emotion for the purposes of show and affectation in order to invoke the experience of valid *ḥuzn*. Al-Ghazzālī explains his recommendation to feign *ḥuzn* and *bukā'* (weeping) by relating means to ends, stating, "While the beginning of these states may be forced, their ends are true."[78] Al-Ghazzālī explains that the reciter affects *ḥuzn* to in order to effect sincere *ḥuzn* in himself and others. This implies that *taḥzīn* is appropriate only if it leads to an authentic experience of *ḥuzn* and then only if the reciter prioritizes his or her spiritual responsibilities over the strategic exploitation of affect in order to manipulate a desired response. Ultimately, the resolution of tensions over "sincerity" (a foundational concept for Sufis especially) returns to the technical, not conceptual or abstract, aspects of practice. As quoted by Nelson, al-Makkī describes the ideal recitation as one in which "the reciter recites promises with longing, admonition with fear, warning with severity, explanation with gentleness."[79] In classical formulations, the reciter should actually feel the emotion the recitation evokes in listeners, and, ideally, the reciter is himself or herself the vehicle for the immediate encounter with the Qur'ān.

The discussions of *ḥuzn* in the classical literature elaborate a reactive, practical, and instrumental system of emotion within Qur'ānic performance. A purely textual view—or one that centers only on the stated "ideals" possibly at the expense of recognizing lived realities—hazards distorting the ways in which affective dynamics develop over time and within actual social systems. Nelson herself encountered the situation that, in modern Egypt where she studied recitation practice, *ḥuzn* did not seem to be a part of the "modern Egyptian lexicon" for recitation. She explains that, while literature on recitation (*tilāwah*) rigorously develops the idea of *ḥuzn*, connecting *ḥuzn* to the technical and performative expression of the meaning of the Qur'ān, only a relatively small number of Muslims in Egypt at the time of her fieldwork were conversant in the advanced vocabulary of *qirā'ah* (reading). Nelson writes that *ḥuzn* nevertheless carried "the same association with the religious ideal" as other aspects of recitation that were more explicit among Egyptians such as accurate memorization, proper vocal articulation, and a stylistic rendering in conformity to the meaning of the Qur'ān.[80] In short, her study seems to imply that *ḥuzn* had become implicit or latent in modern Egyptian recitation.

Although one cannot infer that Egyptians used to cry more in the past in response to expert performances of the recited Qur'ān than they do now, the change that may be deduced from Nelson's comments about *ḥuzn* is that experts once had a more prominent discourse about affective display. In Indonesia, the very Egyptian system Nelson describes was received in a distinctively Southeast Asian way. At a transitional moment in Qur'ānic emotional history in the 1990s, it was apparent in Southeast Asia that Indonesians who had once cried now no longer did. One reason for this change was that learning regimens reconstituted the ideal and instrumental aspects of Qur'ānic emotion around affective, escalating engagement.

As in the previous discussion of *ḥuzn*, Indonesian reciters in the 1990s deployed *rasa* as a Qur'ānic technique in itself. The treatment of *rasa* in Indonesia resembled most closely in Islamic tradition the key Sufi idea of *dhūq*, which also means "taste" and a special kind of perceptivity to subtle realities. Reciters in Indonesia would refer to the specific *dhūq* of a *lagu* or of the rendition of a phrase. *Rasa*, like *dhūq*, encompasses the idea of cultivating a moralized aesthetic of sensibilities and perceptions, like the central Sufi metaphor of polishing the internal mirror of the heart. Like the treatments of affective states in *samā'* and *dhikr*, this quality is also embodied; in *dhikr*, advanced states of cultivated feeling merge with the body to the degree that even the heartbeat conveys these aspects with every beat. In Muslim Indonesia, *rasa* is also an affective quality exerting a presence on all levels of embodiment and evaluation in the melodic recitation of the Qur'ān.

Recitation pedagogy incorporated affect, or *rasa*, into a formalized system as a technique. Even for beginners, the prevalent idea of *rasa*, or "feeling," was conveyed at the most schematic level. *Rasa* bonds beauty, improvisation, and emotion, making recitation both spiritually and practically effective. *Rasa* may be "emotion" in general or specific terms, and in Indonesian recitational practice it also connoted an aesthetic sensibility that provides the basis for beautiful, creative, and controlled performance. A teacher from a rural province of South Sulawesi who worked primarily with beginning-level adolescent students happened to be the person in whose classes I heard the most discussion of *rasa*. At the same time that he would remind his students to "memorize" *(hafal)* their *lagu*, practice *tajwīd* at home, and try to develop control in their voices, he was also striving to develop their *rasa* as a primary component of competent recitation. "The beauty," he would often say, "is in your heart." (This teacher also had the tendency, as did many others, to identify "beauty" with recitation in higher registers.)

The centrality of *rasa* to elementary, systematic instruction is evidenced in the fact that three of the seven summary suggestions that H. Muammar gives at the end of one of his cassettes invoke the idea:

> (1) Practice often so that you know *lagu* and develop *rasa;* (2) don't be *fanatik* about your own *lagu*, and don't assume you're the best so you refuse to listen to and try new things; (3) have a collection of the recitations of the famous *shaikhs* and other Arab materials; (4) don't let your *lagu* interfere with reading [correctly, "*bacaan*"]; (5) recite with *rasa;* (6) eliminate your own "*emosi*" [this connotes negatively valued "upset," as in being "emotional"] so the *lagu* can be "filled up" [with *rasa?*]; (7) be prepared before reading.[81]

Rasa, as indicated in the contrast between negative "*emosi*" (6), cultivated sensibility (1), and a technique of performance (5), is not just a prerequisite or a component of expression, but also the essence of balanced, affective control. It is a technical requirement in this regard. For example, in many classes, when a student would try to ascend too quickly through the registers of a *lagu*, the teacher would comment that he or she needed to develop *perasaan* (a nominal form of "*rasa*") in recitation. More than simply knowing what "feels right," *rasa* allows one to stay within the boundaries of aesthetic sensitivity and technical limits. When I asked H. Burhanuddin whether he had encountered many students not patient enough for *lagu* study, his response linked *rasa* and discipline:

> Yes, there are, there are some who want to be given more right away. They don't even have a fix on the first one *[lagu]* yet, but then they keep wanting to add on the next and then the next. The first one isn't even set yet *(belum mantap)*, but they already want to change to another one. It's all still hazy with them *(masih kabur)*, and they still want more. Yes, it's very hard. It takes a student like this a very long time [*lambat sekali dia*, lit. "he is very slow"], because it's the *rasa* that has to improve [*rasa yang mengangkat*, and he repeated this phrase for emphasis].

Rasa comprises a basic requirement for the development of recitational ability, whether in terms of individual technical artistry or with respect to the affective discipline necessary for aesthetic refinement.

Rasa mediates aspects of technical artistry as well. It is, for example, the basis for apprehending what is, ideally, a match between *lagu*, mood, and meaning in recitation.[82] In general, in Indonesia, competitions and pedagogy had come to structure *lagu* progressions in a way that tended to predominate over textual criteria for modulation. Instead of the star trainers who coached for competition on the national level, it was a champion reciter who spent a good deal of her time teaching older women to recite who often had the most to say about *lagu* corresponding to the meaning of the *āyahs*. Ny. Nurhayati emphasized comprehension, a fact, I think, related to her vision of her work (her "*niyya*," as she called it) of providing religious instruction to women, with the recitation of the Qur'ān being a primary means to that end. Even with students who were struggling with *tajwīd* or basic *murattal lagu*, she would often connect the meaning of the verse to the style in which it was recited. In interviews, she was quick to give examples of how *lagu* mood and meaning could relate, such as using (sad) *lagu hijaz* for an *āyah* about *kuffār* (the "unbelievers," who are doomed). H. Burhanuddin emphasized another aspect of this point, the supremacy of *tajwīd* rules over *lagu* modulation, noting that matching the "rhythm" *(irama)* of the *lagu* and the length and rhythm of a particular *āyah* may restrict melodic and melismatic range.[83] In general, the correspondence of *lagu* mood and meaning was made informally. For example, when a woman once recited an *āyah* containing the phrase "*Wa hua 'l-Ghaffār*" ("He is the Most-Forgiving," one of the Divine Names), Ny. Nurhayati commented that it had been rendered sweetly, a very forgiving *lagu* to match the sense of God being All-Forgiving. She also related this correspondence to "*fasahah*."

The beauty, improvisation, and affective impact that are integral to Islamic traditions of the recited Qur'ān took on distinctive forms in the system of recitation practices in Indonesia in the 1990s. The formal characteristics of Indonesian recitation (especially the use of standardized *lagu*) as well as modes of transmission and learning stylized Qur'ānic ideals of beautification, improvisation, and affect in specific ways. These conditions contributed to a widespread pursuit of Qur'ānic piety among Muslim Indonesians that opened channels of affective experience and pulled practitioners into deepening engagement with the recited Qur'ān. This affective system was also undergoing a process of transformation: gaining power, pervasiveness, and schematicity. A related performance style that privileged aesthetic ideals of spontaneity, deriving from appreciation of virtuoso performances, came to characterize this musicalized system. At the same time, there was a movement toward formalized ideals within Indonesian pedagogical frameworks. For practitioners, this situation resulted in a doubly determined field of evaluation of ability and potential—a system of assessment to which each practitioner seeking this avenue for the perfection of practice was increasingly subject. Whether conceptualized as perfecting exquisite artistry, achieving technical correctness, or attaining the sense of earnestly pious *khushū'*, in all domains the practice of *mujawwad* Qur'ān recitation in Indonesia in the 1990s generated dynamics of religious performance that expanded outward. Under the influences of new kinds of evaluations of the Qur'ānic performances of selves and others that came along with new pedagogy and curriculum, an affective system was changing along with a musical one.

Escalating Expectations and Projects of Piety

In Indonesia in the 1990s, the expanding evaluative criteria for *mujawwad* recitation pushed the boundaries of perceived "orthopraxy" for melodic Qur'ān recitation outward in the directions of two poles simultaneously. On the one hand, there was movement toward an open, expressive ideal of spontaneity that has been strongly elaborated in the "classical" tradition and that was enhanced in Indonesia by the dominance of the influential paradigm of recitational performances from the Arabic-speaking world. On the other hand, as increasing numbers of Indonesians came to consider the ideal of the virtuoso to be potentially attainable, formalization by way of pedagogy strengthened the perception that there was in fact a "right" and "correct" process by which to learn to convey the inimitable beauty of the Qur'ān in voice. When expansive ideals of feeling, improvisation, and musical performance blended with particular competencies and pedagogies, the result was often an escalation of practice. The adaptation of musical and affective systems in Indonesia presented new possibilities for the expression of piety as well as new affective standards for evaluation. Many practitioners found themselves applying these sorts of assessments to their own projects of Qur'ānic piety and amplifying these projects in turn.

An affective system of Qur'ānic learning, in both universalized and contexualized frames, determines a "sense" of orthopraxy with respect to fluid and flexible aspects of recitational practice. This understanding of "affect" differs from the more restricted classification of Qur'ānic emotion as that which is conveyed in a performance or felt as a response, although affective responsiveness and expressions are a component of the musicalized system. This developmental concept of religious affect captures multiple aspects of the evaluation and experience of ritual learning: ideals experienced as expansive, lived realities, and variable levels of competence. In pedagogy, propaedeutic strategies emerge as seemingly attainable goals that guide a practitioner's developing mastery. Such techniques were understood in Qur'ānic Indonesia to be social and cultural products, but in the performance of the "recited Qur'ān," they also become a part of the encounter with revelation. Affect was fundamental to the Indonesian ritual system of Qur'ānic orthopraxy, including the aesthetics and techniques of *rasa* that were used to perform and evaluate controlled improvisation.

Orthopraxy is a form of competence in the recited Qur'ān, whether in the case of a style that references a named performer or with improvisation and emotion in reference to ultimate Qur'ānic ideals of beauty. The "fit" of these ideals and realities is a feeling, an affective sense that was pursued as an end in itself. In the case of *mujawwad* recitation, Indonesian reciters came to have their performances evaluated for competence and orthopraxy on the basis of diverse affective criteria. As a result, persons would assess their own unrealized potential for practice in terms of expansive ideals, mapped into individual practice and projects of learning through personalized styles and specific techniques to capture improvisation and feeling. These conditions led to overall change in a system of practice and performance to which Indonesian Muslims, in turn, increasingly adapted. In Indonesia in the 1990s, when increasing numbers of Muslims were attempting to read the Qur'ān with enhanced technical artistry, fluid norms combined with increasingly formalized standards to determine a relationship not only to ongoing Qur'ānic practice and learning processes, but also to perceptions of individual potential.

Competence tends to be imagined as a discrete property ascribed to individuals (e.g., "A Hajji should 'know *lagu*'") rather than as a continuous process. However, for those who set out to become someone "able to recite with *lagu*," even those following a formalized program, the open-endedness of stylistic, improvisatory, and aesthetic ideals guaranteed that their project would be an open-ended pursuit. Pedagogies embedded flexible ideals within formalized learning processes, while at the same time a proximate ideal of Egyptian experts' style was rendered seemingly attainable though educational regimens. Since expressive aspects of the recited Qur'ān (such as improvisation with a complex modal system or the realization of idealized emotional experience) were understood to inhabit the sacred domain of revelation, the combination of expectations ("closed" orthopraxy with "open" dynamics of performance) often led to an affective dynamic of escalating engagement. When not viewed from the perspective of "expert's culture" but instead in terms of ordinary practitioners who also wanted to "get it right," practitioners often described their own potential to develop competence in terms of cultivating feelings and evaluations of orthopraxy rather than a goal of achieving the artistry of a virtuoso.

Self-understandings in terms of ability as well as contribution to community developed along with Qur'ānic competence in Indonesia in the 1990s. Many Indonesians were becoming increasingly engrossed in a cycle of skill acquisition through the study of melodic modes for Qur'ān recitation. Some were like a certain corporate executive, pulled in by the fascination with aesthetic potential and coming to find themselves practicing piety as a result. Others wished to fulfill the religious obligation to "beautify the Qur'ān with their voices" and found themselves enrolling in projects of lifelong study of Qur'ān recitation along the way. For those who evaluated their own Qur'ānic practice with respect to expectations of orthopraxy, the question could arise, if one does not possess the potential to become a virtuoso, by what criteria should one understand one's own attempts to practice piety? Often evaluations were not based on absolute standards of competence but instead emphasized the affective qualities of practice and the expansive possibilities to influence others through these same modes.

Not every student would prove to have the ability or the sensibility to be able recite like a great Arab *shaikh*. In the field of melodic recitation in Indonesia, the theological problem that arose for many was not the legal permissibility of their particular strategies, but instead the question of how their own potentials and abilities measured up to perceptions of the idealized recited

Qur'ān. This dynamic echoes questions of variable aptitude and ability when measured against extraordinary models found in classical systems of Islamic education and especially within the stratified and "virtuosic" frameworks of Sufism. If recitation with the seven melodic modes was Islamically "correct," what if one could not manage to do it? In Indonesia, self-reflective issues, such as those regarding "talent," could come to influence the subjectivity and the feelings of Qur'ānic practice. The impact of the various methods for teaching "*lagu*," along with the popularization of *mujawwad* reading in Indonesia more generally, raised the question for many of the implications of personal ability ("talent") in melodic recitation if one aspires to the model of the virtuoso as an ordinary practice. A definitive discussion of "talent" in the field of ethnomusicology that theorizes indigenous understandings of "talent" as well as the way that qualities of "cultural talent" are ascribed to ethnographic others has been offered by Indonesianist Michael Bakan.[84] The system of Qur'ān recitation in Indonesia implicated ideas of "talent" (*bakat*, the same word used by Bakan's Indonesian informants) but in a distinctive way in a Muslim religious system. Especially when removed from the structure of the "star system," in Makassar there was a dual aspect to *bakat:* of aptitude, but also of the possibility of pious participation. How one feels about one's own memorizational or musical ability is especially significant if it doubles as one's capacity for religious practice and describes a certain location within the religious community.

With students without much recognized talent for recitation, teachers tried to develop feelings along with technical competence, attempting to instill and encourage "confidence" *(keberanian)*. Several teachers explained that this is their main objective with students who showed little promise of developing into an accomplished *qāri'* or *qāri'ah;* many also stated that developing confidence was also their goal with more proficient students, those who had mastered the basics and needed the confidence to begin to develop their own styles. Teachers of weaker or slower students faced the challenge of determining what about the student's performance was being caused by a feeling of insecurity *(takut)* or embarrassment *(malu)*, and what was actually a matter of capability (a lack of *kemampuan*, or "being able to") in terms of voice or musical competence. (The best coaches would recognize the interdependency between the two.) Teachers would repeat phrases such as "Don't hold anything back" *(Jangan ada yang disimpan)*, "Recite *maksimal*," and, "If your voice can't do it, that's fine, but don't just give up without trying because you're scared" *(jangan kalau faktor takut)*. They were providing an affective education along with a technical one. The potential intensity of the classroom environment for struggling students amplified this effect: not only were they exposing their skill level (and mistakes) to others, but they also faced the added stresses of feeling dizzy, out of breath, and quite possibly frustrated. To encourage "confidence," teachers would combat the sense of impossibility with a running pep talk of perseverance: "Keep trying and one day, *insha'Allah* [God willing], you will be able to."

Nevertheless, the very same teacher who had one of the most sophisticated of the "try, try again" rhetorics at one point acknowledged to his class: "There are some people who just can't recite with *lagu (melagu)*. The people who happen to have this ability are special individuals *(orang tertentu)*, and for the rest who just don't have it, there is still a *target minimal*, which is good *tadarus* with proper *tajwīd*." A question on one of H. Muammar's instructional tapes is "I have followed all of your suggestions from the previous tapes, but I still always lose in competitions—what is my problem?" H. Muammar considers a host of problems the student might be facing. His discussion begins, "There are those who show the same level of effort *(usaha)* and amount of practice *(latihan)*, but the performance *(prestasi)* differs between them because of the quality of the 'raw material.'" He illustrates, "Good paper makes [good material for] a good book, a book full of learning, but bad paper is only good for wrapping fried bananas." Some people, he sums up, are just more talented *(berbakat)* than others to start out with (adding that such people get even better when they work hard).[85]

Whether a case of a practitioner discovering the endless horizons of technical artistry or an ungifted reader measuring himself or herself against world-class *qāri*'s, the evaluation of Qur'ānic practice reveals a possibility of pursuing piety. Indonesians developed this potential through the affective dynamics of open-ended projects that were simultaneously personal and collective. More important to many practitioners was not their heightened skill, but instead the promise of being able to "get it right" according to variable standards and abilities, always in relation to the recited Qur'ān and religious community. Young women who were studying hard at a mosque, for example, agreed that one needed talent to recite the Qur'ān with *lagu* and said they also didn't have any talent; although they said they would never wish to compete, they reported they listened to cassettes as much as possible as recitational models. When I asked whether such listening could actually improve ability or even impart "talent," one young woman said that it instills *motivasi*, and that's better than having any talent; another said that when she was afraid to recite in front of other people, it was because she feared she might not have "interesting" *variasi* to keep the attention of others. For many Indonesians like these teenagers learning to recite the Qur'ān with *lagu*, the project itself was the goal, a potentially permanent motivated state of acquiring piety. For some, the cultivation of heartfelt, *khushū'* emotion as a response to the Qur'ān had become a generative system of reproducing "*khushū*'" aesthetics in voice in order to touch the hearts of others. Some who possessed strong hearts but weak voices nevertheless persevered in pursuing increased technical competence. In spite of the awareness that they would always fall short in evaluations of their competence according to receding horizons of success, the pursuit of orthoprax aesthetics became all the more challenging and appealing as a personal project of piety and potential avenue of contribution to community.

With the recited Qur'an in Indonesia, the performances of virtuosos had come to serve potentially as *kurikulum* for all, and the ideal of improvisatory expression was promoted as a practice of ordinary piety in the 1990s. Formalized pedagogy, while building on a received ideal, nevertheless altered it and also further enhanced ever-expanding expectations for achievement. New "orthoprax" horizons for accomplished performance emerged, placing the homogenizing effect of applied curriculum in tension with the ideal of the spontaneous, improvisatory model of the truly gifted or proficient reciter. Assessments of sentiment, feeling used as a tool of aesthetic sensibility, and the affective recognition of "orthopraxy" that were generated under these conditions determined the self-understandings of aspiring Indonesian reciters at all levels of proficiency. Emotional systems of pedagogy and performance forged for many Indonesians a subjectivity of Qur'ānic practice that took the form of expanding evaluation of potential and escalating expression of pious possibilities.

CHAPTER 5
COMPETING
Promoting Motivated Participation

Qur'ān recitation contests represent a mainstream Southeast Asian expression of the global movement of "Islamic awakening," a phenomenon that in Indonesia emphasized enthusiastically developing Qur'ānic arts, reading, and memorization. Indonesian Muslims recognized that there may be an implicit invitation to try for oneself in the openness of the competition framework, conveying a named "motivating" aspect of piety indirectly even to those who otherwise had no investment in competing. Competitions were understood to be a form of religious education and *da'wah* as well as a popularization of Qur'ānic engagement under the label "the glorification of Islam," *syi'ar* Islam. This conceptualization diminished opposition to contests among religious scholars, by highlighting the overarching goal that the tournaments telegraphed, "motivating" Qur'ānic participation and piety. The "motivation" to ongoing or intensified practice was the object as well as the objective of competition frameworks. Through competitions, a system of Qur'ānic practice developed alongside a goal of instilling emotions of interest and engagement among Indonesian Muslims in the 1990s, driven by the participation of individuals who took their own feeling, or "motivation" to practice, as an object for cultivation.

Immensely popular Qur'ān recitation competitions in the 1990s disseminated a particular form of recitational style and practice throughout Muslim Indonesia, building on religious and social structures as well as the affective systems that have been detailed in the previous chapters. These tournaments enhanced the *motivasi* to Qur'ānic practices, including memorization and calligraphy, and particularly recitation in the *mujawwad* style. Competitions, especially the national tournament, were understood to encourage Indonesians to study Qur'ān recitation though the draws of inspiration (such as admiring of the abilities of others and desiring to emulate them), aspiration (such as wanting to win for personal or group prestige, or perhaps for the prizes that are offered), and participation (often valued as an end in itself). Dimensions of competition practice (the seven standard "*lagu*," or modal melody types, for example) influenced how recitation was practiced overall, as in noncompetitional public performances. Values, standards, and experiences that emerged from competitions along with their training regimens enhanced affective and technical components of practice across multiple levels, even among those who did not compete. The system extended formats and evaluations of "orthoprax" aesthetics as well as affective techniques to ordinary practitioners who then adopted them within increasingly energetic projects of piety.

Recitation contests influenced Qur'ānic engagement by providing structured regimens of practice, enhanced by the affective intensity of real or imagined competition environments. Such regimens influenced larger structures of practice and evaluation. An example is the process by which regional melodic styles (local *lagu*, or "*lagu daerah*") were increasingly labeled as "incorrect" in terms of newer standards conveyed by the competition system. In South Sulawesi, for example, such change occurred in the evaluation and practice of a local melody type, "Lagu Cikoang." Cikoang is an area near Makassar known for its boat festival held around the time of the Birthday of the Prophet, which also includes a famous all-night *dhikr*.[1] When asked what *lagu* Cikoang sounded like, regional contest judges (including ones from the area for which *lagu* Cikoang is named) seemed reluctant to demonstrate, but they identified it as being full of "*naik-turun*" (rise and fall), "like riding a horse." The possibility that it would be used in a competition struck them as laughably silly. They commented that one could not rate it with a score in any case (presumably because of its regular *irama*, or "rhythm")—and besides, "It's just for funerals anyway."

Evaluations of "Cikoang" show the power of competitional ideals, such as "interest" and "motivation," within circumstances of musical, religious, and social change in Qur'ānic Indonesia. Several months after the contest judges had discussed "Cikoang," a teenager from the Cikoang region was happy to demonstrate *lagu* Cikoang. It is based on a nine-beat cycle of two alternations between low and high pitches, with stress on approximately every third beat. This pattern is modified to fit *āyah* phrasing, as in, for example, the first two phrases that would be chanted in almost any recitation:

A - 'u - dhu bi - LLA-hi min ash -shay-TAN - ir - ra - JIM
E♭ G <u>G F G E♭</u> E♭ E♭ E♭ <u>G G F E♭</u>

Bis - mi - LLA - hir - rah - MAN - ir - ra - HIM
G F G E♭ E♭ G G F E♭

The pattern is carried through with minimal variance, favoring the regularity of the cycle over *āyah* length and other considerations. On extended *madd* (duration of vowels), as in the word "*malā'ika*" (angels), the vowel sound was sustained for the correct number of beats according to *tajwīd*, but the pitch continued to vary according to the pattern. Kissing the *muṣḥaf* (text of the Qur'ān) after he had completed his reading, the young man narrated a story about the *lagu* and about Sayyid Jalaluddin al-Aidid. Shaikh Jalaluddin is an important religious figure in the early history of Muslim South Sulawesi who founded a religious order in Cikoang around the turn of the sixteenth to seventeenth centuries. Once upon a time, the story went, Shaikh Jalauddin went to Arabia for a recitation contest. There, all of the reciters used Middle Eastern *lagu* except for him; he stuck with his own *lagu*, "Cikoang." He did this because his *lagu* was different from all the *lagu* of the Arabs. He won the contest because "Lagu Cikoang" stood out, and the distinction drew "attention" in the contest. The young man offered a valorized interpretation of local practice and identity, deploying a strategy that drew on the prevalent competitional idea that difference and "interest" is better. Despite the rejection of Lagu Cikoang for actual competition, his story nevertheless accepted the premise that Indonesian recitation competitions themselves are the authoritative standard for comparison of what is the best in Qur'ānic practice.

For noncompetitors as well as those who did not follow newer national and international standards, Indonesian tournament frameworks still informed the experience and affect of Qur'ānic practice. The reason was their widespread prevalence. By the mid-1990s, competition-style recitation had become the norm for recitation performance at public events, or *acaras*. In Indonesia, public recitation by competition winners at *acaras* and during "broadcast recitation" (as on television) was done in a format of ten-minute segments, deploying the same kinds of *lagu* modulations that a reciter would use in competition, followed by a "poeticization" *(puitisisasi)* of the meanings of the Qur'ānic verses in Indonesian. The performers, such as those who came to an all-day taping of spots for broadcast during Ramadan at the local TVRI (Televisi Republik Indonesia) television station in Makassar, were men and women contest champions. On a call-in radio recitation show, for example, it was obvious that some children were strenuously attempting to emulate the competition style even before receiving any formal instruction. This was usually accomplished by way of uncontrolled melismatic ornamentation, audible especially on the final syllable "*-īm*" (on "*ar-raḥīm*"), of the Bismillah. (Usually, the *ādhān*-like rendition would taper off after a verse or two, to be replaced by a more straightforward *murattal* style.)

Competing is a key frame for performance within religious systems in island Southeast Asia, especially with respect to musical and vocal performances. Although I went to Indonesia to study a form of competition, I was continually surprised by the range of social activities that were actually contests. For example, I spent weeks learning a popular line dance from Papua called the "Sajojo" with women on the Islamic university campus before I realized that we were actually training to compete; in another instance, it took a while to understand that the project of civic beautification in downtown Makassar was a national competition among Indonesian cities, towns, and villages within provinces and districts (Makassar did in fact win this "Adi Pura" competition in 1997). From documented court competitions in gamelan in Java and Bali to *pantung* poetry competitions in Malay-speaking areas, competing is an Indonesian framework for group participation in public events; even the paradigmatic cockfight that Geertz studied was a competition.[2] Not only do competitions provide a structure for balanced or egalitarian presentation of parts of a social system (men and women, different regions, and so on), but in insular and peninsular Southeast Asian cultures, the idea of personal or collective "reputation" (the name, or *nama*, of winners) is often heavily elaborated.[3]

In Muslim Southeast Asia, social expectations of competition activity blended with long-standing Islamic patterns of competing in poetic performance and academic and memorized knowledge, as well as other models of religious virtuosity and accomplishment such as those influenced by sometimes very hierarchical and strongly competitive Sufi systems. Traditions of Arabic poetry competition in the Middle East are also well documented, for example, including those for pre-Islamic Arabia and the Community of the Prophet. In Muslim educational settings, competitions in *ḥadīth* knowledge were also known from the early period of Islam, and some Sufi systems are structured around the comparative appreciation of the spiritual aptitudes of gifted persons.[4] In Southeast Asia, the Qur'ānic idea of communities or individuals "competing in goodness" or "good works" (*Fa'stabiqū'l-khairāt*, as in 2 al-Baqarah 148 and 5 al-Mā'idah 48) formed an Islamic basis for the development of a robust Qur'ān recitation competition system. The Qur'ānic idea of competition for a higher collective goal than mere personal gain was here connected to religious pedagogy, and, consistent with this idea, the Indonesian events themselves were often cast as a form of *da'wah* and education.

Many interpreters of Indonesian cultures have been concerned with the contours of civic "rituals" of the New Order period (which ended with the resignation of President Suharto in 1998). In many analyses of ritual, whether in modern Indonesia or more generally, functional analysis often follows directly from the description of ritual form. Even when something is understood to have happened in a particular ritual, rituals are usually seen to have their temporal and purposive ends in the perpetuation of existing relations of power and authority. A widely shared perspective on the rites of public culture in Indonesia in this period especially—known as ritual *upacara* or civic *acara*—holds that these were repetitive, formulaic events with flat or even dull affective textures that perpetuated preexisting social structures.[5] Furthermore, it is often asserted, dynamics of *acaras* are to be revealed in comparison to other kinds of social activity. In contrast, MTQs are dramatic sites of action. Although some aspects of these events are indeed formulaic (such as the elaborate opening and closing ceremonies), the affective textures of actual tournaments build on the essence of drama. They carry indeterminate outcomes and unforeseeable emotionally charged experiences for the actors involved.

By the decade of the 1990s, a reciprocity of individual and social system had formed around Indonesian Qur'ān competitions that was transformative of each. While elaborate and highly visible, the large-scale promotional frameworks that supported competitions were not a unitary influence on individual motivations, which were simultaneously shaped through the dynamics of preparation, participation, and piety. Sociological function aligned with, but did not completely determine, experience. Individual experience and public discourse instead shared an embracing framework, even as both created it. The structure of Indonesian Qur'ān recitation competitions was highly effective in what was usually the stated goal of "increasing interest in Qur'ān reading," but promotional aspects of competitions did not determine individuals' motivations. Instead, they enhanced and supported multivalent patterns of religious practice. The Indonesians who witnessed the national competition (MTQ) in 1997—and virtually everyone with access to national media had some exposure—saw the framework of Qur'ānic practice being transformed (not just affirmed) by the influence of national competitions. Furthermore, real changes in styles, methods, and approaches within Qur'ānic practice were also taking place among coaches, contestants, judges, patrons, and spectators. The affective charge and dynamism of Qur'ān recitation contests was coming to permeate much recitation practice in Indonesia (whether explicitly "competitive" or not) and fueled its escalation.

Indonesian Qur'ān recitation competitions were widely acknowledged to be highly successful in achieving stated goals of providing the motivation to sustained religious involvement in this period. Promotional frameworks, although evidencing multiple interests, shared *motivasi* as a value. *Motivasi*, like *da'wah*, was an embracing goal conveyed by the competition system, even forming part of some of the practical techniques disseminated to Indonesian Muslims. The salience of the concept is evidenced in the fact that this was the primary reason cited in Indonesian Muslims' explanations of why the activity of competing was not controversial (even among those who had opposed it in the past); in addition, when criticism was offered, it was along the lines that goals of "*motivasi*" were not being achieved. Regimens of training that represented a "charged" virtual competition space conveyed not only the techniques to win contests, but also ways to hierarchize registers of goals under an inclusive affective model of *motivasi*. Pious practitioners who adopted the techniques of "orthoprax" competitional performance embraced the affective quality of *motivasi* self-consciously as a collective ideal and as a personal means to achieve pious goals. When bounded by the competition system, *motivasi* was a strategic "mood"; when viewed from the standpoint of pious practice, it formed part of an expansive motivation. Competitional "moods and motivations" thus propelled enthusiasm to recite the Qur'ān in Indonesia in the 1990s.

The Mood of *Motivasi*

One evening during the weeklong national Qur'ān recitation competition held in Jambi, Sumatra, in 1997, a prominent Muslim intellectual inquired about my research on such events in Indonesia. He asked, did competitions like that one *really* motivate people to recite the Qur'ān? He then rephrased his question as a story, recounting that when he was a boy growing up in the outer islands, his grandmother would make him study how to read the Qur'ān aloud. She told him that if he did not learn how to read properly, he would never be allowed to join the grown-ups at community observances. He would always be made to sit at the back, with the children, no matter how old he got to be. What's more, he would not get to eat along with everyone else, but he would just be given the leftovers, and then only after everybody else was finished. All this, his grandmother warned, would happen if he did not know how to read the Qur'ān. He emphasized how persuasive his grandmother's strategy had been in motivating him to study how to recite. Then he asked one last time, is it true, can the national contest motivate people to recite the Qur'ān as much as his grandmother managed to motivate him?

I thought a bit before trying to give an answer. Many personal goals aligned with the Indonesian recitation competition system: having fun, *da'wah*, participation, winning, contribution to religious community through the "glorification of Islam," and "top-down" ideological interests (such as "national development"), for example. The stated motivations that young people provided for competing were as individual as each person himself or herself. For example, once I asked three teenage boys why they were spending their school vacation training full-time for a corporate recitation contest. The first one said that he initially became interested in competing when he saw the stature *(nama)* of his teacher increase *(naik)* after the teacher had won a local contest; the young man said that he kept up with the contests after that in order to go along with *(ikut-ikut)* his friends. The second young man responded that he wanted someday to become a teacher and that in the future it would be beneficial in the pursuit of that profession to know how to recite well. The third shrugged and said, "It's just what I do" (his "*kebiasaan*"), which could be translated into English with the phrase "just because." These three responses do not and cannot form a framework of contest motivations for individuals (since there are as many personal goals as there are persons). They represent patterns of statements that were typically expressed but not the only ones.

Competitors and coaches recognized a hierarchy of goal registers while they maintained their personal investment in the competition experience. Some said that they started competing for the *juara*, or prizes. Others said it was their parents or another authority figure who had first encouraged them to compete (one coach cited this as a primary factor in young people's participation, adding, "Parents really just want to see their kid up there on the stage"). *Nama* should not be underestimated as a reason for competing, but neither should it be interpreted as purely individualistic self-promotion; a thoughtful coach offered this as the first reason why his students were involved, explaining that kids wanted to increase the *nama* of their region or school (which could also attract sponsorship). Pious goals cross-cut all of these responses. The most common answer given to the question "why compete?" was "*syi'ar Islam*" (the "glorification of Islam"), and, further, the goal was "the practice of piety" *(ibadah)*, "personal" *(pribadi*, or *minat dari dalam)*, or, as one said, "the heart moves on its own" *(hatinya tergerak sendiri)*. Questions about the motivation to compete were also often answered in terms of the *motivasi* that contests supply for individual and collective Qur'ānic engagement. And that, not incidentally, was the question I was also being asked by my colleague. To explain the motivation to Qur'ānic practice that competitions supported and that in turn led Indonesians to support the system requires locating the cultivated Indonesian emotion of *motivasi* and an academic, interpretive idea of "motivation" within a larger theoretical framework.

Often in religious studies, ritual or religious motivation is explained in terms of a mood that functions as an end-state. In their study *The Archetypal*

Actions of Ritual, Humphrey and Laidlaw develop a phenomenological perspective on ritual "intention," also briefly considering the question of ritual motivation. At one point, they pose the question of "not just the immediate reasons for particular rituals but . . . the more general and unfathomable reasons for the continuation of ritual action," asking, "Why do people go on doing it?"[6] Humphrey and Laidlaw provide essentially two types of answers. Both are typical of the thinking about motivated ritual activity in the history of religions. While rejecting that ritual has a "purpose" (and tending to be cognitivist in their overall theory), both of their explanations for ritual action amount to a means-ends situation in which ends are feeling-states. First, they describe a "gap" or "a potential freedom from the everyday and inexorable suffusion of action with personal intentions."[7] The second type of answer Humphrey and Laidlaw provide is in terms of Ludwig Wittgenstein's idea of "depth," seeming to imply that human beings desire to enact a romantic, maybe nostalgic, sense of profundity, mystery, and strangeness.[8] In addition to this kind of depth charge, they also write that ritual affords entrance into "patterns . . . beyond our purposes, beliefs, or intentions," offering the opportunity to step into ritual's "own time" and "perhaps to defy our own transience and death."[9]

Taking the step to consider seriously the "moods and motivations" of progressive religious practice brings on the challenge, however, to view affect in religious systems in terms of the affective dynamics of actual lifeworlds, encompassing everyday emotion as well as the elevated. Religious affect need not be transcendentally death-defying nor inscrutably internal. When ordinary and supraordinary moods are considered in the explanation of the ongoing motivations to religious practice, and when these dynamics are viewed processually in terms of the natural feedback between individuals and social structures, some ritual systems (specifically, voluntary projects of developing ritual piety) reveal themselves to be potentially generative of ongoing activity.

Since the period when symbolic and interpretive perspectives on human behavior (like Geertz') became dominant, scholars have been reluctant to consider the psychological aspects of human activity. In her classic review article of 1984 "Theory in Anthropology since the 1960s," Sherry Ortner provides a glimpse of this state of affairs and further criticizes the absence of sensitive treatments of motivation in the study of social action. Ortner argues:

> At the moment, the dominant theory of motivation . . . is derived from interest theory. The model is that of an essentially individualistic, and somewhat aggressive, actor, self-interested, rational, pragmatic, and perhaps with a maximizing orientation as well. What actors do, it is assumed, is rationally go after what they want, and what they want is materially and politically useful for them

> within the context of their cultural and historical situations. . . . There is, however, a growing body of literature which explores the variable construction of self, person, emotion, and motive in cross-cultural perspective. . . . One may hope for some cross-fertilization between the more sociologically oriented practice accounts, with their relatively denatured views of motive, and some of these more richly textured accounts of emotion and motivation. . . . Finally, an interest approach tends to go hand in hand with seeing action in terms of short-term practical "moves," rather than long-term developmental "projects."[10]

In the fields of the humanities and social sciences, influential frameworks developed since the 1960s (such as those of Bourdieu and Foucault) have not provided theories that adequately explain what motivates religious practice or even action more generally. There has tended either to be an appeal to universalized psychological needs and drives (maximizing self-interest, regenerating the sacred, and so forth), or else there has been an absence of any explicit mechanism at all, as with the idea that action is a by-product of "culture." In the study of human activity in the human sciences, including the study of rituals, an implicit theory of motivation, including applications of Bourdieu's theory of "practice," has typically been some variant of a rational choice model.

Although willing to construct complex universes of interior meaning from semiotic signals, theorists have seemed nervous about the suggestion that one can know what is "in the head" of an individual with respect to motivation. Ironically, this hesitation has not resulted in guarded portrayals of human motivation in actual analysis. Instead, individual motivation has often been treated as the side effect of power relations, a calculation of interest and realpolitik. This perspective tends ultimately to render ritual action in terms of its function, often expressed with respect to religious systems in terms of ritual "efficacy" or large-scale sociological dynamics. If something happens in a ritual (such as a Turnerian inversion), this is often seen to reinforce functionally preexisting social systems or other patterns of order, such as the Durkheimian "sacred." At least since the 1980s, anthropological approaches have often deployed asymmetrical power relations as the determinative mechanism for human action in a top-down psychological structure. Theorists who would not appropriately be labeled "structural-functionalists," for example, nevertheless imply that the purpose of ritual is to produce and reproduce existing power relations, even when ritual is seen as a subversion or resistance to hegemonic power.[11]

Just because competitional discourse highlighted "motivated" long-term interested practice did not mean that this concept had salience for practitioners in the same way for everyone. Some stated interests articulated by contest promotion, for example, clearly were not meaningful for everyone involved. Motivation, as psychological anthropologist Claudia Strauss argues, is "not automatically acquired when cultural messages are imparted." It is not enough for a cultural category to be "widely shared and influential" to conclude that it motivates people, Strauss claims. In order to understand "why people do what they do," she writes, it is insufficient simply to "identify the dominant constructs in a society," since this also requires the specification of culture's relation to action in terms of lived situations and experiences. The aim of a group of scholars in the field of cultural anthropology has been to develop approaches to motivation that address what Strauss has identified as three "complexities of the socialization process": "(1) public social messages may change, be inconsistent, or hard to read; (2) internalizing these messages does not mean copying them in a straightforward way; and (3) motivation is not automatically acquired when cultural descriptions of reality are learned."[12] The goal, as Strauss writes, is to "find the missing links that would explain how ambiguous, conflicting, and potentially impotent social messages become the basis for someone's action."[13]

The program outlined by this academic approach includes three important points. Motivation can be explained, and in a way that recognizes the multiple public messages conveyed by a system; it is possible, and necessary, to investigate the variable ways that individuals adopt (and create) "templates" for action; and affect is a key to understanding these dynamics. Working from this basis, for example, psychological anthropologist Roy D'Andrade offers a theory based on "goal-schemas," resting on "cultural models" with "directive" and affective "force"; his premise is that shared "schemas" serve as goals. D'Andrade treats cognitive "goal-schemas" as motives, or as having "motivational force," evidencing differing degrees of "schematicity" and hierarchical organization (with "means-ends" connections representing one kind of linkage). Goals, D'Andrade explains, are embedded in larger frameworks with the lower levels tending to be "recruited" by higher-level goals. An important aspect of his project is to understand how such schemas are learned, socialized, and internalized.[14]

This group of theorists advocates a "person-centered" approach that emphasizes the power of affect. The model that they propose is cognitive, with a loose idea that affect attaches to ideational frameworks as a "force" or a mode of "internalization," thereby resolving the problems of variance, change, development, and the salience of ideas for individuals. They recognize that cultural constructs "do not automatically deliver motivational force" to lifeworlds; thus affect is a principal component of the connections that they draw. They notice further that motivating "force" may shift over time in life experiences, depending on the contexts of social interactions and cultural frameworks. Strauss, for example, explains that "self concepts are acquired slowly over the course of development as learned social ideologies . . . linked to and energized by memories of powerful life experiences."[15] Feelings, she writes, accompany memories of such life experiences. "Knowing the feelings that people associate with different cultural models as a result of their specific life experiences is crucial to understand what motivates them."[16] Affect is not just a way to recognize actors' motivations, however; in Indonesia, Qur'ānic motivation was itself a salient feeling type promoted by the competition system itself.

Competitions embraced a reciprocal interaction among "top-down" social structures and "bottom-up" individual projects of self-cultivation and community-building. Although dominant discourses influenced motivational registers of religious practice, they did not determine them. Qur'ānic contests in Indonesia and their effects would thus not be best analyzed as a collection of subjects seeking to maximize material self-interest or pursuing "intrinsic rewards" or "self-actualization"[17] any more than they could be satisfactorily described as entirely the effect of a sort of sociological invisible hand. Mechanisms of inspiration that were self-consciously amplified through competition promotion, participation, and preparation included specific affective techniques as well as norms and standards. The system conveyed to ordinary practitioners the affective senses of competing through their pedagogical representation; along with competition standards, competitors as well as non-competitors accepted affective models that they then employed according to their own goals. The modes by which Qur'ān competitions established specific "orthoprax" criteria and techniques that Muslim groups and pious individuals actively sought to adopt included *motivasi* to religious learning and performance as a goal and strategy.

D'Andrade writes that the "top-level" goals that encompass others of a lower order are related to "a person's most general interpretations of what is going on."[18] The question the gentleman asked me regarding what was "going on" in Jambi in 1997 concerned "motivation." I had spent the previous year investigating modes of inspiration for projects of continued Qur'ānic piety in Indonesia; and Indonesians were asking me the same kind of question: do these Qur'ānic regimens impart *motivasi,* and if so how? Although competing may be a natural human motivator, the acknowledgment that *motivasi* was a "top-level" goal of competition practice is not enough to explain how the affective modes of competition were motivational. The heightened intensity of the competition setting lent a power and force to the moods of training and participation and this partially explains how competitions and their emotional valences affected practice from the level of situated details up to large-scale social structures.

A key to understanding the generative aspects of Indonesian Qur'ān recitation competitions for the piety of individuals as well as the Indonesian Muslim public culture of the New Order more widely is the recognition that "motivation" was really an emotion, or in Geertz' language, a religious "mood." In *Language, Charisma, and Creativity,* Thomas Csordas discusses a theory of "motives," which are "orientations" to action (but not exactly "intentions" or "motivations") that "circulate" through a ritual system as a self-referencing "set of terms." These orientations "direct action to another dimension," Csordas writes, and may also direct action "in a strategic sense" in social life. Csordas develops the framework to explain the experiential language of "charisma" in a ritual system, in which motives cycle among a "vocabulary of motives" and a "system of performance" so that they are "not only strategies for action but also instigations to action." In Indonesia in the 1990s, the mood of "*motivasi*" could also be described as such an orientation, emergent in actual practices and pedagogies, and permeating the competition system both inside and apart from actual tournaments with affective and directive force.[19]

Described in public messages, *motivasi* was applied in self-conscious and explicit strategies within motivated projects of piety, along with the other "orthoprax" standards and techniques that the competition system conveyed. When pious noncompetitors adopted the competition framework, its feelings as well as its formats, these bounded affective domains interacted with the expansive aspirations of piety. The affective alignment of bounded and expansive levels of *motivasi* propelled the dynamic of engagement. The goals of realizing perfection enrolled particular strategies of affect, including *motivasi,* while the mood of *motivasi* also resonated with these encompassing ideals. Through promotion, preparation, and participation, the competitions of the 1990s motivated an affective quality of *motivasi* for ongoing practice that described, explained, and inspired an escalating engagement of Qur'ānic piety on personal and public levels in Muslim Indonesia.

Promotion

With Indonesian Qur'ān recitation competitions, or MTQs, the religious proclivities of individuals to practice piety and improve ritual ability interacted with more or less compatible social frameworks and collective systems of meaning. Recitation competition promoters' and participants' interests often aligned, but they could not be said to be identical. Although the frameworks showed a great deal of variation in terms of their interests, consistent across them was the goal of Qur'ānic *motivasi.*

The promotional dynamics of the national competition and more local competitions could be viewed on the level of large-scale interactions of social frameworks of power and authority. Borrowing Howard Federspiel's terminology, one might consider MTQs in terms of the ways in which the frameworks of "Islamic values" and "national development" interacted in cycles of production, reproduction, accommodation, and change.[20] Most contests were framed in terms of the development of the moral values of the younger generation in a rhetorical field that was recognizable for its New Order character, emphasizing IPTEK (*ilmu pengetahuan dan teknologi*, or "research and technology knowledge") and IMTAK (*ilmu takwa*, or "spiritual knowledge"). The idea of the "progress" *(kemajuan)* effected through the promotion of Qur'ān reciting was especially clear in a prison competition I attended, in which Qur'ān recitation (along with table tennis, volleyball, and chess) was related directly to moral reform *(pembinaan)* and to themes of the development of "society" *(masyarakat)*. To focus only on such discourses as if they were automatically determinative, however, risks losing sight of the strategies, experiences, and concerns of those who have the most to do with competitions. The experiences of practitioners do show that the goal of personal "motivation," shared by cultural frameworks, had an impact on individuals. Especially in connection to the national tournament, participants and others also often expressed value in terms of the ideas of "motivating" others to contribute to religious community and the "glorification of Islam."

Images of the Eighteenth National Contest for the Recitation of the Qur'ān invoke the Indonesia of spectacle.[21] A national recitation competition was held every year in Indonesia, the winners of which were eligible to go on to represent Indonesia in international recitation competitions such as those held in Kuala Lumpur and Riyadh.[22] Every three years, the MTQ was held on the maximum scale, with extra divisions open; Jambi 1997 was one of the big ones.[23] The opening ceremony featured some one thousand dancers and five hundred drummers who flooded the newly built arena for a performance of "*tarian massal*" enacting the moment of revelation, and a primary focus of attention was a speech by then-President Suharto.[24] (Starting in the 1970s, the attendance of President Suharto was featured as a prominent component of national MTQs.) The minister of religious affairs presided over the closing awards ceremony, which also showcased a massive movement spectacle, this one featuring a performance by a well-known Indonesian poet as another fifteen hundred bodies symbolically reenacted the moment of divine revelation (they bore long white sheets that rippled across the field). Both events were broadcast live from coasts to coasts, and there was also thorough news coverage of the competition, especially of the grand facilities that the provincial government of Jambi had prepared. Jambi, under the direction of the provincial government, had begun its work years in advance (1992 was usually given as the year), with heavy community support and involvement; the entire city of Jambi—even outlying areas away from the competition arenas—had been decorated with flags, banners, billboards, and festive lights for the occasion.

National MTQs had beginnings more modest than the spectacular event held in Jambi in the summer of 1997, which one contest organizer on the national level described as being "like the Olympics." The first competition formally recognized as "national" was held in 1968 in Makassar, South Sulawesi, and did not include the top-level "official" involvement in evidence at Jambi. The first competition featured contests only in recitation and memorization, in contrast to the multiple events of the 1997 MTQ. Since Makassar 1968, national MTQ events expanded in scale and in activities to include not only the recitation of the Qur'ān and its memorization, but also calligraphy and calligraphic decoration, Qur'ān exegesis (in the Arabic language), teams competing in a kind of "quiz bowl" (short answers on the Qur'ān and Islamic topics, one of the more popular events among spectators), and nonmelodic recitation (*tartil*) for children. Divisions based on age and other criteria (such as sightedness) have also expanded and multiplied.

Typical of national MTQs, the contestants for recitation and memorization events at Jambi sat in sound-proof booths. The main *mimbar* (stage) for melodic recitation had a live video feed for contestants and judges who were backstage. Contestants recited assigned passages of the Qur'ān, while judges from across Indonesia assessed the technical and artistic merits of their performances. Winners were awarded expense-paid Hajj trips and other prizes. In addition to the ceremonies associated with the contests (including, for example, the official swearing in of the judges), national MTQs had also become the occasion for a number of meetings of Muslim groups and organizations,[25] as well as fairs (which featured crafts from across the archipelago and special "houses" constructed to display regional Islamic arts),[26] a massive parade with elaborate floats, Islamic musical theater, and other activities.[27]

The float parade in 1997 was, for the first time, a competition in itself. It opened with representatives of the previous year's overall contest winners (a stately bride and groom couple from West Java in dark sunglasses, carrying balloons), and after local marching bands passed, the parade featured groups representing regional "culture." These groups were dominated by scores of men from East Java (relocated to Sumatra by "*transmigrasi*" programs), who were dressed up—and hammed convincingly—as tough, scary pirates. The real spectacle was the floats. Each province had the opportunity to submit a float to the parade. Guidelines were set up for thematic motifs: encouraged were representations of "traditional houses," usually with contest participants in "traditional [wedding] dress," and I spent much of my time with the group from

Irian Jaya (the area just to the west of Papua New Guinea), who had designed a special costume concept to meet the dual expectations of "tradition" and "Islamic." Invited themes also included Qur'āns and boats of all kinds; many floats combined elements of all of these, and some had imaginative designs that included components such as flowing waterfalls, towering trees, and giant birds. Emblems of the particular region were encouraged. For example, DKI Jakarta had a float of the main mosque, Masjid Istiqlal, and South Sulawesi displayed a proud Bugis schooner featuring the region's famous oath of fealty, "Tadopulli." Even the decorated Qur'ān manuscript "Mushaf Sundawi" had its own float ("not to be judged," said the pamphlet distributed about the project). Provincial governmental departments such as Agriculture and Family Planning had their own floats as well. Agriculture's entry featured two young reciters surrounded by oversized models of local fruit—especially prominent was Jambi's prized durian, fashioned huge, with a piece already sliced out. Only Bali did not have a float entry that year, and instead *jilbab*-clad Balinese women and girls in blue jeans stopped as they passed the provincial governor and official guests on the risers, performing a brief excerpt of Balinese dance before moving on.

In 1997, official MTQ competition events were grouped into seven *cabang* (branches). These were Tilawatil Quran (melodic recitation, for males and females from ages seven to thirty-five, including a subdivision for blind persons); Hifzil Quran (memorization of one, five, ten, twenty, or all thirty *juz'*; age limits increase with each subdivision, up to the maximum age of twenty-four [or married] for all thirty *juz'*); Tafsiril Quran (after demonstrating complete memorization of the text, unmarried contestants under the age of twenty-four conduct thirty minutes of explication of selected Qur'ānic verses, in Arabic); Tartil al-Quran (basic recitation for children under the age of ten with no lowest age limit); Fahmil Quran (questions on Qur'ānic and Islamic topics, posed to a team of three, with gender mix permissible and ages restricted to between thirteen and nineteen); Syarhil Quran (one team of three persons who read the Qur'ān and interpret its moral and legal meaning "poetically" *[secara puitis dan pensyarahan]* into Indonesian for up to twenty minutes); and, finally, Khattil Quran (calligraphy, including divisions for Naskah, Dekorasi, and Hiasan Mushaf, which are script, decorative illumination, and composition and embellishment, respectively, with time limits set at three to four hours; the age limit for these events is forty). A trend over previous years had been the addition of more events that emphasized comprehension of the Qur'ān, such as the Syarhil Quran and the much-admired Tafsiril Quran events.

The national MTQ was hardly the only recitational competition held in Indonesia in these years. There were frequent and popular competitions sponsored by many sorts of associations, institutions, corporations, and individuals. The national MTQ was the best known and the most "official," however, and it had come to provide a model for the many contests that proliferated less formally. Other ongoing national contests have included, for example, the RRI contest (known as the Pekan Tilawatil Quran, or "Week of Qur'ān Recitation," in Ramadan and sponsored by the national broadcasting media); the RRI contest was a national system similar to the national MTQ, with provincial winners sent to Jakarta for the competition. There was also the Musabaqah Tilawatil Quran Antar Sekolah Lanjutan (known as SLTP and SLTA, nationals being held on Hari Pendidikan Nasional [HAR-DIKNAS], or "National Education Day"). Countless other "MTQs" were also conducted among students, employees of banks, hotels, and national utilities such as energy and communications. For example, Pertamina, the national oil company, and Telkom, the national communications company, were two prime sites of recitation training for coaches and students in Makassar. Journalists, police, the military, and the prison system all developed competition systems. For most of these, the judges were drawn from the LPTQ's pool of men and women who were certified by the provincial governor for this function. For the informal contests that continued to proliferate, however, judges could be local mosque teachers. One of the primary assumptions regarding these events was that they inspired greater Qur'ānic activity and involvement.[28]

Although the framework of competitions took on distinctive characteristics in the public culture of Indonesia's New Order, recitation competitions have also been a long-standing feature of Indonesian Islam. Many older people recalled both informal and formal Qur'ān recitation events (some of which were competitions) held in mosques during their childhoods; especially memorable were those held on "*laylat al-Qur'ān*" in Ramadan (lit. "Night of the Qur'ān," also called "Nuzul al-Qur'ān," commemorating the initial descent of the revealed Qur'ān to earth, as invoked in Sūra 97 al-Qadr). Such periodic competitions continued on a local scale in mosques during the time of fieldwork, especially during the fasting month of Ramadan. In relating their memories of recitation competitions, people often highlighted the point that the terms used for these contests were at first of Indonesian origin, and only later (in the 1970s and 1980s) were they replaced by Arabic terms. The notable contest in 1946 in Asahan, North Sumatra, was known as a "*sayembara*," for example. Many people noted that a contest was once called an (Indonesian) "*perlombaan*" and not an (Arabic) "*musābaqah*,"[29] and reciters were once designated "*pelagu*" (those who use *lagu*, or melody) before they were known by the standard Arabic terms "*qāri'/qāri'ah*." The term "*musābaqah*" (based on the Qur'ānic phrase "*Fa'stabiqū'l-khairāt*") may first have been used in Indonesia in

1953, during the second regional contest for the recitation of the Qur'ān in Pontianak, and after that time it clearly gained more popularity. Such semantic changes may have been pointed out in order to stress that competitions began as a local and indigenous phenomenon. This would be consistent with the nostalgic, and ambivalent, mix of pride people showed at the vitality of Qur'ānic activity within local communities (the local terms underscore this sense of distinction) and also a simultaneous deprecation of the earlier forms of contests as less normatively "Islamic" (because a larger Arabic-language framework had not yet been fully realized).

Larger, more organized regional competitions seem first to have been held in Indonesia in the 1920s. A formal competition was held in Sumatra 1946 on the occasion of the Birthday of the Prophet (Mawlid al-Nabi), apparently not without some controversy as to the appropriateness of rendering the revealed Speech of God into a contest. Three years later, a contest was held in Makassar, sponsored by the Panitia Pembangunan Mesjid Raya (Board for the Construction of Mesjid Raya, the city's main mosque for decades until Al-Markaz opened in 1996, just months before the start of my fieldwork). Winners from across South Sulawesi and also from Kalimantan attended the historic event in Makassar. The champions of this contest were designated "*lil imamil qurra*," or "leaders of the readers," indicating the potential social function (or opportunity) associated with contest performance.[30] Contests were reportedly held at the mosque each Ramadan thereafter, and in 1953, the local Radio Republik Indonesia (RRI) station became involved in broadcasting the competition. In the same period (1952), the city of Jakarta also began to hold a contest in Qur'ān recitation on the occasion of the "birthday" of the city,[31] and similar developments in organizing regional competitions seem to have been occurring across the archipelago in these years. Comments by various authorities have suggested that throughout the 1950s, such annual competitions became more widespread because they provided, among other things, a means of selecting a reciter to perform the recitation for public events in the period of the rapid consolidation of "*acara* culture" in the new Republic of Indonesia. By the 1990s, such recitation had become a standard feature of Muslim public culture in Indonesia, and reciters at these formal *acara*s were almost without exception contest champions.[32]

Also in the 1950s, organizations were formed to promote the recitation of the Qur'ān, such as Nahdat al-Qurrā (Revival of the Reciters of the Qur'ān, in East Java); Wihdat al-Qurrā and Muwāfaqāt al-Qurrā (Union of the Reciters of the Qur'ān and Confederation of the Reciters of the Qur'ān, in Makassar);[33] Persatuan Pelajar al-Qur'ān (Association of Students of the Qur'ān, in Pontianak); Jam'iyyatul Qurrā (Organization of the Reciters of the Qur'ān,

Medan), and many others. At the same time, several organizations for *ḥuffāẓ* (memorizers) were also established.[34] In 1951, Wahid Hasyim, then the minister of religious affairs, supported by scholars and reciters of the Qur'ān, became the founder of an organization known as the Jam'iyyat al-Qurrā' wa al-Huffāẓ in Jakarta; this was intended to become a federation for all of the extant organizations. After various branches were founded, the organization held its first national congress in 1953; it carried out the contests in Jakarta and Surabaya in 1958 and 1964 as well as the contest held during the Conference of Islam in Asia and Africa (Bandung, 1965), which included participants from outside Indonesia.[35]

In 1962, the minister of religious affairs, Saifuddin Zuhri, issued a government statement that declared that the quality of Qur'ān recitation among students entering religious schools under the supervision of the ministry was to be improved. Qur'ān recitation contests were seen to be part of the solution to the problem. Soon after, there began a national student *(pelajar)* competition for Qur'ān recitation, held in Jakarta from 1962 to 1968.[36] The Ministry of Religious Affairs would be increasingly active in organizing contests after this time. The educational rationale for recitation contests has been fundamental to their popular conceptualization in Indonesia, as can be seen both in "official" discourse (such as government statements) and in less formal (though no less influential) representations.

In May 1977, the Lembaga Pengembangan Tilawatil Quran was established with the assistance of the Ministry of Religious Affairs and the Department of Home Affairs.[37] The LPTQ began to manage the competitions as well as the promotion of Qur'ānic practices overall, thus consolidating and superseding many previous groups. The LPTQ has officially described itself as a nongovernmental body, operating on and reporting directly to the various levels of government administration (from village and subdistrict to national), with close affiliation to the Ministry of Religious Affairs at each level. One of its primary roles has been to administer contests from the local level up to the national. Its functions are officially stated to be the following: first, to "carry out programs for the development of Qur'ān recitation, memorization, calligraphy, and exhibition of the Qur'ān"; second, to "improve the understanding of the Qur'ān by sponsoring translation, commentary, and classification of verses"; third, to "encourage the practical application of Qur'ānic teachings in Muslims' daily lives."[38]

The upsurge in the MTQ phenomenon and its institutionalization was not limited to Indonesia in these decades. In developing its own recitation contest system, neighboring Malaysia shows a parallel development within the same period. By the 1970s, the Malaysian competition was the primary international extension of the Indonesian national MTQ system; however, even experts who were active in this period acknowledged that it is difficult to ascertain what, if any, direct influence and contact there was between Indonesia and Malaysia in the development of contests for the recitation of the Qur'ān in the years before the Malysian contest became international. In Malaysia, efforts at organized competitions also began in the 1950s. Among the most influential figures for the early development of Malaysian contests was Tunku 'Abdul Rahman, who, as early as 1951, began organizing reading competitions (Musabaqah Membaca al-Qur'ān) in his home state of Kedah; later, relocating to the state of Johor, he organized a statewide competition there. When the Federation of Malaya gained independence from Great Britain in 1957, Tunku 'Abdul Rahman was appointed prime minister, and subsequently, in Ramadan 1960, there was held the first "national" Qur'ān recitation competition in Malaysia, with forty-four state champions competing (four from each of eleven Malaysian states). Similar to the LPTQ in Indonesia, there has been a central organizing committee (part of the government of Malaysia) that oversees the competitions.[39]

In 1961, the Malaysian competition went international, and a total of eleven readers from countries including Brunei, the Philippines, Malaysia, Thailand, and Singapore all took part in the Malaysian contest. Although the first Malaysian competitions were all male, women began to participate soon after, in 1965. This was the year in which Indonesian reciters resumed participating in the Malaysian contest; women had competed in Indonesia all along. The international profile of the Malaysian contest grew outside of Southeast Asia, and in 1976 the competition opened to contestants from Arab nations. Dozens of countries have taken part in the Malaysian competitions, with participation from any one nation limited to two persons, one male and one female. At first, the number of judges was not fixed, but in the mid-1970s, the panel was determined to be nine (the head of which is Malaysian, with others coming from other countries).[40] Just as in Indonesia, the Malaysian contest has been distinguished by the attendance of the prime minister and the Yang di-Pertuan Agong (Supreme Head of State) as well as other dignitaries and spectators; like the Indonesian MTQs, it featured parades, speeches, and a special flag. As in Indonesia, winners were awarded expense-paid Hajj trips.[41] The explicit rationale in Malaysia, as in Indonesia, has been to improve quality and interest in recitation.[42] Malaysia's international tournament had a smaller number of participants, however, compared to the enormous numbers for Indonesia's national tournament (multiply an average of fifty contestants plus ten officials by twenty-seven provinces for an estimate of the number of participants in attendance at Jambi). In Indonesia, internationalization (although valued) has been more minimal,[43] while the maximalization of domestic participation and representation (as well as the continued development of additional contest events) were operative goals.

What is recognized as the first national recitational competition in Indonesia was held in 1968 in Makassar, the site of my fieldwork, about a decade before the official formation of the LPTQ. Although comparative data are difficult to obtain, it seems that South Sulawesi was among the more energetic areas in the archipelago in terms of the organization of competitions in this period, along with parts of Sumatra. Competitions had been held annually at the main mosque, Mesjid Raya, since just after Independence, for almost two decades (relayed since the 1950s by RRI Nusantara III—Makassar, and with official recitation organizations becoming involved with the competition of 1961).[44] In 1967, the year before the historic "first national MTQ" in Makassar, the contest in Mesjid Raya expanded to include participants from regions outside of eastern Indonesia for the first time. Under the direction of the mayor (M. Deng Patompo) and Lieutenant-General Askri (of the Eastern Indonesia Army Division), and under the organizing efforts of the head of RRI Makassar (M. Sani, who had relocated from Medan, northern Sumatra, the year before), the competition evolved into a system that included Medan, Malaysia, and South Sulawesi, with finals held in Medan. The 1968 competition in Makassar, with contestants arriving from throughout the archipelago, was to be given official mention at each national MTQ thereafter as the "first MTQ." This MTQ was seen to be the inception of a national system in which the tournament was held in a different location in Indonesia every year (such as Jambi in 1997).

Competition sponsorship in Indonesia is part of a Muslim tradition of religious patronage, an important mode of the expression of piety and the acquisition of religious merit, available to (and more or less incumbent upon) those who can afford it. The patronage pattern is especially visible in the history of the private and semiprivate endowment of Muslim institutions of education. Qur'ān recitation competitions in Indonesia were widely understood to be a form of religious education, and sponsors of these events, including government affiliates, attained the satisfaction that patrons of religious education are privileged to enjoy. Recitation competition promoters' and participants' interests aligned but were not identical. Contests were a system in which the affecting experience of participants and the public discourse of promotion fed back into one another. Top-level interests did not necessarily determine the direction of all aspects of the shared system; further, since the model was closely tied to individual practice, a reciprocity of individual and social levels within competition structures was often in effect. Although some of the sponsorship and rhetorical framing of the national MTQ was unambiguously political, nationalist, and developmentalist, this did not necessarily render the stated religious goals of the contest patrons, promoters, and participants insincere. Those who promoted and participated in contests at all levels spoke of them in terms that were pious and religious, terms that were appropriate for the awareness that the activity at hand was the voicing of the revealed Speech of God. When values accreted onto a Qur'ānic system came into play, such as New Order developmentalism, their influence was not felt to distort the integrity of revelation from God in the form of the recited Qur'ān.

With MTQs, the religious proclivities of individuals to practice piety and improve ritual ability interacted with more or less compatible social frameworks and collective systems of meaning such as *da'wah*. In this interaction, individual motivations were more than the effects of sociology, however; individual projects of self-cultivation and the complex motivations behind them were also driving competitions. For their part, the form that competitions took and the shape of their modes of evaluation influenced individual practice directly, and they also reinforced the valued sense of a community of religious practice. The intense process of training for and participating in a competition enhanced patterns of individual experience in immediate ways, shaping practitioners' subjectivities with respect to motivation and the valued senses of ability and community.

In Indonesia, the competition pattern blended with other religious values and practices as well as more contemporary concerns, such as, for example, keeping young people out of trouble (or harm's way). For example, one corporate-sponsored competition in Makassar was held not in Qur'ān recitation proper but in oration or speechmaking *(pidato)*, Qur'ān memorization, and recitation of the Barzanji. It was for *pesantren* (religious school) children from throughout the province, demonstrating that the president director of the sponsoring group of companies, like many of South Sulawesi's new industrialists, had old and close ties to the community of traditional Islamic educators. The finals of this competition in 1996 were held on December 31, New Year's Eve, and one stated purpose of the contest was to provide an Islamically positive activity on that night for Muslim youth. There was also benefit for the sponsoring company—not primarily in the form of advertisement, in the sense that corporations benefit from sponsoring sporting events—but in terms of the production of religious merit that would naturally translate into profits. The speeches that opened the corporation's competition event included frequent references to the *barakah*, or blessing, the company would gain from sponsoring the activity. In these speeches, it was presumed that the children would pray for the well-being of the benefactor and his company. I soon witnessed this ideal become a dramatic reality when, just before the competition, a close relative of the president director passed away, and all the competition participants—some eight hundred of them—gathered on the floor of the main front hall of the corporate headquarters and recited the *tahlil* funerary text with the most respected pesantren *kiai* from throughout South Sulawesi sitting in the front to lead them.

Telkom, the national telecommunications company, was one of the first corporate sponsors of recitation contests, having held them approximately every five years for the previous twenty years. Telkom competitions represented avenues for employee development (in the arena of "Sports, Belief, and Culture," as it was called). In this context, the "Islamic values" model of sponsorship combined not only with overarching ideas of national development, but also more potently with the company's desire to develop its human resources. For example, the Qur'ānic verses chosen for recitation in the competition seemed to address common workplace issues, such as idle gossip, as well as more serious moral lapses.[45] A promotion framework such as Telkom's did not so much determine the motivations of participants as it contributed to the multiple or combined goals they pursued. The religious dimensions of motivation were not effaced by companion instrumental aims, such as, in the Telkom example, a decrease in gossip in the workplace. Every one of the verses selected for the Telkom competition is in the Qur'ān and is no less the Qur'ān for the selection process having been intentional.[46] Sponsors' values did influence the attitudes of individuals but often toward the stated goal of increased religiosity rather than the increased cynicism some outsiders might expect. As in the case of the phone company executive who found himself feeling compelled to learn melodic recitation (see chapter 1), this may have come as much as a surprise to participants as it would to outside observers.

The promotional frameworks of the national MTQ could be explained as "invention of tradition"—not in terms of the presence of an imagined past invoked as "tradition" in the present but instead as the creation of new "traditions," with the future (not the past) made palpable. The national MTQ in Jambi in 1997 reverberated with a "first annual" feel. Official symbolism connected with the contest takes up several pages of the official *Guide*, including the color code of the official eighteenth MTQ "*logo*," the seal of the LPTQ and the province of Jambi, as well as the official MTQ "*monumen*" (statue, dedicated to the theme "*Iqro'!*" or "Recite!").[47] The *Guide* also includes the words and music to the official "MTQ Hymn" and the theme song of the event, the "MTQ March." The march lyrics are (translated from Indonesian):

> The Musabaqah Tilawatil Quran resounds, pouring forth unto God
> Our duty is love of God, the Prophet, and the nation

> The land of Indonesia overflows with prosperity and tranquility
> "Blessed country, Forgiving God" [Ar., written as "*Baldatun toyibatun Robbun Ghofur*"] will surely be realized[48]

Both the "March" and the "Hymn" include such nationalist themes. The haunting, minor key of the march was hard to shake, whether performed by a full orchestra, a marching kazoo band, or the human voice. Many Muslim and non-Muslim Indonesians could hum or sing the "MTQ March" because of years of annual exposure through broadcasts and promotion of the events.

The LPTQ's affiliation with the provincial government as well as the Ministry of Religious Affairs brought the full political rhetoric of the state to bear at the national MTQ.[49] Nationalist and developmentalist themes typified the banners that decorated the city of Jambi: "The national MTQ increases belief and piety of the [religious] community as a natural resource for development, leading toward a society that is just, prosperous, and based on Pancasila" or, more succinctly, "The national MTQ increases participation of the [religious] community in national development."[50]

The most overt and programmatic expression of New Order values was evidenced in the opening ceremony (which was the only part of the MTQ that most officials customarily attended). President Suharto's address at the MTQ in 1997, not surprisingly, highlighted national development as well as other familiar themes, such as the idea that the modernization process brings with it the dangers of "excesses" and the potential loss of moral strength for nation-building: "Our people truly desire to become a developed people, prosperous socially and economically. We do not wish, however, to become a people lacking in spirituality *(kering rohaninya)*. Strong religious awareness is the wealth of the spirituality of a people. Only a people that is spiritually strong and prosperous socially and economically can become a great people *(bangsa yang unggul)* in the times to come, [times] that will always be full of challenges."[51]

The president's speech grafted religious language onto the framework of the New Order's nationalist goals in this period. This usage was especially clear in the following statement, which contains an unusual number of Arabic loan words for a presidential address by Suharto. For example, it employs the Islamic designation "Allāh" for "God" (instead of the more neutral Indonesian term "Tuhan"): "We must be quick to give thanks *(pandai bersyukur)* if we enjoy comforts and meet success *(kenikmatan dan keberhasilan)*. In addition, we must also be steadfast in patience and trust [in God, *bersabar dan bertawakal*] if we encounter hardship and setbacks. Allāh (praised be He), in the Qur'ān, has said that He will always be with those who have patience." These words could be interpreted to be addressing Muslims as such, part of an attempt to subordinate goals of the Islamic community (through their interests in religious and political programs) to a proposed top-level schema of national interest. In another example, the speech emphasized the benefits to be derived though community cooperation. In this case, Muslims (imagined homogeneously in terms of idealized interest) are portrayed as having an exemplary role in a form of social development that would align their own goals with national interests. Here, "cooperative" aspects of the schema are imagined to maintain social harmony and also to further national goals:

> The Musabaqah Tilawatil Quran cannot be undertaken with joy and humility *(meriah dan khidmat)* without great solidarity and mutual cooperation *(kebersamman dan kegotongroyongan)*. . . . If this MTQ could be carried out with the mutual cooperation of Muslims *(gotong-royong kaum Muslim)*, then we surely can accumulate more resources *(menghimpun dana lebih besar)* in order to overcome poverty and to prepare scholarships for children whose parents are of poor means. This project, of course, is not an easy one. However, with strong resolve and strength of pure intention *(semangat keikhlasan)*, we can be sure that this effort will yield results.

Compatible frameworks of educational ideals, nation-building, Qur'ānic values, and Muslim solidarity are being proposed in this statement to align hierarchically, with Muslims' goals extended to the interests of the Indonesian people at large.[52] Profoundly committed to ideals of education as many MTQ participants were, it nevertheless does not follow that Indonesian Muslims (or the Indonesian people more generally) would automatically feel their own projects to resonate ideationally or affectively with the president's statement. During the speeches opening the MTQ, in fact, it was instead the model of the internationalization of community that seemed to align most closely with participants' personal and collective self-understanding.

The closing address of the MTQ, delivered by Dr. Tarmizi Taher (the minister of religious affairs), emphasized the global implications of Indonesian Islamic practice. His own developmentalist rhetoric focused primarily on the upcoming era of *globalisasi* and the need for Indonesia to withstand the anticipated assault on moral values that had long been forecasted to accompany the further acceptance of technologies from non-Muslim sources, most notably the United States. In this address, he highlighted a recent request by Muslim educators in the United States to provide Indonesian teachers of Qur'ān reading. American Muslims asking for assistance from Indonesia in order to improve their recitation of the Qur'ān was front page news the following day. (I was not, however, able to determine who these Americans were.)

I did not hear much reflection among MTQ attendees on the familiar nationalist rhetoric of the official speeches (especially the president's), but the minister's mention of American Muslims generated much discussion. His statement struck a chord resonating with the salient goal of the contests as "*syi'ar Islam.*" The welcome message was that Indonesia was taking the lead in the Muslim world in terms of motivating and assisting the growth of Qur'ānic practice, even in what was perceived to be the most unlikely of places: the United States of America. Through Qur'ān recitational practice and its promotion, Indonesians wished to take pride in being at the forefront of worldwide Islamic *da'wah*, and this seemed to be a more forceful project for most than the compatible framework of "national development." It resonated with the promotional idea that competitions could convey *motivasi* to competitors, to other Muslim Indonesians, to Americans, and even to the rest of Muslim-majority and Muslim-minority global communities.

Contests Contested?

Recitation competition in Indonesia was oriented not only to Qur'ānic practice but explicitly to the sense of "motivating" this practice. The beauty of melodic Qur'ān recitation and its affective power to fascinate is well established within the Islamic tradition, and this recognition formed the basis of a self-conscious strategy among those who promoted and participated in competitions. One significant aspect of the Indonesian competition system was its linkage to the Muslim project of "*da'wah*," or "the call" to Muslims to deepen their Islamic faith and piety. A means-ends logic relating to understandings of *da'wah* aligned multiple interests with the competition frameworks. Although the means of contests could be potentially objectionable on some grounds, the ends of increasing "motivation" nevertheless recruited support from broad-based Islamic interests and, further, came over time to decrease such opposition. The lack of controversy around recitation competitions highlighted the ideals of "motivation," and the significance of *motivasi* to the competition system is further shown by the fact that when objection was expressed, it was also along these very lines.

In Indonesia in the mid-1990s, strategies of Islamic *da'wah* tended to highlight participatory activities that were enjoyable and compelling, emphasizing especially the aesthetics of Indonesian Islamic "culture" (sometimes known as "Kesenian yang Bernafaskan Islam," or "Arts with Islamic Flavor"). While the revealed Qur'ān is not to be confused with "culture," it is strongly tied to ideals of Indonesian *da'wah*; the expression most often heard for competitions as *da'wah* was that they were "*syi'ar Islam*," or the "glorification of Islam." The goals and tangible results of this effort came to overshadow potential controversies over the acceptability of particular strategies, especially in the latter years of Indonesia's New Order, as competitions aligned with an interest in presenting Indonesian Islam on the world stage. The discourses concerning the permissibility of contests reveal the logic of *da'wah* and the concomitant acceptance of competitions by virtue of the ideal of the motivating power of competitions.

Qur'ān recitation competitions (for prizes) have been criticized at times in Indonesia. However, by the mid-1990s it was hard to find anyone contesting contests anymore. The acceptance and expansion of contests was seen by those with Islamist commitments to be in part an effect of the key idea of Islamic "*da'wah*," a potent Qur'ānic concept, potentially flexible enough in application so that diverse interests could be readily aligned with it. Specifically, the component of *da'wah* that related to the motivation of ongoing practice had diminished possible religious objections (even where they might have been expected). Decreasing opposition to once-contested practices had occurred across the spectrum of Indonesian Islam in the 1980s and 1990s, including once-maligned "traditional" observances (such as funerary readings).[53] The significance of recitation competitions as "*syi'ar Islam*" had offset possible opposition to the subjection of God's speech to a contest, as the idea of *da'wah* had also done with other Qur'ānic popularizing practices in Indonesia and elsewhere. Although the ideology of the New Order played a role in "coopting" Islamic expression (partially by representing such expression as an aspect of Indonesian national "culture"),[54] the state was not completely responsible for these changes. A "means-ends" logic of *da'wah*, where the ends were viewed to be a more vibrant, popularized, and energetic Qur'ānic engagement, allowed these goals to enroll various perspectives on the practice of recitation competitions in the service of a shared project.

Even *Media Dakwah*, the Islamist publication known for its opposition to New Order interests, had come by the latter 1990s to challenge those who would cynically malign the MTQ.[55] In its coverage of the MTQ in Jambi, *Media Dakwah* opens its "Special Report" (Laporan Khusus) with the following paragraphs:

> The carrying out of the MTQ on a grand scale *(bersifat kolosal)* has always been accompanied by *polemik* or at the very least smaller *pro-kontra* debates about the MTQ that criticize it as a wasteful activity that seems *(berbau)* overly formalized *(seremonial)* and appears to be insignificant *(kurang substantif)* in the face of that which is most *vital*, that is, carrying out works based on the teachings of the Glorious Qur'ān. The MTQ is also judged to be no more than a disturbing

> distraction *(tak lebih hura-hura)*, to the degree that it presents the entirety of the Qur'ān as being [merely] artistic or [just] the beauty of voices. While in fact the MTQ is seen to have value as "*syi'ar Islam*," it still is considered not to match up to the great expense that it consumes. The most cynical voices are without a doubt those that consider the MTQ to be a deliberate effort to deaden the Islamic community's resolve, so that it will not carry out political activities that could endanger the *establishment*.
>
> For whatever reason, the last two or three MTQs have no longer encountered negative, opposing, or cynical voices *(suara minor, kontra, dan sinis)*. The cost of the eighteenth MTQ in Jambi that reached Rp. 12 billion, according to one government official in Jambi responsible for the MTQ speaking to a *Media Dakwah* reporter, could be seen to be rather small (that is, the Rp. 12 billion), when compared with the "performance" *(prestasi)* of the corruptors who have recently succeeded in robbing the nation's finances *(menggasak uang negara)*.[56]

The report continues with a discussion of the losses in the trillions of rupiah that were just coming to light with the previous month's devastating economic crash. Also mentioned are recent social disturbances and unrest (such as a bloody riot in Banjarmasin the previous May). The article continues:

> In contrast [to such tragic events], how very enjoyable was the atmosphere at the MTQ in Jambi. It was so pleasant, so tranquil, and so full of hope for the future for a people that [only wish to] beautify the religious values of Islam. [One feels this] all the more when looking at the bright, beaming children and young people on their way to the various (competition) events of the MTQ. For a whole week, the public kept flooding into the MTQ arena to drink in *(mereguk)* hope for the future to the fullest *(sepuas-puasnya)*. Those who would oppose the MTQ now would seem to be so few *(Makin tipislah sementara pihak untuk menolak penyeleggaraan MTQ)*.[57]

Although Qur'ān competitions (for prizes) had been criticized at times in Indonesia, the amount of opposition does not seem ever to have been very great, and by the mid-1990s, it seems to have all but disappeared in public discourse. Some treatments of competition practice in Indonesia in the 1990s conveyed an air of apology, answering polemical questions no longer being asked. Occasionally cited, for example, was the account that the Prophet approved a poetry competition with a non-Muslim tribe.[58] Citation of Qur'ān verses and *ḥadīth* accounts that emphasize the importance of beautifying the Qur'ān (authoritative statements such as "Beautify the Qur'ān with your voices" and "He is not one of us who does not recite the Qur'ān") echo a conversation that had become one-sided.

Possible objections to Qur'ān-reading contests, like controversy around other religious practices, concerned questions of instrumentality, but the case of competitions also differed a great deal from the religious issues invoked by the "traditional" practices. The issue was not the dangers of imagining or attributing power in a way thought by reformers to be offensive to a normatively Islamic worldview (such as in the case of saints buried at local sites or relations with the dead more generally). Instead, what concerns there were about competitions on legal grounds related to the potentially inappropriate treatment of the unique and miraculous Qur'ān. When older, conservative religious figures were asked whether they recalled objections being raised about recitation contests in previous decades (when "modernists" were especially energetic in attacking "traditionalist" practices and, simultaneously, as the competition system was just forming in Indonesia), they reported it was difficult to recall any such controversy at all, however. In fact, the persons whom I had initially surmised could be the most disapproving of the contests—such as an elderly *kiai* in the region just outside of Makassar who had studied in the Middle East and who served as a high official in South Sulawesi's Islamist insurrectionist government in the 1950s—actually participated in contest judging. This particular individual did recall that there had been another *kiai* in South Sulawesi who lived in a remote area on the other side of the peninsula, who had publicly opposed the competitions. This individual's objection, however, had not been to contests per se, but to the participation of women in them (women's voices being said to be "*aurat*," or indecent for public display).

When asked about past and present objections to the contests, K. H. M. Sayyid Abdullah, the leading national authority, first answered with standard *ḥadīth* verses, adding the Qur'ānic idea that beautiful recitation increases the faith *(iman)* of other Muslims (an implicit argument of ends justifying means). K. H. M. Sayyid Abdullah then went on to say that "95 percent" of Indonesian *'ulamā'* (religious scholars) approved of contests as long as the "intention was for God" *(niyyat Allahi Ta'ala)*, while the other 5 percent—no, that is probably too much, he said, correcting himself—the other *1* percent naturally meant well too but were simply and quite understandably afraid that the Qur'ān might be recited with poor *tajwīd*. As long as such recitation "met the criteria" *(tajwīd)* and was carried out with good intention—and was not treated like "poetry" but as "God's revelation" *(wahyu Allah)*—and "safeguarded" *(dijaga betul*, probably another reference to *tajwīd)*, then it is all just fine with them. He continued, sharing the following thoughts:

> People, they come home from the fields, come home from the office, they come home from trying to make their living in the world, and they play cassettes of recitation. And this adds to their faith [a reference to 8 al-Anfāl 2]. For the ones

> with weak faith, it increases it, and for the ones already strong in their faith, it gets stronger, because they play *(putar)* the Qur'ān [recited with] *lagu*. Everyone *(semua bangsa)* shares in this. There are civil servants and executives and [political] leaders and farmers and fishermen, and how are they all bound together *(ikatan)*? Because Allāh revealed the Qur'ān to all of them so they could listen to it and thereby their faith would be strong and firm and always increasing *(bertambah-tambah)*. And *that's* what the 95 percent think.

The ends (increase in faith) eclipse the means, as long as the "essence" of the Qur'ān is protected by correct intention and the application of *tajwīd*.

Besides *syi'ar Islam*, another meaningful justification for contests (especially among participants) was their potential to counter negative influences, whether in terms of providing constructive activity for youth or by offering an alternative to trends of "Westernization." (One prominent reciter in Jakarta often suggested such an idea by drawing contrasts between the positive activity of Qur'ān recitation and morally questionable "pop" music, for example.) A spirited statement by a young person of precisely the age and social location of many MTQ participants, writing on the topic "The Effort to Prevent the Influence of the West by Way of the MTQ" (Upaya Menangkal Pengaruh Kebudayaan Barat Melalui MTQ), in a chapter of her undergraduate thesis, expresses a typical viewpoint:

> Discussion about Western culture infiltrating *(menyusup masuk)* the world of Islam is not new. Everyone is surprised and struck *(tergigit dan tersentuh)* when they confront *(menyadari)* the Western thought and behavior that has brought such utter chaos and disorder *(memorak poandakan)* to human life. . . .
>
> One action that the *ulama* have found to prevent the influence of the West has been to introduce Islamic culture *(kebudayaan Islam)* by way of the Musabaqah Tilawatil Quran. Since its inception, how much has this effort been able to achieve? According to this author, the effect brought on by the influence of the birth of the MTQ cannot be denied, and in fact it has been wonderful impetus for peace in the world, and on top of that whatever has not already taken on the form of Western culture meshes with the MTQ before it has a chance to be affected by another way of thinking, by which is meant the formation of an Islamic generation that would [otherwise] be totally fanatical for [extremist] Islamic principles. But it's not just they [the "fanatics"] who have come to despise totally everything that smells of the West.[59]

Then, immediately following as an extension of these ideas, the author changes tone, expressing the attitudes of the politically moderate, Islamically committed young people with whom she seems to identify. She argues conclusively that the real value of contests comes with their experiential, affective, and motivational impact:

> With the MTQ, a new generation has become involved actively but nevertheless sympathetically with really feeling the existence of a new [kind of] world outside of their everyday life, because there they find an activity that can bring calmness *(ketenangan)* and beauty in and of itself, and it is the MTQ but not only that that has brought on this new intensity in the desire to study the Qur'ān directly.[60]

Ultimately, this student defines the aims of competing positively and expressly in terms of feeling states that may be induced by MTQ participation. Further, she finally and explicitly assesses competitions in terms of their "top-level" goal: motivating practice. She presents the motivating and educational characteristics as the most salient justification for the activity. This was also the initial, "official" rationale for support of contest activity by the Ministry of Religious Affairs.

Such motivation for escalating involvement in religious practice was not merely for the sake of becoming more busy with the Qur'ān. More meaningfully, it was a project of concentrated and sustained involvement that was understood to carry lasting and transforming effects. Supporting a salient top-level schema of competitions as *motivasi*, there was often detectable another goal, which was internalization and "comprehension" *(faham)* of the Qur'ān. This was explicit in the official and public discourses of the LPTQ and also in emergent trends such as the growing emphasis on contest events that required comprehension, such as "Tafsir." In coaching, for example, K. H. M. Sayyid Abdullah would sometimes refer to the meaning of an *āyah* as its "*da'wah*." Understanding the *da'wah* of the Qur'ān through reading it is more than merely "knowing Qur'ānic Arabic"—itself a potentially lifelong project—but also the development of a sense of intimacy with the Qur'ān that is practice-based.

In both subtle and explicit modes, master reciters would speak idealistically, sometimes touchingly, of the role of Qur'ān reading and Qur'ān competitions for increasing "understanding." The international champion reciter and national expert H. Hasan Basri wrote a characteristic statement: "The Musabaqah Tilawatil Quran represents one activity of *dakwah* that has as its goal the bringing of *motivasi* to the Islamic community and especially its young people so that they are impelled and stimulated with inspired enthusiasm always to study the Qur'ān not only by reading [aloud], but also in comprehending it to the extent that they may fully experience and act on its teaching."[61] When

I asked Ny. Nurhayati, a national champion, "What is the role of competitions in motivating people to recite?" she answered what seemed to be another question (although I believe she understood the one I had posed), speaking about how people would come to know the meaning of the *āyah*s of the Qur'ān. Perhaps because of her dedicated work in teaching women how to read while at the same time extemporaneously explicating meanings of the text of the Qur'ān to them, she was acutely sensitive to such connections.

The salience of competitions' mood and message of *motivasi* in this period is revealed by the terms of the objections that were being made to competitions. The most cutting remarks about competitions were not heard coming from conservative figures or legal scholars (who, in fact, acted as competition judges, especially for memorization). Instead they were expressed in the idealistic and occasionally ambivalent statements made by the competitors and coaches who devoted themselves the most to competitions. While a few admitted (usually disapprovingly) that the prizes were a reason for some to be drawn initially to competition practice and while some expressed theological concern over competitive feelings (one asks on an instructional tape, "Is it OK to pray to win a contest if this would mean that your friends are going to lose?"), issues relating to the rewards for good performance were usually not what was cast as potentially troublesome. Contest organizers on the national level seemed to demonstrate the least ambivalence about the possible tensions of multiple competition goals and the presence of the Qur'ān. As one master coach from Jakarta once said, "If you 're not going [for it in order] to win, what's the use?" *(Kalau tidak menang, apa faidah?).* The comfort displayed by the recitation trainers and competitors is attributable to dedicated years of experience that had given them a pious confidence and ease about what, to them, ultimately matters about competitions. Some, inside and outside of the world of the MTQ, have criticized contests for being too "wide" *(luas)* in the scope of activities (drawing attention away from the Qur'ān itself), while others have criticized them for the opposite reason, for emphasizing only one aspect of the Qur'ān, its recitation (as in the *Media Dakwah* excerpt above).

The most serious concerns, coming from within the system, demonstrated an acute awareness of the ways in which competition practice could have an effect on Qur'ānic engagement, expressing the worry that something might go wrong with the motivating influence of contests. The most pointed criticism was heard when those actually participating in the competition system invoked the term "*qari musiman,*" meaning a "seasonal reciter." The opposite is a "*qari profesional.*" A *qari musiman* works to improve Qur'ānic ability only in preparation for a contest. This represents the problem of good motivation gone bad. Such fair-weather reciters were seen to miss and even subvert the schema of contests as motivating long-term continuous practice. For example, in his book of advice to potential competitors, an active and energetic coach and *ḥāfiẓ* in Makassar, Drs. Syawir Dahlan, discourages the *qari musiman* phenomenon among his students specifically in terms of intentions, emotions, and long-term affective processes:

> Don't let it be that you only study for a week or a month imagining that you'll be able to get it right away. Just like all other kinds of "prizes" *(juara-juara)* that there are in this world, it cannot be rushed *(tergesa-tergesa)*, and in other words it would not yet be possible [for you to win anyway]. Be patient at the beginning and you must also be practicing all the time *(terus menurus)*, and God-willing you *(kita)* will be able to *(bisa)*. In fact many among the [male and female] reciters from all over study the Qur'ān only around the time of the MTQ, and that is what's known as *qari musiman*. Later [at the last minute], when they want to join *(masuk)* in the MTQ all of a sudden or later just as an MTQ is getting close *(menjelang)*, it's only then that they start to want to study all in a big rush *(terburu-buru)*. And if there isn't going to be an MTQ or the MTQ is still a long ways off, then they don't feel like studying and they are reluctant [*malas*, lit. "lazy"] to practice. This cannot be permitted *Lho* . . . ! And this is not only dangerous *(berbahaya)* but even more than that it is really, really DAAANGEROUS *(BERBAHAYYYA)*, and it is not sincere *(ikhlas)*. So just don't go there [*Engga Ussa ya*, colloquial for "there's no need for that"].[62]

Such criticism is for the sake of encouraging students to persevere in their practice year round, aiming at steady long-term improvement (H. Muammar advises on one of his instructional cassettes, for example, to expect an "*evolusi*," not a "*revolusi*"). Although some reciters have been known to say that MTQs have produced too many "*qari musiman*," the fault is almost always seen to lie with the competitor himself or herself and a correspondingly flawed individual goal framework, rather than with the competition system as a whole.

The mood of *motivasi* that practitioners sought to develop in and by competitions was conveyed through the emotional intensity of actual participation and specific strategies of training and preparation. Other pious practitioners who were not seeking to "win a prize" but instead to achieve the new orthoprax standards set by the competition system also sought out competition training regimens and occasionally even the competition format itself. Both competitors and noncompetitors alike incorporated and enhanced the *motivasi* expressed in promotional and critical discourse about competitions as specific techniques and in virtual and actual contest involvement.

Participation

Practice—whether collective or not—occurs on the level of individuals, and a large-scale phenomenon like Qur'ān recitation competition was in a meaningful sense the collective face of persons pursuing goals of increased Qur'ānic ability. Competitions were sites at which features of the Qur'ān, specifically Indonesian features of Qur'ānic practice, and psychological dimensions of religious piety dramatically combined to make Qur'ānic practice something that drew people in compellingly. Patterns of institutions and practice interacted with individuals' goals and experiences in a way that drew new contours, conforming neither to the perspective of any one individual nor to those of institutional discourses. These frameworks, in turn, made available to all a model of motivated practice consistent with psychological experience as well as shared social meanings.

Participation in an MTQ is an intense and transforming experience. Life-changing episodes, like participating in a national competition, had real effects on the people who participated in contests as well as the opportunities available to them. Emotions marking success and failure, engagement and boredom, and anticipation and disappointment influenced the people who tied their energy and identity to contests. A college student cried alone, quietly and with dignity, on a verandah outside her room on the night after she was told the news that she was not selected to go to nationals ("There will always be a job waiting for you in the Ministry of Religious Affairs, and you'll be a respected teacher someday with lots of students"). Another woman bristled, calmly maintaining self-control, when she learned that competitional age criteria had recently been changed, and for this reason she would not be allowed to go to the national MTQ, where she had hoped to look after her own memorization students and to compete herself. Competition engagement shapes who people are, who they understand themselves to be, and the social and emotional opportunities available to them. Less directly, the widespread dissemination of competition standards through pedagogy conveyed affective goals and echoes of competition experiences to competitors and noncompetitors alike.

Attendance at an MTQ, especially a big tournament like a national or international competition, is a memorable (maybe "once-in-a-lifetime") experience for competitors, transformative because of this very intensity. A dramatic example is an international champion's description of attending—and winning—the competition in Saudi Arabia. As he tells it, he had been eating only eggs for days at the event (the food there was too oily, and there was no steamed rice to eat). He had not known when he would be called or what he would be asked to read, so he was ready from the very start. He ended up being the very last contestant on the very last day. He was not told the actual verses that he was to recite until he was up on the *minbar,* having carried up his own *muṣḥaf* with him. Thank God, he said, he managed to open it to the right page! He thought at one point that he had made a mistake and that the officials would stop him right there. But he wasn't stopped; he went straight through. Afterward, they told him he would be reading at the closing ceremony, and he knew then that he must have placed, but he still didn't know with what ranking. Later he was invited into the inside of the Ka'bah by a Moroccan who was remarkably tall ("even taller than Mbak Anna"—and I am tall). In the Ka'bah, he said, it feels as if the whole world just falls away . . . and he began to trail off. Since on Hajj pilgrims circumambulate the structure of the Ka'bah but do not enter into it, everyone listening to the story immediately began to ask, what's the inside of the Ka'bah like? Is it hot or cool? Is it dark? Was there anything on the walls inside? The *qāri'*, however, did not provide details of the Ka'bah's interior but persisted in trying to convey what was most important about the experience to him, which was ineffable, transforming felt emotion. Although an extreme example, it illustrates the unanticipated affective "force" that contest experience may carry for participants.

The affect tied to participation is based on the indeterminacy of tournament events. MTQs were happenings with unpredictable outcomes and unforeseeable experiences for all of the actors involved: winners and losers, as well as their judges. The dynamics of participating in an actual, judged contest rarely matched the expectations of preparation. Many participants, for example, found themselves disoriented by the sudden sense of aloneness in the moments of competing, in a sharp experiential contrast to the solidarity and group identity that otherwise pervades competition preparation and participation. Being singled out is the prerogative and goal of the competitor, but it also creates its own unanticipated stresses. These sometimes led to poor health and poor performance. The moment when the contestant's name is called and he or she breaks away from a protective huddle with the coach or best friend is intense, even for the outside observer to watch. Once a contestant is at the microphone, I have witnessed painful incidents of voices faltering, cracking, and failing, as well as blanking out of various forms, even at the national MTQ. In every competition, it seemed, there were also a few reciters who forgot their coaches' warnings and got lost in the subtleties of their melodic phrasing and subsequently carelessly committed basic errors in *tajwīd,* leading, usually, to significant point deductions.[63]

Memorizers who competed encountered a cognitive discrepancy between the method of memorization and the format for evaluation in an MTQ. Students tended to have memorized the text sequentially, but the competition test

Judging a memorizer from South Sulawesi at the National MTQ, Jambi, 1997

Contestants watching a live video feed of a reciter from South Sulawesi backstage during the main recitation event, National MTQ, Jambi, 1997

takes the form of a series of "spot checks" (often on verses of the Qur'ān that resemble others). The *ḥāfiẓ* or *ḥāfiẓah* attempts to continue reciting a given verse correctly following from the first cue phrase provided by a judge.[64] Mistakes summon a harsh buzzer, and some memorizers became further shaken by the sound. An audible duel could ensue between buzzer and memorizer, speeding up as the contestant's performance became all the more fragmented and confused.

Judges, too, were participants in contests. During a contest, for example, judging altered the relationship between teacher and student, placing them (as an experienced judge once remarked) in a strangely adversarial position. Judges bore the continual responsibility to make subjective evaluations attentively and objectively. The responsibility that judges felt, naturally enhanced by the presence of the Qur'ān, amplified the intensity that typifies the activity of competing.[65] Judging a fellow Muslim's voicing of the Qur'ān is a heavy burden. The responsibility placed on judges echoes the traditional sense of gravity of the role of legal judges (*qāḍī*'s), and MTQ judges would often say that they were charged with a "weighty task" *(tugas berat)*. One coach described judging as being "great but heavy" *(mulia tetapi berat)*: "great," she said, because of "seeing and hearing the reading of the Holy Qur'ān of Allah," but "heavy" because of the obligation to evaluate competitors (often the judge's very own students). She explained, "We have to go to war with whomever we judge" *(yang kita nilai siapa, kita harus berperang dengan)*.

The "Tilawah" category is especially difficult in this regard, because it relies heavily on aesthetic criteria. The three main criteria for judging the "Tilawah" event are "*fasahah*" and "*adab*" (see chapter 2), "*tajwīd*" (see chapter 3), and "*suara dan lagu*" ("voice and *lagu*"; see chapter 4).[66] The system of point values developed over the decades of MTQs, with a major revision occurring in 1989. In later years, there came to be more relative emphasis on *lagu* for judging within this category.[67] *Tajwīd* is the most well-defined in terms of judging standards for the "Tilawah" event (judges are expected to know these rules for themselves). The criteria for judging *tajwīd* are given as

1. *Makharij al-Huruf*, the articulation of letters (such as pronouncing *thā* instead of *sā* or, less seriously, not showing tendencies of local languages);
2. *Shifat al-Huruf*, the weight and emphasis on letters; and *Ahkam al-Madd wa-l-Qasri*, duration of vowels;
3. *Al-Waqf wa-l-Ibtida'*, starts and stops (the seriousness of the mistake is based on the fixed rules as well as the damage to meaning: dropping a negation, "*lā*," at the beginning of an *āyah* is far more serious than dropping an initial "*innā*," meaning "verily," for example);

4. *Ahkam al-Huruf*, other special rules (especially those that only apply for a verse or two of the Qur'ān and thus must be memorized).[68]

There are two kinds of mistakes that can be made: *khatha' jali* (or *kesalahan besar*, a major mistake), and a *khatha' khafi* (*kesalahan kecil*, a minor mistake). A major mistake is one that obscures a letter entirely, changes the meaning, or omits a necessary sound, word, or even *āyah*. A minor error could be, for example, a mistake in terms of one of the rules for the assimilation of consonants (such as *ikhfā'*, *idghām*, or *iqlāb*). Indonesian judges were careful to listen for breaks in continuity in voice and nasalization (sometimes called "*mengkotak-kotakkan*," or "putting into boxes"). They were alert especially for problems with the letter "*rā*" (for which there are special rules about when to make "light" or "heavy"), which tends to be mistakenly pronounced as heavy or rolled. If a mistake is made, the deduction is taken, even if later in the reading the same error is not made when the same situation arises. If the same error is repeated (*kesalahan yang sama dalam satu jenis*, or "the same mistake of one type"), then the mistake is to be counted only once.

The second major area for evaluation of "Tilawah" is *suara dan lagu*, or "voice and melodic mode." For the purpose of evaluation, there are schematized types and categories of *suara*, or voices, including *lembut* (weak) voices. Officially, "good" *(baik)* types of *suara* have been described as the following:

1. Voices that are full [*bulat*, lit. "round"], sweet *(merdu)*, and demonstrate vibrato *(mempunyai getaran)*;
2. Voices that are not off-pitch *[sumbang* or *fals]*, not hoarse *(parau)* or coarse *(kasar)*;
3. Voices that may be controlled *(dapat dikendalikan)*, that is, those that do not disappear *(hilang)* on low tones and that do not become sharply shrill *(melengking runcing)* on high tones. The voice considered good demonstrates mastery of the three registers: low, medium, and high.[69]

The components of *suara* are judged not only on the quality of the voice but also on the management and capacity of the breath *(pengaturan napas)*; the number of *lagu* deployed;[70] the requirement that the reading deploy the three (sometimes four) levels of the melodic mode (*qorar, [nawa], jawab*, and *jawabul jawab*; see chapter 4); transitions, integrity of "melody," and pacing *(peralihan, keutuhan, dan tempo lagu)*; rhythm, style, and variations on the *lagu (irama, gaya, dan variasi)*; and, finally, the close *(lagu penutup)*.[71]

The final judging criterion for the "Tilawah" event is "*fasahah* and *adab*."[72] This came over the years to include the following categories: neatness and "*halus*"-ness (*kercermatan*, *kehalusan*, "*halus*" denoting calm demeanor); fluency (*kefasihan*); rendition of the vowels and (doubled) consonants; rendition of the letters and the (attached) vowels; rendition of words; and the rendition of complete *āyahs*. This final category was once simply known as "*adab*" (while "*fasahah*" was originally grouped with *tajwīd*). Previously, from 1968 (when the MTQ officially began in Makassar) until 1981, the judging criteria for "Tilawah" were oriented more toward the presentation made by the reciter himself or herself. This included "carriage" (*sikap*, also denoting "comportment" or "attitude"), physical movement (*gerak gerik*), clothing coordination (*keserasian pakaian*, meaning especially that nothing clashes badly); and style of reading and facial expression (*gaya membaca dan mimik*).[73]

In contests, tensions may arise because of subjective considerations in judging. One problem that was being addressed at the time of fieldwork was that some judges (at the provincial level and below) were not yet fully familiarized with the difficult melodic system of *lagu*.[74] At the Penataran Dewan Hakim MTQ, Propinsi Sulawesi Selatan (Instructional Meeting for the Judges of Qur'ān Recitation Competitions, Province of South Sulawesi), sponsored by the provincial LPTQ in November 1996, this issue was highlighted. In their five-day meeting, judges from across the province engaged practically every issue connected with the improvement of the quality of Qur'ān recitation and memorization, and especially competition in these areas. Issues discussed included the establishment of training programs for competitors, difficulties in mastering the system of *lagu*, as well as other topics. During the course of the meeting, one of the leaders, Ny. Nurhayati, invited the provincial judges to recite in front of each other one at a time, saying, "How can the judges evaluate the contestants if their knowledge is not greater?" The "*komentar*" that followed each judge's performance (some were seasoned contest winners, while others clearly were not) included praise, dry criticism, jokes (the judge from Takalar was asked if he was planing to do a little bit of "Cikoang" for us), and assessments such as "The recitation of the participant from Luwu practically makes us want to burst into tears" (he had done a fine, although emotive, reading). Ny. Nurhayati later distributed an instructional tape of *lagu* (initially produced by the Ministry of Religious Affairs) so that judges who had demonstrated room for improvement could continue to study at home.

For everyone involved in a competition—contestants and judges alike—the affective texture of competing was woven into an embracing motivated model in which participation (*partisipasi*) was its own reward. A competition is a space of radical participation; in competitions, as at a karaoke party, each contestant has a turn, and exactly the same kind of turn at that. The characterization of competing as act of "*partisipasi*" in Indonesia often seemed to be of a higher order than the idea of a contest as a form of agonistic individualism. The embracing competition schema in effect in Indonesia for contests did not so much resemble a model of aggressive "sportsmanship" but instead of personal contribution to the event as an overall "*sukses*." When competitions, especially recitation competitions, were understood in terms of the Qur'ānic theme of "competing in goodness" (*Fa'stabiqū'l-khairāt*), affective ideals of "goodness" tended to outweigh the realities of competing.

For example, during the last week of Ramadan in 1997, there was a competition in *tadarus* (nonornamented recitation) held at Masjid "Al-Markaz" in Makassar and broadcast by radio. Five teams represented the five subdistricts of the province, and the recitation was on the air just before fast-breaking every evening leading up to the celebration of Idul Fitri (Hari Raya). The judges were not in attendance in the mosque but listened at home on the radio instead. On the first day of competition, minutes before the team of contestants was to go on the air, mosque officials came by a recitation class to invite the teacher to join the competition team. Thinking with a contrasting cultural model of what it means to "compete," I wondered if there was not some kind of rule against that sort of thing. The purpose of the overall event, however, was not so much to designate a "winner" but to broadcast recitation on the air (like national RRI's "Week of the Qur'ān" competition broadcast) and to showcase the centrality of the grand, newly completed mosque to the community. The better the quality of the program, the more the participants and the listeners would share in the *sukses*, thereby enjoy a more meaningful and Qur'ānic Ramadan. Competition was simply the frame for what was essentially a noncompetitive event.

The participatory aspects of such competition frameworks tended to smooth out the more extreme affective textures of winning and losing. At a taping for a televised recitation instructional show at the Makassar TVRI (national television) studio, the host asked the children on the set (who were in town for a recitation contest being held for schoolchildren from throughout the province) who among them was already a contest winner. Ny. Nurhayati (who was accompanying the children and appearing on the broadcast that day) quickly answered, "Oh, everyone *always* wins . . . their very own number!" She was referring to contest registration numbers. Paradoxically, egalitarianism and shared confidence that the competition will be an overall "*sukses*," as a form of *da'wah* especially, allowed for contestants to pursue other goals (such as wanting to take first place; to have community, family, and personal renown increase; or to have a chance to fulfill the personal religious obligation of pilgrimage) without compromising Qur'ānic values, which in Indonesia included the *motivasi* to practice itself. The intensity and indeterminacy of these projects was enhanced by actual competition contexts; more pervasively, their preparatory regimens energized a widespread Muslim revitalization movement focused on Qur'ānic recitation in Indonesia in the 1990s.

Preparation

The experience of performance and preparation conveyed salient aspects of motivation to ongoing practices of Qur'ānic piety within the system of recitation competition practice and training in Indonesia. Ongoing experiences of learning and pedagogy enhanced these dynamics palpably over and above public "meanings" shared in heightened moments of performance. Rehearsals and training regimens conveyed affective strategies to aspiring competitors. Because of the influence of competition training pedagogy in all recitation teaching, pedagogical frameworks propagated the affective texture of preparation widely to all types of aspiring practitioners. The activity of contest preparation shows how patterns of competitional goals also extended to those not preparing to compete, as these affective textures of training were transmitted through the dissemination of pedagogical frameworks. The "mood" of *motivasi* itself along with explicit techniques to relate it to other registers of feeling and experience were transmitted throughout the system of Indonesian Qur'ānic recitation through widespread personal effort.

At the time of fieldwork, there was a movement of interest in Indonesia for study of the recitation of the Qur'ān. Those preparing to compete did not only study, however. They trained. The goal of serious competitors was not merely the general improvement of ability or even improvement with respect to previous "personal bests" but improvement of contest performance. Competitors wanted to achieve maximal performance in the short moments of competition, and this goal influenced pedagogical techniques for all recitation students. A virtual space and time of performance was overlaid and imagined in the learning context; because of the influence of competition training pedagogy in all recitation teaching, this imagined space of recitation competition was becoming an experiential reality for more than just competitors.

Qur'ān reciters prepared for competitions on their own or in groups. When the resources of patronage were available, as for top talent preparing for a national MTQ, there was the opportunity for highly intensive training. In Makassar, for example, aspiring reciters and memorizers, supported by the generosity of a local industrialist, received year-round accommodation at Mesjid Raya, along with daily coaching (this training regime grew in intensity just before the national MTQ). In South Sulawesi, in preparation for the MTQ in 1997, the group of reciters and memorizers who lived year round at Mesjid Raya and practiced every evening was joined by the winners (first through third places) of the provincial MTQ. The selection of the most promising reciters to come to Jakarta, Makassar, and elsewhere was often said to have been made by talent scouts in the villages. Across Indonesia and especially on Java, for example, several well-known reciters also had their own *pesantren* to which reciters and other competitors from across Indonesia would come to live and study, usually with hometown sponsorship. In the months just before the MTQ training intensified, with many reciters traveling to work with the top coaches and with coaches themselves visiting provinces on invitation.

For corporate-sponsored contests, there were also intensive training programs. For example, I observed two months of round-the-clock preparation for reciters from the eastern Indonesia division as they trained for Telkom nationals. The phone company employees, retirees, and the spouses and children of employees who were to compete lived together in a rented house in Makassar, with periodic breaks to return home to visit their families. Participants, many of whom were neither the most accomplished nor the most gifted of Qur'ān reciters, rehearsed continuously the selections that would be in the contest. Training for the Telkom tournament included mock competitions that reproduced the competition setting, including the timing lights and judges' forms.

Norms of competition influenced what was studied in these settings and how it was studied. For some competitions, the readings were known in advance, and it was not uncommon for students to have memorized them. At one training sequence for a corporate competition, the competitors drilled the set readings for the competition continuously. Coaches would also "teach the (con)test" in other ways, such as by giving comments in terms of potential point deductions for mistakes. It was common, for example, to hear discussion about the use of the microphone. K. H. M. Sayyid Abdullah once opened a coaching session, getting everyone's attenion with panegyric praise addressed to the power of the microphone, beginning with "*Yaaaa besiiiih!*" (O [you of] iron). The facial expressions and especially bodily movements of students were subject to scrutiny, especially in order to train reciters' bodies to remain still during recitation. At times, coaches would be explicit about what judges allegedly wanted to hear in terms of vocal quality (suggesting, for example, that judges from Java were especially pleased by exaggerated treatment of plosive consonants). Teachers would give tips on how to conserve breath capacity (such as by reciting in a high register or by being especially careful on sibilant letters such as *s* in order not to let too much air escape wastefully). They would also teach how to "*curi nafas*" (steal a breath), which is a technique of inhaling on certain doubled consonants without the sound being picked up by the microphone and thereby detected by the judges.[75]

Another common coaching subject was how to stand out from the crowd, especially with the use of a surprising "*variasi*" that could get the attention of judges who may have been listening to recitation for many hours. Clothing styles were a common analogy on this point, and my own physical appearance and clothing were occasionally used as an example of the possibility of standing out within a group for being "interesting" and "different," but in a way that was (I was relieved to hear) appropriate and "well-coordinated." H. Muammar, for example, suggests on one of his instructional cassettes that one should develop a personal "*andalan*" (mainstay or specialty) and then enhance that strength with frequent surprises; coaches highlighted especially the ends of *āyahs* as an opportunity to use the power of expectation and rupture to gain attention and to demonstrate technical artistry.

Preparing for competition brings a holistic "training" model into play. Those training to compete wanted to achieve the best performance in the short moments of competition, and this goal influenced pedagogical techniques far more widely as well. In all learning contexts, even instructional cassette tapes for private use, a great deal of attention was placed on the regimen of diet, exercise discipline, and "mental" preparation. Coaches, for example, enumerated foods to be avoided, such as those that are oily and spicy, and ice at all times. Ny. Nurhayati, when once asked on a television show the "secret" to her recitation success, answered that it was never eating ice. Many reciters swore by the traditional honey, its benefits emphasized in classical sources, whereas others turned to local recipes for *obat* or *jamu* (healing drinks) to enhance vocal potential. One published source recommends at the end of its list (which includes ginger and citrus blends) the "sour-tasting drink called SPRITE (Sprait)" to improve performance as well as to prevent the flu (adding that one must thank God for a good voice and also that there is no substitute for practice).[76] There was also a developed discourse about physical activity, such as one's daily jogging discipline. (Some of these stipulations were put into practice, while for some techniques, the sense of "training" generated by discussion alone seemed to be enough.) Teachers often made explicit analogy to sports training, as with the idea of the final "*semes*" (badminton "smash"). Men and women trainers employed prevalent teaching metaphors drawn especially from boxing. The "upper cut" was often likened to an unexpected variation, for example, and a prominent national coach once encouraged a *rast-zinjiran-nawa* alternation by comparing it to "Douglas pummeling one-two-one-two" for the total knockout.

In training for competitions, the competition environment was constantly overlaid on the learning space. A coach would call out, "Yellow light!" or "It's already red!" as a student recited, and everybody could imagine the competition framework in which three colored lights are placed before the reciter in order to regulate the timing of a competition recitation. A reciter usually has ten minutes in which he or she must use, as a general rule, six out of the seven competition *lagu*. As each reciter worked through a reading, no matter how much real class time may have elapsed between vocalization of verses because of the coach's comments, a virtual stopwatch was always running. After a student had worked through a reading for half an hour, a coach might say, "That's been almost three minutes" (on the competition clock) and tell her she must now modulate to another *lagu* in order to fit all the required *lagu* in before her virtual time ran out.

The implication of the training model for Qur'ānic practice more generally was that the virtual space of competition could begin to be imagined by any student who worked with any teacher who had trained, or trained others, for competition. (And instructors' prestige rested on their previous contest wins.) Teachers of noncompetitive reciters often slipped into giving students pointers about competing as a part of general recitation instruction. One example is the instructional cassette series of H. Muammar Z.A., whose MTQ focus has done much to diffuse the competition model of preparation throughout ordinary practice (see chapter 4).

On the cassettes, H. Muammar responds to questions such as: "When I recite at a big *acara* [public event] or an MTQ, I have prepared my reading and my *fisik* for days, but when it comes time to recite, my voice is [suddenly] heavy and can't go high, and all I do is sweat. What can I do?"[77] Muammar's response, paraphrased below, is given in terms of the psychological dynamics of competing:

> You're ready inside and out *(siap lahir dan batin)*, but when it comes time to perform, you just can't do it. This can happen to anyone. Most people have felt it at one time or another, especially reciters at the beginning of their *karir*. You're not sick; it's really a psychological-spiritual problem *(gangguan psykis-jiwaan)*. You've been thinking so much about that moment that you got all wound up and worried and now you've gotten your nerves rattled. Have you ever noticed that in the waiting room at MTQ finals, everyone is always in the restroom? That's a sign of mental problems *(penyakit mental)*. Of course your voice, and everything else, won't be good; you're a person who's terrified *(orang dalam ketakutan)*. Could you sing if someone had just broken into your house at night to rob you? Of course you couldn't. And so then your story's over *(tamatlah riwayatnya)*,

> and the result was just one big zero *(hasilnya adalah nul yang sangat besar).* It [the problem] was all in your mind [all along]. What's the proof that it was all just in your mind? After your turn is over, then you're [suddenly] all right, you don't feel like you need to visit the restroom anymore, and you feel as if *now* you could do it.[78]

Muammar emphasizes the critical importance of emotion management for contest performance. Anyone learning to recite from these tapes would hear such advice on "mental" preparation. This includes, Muammar says, cultivating a sense of confidence and also learning to assess one's own ability realistically by getting used to reciting in front of others, not just alone in your room ("you always feel like you're the biggest hotshot *[jago]* when you're all alone"), reducing sins and interpersonal troubles so that the "voice is light" and one is not distracted when competing (suppose one owed money to a judge—what a distraction that would be), and always to concentrate: "on your voice, *lagu*, whatever's needed, and always practice every day, with concentration."[79] Such advice brings the emotional experience of competing to bear on the learning practice of the ordinary reciter—whether or not he or she would ever actually compete in an MTQ. For pious noncompetitors, these techniques conveyed by the competition system offered ways and means to realize performative ideals within individual projects of religious practice and learning.

The more serious the competition, the more explicit were participants' strategies to balance individual and collective objectives. The training materials that competitors and noncompetitors all used represented and rendered palpable the most intense of imagined competition environments. Competitors recognized a hierarchy of goals when preparing for real competitions this way, while at the same time they retained a personal investment in the competition experience. In the previous discussion of the issue of contest permissibility, a "means-ends" formulation was shown to align lower-order interests with "top-level" goals such as *da'wah*. Participating in an actual contest, in contrast, renders a "goal-goal" identification between individual objectives and shared motivations as competitors negotiated and conflated multiple (and potentially conflicting) goal registers. To illustrate, in a handbook for MTQ competitors, a coach and *ḥāfiẓ* in Makassar, Syawir Dahlan, offers advice on specialized techniques to subordinate personal "*ambisi*" to shared goals:

> When you're competing *(bertanding)* don't be too ambitious *(berambisi)* for getting a prize, yah, [because while] hoping a prize will come your way is permissible *(boleh saja),* don't be too ambitious—are there any asking [who need to ask] why? Because if you *(kita)* are too ambitious, then most of you will end up losing

> your feeling of *ikhlas* [sincerity] to Allah SWT. And even if your heart is not set on winning the prize *(tak diminta-minta)* but nevertheless you do not win a prize, don't let it be the case that you wind up feeling unhappy [*ngomel,* lit. "grumbling"] that it did not happen [because] eventually you'll get discouraged [*putus asa,* lit. "hopeless"]. And, supposing you do just so happen to win the prize, [well then] *Alhamdulillah* [praise God] now you have won a prize, and all the better if it's the first time, but don't let that make you start acting all stuck-up and full of yourself *(terjadi sifat bangga serta angkuh).* Again, hoping to win a prize is permissible but only insofar as it goes *(boleh dan boleh saja).*[80]

Such emotional "dos and don'ts" for competing represent techniques oriented toward both winning and also "successing" the event with respect to internalized social and religious ideals. Dahlan offers further advice for handling emotions in a common competition situation, modeling such strategies in actual application:

> If you listen to one of your opponents and you hear an awesome *(hebat)* voice and *lagu,* don't let that start getting to you, making you freak out or whatever *(jangan semua itu membuat kamu macam-macam),* or getting scared, doubting yourself *(ragu-ragu)* and thinking, "Oh, I know this guy's going to take first for sure." That's not right, you have to be calm and believe in yourself. And if [what it is going to take for you to psych yourself up is that] you have to start telling yourself that what God has given you is better [than what God has given this other person] (this is to boost yourself only as much as you need, *Lho*), then [make sure] you are not [doing this for the sake of] looking down on anyone; [and also] remind yourself that it's not over until it's over when it comes to who's going to be the one who goes home with that prize; and tell yourself, what's [most] important is just that I do my best. And you must be certain *(yakin)* that God's help only comes to His servants who are pure at heart *(sungguh-sungguh).*[81]

This emotional plan is part of Dahlan's lengthier discussion of other technical and affective points, also aimed at realizing multiple and compatible goals within an encompassing framework.

Dahlan's listing of points to remember when competing shows the multiple registers of goals at work for the competitor and how they are to be self-consciously "managed." These include reading the *āyahs* that the judging panel actually provided to you (not, presumably, something else); reading with feelings of *khushu*ʿ (earnest piety) and *ikhlas* (sincerity); being brave, calm, and believing in yourself; not being afraid of the judges or feeling that they are enemies in a struggle (remember they are just people just like you—but of course you must always show them respect); keep in mind the *adab* of reciting, so don't let your eyes wander all over the place and always remember to keep your focus, because when you're up on the *mimbar* it's reciting that's the most important thing (rather than anything else that might be going on in the room); don't recite too fast or too slow; and when you first see the red light flash, you don't have to rush to finish, just take your time, close the Qur'ān with *khushu'* when you're done, and remember always to carry it in your right hand. And, finally, when it is the moment that the winners or finalists are announced and you are not one of them, Dahlan writes, this is when emotions are the key to mediating potential conflicts in goal-schemas:

> Now, this is when your attitude *(sikap)* really counts, because usually in this situation you'll start thinking to yourself right away *(timbul persangkaan),* if only I hadn't made this mistake or that mistake and that kind of thing. Ah, this is really bad [lit. "not good"]. Throw that way of thinking far away from you *(buang sifat itu jauh-jauh),* throw it to the bottom of the deep, deep ocean and replace it with an attitude like this.[82]

Dahlan goes on to describe appropriate emotional comportment in this situation, including *tawakkul* (trust in God), perseverance, remembering that everyone always loses when they're first starting out, and most of all, never, ever to "LOSE HOPE" because that is a "SIN." Further (continuing the list of strategic affirmations that may redirect the force of affect toward higher-level schemas), remember this is all a way to glorify Islam. He closes with a parenthetical statement that indicates that the point of his discussion was to provide effective and instrumental techniques to alter emotional dynamics (and not primarily to affirm self-evident or dominant discourse), writing: "Or you can just go and find some other words of wisdom similar to these, ones that will work for you in encouraging you to apply your best efforts to achieve in the future."[83]

An objective of cultivating *motivasi* encompassed both individual participation and the collective interests that the competition system promoted. Dynamics of promotion, participation, preparation, and piety emergent in competition activities and training practices cross-cut multiple levels of the competition system and fueled energetic projects of learning and performance more widely. These dynamics disseminated specific goals and strategies that practitioners across Indonesia increasingly used as the criteria for Qur'ānic "orthopraxy"; they also conveyed the affective textures of competing and the overall affective ideals of *motivasi* with emotional strategies to support it. Pious practitioners outside of the competition system adopted competition standards and formats within motivated projects of religious learning and performance; they also adopted the competitional mood of *motivasi* as a self-conscious means to pious ends, revealing in the process what these ends mean.

Motivating Motivation as a Religious Movement

The Indonesian competitional system offered a model of orthoprax aesthetics along with accessible training regimens and formats in which all could participate. Promotional frameworks included a "top-down" goal of *motivasi* and means for managing it, which was shown to be salient through the discourses that questioned contests as well as the ways in which competitors framed their own experience. Training regimens conveyed the intensity of the competing experience as well as actual techniques to manage *motivasi* on a wide scale. When competitions are seen from the bottom up, pious practitioners adopted competition formats and techniques, while at the same time they adopted their affective possibilitites, including enhancing the mood of *motivasi* for oneself and for others in the service of expansive goals of piety and as a kind of "orthopraxy" in itself.

Muslims seeking to enhance religious practice in Indonesia in the 1990s would have tended to turn to Qur'ān recitation because of its prominence and in a form that would have been strongly influenced by competitions—and, further, that would probably have drawn heavily on the same resources that those training for competition also deployed. Competitions also worked as a mechanism of motivation by providing specific expectations and clear evaluative criteria for practice, even in diverse and noncompetitional contexts. Norms of practice for the recited Qur'ān were rapidly coming to resemble competition norms in Indonesia in the 1990s. Many actively sought out these norms as a means to affirm that they had in fact gotten their religious performance "right." Motivated practitioners outside of the competition system adopted these strategies and standards and then even began to generate competitions of their own in order to enhance their own motivations to practice.

The competition frame afforded the opportunity for participation in both the immediate experience and the long-term transformative potential of heightened Qur'ānic practice. There is an implicit invitation to try for oneself in the openness of the competition framework, a motivating aspect that may be conveyed indirectly even to those who have no interest in competing. Muslims in Indonesia saw and heard the recitations of proficient reciters and wanted to try for themselves. For memorizers, for example, competitions fostered an increased attention to the aesthetic and technical aspects of reading. This was in addition to a more general escalation of interest in the project of memorizing the Qur'ān (especially among women). Diverse Muslims wanted to "get it right," and as they were borrowing and developing affective techniques and adopting norms and standards for the sense of orthopraxy, they cultivated and applied the expansive sense of competitional "motivation" as a specific feeling-type in order to achieve pious ends.

To illustrate this point to a colleague at the MTQ (who had asked me to summarize the results of my research work by asking a question on the topic of "motivation"), I told a story about Indonesian grandmothers. I mentioned the recitation sessions for women at the locations known as Majelis Ta'lim. There, women were returning to the study of religion, especially though Qur'ān recitation groups. As discussed in previous chapters, in some respects this continued long-standing traditions in the expression of older women's piety. It was also a radically new development, however. The women were meeting not just to share their devotional piety, but to learn together, consciously correcting the vernacular-influenced pronunciation habits they had had since childhood, while also discarding their regional melodic modes in favor of simple variants of competition *lagu*, a stylistic development having little to do with the science of *tajwīd*. And the women kept coming, sometimes two hundred strong on a Sunday afternoon, with many smaller groups forming to meet throughout the weeks. Some grandmothers were starting to break away from the study circles in the mosques in order to join aspiring competition reciters in their teens, coming to identify their personal styles with world-famous *qārī*'s.

When I asked when the groups began, the women and their teachers answered that it was all new, maybe only a few years old. When I asked who or what started all this, they said it all began just a couple of years ago with a competition in *tadarus* (nonornamented recitation) that they held among themselves. After that event, some of them wanted to study recitation, and then some more, and it took off from there. At their Ramadan competition in 1997, the sweeping banner behind the stage read, "By way of the MTQ, we increase interest in Qur'ān reading."[84] Theirs was, emphatically, not an interest in competing in a national MTQ like the one held in Jambi in 1997. Further, it was "interest," and not simply activity, that was the expressed goal. The banner represents an interest in compounding the motivation the women already felt to practice piety, and they did this, in their words, "by way of the MTQ." In holding competitions, the women were not only increasing their interest in reciting, but they were also becoming involved in a widespread framework of practice whose standards of evaluation were changing the ways that normative Qur'ānic practice was understood and experienced in Indonesia. Should they have wished to study with cassettes, for example, they would have used competition-oriented cassettes, and should they have been seeking out teachers, they would have found themselves working with competition participants in the virtual space of an MTQ.

I told the gentleman at the MTQ about the statement made by Drs. H. Burhanuddin about what was motivating the women to study (chapter 4); I said that I had asked teachers why they thought the women were working so hard, holding competitions, and learning to recite like the great Arab *shaikhs*. I explained that an international champion *qāri'* had speculated that maybe the women wanted the assurance that their practice was, once and for all, no question about it, "correct." The competition format provided an open field for continual work and personal betterment, but it also implied a restricted code and standards for evaluating what is correct. This combination is powerful. It promises the possible assurance that one's religious practice is better, better not just because it is judged to be better than somebody else's (in a competition, for example), but better because it feels more *khushu'* (earnestly pious)—and is finally, unambiguously, and officially correct. The women of the Majelis Ta'lim, for example, had a motivated schema in place, and competitions provided a means that instrumentally served their own ends. Once standards for

Final round during a women's semiformal competition, Makassar, Ramadan, 1997

orthopraxy were established and formalized, they had become available to be used not only in competition with others, but also against oneself. In this system, practitioners were adopting the competition system because it offered them specific techniques, affective and otherwise, to apply in the service of their pious goals of "getting it right" and "motivating" their own motivation to engage the Qur'ān.

Like the results of a competition itself, the outcome of the process of Qur'ānic piety that cycled through the system of Indonesian Qur'ān recitation competitions was indeterminate. The Qur'ān engenders an expansive affecting pull to practice. This has been shown to emerge in multiple aspects of Qur'ānic recitational practice—from learning to read to memorizing to mastering the improvisational system of melodic modes. People, motivated for whatever reason—maybe by the possibility of a prize, or religious piety, or both—set out to acquire a particular ability only to find that vast horizons of technical competence open up in practice: the technical artistry of melodic recitation is potentially infinite, especially when one understands that "ideal recitation" renders a relationship between the moods of vocal performance and the meanings of the text. In this expansive sense, competitions enhanced and elaborated upon motivational aspects inherent in Qur'ānic practice. Qur'ān recitation competitions motivated because they amplified the "affecting pull" of Qur'ānic piety and added to it the possibility that one will contribute to community by way of participation in *syi'ar Islam*. Indonesians used competitions to cultivate this very feeling of *motivasi* in the self and for others.

I was observing recitational practice in Indonesia in the latter years of the 1990s, the culmination of at least two decades of continuous development of trends in the growth of Islamic institutions and Muslim communities of practice during the New Order. I was not aware that I was also witnessing the final months of this Indonesian religious and political culture. No one could have foreseen that the period of fieldwork (which also included a general election) was also to be last months of Suharto's New Order regime. The prosperity of mainstream Islamic education was months away from disintegration in the devastating economic collapse of the summer of 1997. The same week as the national MTQ held in Jambi, the ASEAN economy plunged, leading to a chain of events that would include economic disaster, riots, and the resignation of the president within the year. This could be said to represent one of the greatest economic catastrophes any nation had experienced in the preceding fifty years, as Indonesian stock assets rapidly lost their value and, in a matter of months, the segment of the population living below the poverty line increased five times over—by government estimates. Many of the people with whom I had the closest bonds during my fieldwork in Indonesia were from an area of the eastern archipelago noted for tolerance and pluralism but that was tragically scarred by conflict soon after the end of my stay. Even though everything was about to change in the Muslim religious culture of Indonesia after the week of the MTQ in Jambi, the Qur'ān and the piety it engendered through its "moods and motivations" to expansive practice would not. It would instead exert force within new historical and religious conditions of the Islamic call and effort to realize social justice and to recognize Muslim and non-Muslim diversity on an inclusively Qur'ānic basis. And Muslims in Indonesia, as everywhere in global Muslim-majority and Muslim-minority communities, would be motivated and wish to motivate others to read the Qur'ān.

CHAPTER 6

CONCLUSION

An Envy of Goodness

INDONESIANS CARRIED OUT an energetic movement in Qur'ānic practices in the 1990s based on the assurance that the recitation of the Qur'ān inspires others to do the same. The repeated activity of Qur'ānic practice on the part of an individual may motivate that same person to more of that very same practice, and change in systems of piety and learning was effected by individuals as much as the reverse was also the case. Muslims in Indonesia in the 1990s were engaging projects of developing Qur'ānic practical abilities by modeling and applying affective strategies. Within the affective contexts of learning, teaching, rehearsing, and "competing in goodness," they recast senses of self in terms of ongoing practice. Affect was theorized in this system, as it has been in this work, as being relatively autonomous from modes of thinking and bodily sensation. Whatever aspect of the recited Qur'ān practitioners took on as an object—the ability to recite the Qur'ān without a text, processes of reading study, principles and practices of competence and mastery, or feeling about practice itself—affect cycled through multiple domains of practice. In such projects of voluntary Qur'ānic piety and learning, amplified emotion generated ongoing or enhanced involvement in dynamics of continuing or intensifying engagement.

This book has considered four principal kinds of activities or "abilities" *(kemampuan)* in Qur'ānic practice that Indonesians were self-consciously attempting to achieve and to promote during the time of research (1996–1997): memorization, reading, expressive aesthetics, and competing. Building on the recognition that learning is an aspect of all human activity and that religious practice in particular lends itself to long-term projects of self-cultivation, I have demonstrated long-term affective patterns and proclivities that sustain voluntary religious practice in ritualized frames. The argument of each chapter has shown mechanisms by which practitioners recognized themselves to be ongoing Qur'ānic practitioners through modes of learning and feeling. The presentation considered activities that are based on engagement with the structure and style of the Qur'ān (such as memorizing and reading), which were the Qur'ānic "fundamentals" Indonesian Muslims sought to perfect, as well as projects that intersect with socially specific programs of practice, performance, and learning (such as reciting with standard melody types and competing).

Chapters 2 and 3 treated basic aspects of the recited Qur'ān, the fundamentals of Islamic education. Both revealed the interaction of self with the activity of the recited Qur'ān, showing also how educational processes and social roles were formed by the project of maintaining or improving Qur'ānic ability. This occurred especially through affective strategies and challenges, tensions and syntheses, shaping not only institutional structures but subjectivities of ongoing practice as well. Competence as a Qur'ān memorizer is identified as an ongoing practice to be maintained, even after it has once been achieved. Memorizing, as a mode of *adab*, or cultivated Islamic comportment, is best understood not as a "technology of the self" (Foucault); instead subjectivity comes about through continually negotiating cognitive, affective, and social and interactive contexts in order to maintain "preservation." Islamic literature establishes exemplary moral qualities and comportments *(ādāb)* that are incumbent upon one who "carries" the Qur'ān for the community. The subjectivity of the *ḥāfiẓ* as continuous practitioner does not derive solely from these social norms, however, but is simultaneously formed by the practical imperative to repeat constantly for the sake of retention (a problem addressed by the Prophet Muḥammad himself). Cognitive challenges to the memorizer combined with the necessity to rehearse with others so that no errors come into memory organize affective comportment of an ongoing practitioner with respect to the moral, cognitive, and social demands of ability.

The chapter on learning to read showed how affective dimensions of modes of instruction in a basic ability may forge a relationship to a learning process that construes the fundamentals of reading the Qur'ān to be an ongoing project. Because Indonesia is not an Arabic-speaking region, gaining the ability to pronounce the Qur'ān correctly may comprise a long-term, even lifelong project: Indonesian Muslims must learn not only the Arabic alphabet and the complex system of *tajwīd*, but they must also try to eliminate traces of their native languages when pronouncing the sounds of the Qur'ān. Drawing on theories about how "learning identities" are formed through the activity of acquiring competence, I showed that in Indonesia the sentimental processes of pedagogy constituted an identity of learning that highlighted all subjects as potential learners. Two alternative (intellectually competing, but often experientially compatible) pedagogies for learning to read generated a "sense" of self and system with respect to learning to read Qur'ānic Arabic that was built up—and quite literally—from the letters themselves. Further, the widely promoted "modern" method of pedagogy strategically infused practice with enthusiasm for learning, one result being widespread popularity for learning (or relearning) to read among groups of all ages. The basics were thus becoming an affective project of lifelong learning, forged self-consciously through situational experiences, resonances, and associations.

The fourth and fifth chapters are complementary: one showed how expressive aspects projects of ritual learning effected escalation of engagement on a collective scale, while the other revealed how standards applied in study were developed in a system geared to motivate religious "motivation" and a widespread movement in religious revitalization. Both chapters featured self-conscious feeling strategies in relation to changing social systems, showing how emotion informed dynamics of increasing Qur'ānic engagement. A new system of conceptualizing performance in the *mujawwad* style emerged as pedagogy drew practitioners in to attempt to achieve heightened standards of technical artistry. Competence in this style of recitation became increasingly common in Indonesia in the decades leading up to fieldwork, mostly due to the influence of competitions (for which seven modes, or "*lagu,*" were standardized in 1977), evidencing widespread interest in fulfilling the religious injunction to recite "beautifully." *Mujawwad* recitation had become identified on the one hand with the ideal of world-famous *qāri*'s from the Middle East, whose improvised performances were widely understood to be models for ordinary practice; such virtuoso performances had become "*kurikulum*" for ordinary reciters in Indonesia. On the other hand, there also appeared in Indonesia formalized pedagogies for which to develop this kind of expertise, further enhancing the perception that there was a procedure and an attainability, and even an orthopraxy, to these flexible, aesthetic norms such as the ideals and techniques of affective *rasa* (feeling), which informed beauty, control, and spontaneity. A normative system of flexible standards (such as beauty, affect, and the melodic modes themselves) was received and enhanced in Indonesia in historically specific ways as situational ideals for Qur'ānic practice. With emotional aspects of the Qur'ānic system undergoing change along with new musical systems, practitioners reevaluated their Qur'ānic engagement and performance in terms of expansive ideals and escalating projects of piety.

The properties of ongoingness and expansiveness within Qur'ānic engagement became a goal of influential competition training and pedagogy under the rubric of affective "*motivasi*" (motivation). Competitions were widely viewed to be opportunities to engage in enjoyable, Islamically positive activities, and they also appealed to many (and were publicly promoted as) a means of inviting other Muslims to better appreciate Islamic practice. Competitions shaped goals of practice and participation and, further, ultimately framed practice in terms of providing the very quality of "motivation" itself through the affective dynamics of promotion, preparation, and participation. Promotional frameworks (including state ideology), although seen as compatible with Qur'ānic discourse, did not determine individual motivations; rather, participants in competitions pursued multiple or combined goals. Their motivations, in turn, collectively influenced the institutions that were providing the resources to promote Qur'ānic activities. Pedagogical and competitive strategies transmitted by competition practice, especially emotional ones, infused the recited Qur'ān in Indonesia with the motivating discourse of training. Further, the rules of competitions (the seven standard *lagu*, for example) strongly influenced the ways in which recitation was practiced more generally in Indonesia, generating overall expectations (as well as motivation) for the performance of skilled recitation, even in noncompetitive contexts. Practice (competing) related multiple levels of motivation within a framework that was then adopted as a situational goal, or "mood" within projects of piety; the feeling of *motivasi* was a competition goal in itself.

The theory of emotions that matches most closely the one developed here is Sartre's idea that emotions are "perceptions," though modified not to be exactly a "consciousness," but viewed as a "magical" "transformation of the world" in a very real, religious sense.[1] Emotions have been presented here to be a distinctive mode of experience that carries an embodied component but that also determines fields within the domain of thought. In this study, emotions are taken to be a potentially autonomous dimension of experience, not epiphenomenal but instead a time-bound "force" for personal, social, and historical transformation. As such, they have been shown to merge with modes of thought and feeling. We think about our feelings, and sometimes we talk about them; conversely, what we feel shapes and shifts what we think and say. When we "feel" things in our bodies, sometimes the sensation is perceived to be the effect of emotion and, as William James recognized, sometimes what our bodies sense gives rise to emotions. Emotions sometimes drive thoughts and sensations, and sometimes emotions are their effects. At other times, emotion may be experienced as unmediated, such as states of ecstatic love described by some Muslims in the Sufi tradition. Suspending the approach to emotions as embodied states or habits as well as the notion that they are forms of thought allows the historian of religions to view emotions in religious systems as a mode of transformation and often a self-conscious one that may generate action and self-understanding as a religious actor. Emotion in the Qur'ānic systems considered here is both social and individual, and this blending was explicitly theorized and applied in the projects of learning and religious repetition in contemporary Qur'ānic Indonesia.

Theorists including Geertz, J. Z. Smith, Jennings, Humphrey and Laidlaw, and Williams and Boyd have argued that ritual renders a coalescence of "ideals" ("horizons," "maps," "imaginings") and realities; in learning theory, Lave, Strauss, and Holland criticize "two-tier" models of "teaching and learning" and focus on developmental and situational activities; in emotion theory, Katz, Wikan, and others distinguish situational and "transcendental" emotion, while Humphrey and Laidlaw also analyze "emergent moods," highlighting their "double resonance" of levels of affect. Ritual theory, learning theory, and emotion theory all point to a similar conclusion: the self makes and is made by the nesting interaction of ontological levels of affect in progressive religious enactments. These theorists as well as phenomenologists Csordas, Dewey, and Sartre point to the generative property of affective, educative, or religious "motives," "horizons," or "spirals" that propel projects of aesthetics and piety for individuals and social systems.

The key to understanding these dynamics is not just to attenuate "two-tier" models of emotion or learning with intermediate levels of stratification, but instead to consider the whole system as reflexive and recursive rather than a linear progression. The Qur'ān itself points to this idea in its own unique properties of self-referentiality and the ways in which the recited Qur'ān functions in lived worlds as a closed system, textually, practically, and in the expectations of the pious. Classical Qur'ānic theory also indicates this in the ways in which "general" and "specific" are theorized for understanding levels of theology, law, and lexical referentiality within the text itself. When the universal and the particular of the recited Qur'ān, or "transcendent" and "situated" experiences, coalesce—the kind of process Geertz claims is definitional of "religion"—this is not a stable moment in a trajectory of learning repeated activity. It is dynamic, especially through developmental affect. Dynamic interaction between levels of emotion was the mechanism of inspiration for the increase in engagement in the recited Qur'ān among groups and individual Indonesian Muslims in the 1990s.

This approach takes inspiration from theory developed in the book *How Emotions Work* by Jack Katz and resonates as well with Csordas' theory of ritual "motives." In various domains of Qur'ānic activity, there was, first, a register of bounded particularity (which may implicate a shared understanding as well as individual circumstances) and, second, expansive domains (which have salience for religious persons). This first register of affect is feeling that arose or was applied or experienced as bound to particular conditions, understood as temporary or contingent, often within trajectories of learning or development. On this bounded level, emotion was a means, often deployed self-consciously, by which practitioners developed relationships to others and to activity itself along specific lines. This bounded level is not to be understood as essentially private or interior. Often the affective structures were shared; they were, however, applied in what were understood to be conditions with recognized limits, such as the constraints of curriculum and aptitude within learning environments. At the same time, in each particular bounded situation, affect also resonated with a second, less bounded register. In a religiously expansive domain, affect referenced ultimate ideals, such as orthopraxy, practice that is pleasing to God, and manifestation of the presence of revealed Divine Speech. Many of these expansive ideals were also recognized by pious practitioners to be shaped socially. Examples are the *motivasi* Indonesian Qur'ānic practitioners attempted to cultivate (in alphabet songs, by listening to cassettes, and especially in competing) and the aesthetic ideals of affecting, personalized virtuosic performance that they pursued. The bounded level of affect and "transcendental" perceptions did not collapse or become "one and the same" in perfecting Qur'ānic practice, but the bounded was continually being made expansive, while expansive norms were rendered palpable and contingent.

This theorization of creative, dynamic, and generative interaction of two levels of emotion also draws on theorizations of experience within Islamic traditions of esoteric, interiorized, individualized, and devotional piety within institutional structures of piety. Sufis, who base piety on Qur'ānic models and practice both historically and ideationally, have usually systematized religious models of development in terms of two modes of experience. Although the labels are contested and sometimes objectionable in modern contexts, the outlines of this theory remain salient in contemporary projects to energize and personalize Qur'ānic piety. Sufis elaborate, first, the idea of a bounded "state" *(ḥāl)*, a moral quality of experience and perception that is often semipermanent (usually said to be inspired by God); a particular "state" is usually said to occur or recur at any point along the trajectory of spiritual self-cultivation. The second mode is a more enduring "station" *(maqām)*, achieved through long-term effort and understood to be one of many necessary stages along a unilinear series of "stations" along the "path" *(ṭarīqa)* toward the realization of ultimate goals (usually, some form of recognition of Divine Unity).[2] Affect on the bounded or contingent level resembles emotion circumscribed by particular conditions, pedagogies, occasions, or strategies, like a "state." Expansive affect that references ideals of feeling within long-term developmental processes is like a "station." The "states and stations" of the Sufi path are articulated differently by Sufi systems, often deploying the same terms but in different orders, and with named "states" crossing into "stations" and vice versa. In Sufi theory, it is sometimes difficult to tell what is a transient or conditional "state" or a stable "station": states become stations, and stations first appear in flashes as states. Like Sufi understandings of "states" and "stations," both the bounded and expansive levels of affect in revitalized projects of Qur'ānic practice influenced individual lifeworlds. They referenced shared understandings that were undergoing rapid change, even as the self-reflexive recited Qur'ān and its traditions remained constant.

Both bounded and expansive affect are emergent in learning, an activity by which pious practitioners effortfully attempt to extend limited skill or aptitude into the domain of achievable or ultimate mastery. In religious enactments or rituals, affect does more than set off a kind of "charge"; affect transforms. Feeling does not just magnetize a functional field of "force" that internalizes structures of religious systems. Affect, when taken seriously as a component of ritual experience, is the gravity that may ground voluntary ongoing religious engagement, and its ongoing pull engenders long-term changes in the self and system. The propulsive dynamics of bounded and expansive affect, in Qur'ānic as well as phenomenological terminology, blend "horizons" and "self." As in varying conceptualizations of *ḥāl* and *maqām*, they embed within one another recursively: affective ideals are emergent activity, and activity references ideals. Their interaction may take the form of a dialectical cycle that sweeps people up, perhaps in ways they never anticipated. This "motion" of an individual and collective system of piety may be fueled by the intention to have levels of affect align through self-conscious strategies that are "done" as well as the "doings" of emergent "moods and motivations" in religious systems.

While some theories of emotion present affect as secondary to structures of thought and cognition, in the study of religion and society from Durkheim to Geertz, there has also been a tendency to assert that the salient force of religious change within "cultural systems" is affective. The Indonesian movement of Qur'ānic revitalization in the 1990s provides material for reconsidering the idea that dynamism of religious systems may be generated by "feeling." Specifically, the educative characteristics of the Indonesian system reveal how an emotional momentum of persistence and an affective impetus for change may emerge within a particular social and historical system. In the case of Qur'ānic Indonesia in the 1990s, affect maintained structures of ritual engagement with the Qur'ān, while emotion also fueled this involvement within a movement of religious revitalization. For example, social, cognitive, and affective aspects of Qur'ān memorization combined to shape the textual and contextual experience of the ongoing maintenance of the ability to recite the Qur'ān from memory. In contexts of learning, affective strategies for developing proficiency in reading correctly supported practitioners' self-understandings as ongoing learners. The attempt to learn to recite the Qur'ān according to flexible affective and aesthetic norms for technical artistry, according to standards perceived to be fixed in projects of learning, made individual potential a focus of evaluation and escalating effort. Finally, when competitions in Qur'ānic practices are viewed as a coherent form of practice in itself, Indonesian recitation tournaments may be seen to be a framework oriented toward enhancing motivational interest for Qur'ānic practices in personal and collective dimensions.

In the individual and collective dynamics of learning and skill acquisition, affect propelled the movement of Indonesian Qur'ānic religious revitalization recursively. The abilities Indonesian Muslims gained were evaluated not according to the norms that were always absolutely external but based on pious objectives demonstrated by others that could be achieved in the self. The potential for developing competence affected others' practice as well as one's own. A "technology of the self" of Qur'ānic piety in Indonesia in the 1990s doubled as a "technology of the community" as norms instantiated within contexts of learning implicated religious community. Qur'ānic abilities may be perceived as fixed in their idealizations, but they are nevertheless expansive as processes of acquiring competence that continually open horizons not only in experience but also in interaction. To be an ongoing practitioner of the recited Qur'ān is to pursue one's potential "goodness" and to inspire others as well. Jean Lave writes about the social dimension of acquiring competence:

> Notions like those of "intrinsic rewards" in empirical studies of apprenticeship focus quite narrowly on task knowledge and skill as the activities to be learned. Such knowledge is of course important; but a deeper sense of the value of participation to the community lies in becoming part of the community. . . . Moving toward full participation in practice involves not just a greater commitment of time, intensified effort, more and broader responsibilities within the community, and more difficult and risky tasks, but, more significantly, an increasing sense of identity as a master practitioner.[3]

A motivated "sense of identity" was framed in the Indonesian Qur'ānic system in the 1990s not only by collective values but also in terms of individuals' projects of contribution to community. This occurred in social contexts that embraced a reciprocity of individual and shared affective frameworks for adopting, continuing, and improving voluntary religious practice. Many Indonesian Muslims saw themselves as models for others and as representatives of a motivated movement of Qur'ānic *da'wah* while they looked to others and to the movement itself to understand themselves. As Kenneth M. George details in his study of another ritual system in Sulawesi, practitioners "envied" the possibilities of virtuosic and expert religious practice and Qur'ānic commitment in others.[4]

A concern with "ability" (Ind. *kemampuan*) marked religious practice in the contexts I studied.[5] Appreciating, even "envying," the capabilities and aptitudes of others reveals potential in the self. This was a self-conscious aspect of *da'wah* projects such as Qur'ān recitation competitions, but it was also revealed in more subtle forms in other contexts as well, as within the women's reading groups. When women in Qur'ān recitation study circles, for example, asked me to translate passages from the Qur'ān into English (although none was an English speaker), I did not interpret this to be a test. Instead, the invitation seemed to originate in a fascination with ability that has been described throughout the book—all the more compelling because of the contrast of our shared gender with our very different social roles and identities. Here, performing the ability to "read" posed the possibility of transcending the limitations of language as well as cultural and religious boundaries more generally, revealing the potential for "understanding" on multiple levels by way of the exercise of an acquired, practical competency.

During fieldwork with Qur'ān teachers, reciters, and memorizers, I became increasingly aware of the power and versatility of the concept of desired ability to describe and explain the widespread, growing enthusiasm for Qur'ānic practice in Indonesia in this period. By the time I had the opportunity to interview K. H. M. Sayyid Abdullah, I was convinced of the centrality of the idea. K. H. M. Sayyid Abdullah was a figure widely acknowledged throughout Indonesia as having contributed enormously to Qur'ān recitational pedagogies in connection with immensely popular Qur'ān recitation competitions. He was also much respected and greatly admired as Indonesia's premier master coach and a charismatic inspiration for Qur'ān recitation. During our conversation, I asked K. H. M. Sayyid Abdullah about the international spread of Qur'ān recitation competitions. At the same time that his answer illuminated this issue, it also revealed a possible, perhaps characteristic, perspective on the resurgence in Qur'ānic practices at that time, in Indonesia and elsewhere. I asked K. H. M. Sayyid Abdullah whether it would be correct to say that Muslims in other countries had adopted (I used a word meaning "borrowed" by mistake) from Southeast Asia the "*model*" of Qur'ān recitation competitions. His answer was

> Yes. Actually, it's not a "borrowing" [which might imply, presumably, that something is due to be returned], but you know it is really something high and great in religion that appeared all over in a powerful way. It really has to do with

> another kind of process, another situation—not really competitions, and not [exactly] the Qur'ān. In America, for example, sophisticated [scientific] knowledge *(ilmu canggih)* emerged in all sorts of ways. If you take the case of technical and technological knowledge from America, it came ready-made for use by the nation of Indonesia. This [kind of process] is all the more in the case of religion. Not just in America, in Japan, but wherever in whatever [part of the] world—London, anywhere—this [transmission] occurs because knowledge is considered beneficial *(manfaat)*. For the results, we thank and praise God. There's an envy, a [kind of] envy, Mbak, you see? *It's an envy of [for the sake of] goodness* [*kecemburuan untuk kebaikan*, emphasis added].

I heard K. H. M. Sayyid Abdullah saying, in effect, that the impetus to adopt another's practice—whether a case of Indonesian Qur'ān recitation contests catching on elsewhere in the world or the case of the application in Indonesia of useful technologies developed in America (or, also implied, recognizing "benefit" in the religions of others)—arises from the recognition of the desirability of the practice itself. From this perspective, it is as if there is a neutral economy of good things God has put in the world, and who got hold of them first is not the issue. The point is their "greatness" or "goodness," and the desire or "envy" this may produce in others to emulate and adopt great and good things. K. H. M. Sayyid Abdullah's statement suggested the idea that the inherent "goodness" of a practice may be accompanied by a natural desire among people to pursue "goodness" in individual and collective experience.

A well-known *ḥadīth* about a believer's "envy" of a Muslim who is earnest, pious, and diligent and proficient in Qur'ān recitation probably influenced K. H. M. Sayyid Abdullah's statement. The canonical *ḥadīth* report is

> Narrated Abū Huraira: Allāh's Messenger said, "There is no envy except two [kinds, *lā ḥasada illā fī ithnain*]: [first] a person whom Allāh has taught the Qur'ān and he recites it *(yatlūhu)* during the hours of the night and during the hours of the day, and his neighbor hears him and says, 'I wish I had been given what has been given to so-and-so, so that I could do what he does,' and [second] a person whom Allāh has given wealth and he spends it on what is just and right, whereupon another person says, 'I wish I had been given what so-and-so has been given, for then I would do as he does.'"[6] (al-Bukhārī, Muslim)

In the case of the Qur'ān, which Muslims recognize to be God's revelation to humanity, an "envy of goodness" may assume a powerful and unique form that motivates a continuous effort to improve competence in the recited Qur'ān, establishing selves as ongoing practitioners.

Social features of Qur'ānic practices amplify an "envy for goodness" that is natural to a Qur'ānic worldview and that may also be an aspect of the psychology of religious piety more generally. Some of these features are construed by Muslims to be socially constituted *(adab)*, whereas others are understood to have extended from a unique form of authority deriving from the exemplary comportment of the Prophet Muḥammad *(sunnah)*, and still others arise from technical aspects of the revealed and recited Qur'ān (such as, for example, stipulated improvisation and a kaleidoscopic structure that challenges memory). In the case of the Qur'ān, a reflexivity in terms of norms (the Qur'ān instructs as to its own recitation—in fact, the Qur'ān *is* its own recitation) as well as expansive flexibility (with, for example, stipulated improvisatory requirements that systematize spontaneity) enhanced the centrality of Qur'ānic practice for projects of religious self-cultivation among Indonesians. Together, psychological dimensions of repeated practice, the recited Qur'ān, and systems of meaning that enhance these on individual and collective levels forged a compelling emotional draw, "lure," or affective pull to the voluntary practice of Qur'ānic piety in Indonesia in the 1990s. Such practice may be potentially self-sustaining and self-propelling. The desire to be able to recite the Qur'ān in a beautiful, efficacious, or otherwise beneficial way was often coupled with a religious desire to improve in order to inspire others to do the same.

To a religious person for whom voluntary ritual practice is tied to a sense of self-cultivation or to an ongoing relationship with divine or social orders, ritual is progressive, cumulative, and continually to be perfected. Repeated religious practice (in contrast to rituals such as initiations) is not the fixed or given quantity that observers and participants may take it to be; ritual proficiency, as social activity, is processual and continually being relearned. Muslims attest that the meanings of the Qur'ān are layered and cumulative; the same was true for Qur'ānic recitational practice and pedagogies to teach it in Indonesia. In Indonesia in the 1990s, projects of gaining ritual proficiency and competence in the recitation of the Qur'ān were especially amenable to elaboration within educational projects. Individuals pursued enhanced ability *(kemampuan)* in expressions of piety, and groups and organizations, in turn, supported collective projects based on the propensity of individuals to cultivate religious practice. These activities and pedagogies, and the affect and motivations they engendered for individuals, reinforced aspects of ritual practice. They also shaped practitioners' self-understandings as well as their understandings of contribution to community.

This has been a study of contemporary Indonesian Muslims' wish to master Qur'ānic abilities demonstrated by others and the related desire to join in pious Qur'ānic practices with religious community. In Indonesia in the 1990s, such projects of enhancing Qur'ānic engagement constituted expansive and often consistent understandings of selves with respect to ongoing activity determined through affective modes in projects of learning. The effects of such projects that were carried out among numerous individuals along with the conditions of social systems that supported these very projects, combined with the affective dynamics of the "rehearsal" of the Qur'ān itself, explain aspects of a resurgence in Islamic practice in Indonesia in the last decade of the twentieth century.

The ongoing practice of voluntary religious piety may not just be fueled by the wish to emulate others, but may also take shape as an applied "envy" of one's own potential "goodness" and the desire to inspire it in others through example. This mechanism of inspiration led Qur'ānic practitioners in Indonesia in the 1990s to strive collectively to realize the signs of perfected practice that may manifest "on the horizons and in themselves" (41 Fuṣṣilāt 53) within deepening cycles of engagement. It is left up to the reader to draw his or her own conclusions about whether this demonstration, in the end, has simply amounted to a lengthy explanation of some ways to see how the Qur'ān does to people exactly what it said it would do to Muslims all along. In the Indonesian system of the acquisition of Qur'ānic abilities, the Qur'ān itself was reflexively the object and method of learning as well as the standard for evaluation and achievement. The recited Qur'ān comprised a ritual, affective, and educative system determining moods, motivations, and learning trajectories—and, in Indonesia, a movement of religious revitalization. Within the individual and collective programs and projects of ongoing and escalating Qur'ānic piety that transformed Indonesian Muslims in the mid-1990s, the recited Qur'ān was a practice that continually remade transcendent perfection into a pious possibility.

Notes

Chapter 1: Introduction

1. Dra. Hj. Maria Ulfah toured the United States in 1999. Her recitation is featured on the compact disc recording accompanying the book by Michael Sells, *Approaching the Qur'an*. Anne K. Rasmussen accompanied Dra. Hj. Maria Ulfah on her U.S. tour. See Rasmussen, "The Qur'an in Indonesian Daily Life."

2. See Frederick M. Denny, "Qur'ān Recitation Training in Indonesia"; Howard Federspiel, *Popular Indonesian Literature of the Qur'an*; and Anna M. Gade, "An Envy of Goodness."

3. See John R. Bowen, "The Forms Culture Takes," for an overview of tensions between "text-based" and ethnographic perspectives in the anthropology of Southeast Asia. Clifford Geertz has drawn much critical attention along these lines. For example, see William Roff, "Islam Obscured?" and Mark R. Woodward, *Islam in Java*. In "The *Slametan*," Mark Woodward details an important theoretical model for conceptualizing universal, received, and local tradition in the study of Islam.

4. See Anthony Johns, "Coming to Terms with the Qur'ān: A Challenge for Indonesianists," and Peter G. Riddell, *Islam in the Malay-Indonesian World*.

5. See work by Henri Chambert-Loir as well as Christian Pelras and J. Noorduyn. See also works by historians of the early modern era, Leonard Y. Andaya, William Cummings, and Anthony Reid, issues of *Archipel* (vol. 29, 1985) and *Bijdragen tot de Taal-, Land- en Volkenkunde* (vol. 156, no. 3, 2000) that are devoted to the history of South Sulawesi, as well as articles reprinted in Alijah Gordon, ed., *The Propagation of Islam in the Indonesian-Malay Archipelago*.

6. Leonard Andaya, "The Bugis-Makassarese Diasporas."

7. R. Michael Feener, "Shaykh Yusuf and the Appreciation of Muslim 'Saints' in Modern Indonesia." The graves of Prince Diponogoro and especially Sheikh Yusuf are present-day sites of veneration in Makassar.

8. Barbara Sillars Harvey, "Tradition, Islam, and Rebellion: South Sulawesi 1950–1965," and Kees van Dijk, *Rebellion under the Banner of Islam*.

9. See, for example, Nico Kaptein, "The *Berdiri Mawlid* Issue among Indonesian Muslims in the Period from circa 1875 to 1930." Surveys on anti-Sufi polemics in Indonesia in historical perspective appear in the volume edited by Frederick de Jong and Bernd Radtke, *Islamic Mysticism Contested.*

10. Nico Kaptein, *Muhammad's Birthday Festival,* provides historical perspectives that extend much earlier. See also Annemarie Schimmel, *And Muhammad Is His Messenger.* For musical perspectives, see Lois Ibsen Al-Faruqi, "The Mawlid." Text cycles in Southeast Asia such as "The Splitting of the Moon," "The Shaving of the Prophet," and "The Prophet's Night Journey and Ascent" also elaborate events in accounts of the life of the Prophet. R. Michael Feener, "'Knowledge' of the Past in Malay Islamicate Historiography" (unpublished).

11. Such bound volumes also include prayer, such as the "*tahlil*" for the deceased. One such compilation is *Majmu'āt Mawālid wa Ad'īa* (Compilation of Mawlid Texts and Prayers).

12. William Cummings' *Making Blood White* is a book-length study of the history of the textual system of this court tradition. For wider perspectives, see Riddell, *Islam in the Malay-Indonesian World.*

13. James N. Baker, "The Presence of the Name."

14. Jean Lave and E. Wenger, eds., *Situated Learning.*

15. See Jennifer Lindsay, "Cultural Policy and the Performing Arts in South Sulawesi"; R. Anderson Sutton, "Performing Arts and Cultural Politics in South Sulawesi"; and Philip Yampolsky, "Forces for Change in the Performing Arts of Indonesia."

16. The Qur'ānic basis for the idea of *da'wah* is usually taken to be 16 al-Nahl 125, understood to be addressing Prophets as well as ordinary Muslims: "Call [same root as *da'wah*] thou to the way of thy Lord with wisdom and good admonition, and dispute with them in the better way." A good contrast with Indonesian ideals of *da'wah* is the development of modern *da'wah* in neighboring Malaysia. See works by William Roff, especially his "Islamic Movements: One or Many?" See also Kees van Dijk, "*Dakwah* and Indigenous Culture in the Dissemination of Islam." For global perspectives highlighting the Middle East, see Dale F. Eickelman and John W. Anderson, eds., *New Media in the Muslim World,* and Dale F. Eickelman and James Piscatori, *Muslim Politics.*

17. H. Mahfudh Syamsul Hadi, H. Muaddi Aminan, and Cholil Uman, eds., *Rahasia Keberhasilan Dakwah oleh K. H. Zainuddin, M.Z.,* pp. 109–110.

18. H. Hasan Basri, "MTQ dan Peranannya dalam Mengkatkan Semangat Beragama di Kalangan Remaja Muslim," pp. 27–28. Adapted from A. Rosyad Shaleh, *Managemen Dakwah Islam* (Jakarta: Bulan Bintang, 1977), pp. 31–37.

19. Performance program, "Drama Musikan 'Taubat' oleh El Bitrul Pertamina Jakarta (dalam Rangka Memeriahkan MTQ Nasional ke XVIII di Jambi)." Italics in original.

20. For a discussion of the *tahlil* and other controversies in Indonesian context, see John Bowen, *Muslims through Discourse.*

21. An example is the broadcast of Qur'ān recitation from mosque minarets just prior to the times of canonical prayer *(ṣalāt),* which was also controversial when first introduced. Another controversy in the 1990s was about a practice apparently devel-

oped by reciters in Jakarta, in which several reciters read the Qur'ān together melodically, with the performance arranged by a director. The dispute centered on the permissibility of one *āyah* (verse) being divided between two voices, eventually determined to be unacceptable, although different reciters could recite consecutive *āyahs* in turn. Maria Ulfah, "Hukum Melagukan al-Qur'an Secara Bersama."

22. H. Amidhan et al., *The Dynamics of Indonesian Muslim Today,* p. 66.

23. Kenneth M. George, "Designs on Indonesia's Muslim Communities," is an analysis of the conceptual and institutional background of the earlier Mushaf Istiqlal project.

24. The English-language translations of forum topics are taken from *Dynamics of Indonesia Muslim Today,* p. 68. This symposium was the basis for a five-volume book series edited by Aswab Mahasin and others, *Ruh Islam dalam Budaya Bangsa.* Volume 5, "Konsep Estetika," treats general aesthetic concepts, calligraphy, architecture, batik and clothing (with much on women's Islamic fashion, also a popular field for competitions in Indonesia), food, the Internet, and other areas of religious expression; material on Qur'ān recitation is not included.

25. John Pemberton, "Recollections from 'Beautiful Indonesia.'"

26. Art students from Jakarta were the only other visitors to the Baitul Quran on a day that I visited, sitting with sketchbooks in front of the enormous pages mounted on the walls. In a discussion with a designer for the Mushaf Sundawi project, when the issue of identity came up in conversation, the discussion was not about the location of West Java in Indonesia's Muslim culture but instead about the potential international impact that such projects in Indonesia might have: for example, Malaysians following Indonesia in applying local motifs to *muṣḥaf* decoration projects. There was some discussion in Makassar during the time of fieldwork of holding a "Festival Al-Markaz" (modeled on Festival Istiqlal), which would showcase "Islamic culture" acoss eastern Indonesia, from Sulawesi to Ambon, at the new mosque Masjid "Al-Markaz Al-Islami."

27. For perspectives on Islam and politics in the New Order, see B. J. Boland, *The Struggle of Islam in Modern Indonesia,* and works by Robert W. Hefner, especially his *Civil Islam.* See also contributions to Mark Woodward, ed., *Toward a New Paradigm.*

28. Historians of religions have called for recognition of the importance of exploring the oral and aural dimensions of written texts, often in association with their situatedness in ritual practice. Many of these scholars are specialists in Islam, whose consideration of the recited Qur'ān widened a comparative category of "scripture" in the academic study of religion. Islamicists M. Ayoub, F. Denny, W. Graham, R. Martin, K. Nelson, M. Sells, W. Cantwell Smith, as well as others have stressed the necessity to approach the Qur'ān with a performative as well as a textual perspective. The issue of orality-aurality and the Qur'ān is treated by William Graham in many works, including *Beyond the Written Word.* See also works by Wilfred Cantwell Smith on "scripture" and the Qur'ān.

29. Frederick M. Denny, "Exegesis and Recitation" and his "Qur'ān Recitation: A Tradition of Oral Performance and Transmission." I draw on Denny's historical summaries in this section. See also Arthur Jeffery, "The Textual History of the Qur'an," for another historical overview.

30. See Kristina Nelson, *The Art of Reciting the Qur'an,* and Frederick Denny, "Qur'an Recitation," for a bibliography of older works on technical aspects of recitation. There are also works devoted especially to the recitation of the late Sh. 'Abd al-Bāsiṭ 'Abd al-Ṣamad. Other technical treatments are by Lois Ibsen Al-Faruqi, as well as thoughts related to the project of considering the "Islamic Arts." More comparative reflections on the development of Qur'ān recitation are found in Lois Ibsen Al-Faruqi, "What Makes Religious Music Religious?"

31. Besides her *Art of Reciting the Qur'ān,* see also Kristina Nelson, "Reciter and Listener."

32. Paul Kahle, "The Arabic Readers of the Koran," treating issues of the Arabic language and early recitation, and C. M. H. Versteegh, *Arabic Grammar and Qur'anic Exegesis in Early Islam;* see also works by G. H. A. Juynboll.

33. The Qur'ān states: "Surely We Ourselves [God] have sent down the Exhortation [the Qur'ān] and We will most certainly safeguard it" (15 al-Ḥijr 9).

34. There were several other codices in use at that time, as discussed in the scholarship of Arthur Jeffery. For a brief consideration of some technical aspects of recitation and their historical development, see Khalil I. Seeman, "*Tajwīd* as a Source in Phonetic Research."

35. Denny, "Exegesis and Recitation," p. 113.

36. See ibid., p. 115.

37. This version is from al-Bukhārī's collection. There are many other versions of this *ḥadīth* as well as many different interpretations of what the term "modes" *(aḥrūf)* may mean, outlined in Ahmad von Denffer, *'Ulūm al-Qur'ān,* pp. 111–115.

38. Denny, "Exegesis and Recitation," p. 116. Many contemporary professional reciters in the Arabic-speaking world are trained in all seven readings but generally perform in only one style. Most use the reading of Ḥafṣ (d. 796), as is also the case in Indonesia. Dra. Hj. Khadijatus Shalihah published an influential book, *Perkembangan Seni Baca al Quran dan Qiraat Tujuh di Indonesia* (The Development of the Art of Reciting the Qur'ān and the Seven Readings in Indonesia), which emphasizes the diversity of the readings, and this has supported interest among Indonesian reciters in developing expertise in all seven readings.

39. The term occurs only once in this form in the Qur'ān, in 2 al-Baqarah 121 (although there are many instances of verbalized variants).

40. R. Martin, "Tilāwah," p. 529.

41. Denny, "Exegesis and Recitation," p. 97.

42. Ibid., citing also 75 al-Qiyāmah 16–19, and 17 al-Isrā' 110 on modes of reciting the Qur'ān, and 7 al-A'rāf 204–205 on how to listen to it. Compare 25 al-Furqān 32.

43. Denny, "Exegesis and Recitation," p. 120.

44. See Nelson, *Art of Reciting,* for an overview of this material.

45. Frederick M. Denny, "The *Adab* of Qur'ān Recitation."

46. Other names of recitation styles (not in general usage in Indonesia) are *taḥqīq* (slow tempo), *tadwīr* (medium tempo), and *ḥadr* (fast). For an overview of types of recitation and these categories, see Lois Al-Faruqi, "The Cantillation of the Qur'an."

47. William Cummings, *Making Blood White*, especially pp. 158–160, and Russell Jones, "Ten Conversion Myths from Indonesia." The LPTQ survey *Sejarah MTQ di Sulawesi Selatan* (History of the MTQ in South Sulawesi) also cites local court chronicle sources on the amount of the Qur'ān to be recited publicly according to the social status of the deceased.

48. Taufik Abdullah, "Islam and the Formation of Tradition." See the bibliography for selected works of Anthony H. Johns on the history of Sufism in Indonesia as well as the work of Martin van Bruinessen, which includes material on Sufi orders in South Sulawesi specifically.

49. For discussion, see Mark R. Woodward, *Islam in Java*.

50. See George N. Atiyeh, ed., *The Book in the Islamic World*.

51. Darul Aqsha, Dick van der Meij, and Johan Hendrik Meuleman, eds., *Islam in Indonesia*, gives a historical survey of state institutional developments in Islamic education. See also Saya Shiraishi, *Young Heroes*, and, for comparison with Egypt, Gregory Starrett, *Putting Islam to Work*.

52. The phenomenon of Muslim women's Qur'anic study circles is international. For perspectives on Indonesia, see G. G. Weix, "Islamic Prayer Groups in Indonesia," as well as work by Suzanne Brenner.

53. For perspectives on diachronic change and emotional systems highlighting the idea that change in emotion systems over time is not only an effect of change in social structures but also potentially a cause, see Peter N. Stearns and Carol Z. Stearns, "Emotionology," as well as their *Emotion and Social Change*.

54. There are Islamic recited texts famous in Indonesia for inducing weeping, such as the "Tul Kiamat" (attributed, as are many texts in Southeast Asia, to al-Ghazzālī), which treats eschatological themes and is also recited in connection with observances for the dead. Thanks to R. Michael Feener for the citation.

55. The Qur'ān continually asserts itself to be a "guide and a mercy" to humankind, and this claim is a key to apprehending the representation of affective, transformative effect, such as 10 Yūnus 57–58. These ideas are inseparable from the event of revelation, an occurrence associated with the experience of peace (97 al-Qadr), blessing (44 al-Dukhān 3), earth-shattering power, as well as the alternative human responses of acceptance and denial.

56. Anthony Johns, "The Qur'ān on the Qur'ān."

57. A variant of this passage is given as an address for the Prophet in 67 al-Mulk 23, enjoining Muslims to be thankful for God's gifts and bounties.

58. Two out of many possible examples of verses invoking these ideas are 66 al-Taḥrīm 4 and 70 al-Ma'ārij 5.

59. Fazlur Rahman in *Major Themes of the Qur'ān*, pp. 65–79.

60. For a general introduction, see G. E. von Grunebaum, "I'djāz." Surveys of the concept and its application include works by Issa J. Boulatta, such as "The Rhetorical Interpretation of the Qur'an." John Wansbrough treats the history of the relevant controversies in his *Quranic Studies*, pp. 77–84.

61. See Wilfred Madelung, "The Origins of the Controversy Concerning the Cre-

ation of the Qur'an." For a detailed treatment of this position on the issue of Speech, see J. R. T. M. Peters, *God's Created Speech*.

62. There were great number of *i'jāz* texts listed in Ibn al-Nadīm's famous *fihrist* of books available in Baghdad in the early period, suggesting the importance of the concept as well as the energy put into the development of rhetorical analysis that typifies the field. A classical work is Abū Bakr Muḥammad b. al-Ṭayyib al-Baqillānī, *I'jāz al-Qur'ān*, as well as treatments by important persons of letters such as Ibn Qutaiba and al-Jāhiẓ.

63. For perspectives on the translation of the Qur'ān, see also the article by A. L. Tibawi, "Is the Qur'ān Translatable?" for a historical perspective, as well as the article by Raphael Israeli, "Translation as Exegesis."

64. Yusuf Rahman, unpublished paper. Thanks also to Hendrick Maier for discussion.

65. Julia Day Howell, "Sufism and the Indonesian Islamic Revival." In *Islam in Java*, Mark Woodward shows the depth of Sufi systems in a contemporary Indonesian social context.

66. Sirriyeh, *Sufis and Anti-Sufis*.

67. These *ḥadīths* are given in al-Ghazzālī, *The Recitation and Interpretation of the Qur'ān*, pp. 23 and 24, respectively, along with the *ḥadīth* that follows.

68. Al-Ghazzālī, *Recitation and Interpretation*, p. 24. These "abbreviated letters" *(muqaṭṭa'āt)* open 2 al-Baqarah and five other *sūrahs*.

69. Ibid.

70. Al-Makkī, *Qūt al-qulūb fī mu'āmalāt al-maḥbūb*, vol. 1, quoted in Nelson, *Art of Reciting*, p. 97. Nelson cites similar statements in works of the "Sufis" al-Sarrāj al-Tūsī and al-Qurtubī.

71. Talal Asad, *Genealogies of Religion*.

72. Edward L. Deci, *Intrinsic Motivation*.

73. This list is taken from Catherine Lutz and Geoffrey White, "The Anthropology of Emotions," pp. 406–409. Another list of "Ten Problems in the Analysis of Emotion" from the perspective of philosophical psychology, given by Calhoun and Solomon, is more foundational: what counts as an emotion? which emotions are basic? what are emotions about? (intentionality); explaining emotions; the rationality of emotions; emotions and ethics; emotions and culture; emotions and expression; emotions and responsibility; and emotions and knowledge. Cheshire Calhoun and Robert C. Solomon, *What Is an Emotion?* pp. 23–40.

74. Peggy A. Thoits, "The Sociology of Emotions," pp. 318–319.

75. Well-known examples of studies of "vocabularies of emotion" by Indonesianists are Hildred Geertz, "The Vocabulary of Emotion," and Karl Heider, *Landscapes of Emotion*. See also Joel R. Davitz, *The Language of Emotion*. In their review article "The Anthropology of Emotions," Catherine Lutz and Geoffrey White compare such studies to those of color lexicons in the study of culture (p. 416).

76. In her book *Unnatural Emotions*, Catherine Lutz discusses this problem at length.

77. Catherine Lutz and Lila Abu-Lughod, eds., *Language and the Politics of Emotion*.

78. Unni Wikan, *Managing Turbulent Hearts*.

79. In addition to the seminal works on emotions Catherine Lutz, *Unnatural Emotions*, and Michelle Z. Rosaldo, *Knowledge and Passion*, see Geoffrey M. White and John Kirkpatrick, eds., *Person, Self, and Experience*.

80. For another perspective on this definition, see Nancy K. Frankenberry and Hans H. Penner, "Clifford Geertz's Long-Lasting Moods, Motivations, and Metaphysical Conceptions."

81. Clifford Geertz, "Religion as a Cultural System," pp. 90–91, italics in text.

82. The view that Geertz' "moods and motivations" may be understood as a model of ritual or religous internalization contrasts with other perspectives on Geertz' psychology. Claudia Strauss discusses "internalization" in "Models and Motives," pp. 4–8.

83. Geertz, "Religion as a Cultural System," p. 96. One of his points seems to be that there is no single named emotion that is normatively "religious," a key question in the history of the study of religions. Geertz' definition of "motivation" is followed by a quote from psychologist and philosophical behaviorist Gilbert Ryle, author of *The Concept of Mind*, who thought that emotional states were observable through behavior and proclivities to action.

84. Geertz, "Religion as a Cultural System," p. 97.

85. Geertz suggests the visceral "moods and motivations" of symbols with respect to enacted performance in ibid., pp. 114–118.

86. Ibid., pp. 96–97.

87. See discussion in Thomas Csordas, "Embodiment as a Paradigm for Anthropology."

88. Ibid., p. 33.

89. The idea of "religious experience" as the irreducible, affectively based, "essence" of religion (Rudolf Otto, *The Idea of the Holy*, for example) has been challenged as a "protective strategy" in the academic study of religions (for example, by Wayne Proudfoot in *Religious Experience*). Some thinkers (such as William James) have asked, is there such a thing as a "religious emotion" at all? James' answer was "no." William James, *The Varieties of Religious Experience*, p. 28.

90. For a general introduction to Vygotsky's thought, see J. V. Wertsch, *Vygotsky and the Social Formation of Mind*, and Harry Daniels, ed., *An Introduction to Vygotsky*, especially the essay by Jean Lave and Etienne Wenger, "Practice, Person, and Social World." Perspectives on the application of Vygotsky's ideas, including the "zone of proximal development," can be found in J. V. Wertsch, *Culture, Communication, and Cognition*. Also see Lev S. Vygotsky, *The Collected Works of L. S. Vygotsky*, vol. 1; and Vygotsky, *Mind in Society*.

91. Dorothy Holland, "How Cultural Systems Become Desire," p. 63. Emphasis in text.

92. For an assessment of these issues in terms of the impact of Lave's work, see Claudia Strauss, "Beyond 'Formal' and 'Informal' Education." Some of Lave's selected

works are given in the bibliography. For a general overview, see C. Pelissier, "The Anthropology of Teaching and Learning," which includes discussion of Lave's work.

93. Jean Lave, "The Practice of Learning," p. 8.

94. Ibid., pp. 8–9.

95. Ibid., pp. 5–6, 8–9.

96. Ibid., pp. 5–6. Emphasis added.

97. Victor Turner discusses Dewey in "Dewey, Dilthey, and Drama."

98. John Dewey, *Art as Experience*, p. 41.

99. Ibid., p. 65.

100. Ibid., p. 72.

101. Ibid., pp. 58–59, as quoted and discussed in Herbert W. Schneider, "Dewey's Psychology," p. 11.

102. Bertram Morris, "Dewey's Theory of Art," p. 164, quoting Dewey, *Democracy and Education*.

103. Jack Katz, *How Emotions Work*, p. 314. In many theories of emotion, especially moral philosophy back to the time of Aristotle, emotions are theorized as modes of judgment, belief, and assessment of "intensional objects." See Calhoun and Solomon, *What Is an Emotion?* for representative selections.

104. Caroline Humphrey and James Laidlaw, The *Archetypal Actions of Ritual*, p. 249.

105. Ibid. Emphasis in text.

Chapter 2: Memorizing

1. Al-Nawawī, *Al-tibyān fī adab ḥamalat al-Qur'ān* (The Explanation of the Proper Comportment for Carrying the Qur'ān), p. 105. I have changed the translators' "possessor" to "possessing."

2. Jonathan Berkey, *Transmission of Knowledge in Medieval Cairo*, p. 28; George Makdisi, *The Rise of Colleges*, pp. 99–105; Dale F. Eickelman, "The Art of Memory."

3. See work by Taufik Abdullah, Zamasyari Dhofier, and contributions to Charles F. Keyes, ed., *Reshaping Local Worlds*. Recent studies of *pesantren* curriculum and modernization in "traditional" settings include Ronald A. Lukens-Bull, "Two Sides of the Same Coin" and "Teaching Morality."

4. An important study is G. W. J. Drewes, "The Study of Arabic Grammar in Indonesia," referencing the writings of orientalist scholar and colonial administrator Snouk Hugrojne on "Meccan" and "Medinan" pedagogy. See also Sidney Jones, "Arabic Instruction and Literacy in Javanese Muslim Schools," and work by Martin van Bruinessen.

5. Fuller description is in Muntaha Azhari, "Tahfizh al-Qur'an di Indonesia," in Lembaga Pengembangan Tilawatil Quran (LPTQ), *25 Tahun Musabaqah Tilawatil Quran*, pp. 102–104 (originally printed in *Pesantren* 8, vol. 1 [1991]); and Madnuh, "Tradisi Tahfiz al-Qur'an dan Korelasinya dengan Musabaqah Tilawatil Qu'ran dalam Usaha Melestarikan Kemurnian al-Qur'an."

6. A classic study is Clifford Geertz, "The Javanese *Kijaji*." See also references below.

7. Naomi Quinn and Claudia Strauss, "A Cognitive Cultural Anthropology," quoted in Roy G. D'Andrade, "Afterword," p. 229.

8. Strauss, "Models and Motives," p. 16.

9. See the review discussion on "personhood" in George E. Marcus and Michael M. J. Fischer, *Anthropology as Cultural Critique*, pp. 44–73. A discussion in Nancy Chodorow's book *The Power of Feelings*, pp. 144–149, treats anthropology's cross-cultural understanding of the "self," highlighting the contribution of Geertz.

10. Robert David Laing, *The Politics of Experience*, discussed by Bruce Kapferer in "Performance and the Structuring of Meaning and Experience."

11. Katz, *How Emotions Work*, p. 16.

12. A related approach is taken in William M. Reddy, "Emotional Liberty," and the work of Gary Ebersole, who inspired this survey.

13. William James, "What Is an Emotion?" pp. 127–141. This theory is often termed the "James-Lange" theory of emotions.

14. Ibid., p. 128; emphasis in text.

15. Lutz and White, "Anthropology of Emotions," p. 472.

16. See, for example, the foundational studies by Thomas J. Csordas.

17. Elaine Scarry, *The Body in Pain*. As shown by studies of depression undertaken by Arthur Kleinman and Byron Good, these issues may be compounded by cross-cultural questions of translation. See, for example, Kleinman and Good, *The Illness Narratives*.

18. Another approach, typified by George Lakoff and Mark Johnson, for example, sees cognitive conceptual categories and metaphors extending from the body, as in *Metaphors We Live By*. Compare Pierre Bourdieu on "The Body as Geometer," in *Outline of a Theory of Practice*, pp. 114–124.

19. Robert R. Desjarlais, *Body and Emotion*. Other studies of emotions and their aesthetic expression in social contexts have been done by Donald Brenneis, Steven Feld, Bruce Kapferer, Fred R. Myers, and many others.

20. Paul Ekman, Wallace V. Friesen, and Phoebe Ellsworth, *Emotion in the Human Face;* and Richard Schechner, "Magnitudes of Performance," which draws on Eckman's study.

21. Emile Durkheim, *Elementary Forms of the Religious Life*, p. 400, part of chapter 5 on "piacular rites"; and Gary L. Ebersole, "The Function of Ritual Weeping Revisited."

22. M. Rosaldo, unpublished paper, quoted in Robert I. Levy, "Introduction: Self and Emotion," p. 128.

23. M. Rosaldo, "Toward an Anthropology of Self and Feeling," p. 140.

24. Ibid., p. 140. Catherine Lutz makes a similar point in her book *Unnatural Emotions*.

25. M. Rosaldo, "Toward an Anthropology of Self and Feeling," pp. 142–147.

26. Lutz and Abu-Lughod, "Introduction," in *Language and the Politics of Emotion*, ed. Catherine Lutz and Lila Abu-Lughod, pp. 1–23.

27. Rom Harré, "An Outline of the Social Constructionist Viewpoint"; and Claire Armon-Jones, "The Thesis of Constructionism."

28. Lutz and White discuss "commonsense naturalism" in their review article "The Anthropology of Emotions," p. 415, as does Melford E. Spiro in "Some Reflections on Cultural Determinism and Relativism with Special Reference to Emotion and Reason."

29. Katz, *How Emotions Work*, p. 5. In "Embodiment as a Paradigm," Csordas considers new approaches to the "mind-body problem."

30. Katz, *How Emotions Work*, pp. 6–7.

31. Erving Goffman, *Interaction Ritual*, p. 23; and idem, *The Presentation of Self in Everyday Life*.

32. Steven L. Gordon, "The Sociology of Sentiments and Emotion," pp. 585–592. He defines "sentiment" as a "socially constructed pattern linking sensations and expressive gestures with cultural meanings, organized around a relationship to another person" (p. 592).

33. This is the primary distinction given in Theodore D. Kemper, ed., *Research Agendas in the Sociology of Emotions*, in which Hochschild's work also appears.

34. See work by Arlie Russell Hochschild, especially *The Managed Heart*.

35. Unni Wikan, *Managing Turbulent Hearts*.

36. Michel Foucault, *Technologies of the Self*, p. 18.

37. Ibn Khaldūn, *The Muqaddimah*, p. 340. He contrasts this capability with "memorized" knowledge.

38. Ira Lapidus, "Knowledge, Virtue, and Action"; see also Saba Mahmood's discussion of embodied habituation in "Women's Piety and Embodied Discipline."

39. Barbara Metcalf, ed., *Moral Conduct and Authority*; and Katherine Ewing, ed., *Shari'at and Ambiguity in South Asian Islam*.

40. Franz Rosenthal, *Knowledge Triumphant*, pp. 243, 252.

41. Frederick Denny, "The *Adab* of Qur'ān Recitation."

42. For example, see Makdisi, *Rise of Colleges*.

43. Rosenthal, *Knowledge Triumphant*, pp. 70–77.

44. These examples are from Ibn Qutaibah's collected aphorisms on knowledge and *ādāb* in his *'Uyūn Kitāb al-'Ilm wa-l-bayān* (On Knowledge and Eloquent Expression), given in Rosenthal, *Knowledge Triumphant*, pp. 255–263.

45. For al-Askarī, these are all aspects of *ādāb*. The summary of al-Askarī from which this derives is in Rosenthal, *Knowledge Triumphant*, pp. 281–282.

46. There was a later group known as the "readers" *(qurrā')*. Studies of the meaning of the term "reader" and the roles of early Qur'ān readers include work by G. H. A. Juynboll.

47. Ahmad von Denffer, *'Ulūm al-Qur'ān*, p. 33, translating the standard biography of the Prophet by Ibn Hishām, *Sīrah al-Nabī*.

48. Barbara Stowasser, *Women in the Qur'an, Traditions, and Interpretation*.

49. Alexander Knysh, *Islamic Mysticism*, p. 167.

50. Rosenthal, *Knowledge Triumphant*, p. 322.

51. Ibid., p. 316. Related to this, Rosenthal writes, is the question of those whose piety was outstanding but who were perhaps not quite as bright.

52. Quoted in ibid., pp. 172–173.

53. Al-Ghazzāli, *Recitation and Interpretation*, p. 28. The glosses by Quasem, the translator, are modified.

54. Al-Nawawī, "Al-Tibyān," p. 101.

55. Ibid., pp. 102–103.

56. The Qur'ān makes reference to this practice in, for example, 3 Al 'Imrān 113–114. There are also many variants of the *ḥadīth* "The best of believers are those who arise at night," found in the collections of Abū Dāūd and others.

57. Al-Ghazzālī, *Recitation and Interpretation*, p. 30.

58. Al-Nawawī, "Al-Tibyān," p. 101.

59. Al-Ghazzālī, *Recitation and Interpretation*, p. 26.

60. Ibid., p. 31.

61. Ibid., p. 32.

62. Ibid., p. 31.

63. Ibid., p. 29.

64. Ibid., p. 30.

65. Ibid.

66. Al-Nawawī, "Al-Tibyān," p. 105.

67. Al-Rummānī 'Alī b. 'Isā, *Al-Nukāt fi I'jaz al-Qur'ān*.

68. For example, Badr al-Dīn Muḥammad b. 'Abd Allāh al-Zarkashī, *Al-Burhān fī 'Ulūm al-Qur'ān*, and Jalāl al-Dīn al-Suyūṭī, *Al-Itqān fī 'Ulūm al-Qur'ān*.

69. Katz, *How Emotions Work*, p. 314, citing Michael Polanyi, *The Tacit Dimension*.

70. Strauss, "Beyond 'Formal' and 'Informal' Education," pp. 212–213. Strauss refers here to work by Daniel Wagner, Sylvia Scribner, and Michael Cole. An Indonesian reciter, when discussing different strategies of memory, theorized in conversation the possibility of embodied mnemonics, suggested by the "rocking" memorizers enact unreflectively during recall; he hypothesized that memory could be "stored" in the body in some way. This is reminiscent of questions asked about the social embodiment of memory by scholars such as Ulric Neisser, Paul Connerton, and Edward S. Casey.

71. Strauss, "Beyond 'Formal,'" pp. 214–215, citing Howard Gardner, *The Shattered Mind*. Strauss then summarizes results of a test in which Moroccan Qur'ān memorization students outperformed other subjects in "incremental" memory. In this experiment, students were to recall a consecutive sequence of cards shown to them in an exercise much like the "ladder method" described later in the chapter as a technique of Qur'ān memorization (the structure is similar to that of the game American children call "I packed my grandmother's trunk").

72. Jeff Pressing, "Psychological Constraints on Improvisational Expertise and Communication," especially pp. 54–56.

73. Thanks to Wadad Kadi for guidance. See also Norman O. Brown, "The Apocalypse of Islam."

74. Catherine Bell, for example, gives the work of Geertz and Turner critical consideration in her review of methodological perspectives on ritual in *Ritual Theory, Ritual*

Practice. In *The Archetypal Actions of Ritual*, pp. 74–75, Humphrey and Laidlaw also criticize the work of both Turner and Geertz.

75. J. Frits Staal, "The Meaninglessness of Ritual," pp. 4, 8–9.

76. Jonathan Z. Smith, *To Take Place*, p. 103.

77. Compare the synthetic perspective in Stanley Tambiah, "A Performative Approach to Ritual."

78. Staal, "The Meaninglessness of Ritual," p. 3.

79. Jonathan Z. Smith, *To Take Place*, p. 103.

80. Humphrey and Laidlaw, *Archetypal Actions of Ritual;* Thomas Csordas, "Somatic Modes of Attention."

81. William Graham discusses these ideas as well as the framework of "orthopraxy" in "Islam in the Mirror of Ritual"; for an ethnographic perspective on the question of ritual "meaning" in Indonesia, see John Bowen, "*Salāt* in Indonesia." Frederick Denny presents general perspectives on Muslim ritual in "Islamic Ritual: Perspectives and Theories."

82. As with theories from linguistics and aesthetics that have been influenced by Husserlian phenomenology, in Leonard Meyer's influential theory of the expressive "meaning" of music, dynamics of anticipation and expectation are critical. Leonard Meyer, *Emotion and Meaning in Music*, esp. p. 260. See also Al-Faruqi, "What Makes Religious Music 'Religious'?" pp. 26–27. For criticism of this perspective and discussion of alternative approaches, see Elizabeth Tolbert, "Theories of Meaning and Music Cognition." Other classic treatments of music and emotion include those by Susanne Langer, Victor Zuckerkandl, and Peter Kivy. Important phenomenological perspectives on music include works by Don Ihde, Joseph I . Smith, the interactionist perspective of Alfred Schutz, as well as the "experience-near" study of improvisation by David Sudnow, *Ways of the Hand*.

83. Stanley Tambiah, "A Performative Approach to Ritual."

84. Tambiah, "Performative Approach," p. 139. Emphasis in text.

85. Ibid., p. 139.

86. Jonathan Z. Smith, *To Take Place*, p. 109.

87. Margaret Drewal, *Yoruba Ritual*, p. 2.

88. For reflections on Qur'ānic structure and performance, see Richard Martin, "Understanding the Qur'ān in Text and Context."

89. For the basis of the idea of "the principle of interruption," see Walter Benjamin, "The Work of Art in the Age of Mechanical Reproduction," in *Illuminations*, especially p. 238. See also the article by William R. McKenna, "Expectation," in Lester Embree et al., *The Encyclopedia of Phenomenology*, pp. 213–217, and the classic work by Wolfgang Iser, *The Act of Reading*.

90. M. Bakhtin, "Discourse in the Novel," pp. 288–331.

91. Sayyid Hossein Nasr, *Ideals and Realities of Islam*, pp. 47–48, also quoted in Norman O. Brown, "The Apocalypse of Islam," and Nelson, *Art of Reciting*. See also the in-depth discussion given in Hussein Abdul-Raof, *Qur'ān Translation*.

92. These are treated systematically in treatises on the Qur'ān, such as the one

by ʻAlī b. ʻIsā al-Rummanī (d. 966), *Al-Nukāt fī Iʻjāz al-Qur'ān* (translated by Andrew Rippin and Jan Knappert as "The Nature of the Qur'an") which draws on previous treatments in the study of the "inimitable" Qur'ān such as al-Jāhiẓ.

93. Nelson, *Art of Reciting*, p. 10.

94. Michael Sells' work includes close analysis of "sound figures." Sells studies *sūrahs* in terms of the "syntactical, phonological, and rhythmic grids" and four modes of Qur'ānic discourse: the "semantic, acoustic, emotive, and gender modes."

95. See works by Roman Jakobson on linguistic structure and by Stephen Feld on linguistic structure and music.

96. Roman Jakobson, "Linguistics and Poetics," pp. 353–357.

97. See examples in Sells, *Approaching the Qur'ān*. Nelson, *Art of Reciting*, pp. 7–13, discusses features of rhyme, rhythm, assonance, and the sound of Qur'ān recitation, also drawing examples from Meccan *sūrahs*.

98. See Muhammad Abdel Haleem's article "Contexts and Internal Relationships." Abdel Haleem applies the classical ideas of *maqām* (context) and *maqāl* (distinctive forms of speech) to one *sūrah* of the Qur'ān, 55 al-Raḥmān.

99. Frances Yates, *The Art of Memory*.

100. Anthony H. Johns, "The Qur'ānic Presentation of the Joseph Story," and Brown, "The Apocalypse of Islam," discuss regular and irregular narrative modes.

101. Sūrah Hūd 28, 63, and 88 are an example of formulaic expression ending each of the accounts of Prophets presented sequentially in the *sūrah*, each with a slightly different wording.

102. The two illustrations that follow are commonly cited in Indonesia as examples of the difficulty of memorization. Others are 2 al-Baqarah 59 and 7 al-Aʻrāf 162.

103. Kristina Nelson also cites this example in *Art of Reciting the Qur'an* but with a different total number, probably due to different criteria for counting the multiple variants.

104. Abdel Haleem, "Dynamic Style." Treatments of *iltifāt* are to be found in the writings of the great linguist and exegete al-Zamakhsharī (b. 1075), as well as al-Zarkashī (d. 1391) and Ibn al-Athīr (d. 1239).

105. Abdel Haleem, "Dynamic Style," pp. 184, 186–188.

106. Ibid., pp. 186–187, translating al-Zarkashī, *Al-Burhān fī wujūh al-bayān*, vol. 3 (Baghdad, 1967), pp. 314–315.

107. Ibid., pp. 196–197. Abdel Haleem lists other aspects of "dynamic style" in the Qur'ān that complement *iltifāt* as omission of the verb "say" and its derivative, so God speaks directly; dialogue (especially at Judgment, and in Paradise and Hell); "interactive" style, in which the Qur'ān inserts direct comments on situations (God's voice interrupting the prayer of believers, for example, in 2 al-Baqarah 285–286); the "high frequency of the affective sentence" *(al-jumlah al-inshā'iyyah)*, which are statements that cannot be said to be true or false; and various emphatic rhetorical styles. Abdel Haleem, "Dynamic Style," pp. 208–209.

108. Rosenthal, *Knowledge Triumphant*, p. 282.

109. Makdisi, *Colleges*, pp. 99–102.

110. Ibid., p. 100 (Makdisi's translation), citing the biographical dictionary by Taj al-Dīn Subkī, *Tabaqāt al-Shāfiʿīya al-kubrā*.

111. Makdisi, *Colleges*, pp. 103–104, discusses *mudhākara*.

112. Ibid., p. 104, citing the manuscript by al-Khāṭīb al-Baghdādī *Al-faqīh wa 'l-mutafaqqih*.

113. Dale Eickelman highlights this idea in his writings on Islamic "traditional" education.

114. LPTQ, *25 Tahun*, p. 109, excerpting from a source cited as Muntaha Azhari (1991).

115. 'Abd al-Rahmān Aby Zayd b. Muḥammad Ibn Khaldūn, *The Muqaddima*, pp. 416–433.

116. H. A. Muhaimin Zen, *Tata Cara*, p. 39.

117. Ibid., pp. 48–49.

118. Ibid., pp. 51–52.

119. Berkey, *Transmission*, p. 29, citing for this information al-'Askarī, *Al-ḥathth 'alā ṭalab*.

120. Zen, *Tata Cara*, p. 271, includes prayers for memory, for example.

121. Ibid., p. 39.

122. Ibid., pp. 40–41.

123. Ibid. Emphasis added.

124. Makdisi, *Colleges*, p. 102, citing al-Khāṭīb al-Baghdādī, *Al-faqīh wa 'l-mutafaqqih*.

125. Zen, *Tata Cara*, p. 236.

126. Ibid., pp. 235–236.

127. Ibid., p. 234.

128. Ibid., p. 235.

129. Ibid.

130. Ibid., pp. 235–236.

Chapter 3: Reading

1. James N. Baker, "The Presence of the Name," p. 108.

2. Most recently, Andrew Beatty shows this tendency in his ethnography *Varieties of Javanese Religion*, pp. 120–124. In *The Religion of Java*, Clifford Geertz characterizes the "*santri*" *pesantren* educational system by the activity of "chanting," emphasizing (as did modernist "*santri*" informants) the issue of comprehension (pp. 186, 220). In "Art as a Cultural System," Geertz shows more sensitivity to the depth of pious possibilities of Qur'ān reading.

3. Denny, "Exegesis and Recitation," p. 98, quoting from Anwar Chejne, *The Arabic Language: Its Role in History*.

4. "*Iqrā'*" (lit. "Read!, Recite!") is a reference to the eponymous first word of *sūrah* 96 (also called "al-'Alaq"), which some have said was the first to be revealed to the Prophet Muḥammad. Other "modern" Indonesian methods are said to include Muhafakah (memorizing "everyday words"); Muqoronah (relying heavily on roman-

ized transliteration); Wasilah (deploying pictographs); al-Barqy (a method relying on building words from consecutive letters); Qiroati (very similar to Iqra'); and a curriculum developed by the Lembaga Bahasa dan Ilmu al-Quran (LBIQ), Jakarta, known as "SAS." I did not observe the first three of these methods in use; they are cited in M. Chairul Mu'min, *Petunjuk Praktis Mengelola TK al-Quran*, pp. 32–33. H. Maqbul Rasyid mentions several other names of curricula, such as al-Jabbari from West Java, al-Banjari from Banjarmasin, and Hattaiyah from Pekanbaru-Riau, writing that there had been interest within the Ministry of Religious Affairs in compiling and standardizing these regional methods. H. Maqbul Rasyid, "Sistem Pengajaran Membaca AlQuran di Taman Pendidikan AlQuran (TPA)," pp. 40–42.

5. Another "traditional" method was Tarkibiyah, said to be very close to Baghdadi, but I did not encounter a case of it in use.

6. The seminal article is Eickelman, "The Art of Memory." Studies of traditional education in Morocco addressing the question of learning "by rote" include work by Jarmo Houtsonen, Daniel A. Wagner, Abdelhamid Lotfi, and Jennifer E. Spratt. Perspectives on literacy that highlight parts of the Muslim world include work by Brinkley Messick and foundational work by Jack Goody, Walter J. Ong, and Brian Street. For a general overview of the issues, see James Collins, "Literacy and Literacies." Recent anthropological work on contemporary social structures of Islamic schooling includes Gregory Starrett, *Putting Islam to Work*.

7. One of many notable exceptions to this is Dale Eickelman, *Knowledge and Power in Morocco*.

8. Timothy Mitchell, *Colonising Egypt*, pp. 85–87.

9. Brinkley Messick, *The Calligraphic State*.

10. Ibid., pp. 21–30, referring to "learning by rote." The poems are "al-Suyūṭī's Thousand" on *ḥadīth* and "Ibn Mālik's Thousand" on grammar (Messick also mentions a Shafi'ī *fiqh* verse-text by Ibn al-Wardī that had previously been in use in the area). Ibid., p. 27.

11. An example is the work of Ibn Muẓaffar, a fifteenth-century scholar who set a number of important pedagogical works in verse, such as a compendium of Shāfi'ī law and a short treatise on the methodology of *ḥadīth* study. Jonathan Berkey, *The Transmission of Knowledge in Medieval Cairo*, p. 28. One of the earliest treatises on recitation is in the form of a fifty-one line verse-text attributed to Ibn Khāqān (d. 937–938).

12. Unlike theorists influenced by Eric Hobsbawm and Terrence Ranger, who have highlighted the "inventedness" of traditions that claim to be more ancient than they actually are, "Islamic education," in a significant way, is not "invented." Hobsbawm and Ranger, eds., *The Invention of Tradition*; compare the approach to contemporary Islamic systems of "tradition" in Marilyn Robinson Waldman, "Tradition as a Modality of Change." The approach to "tradition" as a perceptive "feeling" developed here was originally inspired by Sartre's writing on emotion as a mode of consciousness.

13. Bahasa Indonesia, the national language, has been written in romanized letters for most of the twentieth century and especially since Indonesian independence.

14. In most theories of ritual in the history of religions, repetition is the departure point for further analysis (Eliade's basic concept of the "regeneration of the sacred" is a primary illustration). Cumulative effects of ritual practice are usually not the question in these investigations, however. Instead, scholars have tended to consider whether ritual repetition necessarily includes diachronic change and, if so, how change (or lack of it) is to be explained in terms of ritual form.

15. Theodore W. Jennings, Jr., "On Ritual Knowledge," pp. 118–119.

16. Ibid., p. 122.

17. For example, Richard Schechner, *Between Theater and Anthropology*, and the work of Victor Turner.

18. Jean Lave, "The Practice of Learning," pp. 5–6.

19. For example, in her book *Affecting Performance*, Corinne Kratz considers initiation rituals; unlike her predecessors in the study of "rites of passage," she draws attention to the experiential transformation this performance effects on the self-understanding of initiates, which accompanies the reconstituted social roles. She argues that ritual is transformative by way of its emotional and psychological textures. Her important work, however, does not consider the kind of ritual that would help further understanding of the transformations affected by repeated, nonobligatory devotional piety, such as Qur'ān recitation.

20. In Catherine Bell's only mention of ritual and education in her book *Ritual: Perspectives and Dimensions*, mention is not made of how people get their *religious* education, whether in general or in terms of how practitioners are schooled in the performance of ritual in specific. Bell, *Ritual*, p. 152, n. 4. Humphrey and Laidlaw discuss and theorize learning a ritual in *Archetypal Actions*, pp. 111–132 and elsewhere.

21. Williams and Boyd's *Ritual, Art, and Knowledge*, a rich theorization of developmental engagement with ritual through repetition, separates repeated "pedagogy" and the changing learning dynamics inherent in repeated ritual performance. Ron G. Williams and James W. Boyd, *Ritual, Art, and Knowledge*, p. 64, cf. pp. 115–117.

22. Lave and Wenger, eds., *Situated Learning*, pp. 4, 121.

23. Lave, "The Practice of Learning."

24. Kristina Nelson treats *tajwīd* in detail in *The Art of Reciting the Qur'an*, pp. 14–18.

25. Denny, "Exegesis and Recitation," p. 121, translating from Ibn al-Jazarī, *Al-Nashr fī qirā'āt al-'ashr*. Denny writes that this is an elaboration of al-Dānī 's statement "between *tajwīd* and its neglect is simply practice for him who tends to it carefully with his jaw."

26. For a discussion of *tajwīd* pedagogy in Indonesia, see Denny, "Qur'ān Recitation Training in Indonesia."

27. I draw examples in the pages to follow from Syed Kaleemullah Husainī, *Easy Tajwīd*. I have also followed closely key points in the encyclopedia article "Koran, Chanting," while also drawing many examples from it. This discussion is limited to matters of sound production in a single, established "reading" rather than treating the issue of "variant readings." As in Egypt, the reading in Indonesia is customarily Ḥafṣ,

although there was interest at the time of research among advanced *qāri*'s in mastering other readings such as Warsh.

28. The example is from Husainī, *Easy Tajwīd.*

29. There is another classification known as "*qalqalah*" letters.

30. "Koran, Chanting," p. 232.

31. There are other special cases of rules related to the assimilation of sounds that present themselves immediately to the beginner, such as the *lām al-jalāla,* the doubled *l* sound in the name of God (Allāh). If the name of God is prefixed by the short vowel *i* (as happens with prepositions meaning "with," "by," and "to"), the double *l* is softened and the following long *ā* takes on a "leaning" *(imālah)* toward the *l* sound. An example is the light pronunciation in the formula the Bismillah, "In the name of God," as well as the second phrase of the *shahādah* (and Muḥammad is the messenger of God), as opposed to the first (there is no god but God), where the long *ā* in the Divine Name remains heavy. The examples are given in ibid.

32. See and hear Michael Sell's treatment of the *ādhān* in *Approaching the Qur'an* and accompanying sound recording.

33. These are *wājib* or *muttaṣil* (compulsory or joint) *madd* (occurring within a single word); *jā'iẓ* or *munfaṣil* (permissible or separating) *madd* (occurring between two adjacent words); *ṣilah* or *talaffuẓī* (temporary) *madd;* and *lāẓim* (permanent or essential) *madd,* of which there are four additional subtypes. An explanation is in Husainī, *Easy Tajwīd.*

34. There is a further stop, called "waiting" *(intiẓārī),* which covers the combination of *qirā'āt* (variant readings), such as Ḥafṣ and Shu'bah. Further explanation is in Husainī, *Easy Tajwīd,* and the article "Koran, Chanting."

35. In some written copies of the Qur'ān, these are designated by the letters "*mīm*" and "*'ayn,*" which stand for the term "*mu'āniqah,*" meaning that the phrase or the word may be understood to "embrace" the passage that either precedes or follows it. They are sometimes also marked by three dots. An example is in 2 al-Baqarah 2. In addition to this, scholars have also added approximately eight more marks in common use, such as one that indicates that some scholars have said that there is a stop but others have not *(q-l-ā),* marks for weak preferences, and places in which it is permitted to pause but not to take a breath (marked *w-q-f-h*). For more explanation, see Husainī, *Easy Tajwīd.*

36. In contrast, one Indonesian teacher encouraged the use of translations as a way to perfect *tajwīd.* For example, he said that the way to distinguish between two common words, "*ānā*" (I) and "*ānnā*" (that), was to recognize that the "*ana*" that means *saya*/myself does not have a doubled *(tashdīd) nūn.* This is not a method with broad application, since it requires reference to Indonesian interpretation, and the cases in which this procedure would actually be of any help are few.

37. This is similar to the Vygotskian idea that a "mature concept" is the coalescence of "scientific" and "everyday" concepts. For an overview of these ideas in learning theory, related to interpretations of Vygotsky's idea of a socially interactive "zone of proximal development," see Lave and Wenger, eds., *Situated Learning,* pp. 48–49.

38. For a general discussion of affect, language, and identity, see Niko Besnier, "Language and Affect." Here I draw especially on Judith T. Irvine, "Registering Affect."

39. Irvine, "Registering Affect," p. 127, citing Michael A. Halliday, "The Users and Uses of Language."

40. Irvine, "Registering Affect," p. 128.

41. For an example of this approach to speech and identity in an Indonesian context, see Joseph Errington, *Language and Social Change in Java.*

42. See also P. L. Amin Sweeney, *A Full Hearing.*

43. H. Mahfudh Syamsul Hadi, H. Muaddi Aminan, and Cholil Uman, eds., *Rahasia Keberhasilan Dakwah oleh K. H. Zainuddin,* M.Z., pp. 250–251.

44. Memorizers, for example, would sometimes call attention to the fact that they did not get the recognition of *qāri*'s. Melodic reciters themselves, who accompanied big-name preachers on tour to recite before the speaker came on the stage, have been heard to remark that they also receive less attention than that given to the accompanying performance. ("*Qari* time is *becak* [cycle rickshaw] time," as an expression among reciters went.)

45. Correction of *sh*, as in the word "*shaiṭān*" (Satan), is often heard because it occurs in the formula that opens all recitation: "I take refuge from accursed Satan." As one teacher would often remind her students, "The devil won't go away if you mispronounce his name."

46. In classical *i'jāz* works there is a discussion of the "harmonious letters" in the Qur'ān. Ibn 'Arabi and Ibn Tustarī, both great esoteric thinkers, as well as others, elaborated this kind of piety in their writings. Annemarie Schimmel treats the phenomenon of esoteric understandings of the symbols of the Arabic alphabet in *Calligraphy and Islamic Culture,* especially pp. 77–114.

47. Treatises on recitation, such as al-Makkī, often delineate similar lists of "tasks," also with Sufi influence.

48. These External Rules are given in al-Ghazzālī, *Recitation and Interpretation of the Qur'ān,* pp. 34–47.

49. Ibid., p. 43.

50. Al-Ghazzālī's Mental Tasks are given in ibid., pp. 56–82.

51. Ibid., p. 62.

52. William Cummings, *Making Blood White,* discusses the development of literacy and writing in the history and historiography of early modern Makassar. For comparative cases of a writing system being received or developed along with a religious system in Southeast Asia, see William A. Smalley, Chia Koua Vang, and Genia Yee Yang, *Mother of Writing* (Laotian Hmong); Vincente L. Rafael, *Contracting Colonialism,* pp. 39–55 (the Catholic Philippines); and Raechelle Rubinstein, *Beyond the Realm of the Senses* (Hindu Bali).

53. The Arabic script is called, for example, "Huruf Arab Melayu" in Ambon, "Huruf Serang [Seram]" in Buginese and Makassarese areas as well as Buton (but not in Seram itself), "Huruf Pegon" on Java, and on the Malay peninsula, it is known as "Jawi." Thanks to R. Michael Feener for discussion.

54. The Arabic alphabet starts with the letter "*ā*," or "*ālif*" (not given in the example here). Superscript indicates *tanwīn* declensional case ending. The version shown is that taught at IAIN Alauddin, Makassar, in 1997 as "*Al-Tamrīnāt fī makhārij al-hurūf wa al-tajwīd*." It appears with slight variation in Chairul Mu'min, *Petunjuk Praktis*, pp. 74–76, titled "Titian Makharijul Huruf." Other variants were taught at IAIN Alauddin as well.

55. Hendi Indyawan, *Belajar Mudah Huruf al-Quran*.

56. "Huruf Sambung" by Drs. H. Tasyrifin Karim, on *Lagu-Lagu Belajar Cepat Membaca al-Qur'an* (sound recording).

57. Berkey, *Transmission*, p. 23, and elsewhere. Rosenthal, *Knowledge Triumphant*, pp. 290–294 surveys works on the *adab* of teachers.

58. Berkey, *Transmission*, p. 26, citing Badr al-Dīn b. Jamā'a, *Tadhkirāt al-sāmi' wa'l-mutakallim*, p. 123.

59. Berkey, *Transmission*, p. 26, quoting Muḥammad b. 'Abd al-Raḥmān al-'Uthmānī.

60. Berkey, *Transmission*, p. 52.

61. Ibid., pp. 38–39, citing Ibn Jamā'a, *Tadhkirāt*. Berkey also quotes al-Nawawī's advice on how to respond to an instructor who falls asleep when teaching class.

62. "Juz' 'Amma" begins with the word "*'amma*" in 78 al-Nabā' 1, "*'amma yatasā'ilūn*" (Concerning what are they disputing?).

63. Studying alone traditionally was an aural, not a silent, activity, involving active vocal enunciation of the text. Berkey, *Transmission*, p. 27.

64. Chairul Mu'min, *Petunjuk Praktis*, pp. 34–35.

65. "Lagu Pembuka," by Drs. H. Tasyrifin Karim, on *Lagu-Lagu Belajar Cepat*.

66. Persatuan Pengajian Anak-anak Kotagede dan Sekitarnya, or "Consolidation of Children's Recitation of the Kotagede Region," later known as BAKOPA, or Badan Koordinasi Pengajian Anak-anak, "Coordinating Body for Children's Recitation."

67. Team Tadarus "AMM," *Pedoman Pengelolaan, Pembinaan dan Pengembangan* "M3A," p. 1.

68. Ibid., p. 2. Emphasis in text.

69. Ibid. Emphasis in text. R. Michael Feener has pointed out that this resembles the phenomenon of *kaderisasi* (from the word "cadre"), a term for campus *da'wah* strategies in Indonesia and Malaysia, especially in the 1970s (and, in fact, a derivative of the term appears in a manual that was in popular circulation among college students in the field of education). This was also the period in which the organizations that were to consolidate into the LPTQ were forming. Contrast the Qur'ānic educational directives of the Egyptian schoolteacher and religious leader Ḥasan al-Bannā.

70. Team Tadarus "AMM," *Pedoman*, pp. 3–4.

71. For kindergarten and elementary school levels, there was TKA-TPA; at the junior high level, the program was known as TKAL-TPAL (Taman Kanak-kanak Al-Quran Lanjutan and Taman Pendidikan Al-Quran Lanjutan), and at the high school level, TQA (Talimul Quran Lil Aulad). At the Team Tadarus "AMM" center in Yogyakarta, as well as in Jakarta, all of these levels of instruction were available.

72. Team Tadarus "AMM," *Pedoman*, p. 10.

73. Masjid "Al-Markaz" in Makassar had its first *wisuda* in January 1997, with much local media coverage. President Suharto and the first lady attended at least one TPA *wisuda* in Yogyakarta.

74. As'ad Humam, *Buku Iqro'*.

75. For comparison of ideological change and the adaptation of affective systems of ritual speech in the New Order, for example, see work by Kenneth M. George and Joel Kuipers.

76. *"Diyakini, dipelajari, dibacakan, dihafal. . . . Itu ilmu harus diberikan sama orang lain. . . . Itu amanat. . . . Saya harus menghargai kemauan mereka."*

Chapter 4: Expression

1. R. Anderson Sutton, *Variation in Central Javanese Gamelan Music;* and John Pemberton, "Musical Politics in Central Java."

2. In Indonesia, the term *"maqām"* was almost never heard. In Malaysia, melodic recitation is sometimes known by the Arabic term *"tarannum."* See Kristina Nelson, *The Art of Reciting the Qur'an*, pp. 110–116, and work by Lois Al-Faruqi.

3. Nelson's primary discussions of the idea of "ideal recitation" are given in *Art of Reciting*, pp. 52–100 and 136–152, as well as in "Reciter and Listener."

4. For example, Ali J. Racy, "Creativity and Ambiance."

5. Variants of this term appear multiple times in the Qur'ān, often translated as "humility," as in 17 al-Isrā' 109: "They fall down upon their faces weeping, and it increases them in humility *(khushū')*." Nelson writes that a "key" to understanding "ideal recitation" is the meanings of the terms *"khūshū'"* and *"khashyah"* (from the verbs *"khasha'a"* and *"khashā,"* respectively). Nelson, *Art of Reciting*, pp. 97–98. Drs. H. Burhanuddin's own recitation has been described by other accomplished reciters as being an especially *"khushū'"* style.

6. Thomas J. Csordas develops a theory of ritual "creativity, constraint and the sacred" in his ground-breaking study *Language, Charisma, and Creativity*.

7. This idea of "proximate ideals" has resonance with many theoretical approaches. Jack Katz, for example, cites Michael Polanyi, *Personal Knowledge*, in *How Emotions Work*, p. 336. It also sounds similar to Vygotsky's "zone of proximal development," and somewhat misleadingly so. One possible definition of Vygotsky's complicated concept is "the distance between the actual developmental level as determined by independent problem solving and the level of potential development as determined through problem solving under adult guidance or in collaboration with more capable peers." James Wertsch, "Introduction," in *Culture, Communication, and Cognition*, p. 11, citing Lev S. Vygotsky, *Mind in Society*, p. 86. This concept provides, among other things, a transactional understanding of learning, which (although featured in chapter 2) is not the emphasis here.

8. Frederick M. Denny, *An Introduction to Islam*, p. 98; a lengthier discussion of the key concept of "orthopraxy" in Islamic systems is William Graham, "Islam in the Mirror of Ritual." See also the discussion of "orthopraxy" and the comparative study of ritual given by Bell in *Ritual*, pp. 191–197.

9. Humphrey and Laidlaw, *Archetypal Actions of Ritual*, p. 11, and especially the chapter "Getting It Right," pp. 111–132.

10. Jeanne Bamberger and Evan Ziporyn, "Getting It Wrong."

11. Geertz, "Religion as a Cultural System," p. 113. Emphasis added.

12. In "Religion as a Cultural System," Geertz writes: "The acceptance of authority that underlies the religious perspective that ritual embodies thus flows from the enactment of the ritual itself. By inducing moods and motivations—and ethos—and defining an image of cosmic order—a world view—by means of a single set of symbols, the performance makes the model *for* and a model *of* aspects of religious belief mere transpositions of one another" (p. 118; emphasis in original).

13. Jonathan Z. Smith, "The Bare Facts of Ritual," p. 56.

14. Jennings, "On Ritual Knowledge," p. 119. Williams and Boyd draw on Jennings in their discussion of ritual repetition as well, and this statement is also cited in Williams and Boyd, *Ritual, Art, and Knowledge*, p. 66.

15. Jennings writes: "A ritual is falsified to the extent to which it cannot serve as a paradigm for significant action outside the ritual itself and is validated to the extent to which it does function this way." Jennings, "On Ritual Knowledge," pp. 119–120, also cited in Williams and Boyd, *Ritual, Art, and Knowledge*, p. 66.

16. Holland, "How Cultural Systems Become Desire," p. 85.

17. Benjamin Brinner, *Knowing Music, Making Music*. See also the seminal article by John Blacking "Towards a Theory of Musical Competence"; and Linda M. Gruson, "Rehearsal Skill and Musical Competence."

18. Brinner, *Knowing Music, Making Music*, p. 28.

19. In *Archetypal Actions*, Humphrey and Laidlaw offer a skeleton of their main argument, explaining how "action may be said to be ritualized when the actor has taken up what we call the 'ritual commitment,' a particular stance with respect to his or her own action" (pp. 88–89).

20. Humphrey and Laidlaw, *Archetypal Actions*, p. 99.

21. Ibid., p. 267.

22. Ibid., p. 150.

23. For concise treatments of key concepts such as "horizon," "gestalt," and "potential" in the phenomenological tradition, see *The Encyclopedia of Phenomenology*, especially the essay "Expectation," by William R. McKenna, pp. 213–217.

24. Williams and Boyd, *Ritual, Art, and Knowledge*, pp. 78–79.

25. Ibid., p. 78. Emphasis in text.

26. Humphrey and Laidlaw, *Archetypal Actions*, p. 238. Humphrey and Laidlaw's theory of "emergent moods" in ritual presents emotion as a distinctive mode of ritual repetition that stands apart from representation, cognition, and even "attention." An "emergent mood" manifests when "the self is 'filled' with an emotionally experienced image created through particular, repeated, physical actions . . . now involving channeled emotional projection and identification rather than representation." They relate it to Merleau-Ponty's idea of "abstract action." *Archetypal Actions*, p. 244.

27. Katz, *How Emotions Work*, p. 7.

28. Ibid.

29. Ibid., p. 34.

30. Ibid., p. 332.

31. The traditions are cited from Nelson, *Art of Reciting,* pp. 69, 77.

32. A treatment of these issues is Lois Ibsen Al-Faruqi, "Music, Musicians, and Muslim Law"; see also Al-Faruqi, "The Status of Music in Muslim Nations"; Sayyed Hossein Nasr, "Islam and Music"; and Nelson, *Art of Reciting,* pp. 34–35, 153–187.

33. Chapter 3 of Nelson, *Art of Reciting,* is dedicated to *samāʿ* (pp. 32–51). There are actually several sorts of disputes in the history of Islamic thought and practice that can be termed a "*samāʿ* polemic," most notably the controversy over Sufi practices that deploy bodily experience (almost always music, but sometimes also dance) as self-conscious strategies of attaining heightened states of religious awareness. When the *samāʿ* question refers to the use of melody in Qur'ān recitation, the problem may be, more specifically, what melodic practices are being deployed (for example, "sacred" or "secular" melody) and with what intent and understanding of affective agency. Alexander Knysh also provides an overview in *Islamic Mysticism,* pp. 322–332, and al-Ghazzālī, *Recitation and Interpretation of the Qur'ān,* takes up the classical question of *samāʿ* in detail.

34. See relevant contributions by Bohlman, Horsley et al., and Powers to the *New Grove Dictionary of Music and Musicians* as well as survey works by George Farmer, Amnon Shiloah, Habib Hasan Touma, and Owen Wright.

35. Philip Bohlman, "Middle East." Also see works by Scott Marcus, such as "The Periodization of Modern Arab Music Theory," and works by Habib Hasan Touma, such as "The *Maqām* Phenomenon."

36. For example, see U. Wegner, "Transmitting the Divine Revelation."

37. *Makawi maqāmāt* are often named as *banjaka, hijaz, mayya, rakby, jiharka, sikah,* and *dukkah.* This list is the same within various historical summaries of *lagu* in Indonesia. Given the actual variability of musical practice "on the ground," it is likely that the list itself may have seen significant systematization. M. Ali bin Abu Bakar, *Seni Lagu al-Quran di Malaysia;* and Khadijatus Shalihah, *Perkembangan Seni Baca al Quran.*

38. Khadijatus Shalihah, author of *Perkembangan Seni Baca al Quran dan Qiraat Tujuh di Indonesia,* related in an interview that she wrote her influential book in part to clarify this popular conflation from the perspective of the Qur'ānic sciences.

39. H. Muammar, *Kunci Sukses M.T.Q.*, vol. 8.

40. Nelson, *Art of Reciting,* p. 111, writes that *qāri*'s in Egypt customarily practiced *mujawwad* recitation of a text other than the Qur'ān.

41. The classic survey on this topic is Muhammad Talbi, "*Lā Qirā'ah bi'l-Alḥān.*"

42. Labīb al-Saʿīd, *The Recited Koran,* discusses the development of *murattal* recording and broadcast in Egypt. Nelson gives a history of radio broadcast of the Qur'ān in Egypt in *Art of Reciting,* pp. 142–152. Broadcast began in 1934, and in 1964 a special station was established expressly devoted to Qur'ān recitation. This was at the same time that the Ministry of Religious Endowments and Dr. Labīb al-Saʿīd produced a recording of the entire Qur'ān in *murattal* style.

43. *Qasida* in Indonesia differs somewhat from the Arabic meaning of the term

"*qaṣīdah*," a "religious song," usually in Arabic but possibly in other languages. In Indonesia, women reciters especially perform *qasida*, although it was not as popular as other styles of religiously oriented music, such as *dangdut*. On the recording industry in Egypt and elsewhere, see works by S. El-Shawan Castelo-Branco, Ali Jihad Racy, and the general discussion in Peter Manuel, *Cassette Culture*.

44. See Virginia Danielson, "The Qur'an and the *Qasidah:* Aspects of the Popularity of the Repertory Sung by Umm Kulthum," and her book *The Voice of Egypt*, as well as other works by Danielson and Racy.

45. There was a similar development in Malaysia. Abu Bakar, *Seni Lagu al-Quran di Malaysia*.

46. LPTQ, *25 Tahun Musabaqah Tilawatil Quran* lists some of the figures who visited Indonesia as 'Abd al-Bāsiṭ, al-Tantawī, Maḥmūd Majid, Muṣṭafā Isma'īl, Maḥmūd Khalīl, and al-Ḥusarī (p. 93).

47. Another opinion from a national champion was "You know, you can't apply the [melodic] styles of the Egyptian *shaikhs* with any precision." This reciter had, however, one of the most extensive repertoires of Egyptian recitation performances committed to memory. She emphasized that the challenge was not to imitate the melody of the Egyptian *qāri*'s as much as their "*bobot*," or vocal quality.

48. In *Music of Death and New Creation*, Michael Bakan traces the development of particular "styles" of performance of Balinese ensemble *gamelan beleganjur* in Indonesia, especially in relation to a competition system that developed in the same period (pp. 115–170).

49. For example, one international champion preferred Sh. Mutawallī; H. Muammar Z.A. follows the style of 'Antar (who is not appreciated by all). I listened with Ny. Nurhayati to a cassette of her own favorite, Raghīb Muṣṭafā Ghalwash, that had recently arrived from Cairo, as she enthusiastically repeated the especially fine examples of technical artistry as they played. Other well-known reciters are Kāmil Yūsuf al-Bahtimī, Abū al-'Ainain al-Shuaishā', al-Tablawī, al-Minshawī, as well as others.

50. At the end of his cassette series, H. Muammar criticizes students who think they do not need a teacher, picking the example of students who recite from transliterations of the Qur'ān in Latin letters. Muammar, *Kunci Sukses M.T.Q.*, vol. 8. He adds, however, that one must also be aware that teachers can make mistakes because of their regional dialects (demonstrating several, excusing himself before each one).

51. Most national coaches were pleased and confident in saying, however, that by the 1990s the overall vocal characteristics *(bobot)* had become the same all over the Indonesian archipelago and that the quality level of *lagu* in recitation was very high (although concerns about shortcomings in *tajwīd* were also often expressed). According to K. H. M. Sayyid Abdullah, everyone was now "following Cairo."

52. Works on Arab music and improvisation include titles by Al-Faruqi, Racy, and Touma.

53. See the seminal work by Bruno Nettl, "Thoughts on Improvisation," and his more recent introduction to *In the Course of Performance*, as well as Edward T. Hall, "Improvisation as an Acquired, Multilevel Process." See also Imogene Horsley, Michael

Collins, and Nazir A. Jairazbhoy, "Improvisation." Another important work is Paul Berliner, *Thinking in Jazz*.

54. This is so that the human technical artistry of melodic expression would not be confused with revelation. Very rarely, the melody types were notated with a system of wavy lines, like the trace of a teacher's hand indicating rise and fall in pitch. Many handbooks did, however, include modulation guidelines for set "readings" for specific occasions, with the *lagu* suggestions corresponding to each verse marked in the margins.

55. M. Misbachul Munir, *Pedoman Lagu-lagu Tilawatil Qur'an dilengkapi dengan Tajwid dan Qasida*, p. 21. It seems that the Egyptian *qāri*'s who traveled to Indonesia in order to teach and perform in Indonesia were adamant on the point that musical notation could not be used for the *maqāmāt*.

56. "*Variasi*" are often first learned in actual practice as set pieces as well. The movement from fixed paradigms to spontaneous improvisation is imagined as a smooth, natural transition. For comparison, see R. Anderson Sutton, "Do Javanese Gamelan Musicians Really Improvise?"

57. Andrew N. Weintraub, "Theory in Institutional Pedagogy and 'Theory in Practice' for Sundanese Gamelan Music." Nelson describes the process of "imitation" as a pedagogical technique in recitation in *Art of Reciting*, pp. 181–183, and contrasts it to other concerns.

58. See the classic article by Harold S. Powers, "Mode." Compare the use of the term "*lagu*" in gamelan systems described in Sumarsam, *Gamelan*, p. 155, and R. Anderson Sutton, "Concept and Treatment in Javanese Gamelan Music."

59. This mode of teaching has been termed "directed emulation" and is common in Southeast Asian music pedagogy. Brinner, *Knowing Music, Making Music*, pp. 149–150.

60. Nelson identifies the genre of "*tawāshiḥ*" as a "bridge between recitation and secular singing" in Egypt and reports that some *qāri*'s would perform in this improvisatory style, along with the genre of *ibtihālāt* (a solo improvisation on a poetic text). *Art of Reciting*, p. 159. In Indonesia, the *tawshih* were very much set pieces and were only used for instruction. Not all Indonesian teachers used the *tawshih*, however.

61. They may be used as the basis of *murattal* recitation, for which the characteristic melodic movement is applied in a simplified improvisational form; they are, however, most closely associated with *mujawwad* recitation.

62. Earle H. Waugh, *The Munshidīn of Egypt*. Michael Sells transliterated the text of "Arā Tairan" for the musical transcription given by Anne K. Rasmussen in "The Qur'an in Indonesian Daily Life."

63. Maria Ulfah, *Pedoman Praktis Belajar Lagu Tilawatil Qur'an*. The idea of the "hundred times method," for example, illustrates this idea; with this idealized teaching method, the *lagu* is repeated multiple times along with its name, until the identification is made. I did not see or hear of an instance in which this method actually was used (although perhaps it was being deployed on Java). I have observed *lagu* taught by coaches by calling out *lagu* switches to their students, *āyah* by *āyah*.

64. This is the only *lagu* for which I encountered variants in the use of *tawshih*, such as on the two-cassette instructional recordings Hj. Maria Ulfah, *Pedoman Praktis Belajar Lagu*. For a musicological analysis of *lagu bayati*, see Habib Hasan Touma, *Der Maqam Bayati im Arabischen Taqsim*.

65. For theory and comparison with instrumental performance, see Scott Marcus, "Modulation in Arabic Music."

66. For example, Misbachul Munir, *Pedoman Lagu-lagu*, pp. 56–140, and M. Syawir Dahlan, *Pedoman untuk Sukses dalam* M.T.Q., pp. 64–78. Besides occasions such as Mawlid al-Nabi (The Birthday of the Prophet), Isra' dan Mi'raj (The Prophet's Night Journey and Ascent), Nuzul al-Qur'ān (Night of the Qur'ān, in Ramadan), and also housewarmings, weddings, and so forth, the source includes readings for civic and public events, such as Laporan Umum Organisasi (Official Report by an Organization), graduations, sporting events, national holidays, and even "*transmigrasi*."

67. Judith Becker, *Gamelan Stories*, and her "Tantrism, *Rasa*, and Javanese Gamelan Music"; V. I. Braginsky, "The Concept of 'the Beautiful' *(Indah)* in Malay Classical Literature and Its Muslim Roots," and Paul Stange, "The Logic of *Rasa* in Java." Geertz grafts the idea of *rasa* onto a theory of "meaning" in "Ethos, World View, and the Analysis of Sacred Symbols," pp. 134–136. For more discussion of *rasa* and religion, see Donna Wulff, "Religion in a New Mode."

68. Nelson, *Art of Reciting*, p. 44.

69. Ibid., p. 99. Ethnomusicological discussions of weeping, sung weeping, and wept song include work by Steven Feld and, in the history of religions, Ebersole, "The Function of Ritual Weeping Revisited."

70. Other examples are given in Nelson, *Art of Reciting*, pp. 97–98.

71. Jalāl al-Dīn al-Suyūṭī, *Al-Itqān fī 'Ulūm al-Qur'ān*, cited in Nelson, *Art of Reciting*, p. 90.

72. Nelson, *Art of Reciting*, p. 95, also citing statements by al-Makkī, al-Sarrāj, al-Jawziyyah, al-Ghazzālī, and others.

73. Al-Ghazzālī, *Recitation and Interpretation*, p. 44. Al-Suyūṭī writes, "and if *ḥuzn* and weeping do not attend him in that state, then let him weep for lack of it." *Al-Itqān*, vol. 1, p. 109, quoted in Nelson, *Art of Reciting*, p. 102.

74. Nelson, *Art of Reciting*, p. 90.

75. See ibid., p. 93, for discussion and examples.

76. Al-Suyūṭī, *Al-Itqān*, vol. 1, p. 109, quoted by Nelson and discussed along with similar statements such as those in al-Ghazzālī, *Iḥyā' 'Ulūm al-Dīn*, in *Art of Reciting*, pp. 89–91.

77. Al-Qurtubī, quoted in Nelson, *Reciting the Qur'ān*, p. 96. Ibn al-Jazarī, *Al-tamhīd fī 'ilm al-tajwīd*, p. 4, criticizes the "hypocrisy" of this; quoted in Nelson, *Art of Reciting*, p. 96.

78. Al-Ghazzālī, *Iḥyā' 'Ulūm al-Dīn*, vol. 8, p. 1167, quoted in Nelson, *Art of Reciting*, p. 99. A more common formulation of this idea, found in the writings of al-Ghazzālī and others, is "When you recite . . . weep, and if the eyes of any one of you do not

weep, then let his heart weep, for from *ḥuzn* springs weeping." Al-Ghazzālī, *Iḥyā' 'Ulūm al-Dīn*, quoted in Nelson, *Art of Reciting*, p. 90.

79. Al-Makkī, *Qūt al-qulūb*, quoted in Nelson, *Art of Reciting*, p. 97. Nelson also cites al-Zarkashī on this point.

80. Nelson, *Art of Reciting*, p. 96.

81. Muammar, *Kunci Sukses* M.T.Q., vol. 5, paraphrased.

82. "*Taswīr al-ma'nā*" is the term for this, although I never heard this expression used in Indonesia, just as attention was rarely focused on the concept itself. In Indonesia, "moods" of *lagu* are occasionally listed as "happy" and "sad": "happy melodies" *(bernada gembira)* are *bayati*, *rast*, and *nahawand*; the "sad" *(sedih)* ones are *sikah*, *jiharka*, *hijaz*, and *soba*. These are listed, for example, in Misbachul Munir, *Pedoman Lagu-lagu Tilawatil*, p. 25. H. Burhanuddin gave an example by reciting an *āyah* about "the terrifying fire" and "tortures of hell" *(nar yang menakutkan* and *siksaan neraka)* using *lagu soba* (adding that *hijaz* would also be good). Nelson's discussion of *ma'nā* (meaning) and *maqām* is in *Art of Reciting*, pp. 62–68.

83. The technical difficulties of applying the modal system to the style of the Qur'ān are also discussed in Nelson, *Art of Reciting*, pp. 153–187.

84. Here, I translate the Indonesian concept of *bakat* as "talent," linking it to the more general idea of whether one possesses "capability" *(kemampuan)*, a quality that may be seen to be either inborn or acquired. A discussion of "cultural talent" is in Bakan, *Music of Death and New Creation*, pp. 214–215, 268–269. Henry Kingsbury, *Music, Talent, and Performance*, is a classic study in the context of a Western art-music conservatory, while Steven Feld also gives the concept some treatment in his article "Sound Structure as Social Structure."

85. Muammar, *Kunci Sukses* M.T.Q., vol. 8. Top reciters took it for granted that one would need talent *(bakat)* in order to recite like they did and would also say so privately.

Chapter 5: Competing

1. Gilbert Harmonic, "La fête du grand *maulid* à Cikoang."

2. For example, Sumarsam, *Gamelan*, p. 40; John R. Bowen, "Islamic Transformations"; Geertz, "Deep Play." Michael Bakan's study of Balinese *gamelan beleganjur* in the same period as the development of the Qur'ān recitation competition system demonstrates how competition restructured an Indonesian musical system originally derived from a type of ritual accompaniment into an autonomous stylistic and institutional form. See Bakan, *Music of Death and New Creation*.

3. For comparison of this idea as a concept elaborated in the Malay world, see Amin Sweeney, *Reputations Live On*, and the discussion of *nama* given in Milner, *Kerajaan*.

4. Saad Abdullah Sowayan, "'Tonight My Gun Is Loaded'"; and George Makdisi, *The Rise of Colleges*, p. 104.

5. John Pemberton, *On the Subject of "Java,"* esp. pp. 189–197.

6. Humphrey and Laidlaw, *Archetypal Actions*, p. 265.

7. Ibid., p. 99.

8. Wittgenstein makes reference to "depth" *(Tiefe)* in *Remarks on Frazer's "Golden Bough,"* p. 15e, although in *Archetypal Actions*, Humphrey and Laidlaw cite page 17e, another statement about affect and perception (p. 160).

9. Humphrey and Laidlaw, *Archetypal Actions*, p. 267.

10. Sherry B. Ortner, "Theory in Anthropology since the Sixties," pp. 152–153.

11. Victor Turner, *The Ritual Process*, esp. p. 176; and Bourdieu, *Outline of a Theory of Practice*, esp. p. 165. See also Bell, *Ritual Theory, Ritual Practice*, p. 140.

12. Claudia Strauss, "Models and Motives," in *Human Motives and Cultural Models*, p. 10.

13. Ibid., p. 2.

14. D'Andrade outlines the project in "Schemas and Motivation," pp. 30–38.

15. Strauss, "Models and Motives," p. 14.

16. Ibid., p. 14, citing Michelle Z. Rosaldo, "Toward an Anthropology of Self and Feeling."

17. Deci, *Intrinsic Motivation*, p. 61.

18. D'Andrade, "Schemas and Motivation," p. 30.

19. Csordas, *Language, Charisma, and Creativity*, pp. 191–201, esp. p. 194.

20. Howard Federspiel, *Popular Indonesian Literature of the Qur'an*, pp. 23–27.

21. For description of a previous MTQ by a historian of religions, see Frederick Denny, "The Great Indonesian Qur'an Chanting Tournament," which describes in detail the fifteenth MTQ in Pontianak, Kalimantan. Clifford Geertz' ideas of spectacle and the Indonesian "exemplary center" and "theater state" in an Islamic framework can be found in Clifford Geertz, *Negara*, and *Islam Observed*. Ethnomusicologist Anne K. Rasmussen also observes competitions and the "festivalization of Islam" in "The Qur'an in Indonesian Daily Life."

22. Besides the Malaysian and Saudi competitions, there were major international Qur'ān recitation competitions held in Thailand, Iran, Turkey, Egypt, as well as other countries. The Egyptian Ministry of Religious Affairs, for example, was charged in 1981 with the task of carrying out recitation competitions, with a similar rationale as that expressed in Indonesia and elsewhere: to encourage study, recitation, and memorization of the Qur'ān. Indonesian competition coaches often referred to the Egyptian contests, admiring especially their integration of recitation *(tilāwah)* and memorization *(taḥfīẓ)*.

23. The competition system includes contests from the *kecamatan* (district) level up to the national. Contestants have been known to compete in regions other than the one of current residence, sometimes on invitation. The contest was once held every other year, but starting in 1985 the MTQ began to be held every three years, with an "STQ" ("Seleksi") in off years. (The "Selection" determined the reciter who would go to the international competition in Malaysia in the following month of Ramadan.) At each MTQ and STQ, there was a meeting of the LPTQ to determine the shape of contests in the coming years.

24. The performance genre "*tarian massal*" is a distinctive Indonesian performing

art, probably derived from marching drills but with highly expressive movement forms. It is a massive spectacle of coordinated movement and costumed color. The opening performance also featured "traditional" Jambi drumming and folk songs as well as a "*jaget*" dance style that was well known in the area. The choreographer of the *tarian massal* performances was nationally known and featured in news coverage.

25. In Jambi in 1997, these included the National LPTQ Conference, ASEAN Artists' Dialog, the Meeting of the Asia Pacific Committee on Islamic Dakwah, and other meetings with an ASEAN focus, as well as seminars on Islam, such as a Congress on the Quran.

26. The house from nearby Kerinci proudly displayed what was said to be the longest batik calligraphy in the world. The structure was continuously packed with visitors. There was also a special pavilion erected to display items from the Museum Istiqlal exhibit in Jakarta, including illuminated texts from the period of the coming of Islam.

27. I collected no fewer than five separately published booklets of the official contest-related *acara*, or formal events (such as the opening parade or the closing of the crafts fair); one of them was devoted entirely to the hour-by-hour itinerary of President Suharto while staying in Jambi.

28. The Ministry of Religious Affairs also sponsored contests in hymn singing and recitation of Sanskrit texts for the Protestant and Hindu communities, respectively. Departemen Agama, *Ministry of Religious Affairs: Tasks and Functions*, p. 25.

29. "The Contest of the Recitation of the Qur'ān in Indonesia," p. 4.

30. LPTQ, Propinsi Sulawesi Selatan, *Sejarah MTQ di Sulawesi Selatan* (History of the MTQ in South Sulawesi).

31. "The Contest of the Recitation," p. 4.

32. The competition-*acara* connection continued in 1997: for example, after the closing ceremony of the MTQ in Jambi, the male and female winners of the adult division were flown immediately to Jakarta to perform at the celebration of the Prophet's Birthday at the Istiqlal Mosque in Jakarta, which was broadcast nationally and attended by the president. The winner of the Radio Republik Indonesia contest, held during Ramadan, would go on to recite at the Nuzūl al-Qur'ān (Night of the Qur'ān) celebration held at the end of Ramadan in the Istiqlal Mosque, which was also known for presidential attendance. Such televised *acara* were so significant that the celebration of Nuzūl al-Qur'ān at the Al-Markaz mosque in Makassar was delayed until the night after the television broadcast of the main Nuzūl al-Qur'ān event from Jakarta.

33. In South Sulawesi, I heard passing reference to many more groups that had once existed, although it is likely that many of these were less formal associations. It was reported that before 1977, the rivalry among them was intense at times.

34. "The Contest of the Recitation," p. 4.

35. Ibid., pp. 4–5.

36. Ibid., p. 5.

37. LPTQ, *25 Tahun Musabaqah Tilawatil Quran*, mentions many organizations in West Sumatra, Java, and Jakarta that developed in the early 1970s and came together in the form of the LPTQ (pp. 58–59). See also the discussion of the concurrent development of Team Tadarus "AMM" in the same period in chapter 4.

38. "The Contest of the Recitation," pp. 5–6.

39. The source *Seni Lagu al-Qur'ān di Malaysia* by Bin Abu Bakar treats the history of the Majelis Tilawah al-Quran on pp. 120–130 and outlines contest rules and organization for recitation and memorization events on pp. 136–159. See also Lois Al-Faruqi, "Qur'an Reciters in Competition in Kuala Lumpur," p. 222; the primary source for this article is the Malaysian embassy in Washington, D.C.

40. Al-Faruqi, "Qur'an Reciters in Competition," p. 222.

41. In Indonesia, contest champions received additional recognition in the form of other prizes and awards.

42. Al-Faruqi, "Qur'an Reciters in Competition," pp. 226–227.

43. In Jambi in 1997, although attendance of non-Indonesians was hoped for, the number of foreign guests at the MTQ was relatively small. The *Independent*, the local Jambi paper, ran special MTQ coverage, which included a page in English; it was reported by the paper itself that the president asked specifically for a copy of the *Independent* in order to see its value to foreign guests and had expressed his approval personally, especially of the English-language coverage. International groups attending this MTQ included groups from Brunei, Malaysia, a South African delegation, as well as a group of international students from ASEAN countries studying at IAIN campuses.

44. LPTQ, Sulawesi Selatan, *Sejarah MTQ di Sulawesi Selatan*, p. 26.

45. The many readings included verses from 49 al-Ḥujurāt and also 24 al-Nūr 1–10, for example (as well as excerpts with other themes, such as 24 al-Nūr 34, the "Verse of Light").

46. The case of the selections for the *pidato*, or "oration," event reflected the kind of individual and situational choices that religious sermon makers make (as at Friday congregational worship). Whereas some topics were contextually neutral, such as those emphasizing personal and social responsibility, like "Humanity's Stewardship to Create Prosperity on Earth" (based on 2 al-Baqarah 30), "Living a Balanced Life" (28 al-Qaṣaṣ 77), and "Good and Bad Lives Are the Result of Human Actions" (30 al-Rūm 41), others were more specific to context: "Work and Profession as Trusteeship/Responsibility" (4 al-Nisā' 58) and "The Implementation of Faith, *Hijrah*, and *Jihad* in Daily Work" (Implementasi Iman, Hijra, dan Jihad dalam Pelaksanaan Tugas Sehari-hari, 2 al-Baqarah 218).

47. *Panduan Penyelenggaraan MTQ National XVIII 1997 Jambi*, pp. 112–119, 123–125. The explication of the symbolism of graphic design has been a principal mode of pedagogy for the state ideology of Pancasila.

48. Lyrics are attributed in the 1983 edition of the national LPTQ's *Pedoman Pengembangan Tilawatil Qur'an* to Agus Sanaryo, arrangement by M. Tholfur Syairor. There are two other verses (rarely heard), which invoke nationalist themes such as Pancasila.

49. The introduction to the handbook for the MTQ in Jambi, *Panduan Penyelenggaraan*, lists two of the three "*thema*" (themes) of the contest as "successing" the general meeting of the National Assembly (Sidang Umum MPR) in 1998, the meeting of the National Assembly which was to ratify the president for another term. Tucked away in the opening pages of the handbook, this was the only mention of the Indonesian

political process at the MTQ. The national election had been held two months before, in May.

50. These are, in Indonesian: "*MTQ nasional meningkatkan keimanan dan ketakwaan umat sebagai modal dasar pembangunan menuju masyarakat adil makmur berdasarkan Pancasila*" and "*MTQ nasional meningkatkan partisipasi umat dalam pembangunan nasional.*" Other notable slogans prominent on banners around Jambi were "With disciplined traffic patterns we make the eighteenth MTQ a success" (on the new bus station built in the center of town in preparation for the MTQ); "The national MTQ enhances the work ethic and the inculcation of national discipline"; and "The national MTQ improves the quality of humanity in Indonesia who possess knowledge and elevated morals leading to a society that is forward-looking and self-sufficient."

51. President Suharto, opening address at the Eighteenth National MTQ, July 7, 1997.

52. President Suharto, July 7, 1997. The theme of cooperation *(gotong royong)* among Muslims was highlighted especially in local and national news coverage of this speech as well as in Muslim-oriented sources like *Media Dakwah.* A central theme of President Suharto's speeches on religion in the New Order years was, not surprisingly, the connection of Islam to schemas of national development. See Djohan Effendi et al., *Agama Islam dalam Pembangunan Nasional* (Islamic Religion in National Development: A Collection of Speeches by President Suharto).

53. For discussion, see John Bowen, *Muslims through Discourse.*

54. See Pemberton, *On the Subject of "Java."*

55. For discussion of this Islamist publication in the 1990s, see William R. Liddle, "*Media Dakwah* Scripturalism." Robert W. Hefner's article "Print Islam" also discusses *Media Dakwah* in detail, as does his lengthy study of Islamic movements in the New Order in *Civil Islam.*

56. "MTQ Pamungkas Abad XX," *Media Dakwah* no. 278, (August 1997/Rabiul Awal 1418), p. 54. The article reports elsewhere that no more than one-fifth of the funding for the MTQ came from the Indonesian government by way of the Ministry of Religious Affairs; the rest came from other sources, listed in the conclusion to the official handbook for the tournament, *Panduan Penyelenggaraan MTQ National XVIII 1997 Jambi.* At the time of the eighteenth MTQ, the Indonesian rupiah was approximately two thousand to the U.S. dollar.

57. "MTQ Pamungkas Abad XX," p. 56.

58. For example, Hasan Basri, "MTQ dan Peranannya," p. 65, citing al-Maraghī's *tafsīr* (Qur'ān exegesis).

59. Sy. Aliyah, "MTQ Sebagai Sarana Pengembangan Kebudayaan Islam," pp. 60–61.

60. Ibid., p. 61.

61. Hasan Basri, "MTQ dan Peranannya," p. 64.

62. M. Syawir Dahlan, *Pedoman untuk Sukses dalam M.T.Q.*, p. 25. Capitalization in text.

63. There are also stories of contestants winning on the merit of their artistic expression even though they made a significant technical mistake, such as missing an

obligatory stop *(waqf)*. One coach told about a contestant allegedly winning finals in a contest even though an entire *āyah* was dropped.

64. Memorizers could sometimes be seen attending competition rounds and marking the parts of the Qur'ān that were the "questions" in the judges' packets, perhaps recognizing that with a limited number of packets in circulation in a given competition, the questions were bound to be repeated later.

65. Hasan Basri, for example, includes many pages of discussion of the moral responsibilities of contest judges (citing authoritative statements from the Qur'ān and *ḥadīth*) in his "MTQ dan Peranannya," pp. 36–45.

66. The overview of judging criteria for *tilawah* that follows is adapted from Hasan Basri, "MTQ dan Peranannya," pp. 45–63, one of the more detailed explanations of judging criteria available. His explanation draws on personal experience and also the LPTQ's official guide, *Pedoman Musabaqah Tilawatil Quran* (1987), p. 11, which has also been consulted for this summary.

67. The original system employed a scale of forty to one hundred points for *tajwid* and *fasahah*, forty to eighty for *suara* and *lagu*, and forty to sixty for *adab*. In an intermediate system (1989), maximal point values added up to one hundred (about thirty points per area, with additions and deductions), but the calculation of points differed according to area. By the 1990s, the system had changed to reflect more of an emphasis on *lagu* over *tajwid*, with *lagu* (once "*suara dan lagu*") increased from a basic thirty points to count for forty possible points and with *tajwid* reduced from forty to a maximum of thirty. LPTQ, *Pedoman Musabaqah* (1987); and LPTQ, *25 Tahun*, p. 4.

68. For the last category, there are special handbooks of such "trouble spots" for reciters, just as there are for memorizers (as discussed in chapter 2). Examples of such verses are 18 al-Kahf 1, 36 Yā Sīn 52, 75 al-Qiyāmah 27; also included are instances of missing unusual and difficult aspects of *tajwīd*.

69. Hasan Basri, "MTQ dan Peranannya," p. 49. A later guide from the LPTQ gives a complete treatment of this aspect, using (as is sometimes done) Western-style musical categories to describe voices, such as "alto," "soprano," and so on. LPTQ, *Pedoman Pelatihan Tilawatil Quran* (1996), pp. 43–44.

70. For adults *(dewasa)*, six *lagu* are minimal; for adolescents *(remaja)* and blind persons *(tuna netra)*, five; and for children *(kanak-kanak)*, four. In final rounds of any MTQ, *lagu* selection is entirely open.

71. For all but MTQ final rounds, the opening and closing *lagu* used must be *bayati*.

72. "*Fasahah*" is defined in competitional context as "articulating well, clarity of words, and distinct meaning" *(pandai bicara, kata yang jelas, nyata maksudnya)*. LPTQ, *Pedoman Pelatihan*, p. 27. On p. 28, the source states reciters should know the meaning of what they recite.

73. Hasan Basri, "MTQ dan Peranannya," pp. 49–50.

74. There were reports of problems when judges with basic proficiency nevertheless could not "understand" or recognize a *lagu* variation being used by an outstanding reciter.

75. An example given for this technique is the common word "*ḥattā*" (until), with which one can inhale through the nose between the *ḥat-* and the *-tā* syllables; another

example is doubled labial consonants, as in the word "*rabb.*" Students are instructed not to move their bodies when inhaling if they ever steal a breath so that they won't be "found out" *(diketahui).*

76. Dahlan, *Pedoman untuk Sukses*, pp. 42–47.

77. H. Muammar Z.A., *Kunci Sukses M.T.Q.*, vol. 7.

78. Ibid., vol. 8.

79. Ibid.

80. Dahlan, *Pedoman untuk Sukses*, pp. 32–33.

81. Ibid., p. 34.

82. Ibid., p. 35.

83. Ibid., pp. 36–37. Emphasis in text.

84. "*Melalui Musabaqah Tadarus Al-Quran Kita Tingkatkan Minat Baca Al-Quran.*" In a fascinating discussion, Saba Mahmood writes about women in mosque groups in Cairo in the same time period (1995–1997) cultivating dispositions and "creating the desire to pray" as both an "ends and a means" to piety in "Women's Piety and Embodied Discipline," pp. 102–114.

Chapter 6: Conclusion

1. Jean-Paul Sartre, *Sketch for a Theory of the Emotions*, esp. pp. 63–93. See also Robert C. Solomon, "Sartre on Emotions."

2. In the field of Arabic grammar, "*ḥāl*" is key term for verbal tense aspect, deployed in Bahasa Indonesia as a term for "condition" or "state" more generally. "*Maqām*" is also a term in Arabic art music, the "place" or pitch class and melody type upon which one improvises in a "mode."

3. Lave and Wenger, eds., *Situated Learning*, p. 111.

4. Kenneth George, *Showing Signs of Violence*.

5. Benjamin Brinner highlights the question "How do they do what they do?"—implying fascination with the ability of others—in Indonesian context on the very first page of his book *Knowing Music, Making Music*.

6. A variant of the report above, apparently emphasizing the role of the *qāḍī'* (judge), states, "Two people to be envied are the person who spends prosperity given by God and a person who is given wisdom by God and renders judgment by it *(yaqḍī bihā)* and teaches it to others." Al-Bukhārī, cited in Franz Rosenthal, *Knowledge Triumphant*, p. 80. It is also related that the Prophet said, "A man who reads the Qur'ān and who then feels that another man has been bestowed [by God] more than he himself has been bestowed has truly considered small what God has considered great." Other *ḥadīth* material emphasizes the detestability of human jealousy, such as the report that the Prophet said, "Avoid jealousy for this destroys good deeds as a fire destroys wood" (Abū Dāūd). In 2 al-Baqarah 109, the Qur'ān states: "Many People of the Book [non-Muslims] would like to turn you back into disbelievers after your [profession of] faith, out of their envy." Elsewhere, in 113 al-Falaq, the Qur'ān evokes the idea that envy brings misfortune on the envied person; in this *sūrah*, the reader seeks refuge with God "from the evil of the envier who envies."

Selected Bibliography

Abdel Haleem, Muhammad. "Context and Internal Relationships: Keys to Quranic Exegesis." In *Approaches to the Qur'ān*, pp. 71–99. Edited by G. R. Hawting and Abdul-Kader A. Shareef. New York: Routledge, 1993.

———. "Dynamic Style." In *Understanding the Qur'ān: Themes and Style*, pp. 184–210. London: I. B. Tauris Publishers, 1999.

———. "Grammatical Shift for Rhetorical Purposes: *Iltifāt* and Related Features of the Qur'ān." *Bulletin of South Asian Studies* (London), 60, no. 3 (1992): 409–410.

Abdul-Raof, Hussein. *Qur'ān Translation: Discourse, Texture, and Exegesis*. Richmond, Surrey: Curzon, 2001.

Abdullah, Taufik. "Islam and the Formation of Tradition: A Comparative Perspective." *Itinerario* 13 (1989): 17–36.

———. "The Pesantren in Historical Perspective." In *Islam and Society in Southeast Asia*, edited by Taufik Abdullah and S. Siddique, pp. 80–107. Singapore: Institute for Southeast Asian Studies, 1986.

bin Abu Bakar, M. Ali. *Seni Lagu al-Quran di Malaysia*. Kuala Lumpur: Darul Fikir, 1991.

Al-Faruqi, Lois Ibsen. "Accentuation in Qur'ānic Chant: A Study in Musical *Tawāzun*." *Yearbook for Traditional Music* 10 (1978): 53–68.

———. *An Annotated Glossary of Arabic Musical Terms*. Westport, Conn.: Greenwood Press, 1981.

———. "The Cantillation of the Qur'an." *Asian Music* 19, no. 1 (1987): 2–25.

———. "The *Mawlid*." *World of Music* 3, no. 1986 (1986): 79–89.

———. "Music, Musicians, and Muslim Law." *Asian Music* 17, no. 1 (1985): 13–36.

———. "Ornamentation in Arabian Improvisational Music: A Study of Interrelatedness in the Arts." *World of Music* 20, no. 1 (1978): 17–28.

———. "Qur'ān Reciters in Competition in Kuala Lumpur." *Ethnomusicology* 31, no. 2 (1987): 221–228.

———. "The Status of Music in Muslim Nations: Evidence from the Arab World." *Asian Music* 12, no. 1 (1980): 56–85.

———. "Structural Segments in the Islamic Arts: The Musical 'Translation' of a Characteristic of the Literary and Visual Arts." *Asian Music* 16, no. 1 (1984): 59–82.

———. "What Makes Religious Music 'Religious'?" In *Sacred Sound: Music in Religious Thought and Practice*, edited by Joyce Irwin, pp. 21–34. Chico, Calif.: Scholars Press, 1983.

Amidhan, H., et al. *The Dynamics of Indonesian Muslim Today*. Translated by ADZAN Team. Jakarta: Department of Religious Affairs, 1993.

Andaya, Leonard Y. "The Bugis-Makassarese Diasporas." *Journal of the Malaysian Branch of the Royal Asiatic Society* 68, no. 1 (1995): 119–138.

———. *The Heritage of Arung Palakka: A History of South Sulawesi (Celebes) in the Seventeenth Century*. The Hague: Martinus Nijhoff, 1981.

———. "Kingship-*Adat* Rivalry and the Role of Islam in South Sulawesi." *Journal of Southeast Asian Studies* (Singapore), 15, no. 1 (1984): 22–42.

———. *The World of Maluku: Eastern Indonesia in the Early Modern Period*. Honolulu: University of Hawai'i Press, 1993.

Aqsha, Darul, Dick van der Meij, and Johan Hendrik Meuleman, eds. *Islam in Indonesia: A Survey of Events and Developments from 1988 to March 1993*. Vol. 26. Jakarta: INIS (Indonesia-Netherlands Cooperation in Islamic Studies), 1995.

Armon-Jones, Claire. "The Thesis of Constructionism." In *The Social Construction of Emotions*, edited by Rom Harré, pp. 32–56. Oxford: Blackwell, 1986.

Asad, Talal. "Anthropological Conceptions of Religion: Reflections on Clifford Geertz." *Man* 18 (1983): 237–259.

———. *Genealogies of Religion: Discipline and Reasons of Power in Christianity and Islam*. Baltimore: Johns Hopkins Univerity Press, 1993.

Atiyeh, George, ed. *The Book in the Islamic World: The Written Word and Communication in the Middle East*. Albany: SUNY Press, 1995.

Bakan, Michael B. *Music of Death and New Creation: Experiences in the World of Balinese Gamelan Beleganjur*. Chicago: University of Chicago Press, 1999.

Baker, James N. "The Presence of the Name: Reading Scripture in an Indonesian Village." In *The Ethnography of Reading*, edited by Jonathan Boyarin, pp. 98–138. Berkeley: University of California Press, 1993.

Bakhtin, Mikhail M. "Discourse in the Novel." In *The Dialogic Imagination: Four Essays by M. M. Bakhtin*, translated and edited by C. Emerson and M. Holquist, pp. 288–331. Austin: University of Texas Press, 1994 [1981].

Bamberger, Jeanne, and Evan Ziporyn. "Getting It Wrong." *World of Music* 34, no. 3 (1992): 22–56.

al-Bāqillānī, Abū Bakr Muḥammad ibn al-Ṭayyib. *I'jāz al-Qur'ān*. Cairo: Dar al-Ma'arif, 1963.

Bauman, Richard, ed. *Verbal Art as Performance*. Prospect Heights, Ill.: Waveland Press, 1984.

Beatty, Andrew. *Varieties of Javanese Religion: An Anthropological Account*. Cambridge: Cambridge University Press, 1999.

Becker, Judith. *Gamelan Stories: Tantrism, Islam, and Aesthetics in Central Java*. Tempe: Arizona State University, 1993.

———. "Tantrism, *Rasa*, and Javanese Gamelan Music." In *Enchanting Powers: Music in the World's Religions*, edited by Lawrence E. Sullivan, pp. 15–60. Cambridge, Mass.: Harvard University Press, 1997.
Bell, Catherine. *Ritual: Perspectives and Dimensions*. New York: Oxford University Press, 1997.
———. *Ritual Theory, Ritual Practice*. New York: Oxford University Press, 1992.
Benda, Harry J. *The Crescent and the Rising Sun: Indonesian Islam under the Japanese Occupation, 1942–1945*. The Hague: W. van Hoeve, 1958.
Benjamin, Walter. *Illuminations: Essays and Reflections*. Translated and edited by Hannah Arendt. New York: Schocken, 1968.
Berkey, Jonathan. *Transmission of Knowledge in Medieval Cairo: A Social History of Islamic Education*. Princeton: Princeton University Press, 1992.
Berliner, Paul. *Thinking in Jazz: The Infinite Art of Improvisation*. Chicago: University of Chicago Press, 1994.
Besnier, Niko. "Language and Affect." *Annual Review of Anthropology* 19 (1991): 419–451.
———. *Literacy, Emotion, and Authority: Reading and Writing on a Polynesian Atoll*. Cambridge: Cambridge University Press, 1995.
Blacking, John. "Towards a Theory of Musical Competence." In *Man: Anthropological Essays Presented to O. F. Raum*, pp. 19–34. Cape Town: C. Struik, 1971.
Bohlman, Philip V. "Middle East." In *The New Grove Dictionary of Music and Musicians*, edited by Stanley S. Sadie, vol. 16, pp. 626–638. New York: Macmillan, 2001.
———. "The Recitation of the Qur'an." Paper presented at the University of Chicago Divinity School, 1993.
Boland, B. J. *The Struggle of Islam in Modern Indonesia*. The Hague: Martinus Nijhoff, 1982.
Boulatta, Issa J. "The Rhetorical Interpretation of the Qur'an: *I'jāz* and Related Topics." In *Approaches to the History of the Interpretation of the Qur'an*, edited by Andrew Rippin, pp. 139–157. Oxford: Clarendon, 1988.
———, ed. *Literary Structures of Religious Meaning in the Qur'ān*. London: Curzon, 2000.
Bourdieu, Pierre. *Outline of a Theory of Practice*. New York: Cambridge University Press, 1991 [1977].
Bourdieu, Pierre, and Jean-Claude Passerson. *Reproduction in Education, Society, and Culture*. London and Beverly Hills: Sage, 1977.
Bowen, John R. "The Forms Culture Takes: A State-of-the-Field Essay on the Anthropology of Southeast Asia." *Journal of Asian Studies* 54, no. 4 (1995): 1047–1078.
———. "Islamic Transformations: From Sufi Poetry to Gayo Ritual." In *Indonesian Religions in Transition*, edited by Rita Smith Kipp and Susan Rodgers, pp. 113–135. Tucson: University of Arizona Press, 1987.
———. *Muslims through Discourse: Religion and Ritual in Gayo Society*. Princeton: Princeton University Press, 1993.

———. "*Ṣalāt* in Indonesia: The Social Meanings of an Islamic Ritual." *Man* (n.s.), 24, no. 4 (1989): 299–318.

Braginsky, V. I. "The Concept of 'the Beautiful' *(Indah)* in Malay Classical Literature and Its Muslim Roots." *Persidangan Antarabangsa Pengajian Melayu* (1979).

———. "Some Traces of the Theory of *Rasa* in Malay Classical Literature." In *Sanskrit and World Culture*, edited by F. Gruner, pp. 191–197. Berlin: Akademie Verlag, 1986.

Brenneis, Donald. "Performing Passions: Aesthetics and Politics in an Occasionally Egalitarian Community." *American Ethnologist* 14 (1987): 236–250.

Brenner, Suzanne April. *The Domestication of Desire: Women, Wealth, and Modernity in Java*. Princeton: Princeton University Press, 1998.

———. "Reconstructing Self and Society: Javanese Muslim Women and the 'Veil.'" *American Ethnologist* 23 (1996): 673–697.

Brinner, Benjamin. *Knowing Music, Making Music: Javanese Gamelan and the Theory of Musical Competence and Interaction*. Chicago: University of Chicago Press, 1995.

Brown, Norman O. "The Apocalypse of Islam." *Social Text* 3, no. 8 (1983): 155–171.

Bruinessen, Martin van. "*Kitab Kuning:* Books in Arabic Script Used in the Pesantren Milieu." *Bijdragen tot de Taal-, Land- en Volkenkunde* 146 (1990): 226–269.

———. *Kitab Kuning: Pesantren dan Tarekat (Tradisi-tradisi Islam di Indonesia)*. Bandung: Penerbit Mizan, 1995.

Bruner, Edward M. "Experience and Its Expressions." In *The Anthropology of Experience*, edited by Victor W. Turner and Edward M. Bruner, pp. 3–30. Urbana and Chicago: University of Illinois Press, 1986.

Calhoun, Cheshire, and Robert C. Solomon, eds. *What Is an Emotion? Classical Readings in Philosophical Psychology*. New York: Oxford University Press, 1984.

Capwell, Charles. "Contemporary Manifestations of Yemeni-Derived Songs and Dance in Indonesia." *Yearbook for Traditional Music* 27 (1995): 76–89.

Casey, Edward S. *Remembering: A Phenomenological Study*. Bloomington: Indiana University Press, 1987.

Castelo-Branco, S. El-Shawan. "Some Aspects of the Cassette Industry in Egypt." *World of Music* 29, no. 2 (1987): 32–45.

Chairul Mu'min, M. *Petunjuk Praktis Mengelola TK al-Qur'an*. Jakarta: Fikahati Aneska, 1995.

Chambert-Loir, Henri. "*Dato' ri Bandang:* Légendes de l'islamisation de la région de Célèbes-Sud." *Archipel* 29 (1985): 137–163.

Chodorow, Nancy. *The Power of Feelings: Personal Meaning in Psychoanalysis*. New Haven, Conn.: Yale University Press, 1999.

Connerton, Paul. *How Societies Remember*. New York: Cambridge University Press, 1989.

"The Contest of Recitation of the Qur'ān in Indonesia: History of a Quarter Century." *Studia Islamika* 1, no. 2 (1994): 1–6 (special insert).

Csordas, Thomas J. "Embodiment as a Paradigm for Anthropology." *Ethos* 18, no. 1 (1990): 5–47.

———. "Genre, Motive, and Metaphor: Conditions for Creativity in Ritual Language." *Cultural Anthropology* 2 (1987): 445–469.
———. *Language, Charisma, and Creativity: The Ritual Life of a Religious Movement.* Berkeley: University of California Press, 1997.
———. *Sacred Self: A Cultural Phenomenology of Charisma and Healing.* Berkeley: University of California Press, 1995.
———. "Somatic Modes of Attention." *Cultural Anthropology* 8, no. 2 (1993): 135–157.
———. ed. *Embodiment and Experience: The Existential Ground of Culture and Self.* New York: Cambridge University Press, 1994.
Cummings, William. *Making Blood White: Historical Transformations in Early Modern Makassar.* Honolulu: University of Hawai'i Press, 2002.
———. "The Melaka Malay Diaspora in Makassar, c. 1500–1699." *Journal of the Malaysian Branch of the Royal Asiatic Society* 71, no. 1 (1998): 106–121.
Dahlan, M. Syawir. *Pedoman untuk Sukses dalam M.T.Q.* Ujung Pandang (Makassar): Pimpinan Pendidikan Ilmu al-Qur'an "Al-Muzahwirah," n.d.
D'Andrade, Roy G. "Afterword." In *Human Motives and Cultural Models*, edited by Roy G. D'Andrade and Claudia Strauss, pp. 225–232. Cambridge: Cambridge University Press, 1992.
———. "Schemas and Motivation." In *Human Motives and Cultural Models*, edited by Roy G. D'Andrade and Claudia Strauss, pp. 23–44. Cambridge: Cambridge University Press, 1992.
Daniels, Harry, ed. *An Introduction to Vygotsky.* New York: Routledge, 1966.
Danielson, Virginia. "'*Min al-Mashaikh*': A View of the Egyptian Musical Tradition." *Asian Music* 22, no. 1 (1990): 113–127.
———. "The Qur'an and the *Qasidah*: Aspects of the Popularity of the Repertory Sung by Umm Kulthum." *Asian Music* 19, no. 1 (1987): 26–45.
———. *The Voice of Egypt: Umm Kulthūm, Arabic Song, and Egyptian Society in the Twentieth Century.* Chicago: University of Chicago Press, 1997.
Davitz, Joel R. *The Language of Emotion.* New York: Academic Press, 1969.
Deci, Edward L. *Intrinsic Motivation.* New York: Plenum Press, 1975.
Denffer, Ahmad von. *'Ulūm al-Qur'ān: An Introduction to the Sciences of the Qur'ān.* London: The Islamic Foundation, 1983.
Denny, Frederick M. "The *Adab* of Qur'ān Recitation: Text and Context." In *International Congress for the Study of the Qur'an*, edited by A. H. Johns, pp. 143–160. Canberra: Australian National University, 1981.
———. "Exegesis and Recitation: Their Development as Classical Forms of Qur'anic Piety." In *Transitions and Transformations in the History of Religions: Essays in Honor of Joseph M. Kitagawa*, edited by Frank E. Reynolds and Theodore M. Ludwig, pp. 91–123. Leiden: Brill, 1980.
———. "The Great Indonesian Qur'an Chanting Tournament." *The World and I: A Chronicle of Our Changing Era* 6 (1986): 216–223.
———. *An Introduction to Islam.* New York: Macmillan, 1985.

———. "Islamic Ritual: Perspectives and Theories." In *Approaches to Islam in Religious Studies*, edited by Richard Martin, pp. 63–77. Tucson: Univeristy of Arizona Press, 1985.
———. "Qur'an Recitation: A Tradition of Oral Performance and Transmission." *Oral Tradition* 4, no. 1–2 (1989): 5–26.
———. "Qur'ān Recitation Training in Indonesia: A Survey of Contexts and Handbooks." In *Approaches to the History of the Interpretation of the Qur'ān*, edited by Andrew Rippin, pp. 288–306. Oxford: Clarendon Press, 1988.
Departemen Agama (Ministry of Religious Affairs, Indonesia). *Juz 'Amma dan Terjemahannya Dilengkapi Iqro', Cara Cepat Belajar Membaca Al-Qur'an*. 6 "Iqra'" volumes bound as one. Jakarta: Proyek Pengadaan Kitab Suci Al-Qur'an, Departemen Agama R.I., 1993–1994.
———. *Ministry of Religious Affairs: Tasks and Functions*. Jakarta: Publishing Team, Ministry of Religious Affairs, 1996.
———. *Pedoman Pelatihan Tilawatil Quran*. Jakarta: Ditjen Bimas Islam dan Urusan Haji, Proyek Bimbingan Dakwah Agama Islam (Pusat), 1996.
Desjarlais, Robert R. *Body and Emotion: The Aesthetics of Illness and Healing in the Nepal Himalayas*. Philadelphia: University of Pennsylvania Press, 1992.
Dewey, John. *Art as Experience*. New York: Minton, Balch, and Company, 1934.
Dhofier, Zamakhsyari. *The Pesantren Tradition: A Study of the Role of the Kyai in the Maintenance of the Traditional Ideology of Islam in Java*. Tempe: Program for Southeast Asian Studies, Arizona State Univerity, 1999.
van Dijk, Kees. "*Dakwah* and Indigenous Culture: The Dissemination of Islam." *Bijdragen tot de Taal-, Land- en Volkenkunde* 154, no. 2 (1998): 218–235.
———. *Rebellion under the Banner of Islam: The Darul Islam Movement in Indonesia*. The Hague: Martinus Nijhoff, 1981.
Douglas, Mary, and Steven Ney. *Missing Persons: A Critique of the Social Sciences*. Berkeley: University of California Press, 1998.
Downey, Greg. "Incorporating Capoeira: Phenomenology of a Movement Discipline." Ph.D. dissertation, University of Chicago, 1998.
Drewal, Margaret Thompson. *Yoruba Ritual: Performers, Play, Agency*. Bloomington: Indiana University Press, 1992.
Drewes, G. W. J. "The Study of Arabic Grammar in Indonesia." In *Acta Orientalia Neerlandica: Proceedings of the Congress of the Dutch Oriental Society (May 1970)*, edited by P. W. Westman, pp. 61–70. Leiden: E. J. Brill, 1971.
Durkheim, Emile. *Elementary Forms of the Religious Life*. Translated by Karen E. Fields. New York: Free Press, 1995 [1912].
———. *Moral Education: A Study of the Theory and Application of the Sociology of Education*. New York: The Free Press, 1961.
Eagleton, Terry. *The Ideology of the Aesthetic*. Oxford: Blackwell, 2000 [1990].
Ebersole, Gary L. "The Function of Ritual Weeping Revisited: Affective Expression and Moral Discourse." *History of Religions* 39, no. 3 (2000): 211–246.
Effendi, Djohan, Moeslim Abdurrahman, Amidhan, Soenarto Soedarno, and Saafroe-

din Bahar, eds. *Agama dalam Pembangunan Nasional: Himpunan Sambutan Presiden Soeharto.* Jakarta: Pustaka Biru, 1981.

Eickelman, Dale F. "The Art of Memory: Islamic Education and Its Social Reproduction." *Comparative Studies in Society and History* 20, no. 4 (1978): 485–516.

———. *Knowledge and Power in Morocco: The Education of a Twentieth-Century Notable.* Princeton: Princeton University Press, 1985.

———. "The Study of Islam in Local Contexts." *Contributions to Asian Studies* 17 (1982): 1–16.

Eickelman, Dale F., and Jon W. Anderson, eds. *New Media in the Muslim World: The Emerging Public Sphere.* Bloomington: Indiana University Press, 1999.

Eickelman, Dale F., and James Piscatori. *Muslim Politics.* Princeton, N.J.: Princeton University Press, 1996.

Ekman, Paul, Wallace W. Friesen, and Phoebe Ellsworth. *Emotion in the Human Face.* New York: Pergamon Press, 1972.

Embree, Lester, et al., eds. *Encyclopedia of Phenomenology.* Dordrecht and Boston: Kluwer Academic Publishers, 1997.

Errington, Joseph. *Language and Social Change in Java.* Athens: Ohio University Press, 1984.

Ewing, Katherine Pratt. *Arguing Sainthood: Modernity, Psychoanalysis, and Islam.* Durham: Duke University Press, 1997.

———, ed. *Shari'at and Ambiguity in South Asian Islam.* Berkeley: University of California Press, 1988.

Farmer, Henry George. *History of Arabian Music to the XIIIth Century.* London: Luzac, 1929.

Federspiel, Howard. *Popular Indonesian Literature of the Qur'an.* Ithaca, N.Y.: Cornell Modern Indonesia Project, Cornell University, 1994.

Feener, R. Michael. "'Knowledge' of the Past in Malay Islamicate Historiography." Unpublished paper, n.d.

———. "Shaykh Yusuf and the Appreciation of Muslim 'Saints' in Modern Indonesia." *Journal for Islamic Studies* (Cape Town), 18–19 (1999): 112–131.

Feld, Steven. "Linguistic Models in Ethnomusicology." *Ethnomusicology* 18, no. 2 (1974): 179–217.

———. *Sound and Sentiment: Birds, Weeping, Poetics, and Song in Kaluli Expression.* Philadelphia: University of Pennsylvania Press, 1982.

———. "Sound Structure as Social Structure." *Ethnomusicology* 28, no. 3 (1984): 383–409.

Feld, Steven, and A. A. Fox. "Music and Language." *Annual Review of Anthropology* 23 (1995): 25–53.

Foucault, Michel. *Technologies of the Self: A Seminar with Michel Foucault.* Amherst: University of Massachusetts Press, 1988.

Frankenberry, Nancy K., and Hans H. Penner. "Clifford Geertz's Long-Lasting Moods, Motivations, and Metaphysical Conceptions." *Journal of Religion* 79, no. 2 (1999): 617–640.

Gade, Anna M. "An Envy of Goodness: Learning to Recite the Qur'an in Modern Indonesia." Ph.D. dissertation, University of Chicago Divinity School, 1999.

———. "Motivating the 'Motivation' to Recite the Qur'ān in Indonesia." Paper presented in the Religion and Culture Workshop, Princeton University, 2000.

———. "Oral Statement and Affective Voice." Paper presented at the University of Chicago Divinity School, 1996.

———. "The Recitation of the Qur'ān in Indonesia: Text and Context." Paper presented at the Middle East Studies Association Annual Meeting (Washington, D.C.), 1999.

———. "Taste, Talent and the Problem of Internalization: A Qur'ānic Study in Religious Musicality from Southeast Asia." *History of Religions* 41, no. 4 (2002): 328–368.

Geertz, Clifford. "Art as a Cultural System." *Modern Language Notes* 91 (1976): 1473–1499.

———. "Deep Play: Notes on the Balinese Cockfight." In *The Interpretation of Cultures: Selected Essays by Clifford Geertz*, pp. 412–454. New York: Basic Books, 1973.

———. "Ethos, World View, and the Analysis of Sacred Symbols." In *The Interpretation of Cultures: Selected Essays by Clifford Geertz*, pp. 134–136. New York: Basic Books, 1973.

———. *Islam Observed: Religious Development in Morocco and Indonesia*. Chicago: University of Chicago Press, 1968.

———. "The Javanese *Kijaji*: The Changing Role of a Cultural Broker." *Comparative Studies in Society and History* 2 (1960): 288–249.

———. *Negara: The Theatre State in Nineteenth Century Bali*. Princeton, N.J.: Princeton University Press, 1980.

———. "Religion as a Cultural System." In *The Interpretation of Cultures: Selected Essays by Clifford Geertz*, pp. 87–125. New York: Basic Books, 1973.

———. *The Religion of Java*. Glencoe, Ill.: Free Press, 1960.

Geertz, Hildred. "The Vocabulary of Emotion: A Study of Javanese Socialization Processes." In *Culture and Personality: Contemporary Readings*, edited by Robert A. LeVine, pp. 249–264. Chicago: Aldine, 1974 [1959].

George, Kenneth M. "Designs on Indonesia's Muslim Communities." *Journal of Asian Studies* 57, no. 3 (1998): 693–713.

———. *Showing Signs of Violence: The Cultural Politics of a Twentieth-Century Headhunting Ritual*. Berkeley: University of California Press, 1996.

———. "Violence, Solace, and Ritual: A Case Study from Island Southeast Asia." *Culture, Medicine, and Psychiatry* 19, no. 2 (1995): 225–260.

al-Ghazzālī, Abū Ḥāmid Muḥammad ībn Muḥammad al-Tūsī. *Invocations and Supplications (Kitāb al-adhkār wa'l-da'awāt, Iḥyā' 'Ulūm al-Dīn, Book 9)*. Translated by Kojiro Nakamura. Cambridge: The Islamic Texts Society, 1973.

———. *The Jewels of the Qur'ān: al-Ghazālī's Theory (Kitāb Jawāhir al-Qur'ān)*. Translated by Muhammad Abul Quasem. London: Kegan Paul International, 1977.

———. *The Recitation and Interpretation of the Qur'ān, Al-Ghazālī's Theory (Iḥyā' 'Ulūm al-Dīn, Book 8).* Translated by Muhammad Abul Quasem. Boston: Kegan Paul International, 1983 [1982].
Goffman, Erving. *Interaction Ritual: Essays in Face-to-Face Behavior.* Chicago: Aldine Publishing Company, 1967.
———. *The Presentation of Self in Everyday Life.* New York: Doubleday Anchor, 1959.
Goody, Jack, ed. *Literacy in Traditional Societies.* Cambridge: Cambridge University Press, 1968.
Gordon, Alijah, ed. *The Propagation of Islam in the Indonesian-Malay Archipelago.* Kuala Lumpur: Malaysian Sociological Research Institute, 2001.
Gordon, Steven L. "The Sociology of Sentiments and Emotion." In *Social Psychology: Sociological Perspectives*, edited by Morris Rosenberg and Ralph H. Turner, pp. 562–592. New York: Basic Books, 1981.
Graham, William A. *Beyond the Written Word: Oral Aspects of Scripture in the History of Religion.* New York: Cambridge University Press, 1987.
———. *Divine Word and Prophetic Word in Early Islam: A Reconsideration of the Sources, with Special Reference to the Divine Saying or Ḥadith Qudsī.* The Hague: Mouton, 1977.
———. "Islam in the Mirror of Ritual." In *Islam's Understanding of Itself*, edited by Richard G. Hovannisian and Jr. Speros Vryonis, pp. 53–72. Malibu, Calif.: Undena Publications, 1983.
———. "Qur'ān as Spoken Word: An Islamic Contribution to the Understanding of Scripture." In *Approaches to Islam in Religious Studies*, edited by Richard Martin, pp. 23–40. Tucson: University of Arizona Press, 1985.
———. "Scripture as Spoken Word." In *Rethinking Scripture: Essays from a Comparative Perspective*, edited by Miriam Levering, pp. 129–169. Albany: State University of New York Press, 1989.
———. "Those Who Study and Teach the Qur'ān." In *International Congress for the Study of the Qur'an*, edited by A. H. Johns, pp. 9–28. Canberra: Australian National University, 1981.
Grunebaum, G. E. von. "*I'djāz.*" In *Encyclopedia of Islam* (new ed.), pp. 1018–1020. Leiden: Brill, 1986.
Gruson, Linda M. "Rehearsal Skill and Musical Competence: Does Practice Make Perfect?" In *Generative Processes in Music: The Psychology of Performance, Improvisation, and Composition*, edited by John Slobada, pp. 91–112. Oxford: Clarendon Press, 1988.
Hadi, H. Mahfudh Syamsul, H. Muaddi Aminan, and Cholil Uman, eds. *Rahasia Keberhasilan Dakwah oleh K. H. Zainuddin*, M.Z. Surabaya: Ampel Suci, 1994.
Hall, Edward T. "Improvisation as an Acquired, Multilevel Process." *Ethnomusicology* 36, no. 2 (1992): 223–235.
Harmonic, Gilbert. "La fête du grand *maulid* à Cikoang: regard sur une tarekat dite 'shi'ite' en Pays Makassar." *Archipel* 29 (1985): 175–191.
Harré, Rom. "An Outline of the Social Constructionist Viewpoint." In *The Social Con-*

struction of Emotions, edited by Rom Harré, pp. 12–14. London: Basil Blackwell, 1986.
Harvey, Barbara Sillars. "Tradition, Islam, and Rebellion: South Sulawesi 1950–1965." Ph.D. dissertation, Cornell University, 1974.
Hasan Basri, H. "MTQ dan Peranannya dalam Mengkatkan Semangat Beragama di Kalangan Remaja Muslim." S1 (B.A.) thesis, IAIN "Alauddin," Ujung Pandang (Makassar), 1990.
Hefner, Robert W. *Civil Islam: Muslims and Democratization in Indonesia*. Princeton, N.J.: Princeton University Press, 2000.
———. "Islam, State, and Civil Society: ICMI and the Struggle for the Indonesian Middle Class." *Indonesia* 56 (1993): 1–36.
———. "Print Islam: Mass Media and Ideological Rivalries among Indonesian Muslims." *Indonesia* 64 (1997): 77–103.
Hefner, Robert W., and Patricia Horvatich, eds. *Islam in an Era of Nation-States: Politics and Religious Renewal in Muslim Southeast Asia*. Honolulu: University of Hawai'i Press, 1997.
Heider, Karl G. *Landscapes of Emotion: Mapping Three Cultures of Emotion in Indonesia*. Cambridge: Cambridge University Press, 1991.
Hobsbawm, Eric, and Terrence Ranger, eds. *The Invention of Tradition*. New York: Cambridge University Press, 1992.
Hochschild, Arlie Russell. "Emotion Work, Feeling Rules, and Social Structure." *American Journal of Sociology* 85 (1979): 551–575.
———. *The Managed Heart: Commercialization of Human Feeling*. Berkeley: University of California Press, 1983.
Holland, Dorothy C. "How Cultural Systems Become Desire: A Case Study of American Romance." In *Human Motives and Cultural Models*, edited by Roy G. D'Andrade and Claudia Strauss, pp. 61–89. Cambridge: Cambridge University Press, 1992.
Hood, Mantle. "The Challenge of Bi-Musicality." *Ethnomusicology* 4 (1960): 55–59.
Horsley, Imogene, Michael Collins, and Nazir A. Jairazbhoy. "Improvisation." In *The New Grove Dictionary of Music and Musicians*, edited by Stanley Sadie. London: Macmillan, 1980.
Houtsonen, Jarmo. "Traditional Qur'anic Education in a Southern Moroccan Village." *International Journal of Middle East Studies* 26 (1994): 489–500.
Howell, Julia Day. "Sufism and the Indonesian Islamic Revival." *Journal of Asian Studies* 60, no. 3 (2001): 701–730.
Humam, As'ad. *Buku Iqro': Cara Cepat Belajar Membaca Al-Qur'an*. 6 vols. bound as one. Kotagede, Yogyakarta: Team Tadarus "AMM," 1990.
Humphrey, Caroline, and James Laidlaw. *The Archetypal Actions of Ritual: A Theory of Ritual Illustrated by the Jain Rite of Worship*. Oxford: Clarendon, 1994.
Husainī, Syed Kaleemullāh. *Easy Tajwīd: A Text Book on Phonetics and Rules of Pronunciation and Intonation of the Glorious Qur'ān*. Translated by Syed Noorullāh Khādrī and Quadir Husain Khan. Chicago: Muslim Community Center, 1990 [1982].

Ibn Khaldūn, 'Abd al-Raḥmān Abū Zayd ībn Muḥammad. *The Muqaddimah: An Introduction to History*. Translated by Franz Rosenthal. Abridged and edited by N. J. Dawood. Princeton, N.J.: Princeton University Press, 1969.

Ibn Naqīb Al-Miṣrī, Aḥmad. *Reliance of the Traveller: A Classic Manual of Islamic Sacred Law ('Umdat al-Ṣālik)*. Translated with commentary and appendices by Nuh Ha Mim Keller. Beltsville, Md.: Amana Publications, 1994 [1991].

Ihde, Don. *Listening and Voice: A Phenomenology of Sound*. Athens: Ohio University Press, 1976.

Indyawan, Hendi. *Belajar Muda Huruf al-Quran*. Bandung: Penerbit Mizan, 1996 [1994].

Irvine, Judith T. "Registering Affect: Heteroglossia in the Linguistic Expression of Emotion." In *Language and the Politics of Emotion*, edited by Catherine Lutz and Lila Abu-Lughod, pp. 126–161. Cambridge: Cambridge University Press, 1993 [1990].

———. "Status and Style in Language." *Annual Review of Anthropology* 14 (1986): 557–581.

Irwin, Joyce, ed. *Sacred Sound: Music in Religious Thought and Practice*. Journal of the American Academy of Religion Thematic Study, vol. 50, no. 1. Chico, Calif.: Scholars Press, 1983.

Iser, Wolfgang. *The Act of Reading: A Theory of Aesthetic Response*. Baltimore: Johns Hopkins University Press, 1978.

Israeli, Raphael. "Translation as Exegesis: The Opening *Sura* of the Qur'an in Chinese." In *Islam: Essays on Scripture, Thought, and Society*, edited by Peter G. Riddell and Tony Street, pp. 81–103. Leiden: Brill, 1997.

Jakobson, Roman. "Linguistics and Poetics." In *Style and Language*, edited by T. Sebeok, pp. 350–377. Cambridge, Mass.: MIT Press, 1960.

———. *Six Lectures on Sound Meaning*. Cambridge, Mass.: MIT Press, 1979.

Jakobson, Roman, and Linda Waugh. *The Sound Shape of Language*. Bloomington: Indiana University Press, 1979.

James, William. "The Emotions." In *Principles of Psychology*, pp. 442–485. New York: Dover, 1950 [1890].

———. *The Varieties of Religious Experience*. New York: Penguin, 1982.

———. "What Is an Emotion?" In *What Is an Emotion? Classical Readings in Philosophical Psychology*, edited by Cheshire Calhoun and Robert C. Solomon, pp. 127–141. New York: Oxford University Press, 1984 [1884].

Jeffery, Arthur J. "The Textual History of the Qur'an." *Journal of the Middle Eastern Society* 1947: 35–49.

Jennings, Theodore W., Jr. "On Ritual Knowledge." *Journal of Religion* 62, no. 2 (1982): 111–127.

Johns, Anthony H. "Coming to Terms with the Qur'an: A Challenge for Indonesianists." *Review of Indonesian and Malaysian Affairs* 22, no. 1 (1988): 69–93.

———. "Islam in the Malay World: An Explatory Survey with Some Reference to Quranic Exegesis." In *Islam in Asia*, edited by Raphael Israeli and Anthony H. Johns, pp. 115–161. Jerusalem: Magnes Press, 1984.

———. "The Qur'anic Presentation of the Joseph Story: Naturalistic or Formulaic Language?" In *Approaches to the Qur'an*, edited by G. R. Hawting and Abdul-Kader A. Shareef, pp. 37–70. New York: Routledge, 1993.
———. "The Qur'ān on the Qur'ān." In *International Congress for the Study of the Qur'ān*, edited by A. H. Johns, pp. 1–8. Canberra: Australian National University, 1981.
———. "Sufism in Southeast Asia: Reflections and Reconsiderations." *Journal of Southeast Asian Studies* 26, no. 1 (1995): 169–183.
Jones, Gavin W. "Religion and Education in Indonesia." *Indonesia* 22 (1976): 19–56.
Jones, Russell. "Ten Conversion Myths from Indonesia." In *Conversion to Islam*, edited by Nehemia Levtzion, pp. 129–158. New York: Holms and Meier Publishers, 1979.
Jones, Sidney. "Arabic Instruction and Literacy in Javanese Muslim Schools." *International Journal of the Sociology of Language* 42 (1983): 83–94.
———. "The Javanese Pesantren: Between Elite and Pesantry." In *Reshaping Local Worlds: Formal Education and Cultural Change in Rural Southeast Asia*, edited by Charles F. Keyes, pp. 19–41. New Haven, Conn.: Yale Center for International and Area Studies, 1991.
de Jong, Frederick, and Bernard Radtke, eds. *Islamic Mysticism Contested: Thirteen Centuries of Controversies and Polemics*. Leiden: Brill, 1999.
Juynboll, G. H. A. "The Position of Qur'ān Recitation in Early Islam." *Journal of Semitic Studies* 19 (1974): 240–251.
———. "The *Qurrā'* in Early Islamic History." *Journal of the Economic and Social History of the Orient* 16 (1973): 113–129.
Kagan, Jerome. "The Idea of Emotion in Human Development." In *Emotions, Cognition, and Behavior*, edited by Carroll E. Izard, Jerome Kagan, and Robert B. Zajonc, pp. 38–72. Cambridge: Cambridge University Press, 1984.
Kahle, Paul. "The Arabic Readers of the Koran." *Journal of Near Eastern Studies* 8 (1949): 65–71.
Kapferer, Bruce. *A Celebration of Demons: Exorcism and the Aesthetics of Healing in Sri Lanka*. Bloomington: Indiana University Press, 1983.
———. "Performance and the Structuring of Meaning and Experience." In *The Anthropology of Experience*, edited by Victor Turner and Edward M. Bruner, pp. 188–206. Urbana: University of Illinois Press, 1986.
Kaptein, Nico J. G. "The *Berdiri Mawlid* Issue among Indonesian Muslims in the Period from circa 1875 to 1930." *Bijdragen tot de Taal-, Land- en Volkenkunde* 149 (1993): 124–153.
———. *Muhammad's Birthday Festival: Early History in the Central Muslim Lands and Development in the Muslim West until the 10th/16th Century*. Leiden: Brill, 1993.
Kassis, Hanna E. *A Concordance of the Qur'ān*. Berkeley: University of California Press, 1983.
Katz, Jack. *How Emotions Work*. Chicago: University of Chicago Press, 1999.
Kemper, Theodore D., ed. *Research Agendas in the Sociology of Emotions*. Albany: SUNY, 1990.

Keyes, Charles F., ed. *Reshaping Local Worlds: Formal Education and Cultural Change in Rural Southeast Asia*. New Haven, Conn.: Yale Center for International and Area Studies, 1991.

Kingsbury, Henry. *Music, Talent, and Performance: A Conservatory Cultural System*. Philadelphia: Temple University Press, 1988.

Kivy, Peter. *Music Alone: Philosophical Reflections on the Purely Musical Experience*. Ithaca, N.Y.: Cornell University Press, 1990.

———. *Sound Sentiment: An Essay on the Musical Emotions*. Philadelphia: Temple University Press, 1989.

Kleinman, Arthur, and Byron Good, eds. *The Illness Narratives: Suffering, Healing, and the Human Condition*. New York: Basic Books, 1988.

Kleinman, Arthur, and Joan Kleinman. "Suffering and Its Professional Transformation: Toward an Ethnography of Interpersonal Experience." In *Things as They Are: New Directions in Phenomenological Anthropology*, edited by Michael Jackson, pp. 169–195. Bloomington: Indiana University Press, 1996.

Knysh, Alexander. *Islamic Mysticism: A Short History*. Leiden: Brill, 2000.

"Koran, Chanting." In *The Concise Encyclopedia of Islam*, edited by Cyril Glassé, pp. 232–241. New York: HarperSanFrancisco, 1989.

Kratz, Corinne A. *Affecting Performance: Meaning, Movement, and Experience in Okiek Women's Initiation*. Washington, D.C.: Smithsonian Institution Press, 1994.

Kuipers, Joel C. *Language, Identity, and Marginality in Indonesia: The Changing Nature of Ritual Speech on the Island of Sumba*. Cambridge: Cambridge University Press, 1998.

———. *Power in Performance: The Creation of Textual Authority in Weyewa Ritual Speech*. Philadelphia: University of Pennsylvania Press, 1990.

Laderman, Carol, and Marina Roseman, eds. *The Performance of Healing*. New York: Routledge, 1996.

Lagu-Lagu Belajar Cepat Membaca al-Qur'an. Sound recording. Jakarta: Badan Komunikasi Pemuda Remaja Masjid, n.d.

Lakoff, George, and Mark Johnson. *Metaphors We Live By*. Chicago: University of Chicago Press, 1980.

Langer, Suzanne. *Feeling and Form: A Theory of Art*. New York: Charles Scribner's Sons, 1953.

———. *Philosophy in a New Key*. Cambridge, Mass.: Harvard University Press, 1999 [1942].

Lapidus, Ira. "Knowledge, Virtue, and Action: The Classical Muslim Conception of *Adab* and the Nature of Religious Fulfillment in Islam." In *Moral Conduct and Authority: The Place of Adab in South Asian Islam*, edited by Barbara Metcalf, pp. 38–61. Berkeley: University of California Press, 1984.

"Laporan Khusus" (Special Report): "MTQ Pamungkas Abad XX." *Media Dakwah*, August (Rabuil Awal), 1418/1997: 54–61.

Lave, Jean. "A Comparative Approach to Educational Forms and Learning Processes." *Anthropology and Education Quarterly* 13, no. 2 (1982): 181–187.

———. "The Practice of Learning." In *Understanding Practice: Perspectives on Activity*

and Context, edited by Seth Chaiklin and Jean Lave, pp. 3–34. New York: Cambridge University Press, 1993.
Lave, Jean, and Etienne Wenger. "Practice, Person, Social World." In *An Introduction to Vygotsky*, edited by Harry Daniels, pp. 143–150. New York: Routledge, 1996.
———, eds. *Situated Learning: Legitimate Peripheral Participation*. Cambridge: Cambridge University Press, 1991.
Lawson, E. Thomas, and Robert N. McCauley. *Rethinking Religion: Connecting Cognition and Culture*. New York: Cambridge University Press, 1993 [1990].
Lee, Soon Tong. "Technology and the Production of Islamic Space: The Call to Prayer in Singapore." *Ethnomusicology* 43, no. 1 (1999): 86–100.
Leiser, Gary. "Notes on the *Madrasa* in Medieval Islamic Society." *Muslim World* 17 (1986): 16–23.
Lembaga Bahasa dan Ilmu al-Qur'an. *Belajar Membaca al-Qur'an dengan Lagu*. Jakarta: LBIQ, 1991.
———. *Belajar Membaca al-Qur'an dengan Tajwid*. Jakarta: LBIQ, 1985.
———. *Belajar Seni Suara Baca al-Qur'an: Teori dan Praktek*. Jakarta: LBIQ, 1997.
Lembaga Pengembangan Tilawatil Qur'an Nasional. *25 Tahun Musabaqah Tilawatil Quran dan 17 Tahun Lembaga Pengembangan Tilawatil Quran*. Jakarta: LPTQ Nasional, 1994.
———. *Pedoman Lembaga Pengembangan Tilawatil Qur'an*. Jakarta: LPTQ Nasional, 1992.
———. *Pedoman Musabaqah al-Qur'an: Hasil Rapat Kerja Nasional (Rakernas) VI*, 1987. Jakarta: LPTQ Nasional, 1987.
———. *Pedoman Pelatihan Tilawatil Quran*. Jakarta: LPTQ Nasional, 1996.
———. *Pedoman Pengembangan Tilawatil Qur'an*. 4 vols: 1983; 1992; 1995 (Seri I); 1995 (Seri III). Jakarta: LPTQ Nasional, 1983–1995.
Lembaga Pengembangan Tilawatil Qur'an, Propinsi Sulawesi Selatan. *Sejarah MTQ di Sulawesi Selatan*. Ujung Pandang: LPTQ Tk. Prop. Sulsel, 1985.
Leppert, R., and S. McClary, eds. *Music and Society: The Politics of Composition, Performance, and Reception*. Cambridge: Cambridge University Press, 1987.
Levy, Robert I. "Introduction: Self and Emotion." *Ethos* 11, no. 3 (1983): 128–134.
Liddle, R. William. "*Media Dakwah* Scripturalism: One Form of Islamic Political Thought and Action in New Order Indonesia." In *Toward a New Paradigm: Recent Developments in Indonesian Islamic Thought*, edited by Mark R. Woodward, pp. 323–356. Tempe: Program for Southeast Asian Studies, Arizona State University, 1996.
Lindsay, Jennifer. "Cultural Policy and the Performing Arts in South Sulawesi." *Bijdragen tot de Taal-, Land- en Volkenkunde* 151, no. 4 (1995): 656–671.
Lock, Margaret. "Cultivating the Body: Anthropology and Epistemologies of Bodily Practice and Knowledge." *Annual Review of Anthropology* 22 (1993): 133–155.
Lockard, Craig A. *Dance of Life: Popular Music and Politics in Southeast Asia*. Honolulu: University of Hawai'i Press, 1998.
Lukens-Bull, Ronald A. "Teaching Morality: Javanese Islamic Education in a Globalizing Era." *Journal of Arabic and Islamic Studies*, no. 3 (2000): 26–47.

———. "Two Sides of the Same Coin: Modernity and Tradition in Islamic Education in Indonesia." *Anthropology and Education Quarterly* 32, no. 3 (2001), pp. 350–372.

Lutz, Catherine A. "Emotion, Thought, and Estrangement: Emotion as a Cultural Category." *Cultural Anthropology* 1, no. 3 (1986): 286–309.

———. "Motivated Models." In *Human Motives and Cultural Models*, edited by Roy G. D'Andrade and Claudia Strauss, pp. 181–190. Cambridge: Cambridge University Press, 1992.

———. *Unnatural Emotions: Everyday Sentiments on a Micronesian Atoll and Their Challenge to Western Theory*. Chicago: University of Chicago Press, 1988.

Lutz, Catherine, and Lila Abu-Lughod, eds. *Language and the Politics of Emotion: Studies in Emotion and Social Interaction*. Cambridge: Cambridge University Press, 1993 [1990].

Lutz, Catherine, and Geoffrey White. "The Anthropology of Emotions." *Annual Review of Anthropology* 15 (1986): 405–436.

Lynch, Owen M., ed. *Divine Passions: The Social Construction of Emotion in India*. Berkeley: University of California Press, 1990.

Madelung, Wilfred. "The Origins of the Controversy Concerning the Creation of the Qur'an." In *Religious Schools and Sects in Medieval Islam*, pp. 504–525. London: Variorum Reprints, 1985.

Madnuh. "Tradisi Tahfiz al-Qur'an dan Korelasinya dengan Musabaqah Tilawatil Qur'an dalam Usaha Melestarikan Kemurnian al-Qur'an." S1 (B.A.) thesis, IAIN "Syarif Hidayatullah," Jakarta, 1996.

Mahasin, Aswab, et al., eds. *Ruh Islam dalam Budaya Bangsa: Konsep Estetika*, vol. 5: *Ruh Islam dalam Budaya Bangsa*. Jakarta: Yayasan Festival Istiqlal, 1996.

Mahmood, Saba. "Women's Piety and Embodied Discipline: The Islamic Resurgence in Contemporary Egypt." Ph.D. dissertation, Stanford University, 1998.

Majmu'āt Mawālid wa Ad'īa. Semarang: Maktabat Taha Futara, n.d.

Makdisi, George. "Institutionalized Learning as a Self-Image of Islam." In *Islam's Understanding of Itself*, edited by Richard G. Hovannisian and Jr. Speros Vryonis, pp. 73–88. Malibu, Calif.: Undena Publications, 1983.

———. *The Rise of Colleges: Institutions of Learning in Islam and the West*. Edinburgh: University Press, 1981.

Manuel, Peter. *Cassette Culture: Popular Music and Technology in North India*. Chicago: University of Chicago Press, 1993.

Maqbul Rasyid, H. "Sistem Pengajaran Membaca AlQuran di Taman Pendidikan Al-Quran (TPA): Studi Kasus di TPA Al-Markaz Al-Islami Ujungpandang." S2 (M.A.) thesis, IAIN "Alauddin," Ujung Pandang (Makassar), 1997.

Marcus, George E., and Michael M. J. Fischer. *Anthropology as Cultural Critique: An Experimental Moment in the Human Sciences*. Chicago: University of Chicago Press, 1986.

Marcus, Scott. "Modulation in Arabic Music: Documenting Oral Concepts, Performances, Rules, and Strategies." *Ethnomusicology* 36, no. 2 (1992): 171–195.

———. "The Periodization of Modern Arab Music Theory: Continuity and Change in the Definition of *Maqāmāt*." *Pacific Review of Ethnomusicology* 5 (1989): 33–48.
Martin, Richard C. "Structural Analysis of the Qur'ān: Newer Approaches to the Study of Islamic Texts." *Journal of the American Academy of Religion*, thematic issue (Studies in *Qur'ān* and *Tafsīr*), vol. 47, no. 4S (1979): 665–684.
———. "*Tilāwah*." In *The Encyclopedia of Religion*, edited by Mircea Eliade et al., vol. 10, pp. 526–530. New York: Macmillan, 1986.
———. "Understanding the Qur'ān in Text and Context." *History of Religions* 21, no. 4 (1982): 361–384.
Mauss, Marcel. "Techniques of the Body." *Economy and Society* 2, no. 1 (1973 [1934]): 70–88.
Merleau-Ponty, M. *The Phenomenology of Perception*. Translated by Colin Smith. New York: Routledge, 1962.
Messick, Brinkley. *The Calligraphic State: Textual Domination and History in a Muslim Society*. Berkeley: University of California Press, 1996 [1993].
———. "Legal Documents and the Concept of 'Restricted Literacy' in a Traditional Society." *International Journal of the Sociology of Language* 42 (1983): 41–52.
Metcalf, Barbara, ed. *Moral Conduct and Authority: The Place of Adab in South Asian Islam*. Berkeley: University of California Press, 1984.
Meyer, Leonard B. *Emotion and Meaning in Music*. Chicago: University of Chicago Press, 1956.
Milner, A. C. *Kerajaan: Malay Political Culture on the Eve of Colonial Rule*. Tucson: University of Arizona Press, 1982.
Misbachul Munir, M. *Pedoman Lagu-Lagu Tilawatil Qur'an dilengkapi dengan Tajwid dan Qasida*. Surabaya: Apollo, 1994.
Mitchell, Timothy. *Colonising Egypt*. Cambridge: Cambridge University Press, 1988.
Morris, Bertram. "Dewey's Theory of Art." In *Guide to the Works of John Dewey*, edited by Jo Ann Boydston, pp. 156–182. Carbondale and Edwardsville: Southern Illinois University Press, 1970.
Muammar, H. *Kunci Sukses M.T.Q.: Bimbingan Tilawatil Qur'an*. Sound recording (eight cassettes). Jakarta: P. T. Cipta Inda Record, 1979.
Munro, Donald, John F. Schumaker, and Stuart C. Carr, eds. *Motivation and Culture*. New York: Routledge, 1997.
Myers, Fred R. *Pintupi Country, Pintupi Self: Sentiment, Place, and Politics among Western Desert Aborigines*. Berkeley: University of California Press, 1991.
Nasr, Sayyid Hossein [Sayyed Hosein]. *Ideals and Realities of Islam*. London: Allen and Unwin, 1971.
———. "Islam and Music: The Legal and Spiritual Dimensions." In *Enchanting Powers: Music in the World's Religions*, edited by Lawrence E. Sullivan, pp. 219–236. Cambridge, Mass.: Harvard University Press, 1997.
al-Nawawī, Abū Zakariyā' Yaḥya ibn Sharaf al-Dīn. "Al-Tibyān fī Adab Ḥamalat al-Qur'ān" (The Explanation of the Proper Comportment for Carrying the Qur'ān). In *Textual Sources for the Study of Islam*, translated and edited by

Andrew Rippin and Jan Knappert, pp. 100–105. Chicago: University of Chicago Press, 1986.
Neisser, Ulric, ed. *Memory Observed: Remembering in Natural Contexts.* New York: W. H. Freeman, 1982.
Neisser, Ulric, and Eugene Winograd, eds. *Remembering Reconsidered: Ecological and Traditional Approaches to the Study of Memory.* Cambridge and New York: Cambridge University Press, 1988.
Nelson, Kristina. *The Art of Reciting the Qur'an.* Austin: University of Texas Press, 1985.
———. "Reciter and Listener: Some Factors Shaping the *Mujawwad* Style of Qur'anic Reciting." *Ethnomusicology* 26, no. 1 (1982): 41–48.
Nettl, Bruno. "Introduction: An Art Neglected in Scholarship." In *In the Course of Performance: Studies in the World of Musical Improvisation,* edited by Bruno Nettl and Melinda Russell, pp. 1–26. Chicago: University of Chicago Press, 1998.
———. "Thoughts on Improvisation: A Comparative Approach." *The Musical Quarterly* 60 (1974): 1–19.
Noorduyn, J. *A Critical Survey of Studies on the Languages of Sulawesi.* KITLV Bibliographic Series, vol. 17. Leiden: KITLV Press, 1991.
———. "De Islamering van Makasar." *Bijdragen tot de Taal-, Land- en Volkenkunde* 112, no. 3 (1956): 454–494.
Ong, Walter J. *Orality and Literacy.* London: Methuen, 1982.
Ortner, Sherry B. "Theory in Anthropology since the Sixties." *Comparative Studies in Society and History* 26, no. 1 (1984): 247–266.
Otto, Rudolf. *The Idea of the Holy.* Translated by John W. Harvey. London: Oxford, 1950.
Panduan Penyelenggaraan MTQ National XVIII 1997 Jambi (Guide to the Organization of the Eighteenth National MTQ in Jambi). Jambi: Panitia Penyelenggara MTQ Nasional XVIII 1997, 1997.
Pelissier, C. "The Anthropology of Teaching and Learning." *Annual Review of Anthropology* 20 (1992): 75–95.
Pelras, Christian. "Religion, Tradition, and the Dynamics of Islamization in South Sulawesi." *Archipel* 29 (1985): 107–135.
Pemberton, John. "Musical Politics in Central Java (or How Not to Listen to a Javanese Gamelan)." *Indonesia* 44 (1987): 17–30.
———. *On the Subject of "Java."* Ithaca, N.Y.: Cornell University Press, 1994.
———. "Recollections from 'Beautiful Indonesia' (somewhere beyond the postmodern)." *Public Culture* 6, no. 2 (1994): 241–262.
Perlman, Marc. "The Social Meanings of Modal Practices: Status, Gender, History, and *Pathet* in Central Javanese Music." *Ethnomusicology* 42, no. 1 (1998): 45–80.
Peters, J. R. T. M. *God's Created Speech: A Study in the Speculative Theology of the Mu'tazilī Wadī'l-Qudāt Abū'l-Ḥasan 'Abd al-Jabbār b. Aḥmad al-Ḥamdānī.* Leiden: Brill, 1976.
Plutchik, Robert, and Henry Kellerman, eds. *Emotion, Theory, Research, Experience,* vol. 1: *Theories of Emotion.* 4 vols. New York: Academic Press, 1980.

Polanyi, Michael. *The Tacit Dimension*. Garden City, N.Y.: Doubleday, 1966.

Powers, Harold S. "Mode." In *The New Grove Dictionary of Music and Musicians*, edited by Stanley S. Sadie, vol. 16, pp. 775–860. New York: Macmillan, 2001.

Pressing, Jeff. "Improvisation: Methods and Models." *In Generative Processes in Music: The Psychology of Performance, Improvisation, and Composition*, edited by John Slobada, pp. 129–178. Oxford: Clarendon Press, 1988.

———. "Psychological Constraints on Improvisational Expertise and Communication." In *In the Course of Performance: Studies in the World of Musical Improvisation*, edited by Bruno Nettl and Melinda Russell, pp. 47–68. Chicago: University of Chicago Press, 1998.

Proudfoot, Wayne. *Religious Experience*. Berkeley: University of California Press, 1985.

Qā'ida Baghdadiyya ma' Juz' 'Amma. Semarang: Maktaba wa Matba'at Taha Futara, n.d.

Racy, Ali Jihad. "Arabian Music and the Effects of Commercial Recording." *World of Music* 20, no. 1 (1978): 47–57.

———. "Creativity and Ambience: An Ecstatic Feedback Model from Arabic Music." *World of Music* 33, no. 3 (1991): 7–28.

———. "Improvisation, Ecstacy, and Performance Dynamics in Arabic Music." In *In the Course of Performance: Studies in the World of Musical Improvisation*, edited by Bruno Nettl and Melinda Russell, pp. 95–112. Chicago: University of Chicago Press, 1998.

———. "The Many Faces of Improvisation: The Arab *Taqāsīm* as a Musical Symbol." *Ethnomusicology* 44, no. 2 (2000): 302–320.

———. "Musical Aesthetics in Present Day Cairo." *Ethnomusicology* 34, no. 1 (1982): 143–162.

Radscheit, Matthias. "*I'gaz al-Qur'an* im Koran?" In *The Qur'an as Text*, edited by Stefan Wild, pp. 113–124. Leiden: Brill, 1996.

Rafael, Vincente L. *Contracting Colonialism: Translation and Christian Conversion in Tagalog Society under Early Spanish Rule*. Durham: Duke University Press, 1993.

Rahman, Fazlur. *Major Themes of the Qur'ān*. Minneapolis: Bibliotheca Islamica, 1989.

Rasmussen, Anne. "The Arab Musical Aesthetic in Indonesian Islam." Paper presented at the Middle East Studies Association Annual Meeting (Washington, D.C.), 1999.

———. "The Qur'an in Indonesian Daily Life: The Public Project of Musical Oratory." *Ethnomusicology* 45, no. 1 (2001): 30–57.

Reddy, William M. "Emotional Liberty: Politics and History in the Anthropology of Emotions." *Cultural Anthropology* 14, no. 2 (1999): 256–288.

Reid, Anthony. "The Rise of Makassar." *Review of Indonesian and Malaysian Affairs* 17 (1983): 117–160.

Renard, John. *Islam and the Heroic Image: Themes in Literature and the Visual Arts*. Columbia: University of South Carolina Press, 1993.

Ricklefs, M. C. *A History of Modern Indonesia since c. 1300*. Second ed. Stanford, Calif.: Stanford University Press, 1993 [1981].

Riddell, Peter G. *Islam in the Malay-Indonesian World: Transmission and Responses*. Honolulu: University of Hawai'i Press, 2001.

Roff, William R. "Islamic Movements: One or Many?" In *Islam and the Political Economy of Meaning*, edited by William Roff, pp. 31–52. Berkeley: University of California Press, 1987.
———. "Islam Obscured? Some Reflections on Studies of Islam and Society in Southeast Asia." *Archipel* 30, no. 1 (1985): 7–34.
———. *The Origins of Malay Nationalism*. Kuala Lumpur: University of Malaya Press, 1967.
Rosaldo, Michelle Z. *Knowledge and Passion: Ilongot Notions of Self and Social Life*. Cambridge: Cambridge University Press, 1980.
———. "The Shame of Headhunters and the Autonomy of the Self." *Ethos* 11 (1983): 135–151.
———. "Toward an Anthropology of Self and Feeling." In *Culture Theory: Essays on Mind, Self, and Emotion*, edited by Richard A. Shweder and Robert A. LeVine, pp. 137–158. Cambridge: Cambridge University Press, 1984.
Rosenthal, Franz. *Knowledge Triumphant: The Concept of Knowledge in Medieval Islam*. Leiden: Brill, 1970.
Rubinstein, Raechelle. *Beyond the Realm of the Senses: The Balinese Ritual of Kakawin Composition*. Leiden: KITLV Press, 2000.
al-Rummānī 'Ali bin 'Isa. "*Al-Nukāt fi I'jāz al-Qur'ān*." In *Textual Sources for the Study of Islam*, translated and edited by Andrew Rippin and Jan Knappert, pp. 49–58. Chicago: University of Chicago Press, 1986.
Ryle, Gilbert. *The Concept of Mind*. London: Hutchinson, 1963.
Said, Edward. *Orientalism*. New York: Vintage Books, 1979.
al-Sa'īd, Labīb. *The Recited Koran: History of the First Recorded Version (Al-Jam' al-Sawtī al-Awwal li'l-Qur'ān al-Karīm)*. Translated by Bernard Weiss, M. A. Rauf, and Morrow Berger. Princeton, N.J.: Darwin Press, 1975.
Sartre, Jean-Paul. *Sketch for a Theory of the Emotions*. Translated by Philip Mairet. London: Methuen, 1962.
Scarry, Elaine. *The Body in Pain*. New York: Oxford University Press, 1985.
Schachter, Daniel L. *Searching for Memory: The Brain, the Mind, and the Past*. New York: Basic Books, 1996.
Schechner, Richard. *Between Theater and Anthropology*. Philadelphia: University of Pennsylvania Press, 1985.
———. "Magnitudes of Performance." In *The Anthropology of Experience*, edited by Victor Turner and Edward M. Bruner, pp. 344–372. Urbana and Chicago: University of Illinois Press, 1986.
Schimmel, Annemarie. *And Muhammad Is His Messenger: The Veneration of the Prophet in Islamic Piety*. Chapel Hill: University of North Carolina Press, 1985.
———. *Calligraphy and Islamic Culture*. New York: New York University Press, 1984.
Schneider, Herbert W. "Dewey's Psychology." In *Guide to the Works of John Dewey*, edited by Jo Ann Boydston, pp. 1–14. Carbondale and Edwardville: Southern Illinois University Press, 1970.
Schutz, Alfred. "Making Music Together." In *Collected Papers*, vol. 2: *Studies in Social*

Theory, edited by Arvid Brodersen, pp. 159–178. The Hague: Martinus Nijhoff, 1976.
Schuyler, Philip D. "Music Education in Morocco: Three Models." *World of Music* 21, no. 3 (1979): 91–131.
Scribner, Sylvia, and Michael Cole. *The Psychology of Literacy*. Cambridge, Mass.: Harvard University Press, 1980.
Sears, Laurie. "Introduction." In *Fantasizing the Feminine in Indonesia*, edited by Laurie Sears, pp. 1–44. Durham, N.C.: Duke University Press, 1996.
Seeman, Khalil. "*Tajwīd* as a Source in Phonetic Research." *Wiener Zeitschrift für die Kunde des Morganlandes* 58 (1962): 112–120.
Sells, Michael. *Approaching the Qur'an: The Early Revelations*. Book and sound recording. Ashland, Ore.: White Cloud Press, 1999.
———. "Sound and Meaning in *Sūrat al-Qāri'a*." *Arabica* 40 (1993): 403–440.
———. "Sound, Spirit, and Gender in *Sūrat al-Qadr*." *Journal of the American Oriental Society* 111, no. 2 (1991): 239–259.
Seremetakis, Nadia C., ed. *The Senses Still: Perception and Memory as Material Culture in Modernity*. Chicago: University of Chicago Press, 1996 [1994].
Shalihah, Khadijatus. *Perkembangan Seni Baca al Quran dan Qiraat Tujuh di Indonesia*. Jakarta: Pustaka Alhusna, 1983.
Shiloah, Amnon. "The Arabic Concept of Mode." *Journal of the American Musicological Society* 34 (1981): 19–42.
———. *Music in the World of Islam: A Socio-Cultural Study*. Detroit: Wayne State University Press, 1996.
———. *The Theory of Music in Arabic Writings, c. 900–1900*. Munich: Henle, 1979.
Shiraishi, Saya. *Young Heroes: The Indonesian Family in Politics*. Ithaca, N.Y.: Southeast Asia Program Publications, Cornell University, 1997.
Shweder, Richard. "Anthropology's Rebellion against the Enlightenment, or There's More to Thinking Than Reason and Evidence." In *Culture Theory: Essays on Mind, Self, and Emotion*, edited by Richard A. Shweder and Robert A. LeVine, pp. 27–66. Cambridge: Cambridge University Press, 1984.
Shweder, Richard A., and Maria A. Sullivan. "Cultural Psychology: Who Needs It?" *Annual Review of Pschology* 44 (1993): 497–523.
Siegel, James T. *The Rope of God*. Ann Arbor: University of Michigan Press, 2000 [1969].
Sirriyeh, Elizabeth. *Sufis and Anti-Sufis: The Defense, Rethinking and Rejection of Sufism in the Modern World*. London: Curzon Press, 1999.
Smalley, William A., Chia Koua Vang, and Genia Yee Yang. *Mother of Writing: The Origin and Development of a Hmong Messianic Script*. Chicago: University of Chicago Press, 1990.
Smith, I. Joseph. *The Experiencing of Musical Sound: Prelude to a Phenomenology of Music*. New York: Gordon and Breach, 1979.
Smith, Jonathan Z. "The Bare Facts of Ritual." *History of Religions* 20, nos. 1–2 (1987): 112–127.

———. "Reductionism." In *The HarperCollins Dictionary of Religion*, edited by Jonathan Z. Smith and William Scott Green, pp. 882–884. San Francisco: HarperCollins, 1995.
———. *To Take Place: Toward Theory in Ritual*. Chicago: University of Chicago Press, 1987.
Smith, Wilfred Cantwell. "Scripture as Form and Concept: Their Emergence for the Western World." In *Rethinking Scripture: Essays from a Comparative Perspective*, edited by Miriam Levering, pp. 29–57. Albany: State University of New York Press, 1989.
———. *What Is Scripture? A Comparative Approach*. Minneapolis: Fortress Press, 1993.
Solomon, Robert C. "Getting Angry: The Jamesian Theory of Emotion in Anthropology." In *Culture Theory: Essays on Mind, Self, and Emotion*, edited by Richard Shweder and Robert LeVine, pp. 238–254. Cambridge: Cambridge University Press, 1984.
———. "Sartre on Emotions." In *The Philosophy of Jean-Paul Sartre*, edited by Paul A. Schlipp, pp. 211–228. La Salle, Ill.: Open Court, 1981.
Sowayan, Saad Abdullah. "'Tonight My Gun Is Loaded': Poetic Dueling in Arabia." *Oral Tradition* 4, nos. 1–2 (1989): 151–173.
Spindler, George D., and Louise Spindler. "Do Anthropologists Need Learning Theory?" *Anthropology and Education Quarterly* 13, no. 2 (1982): 109–124.
Spiro, Melford E. "Some Reflections on Cultural Determinism and Relativism with Special Reference to Emotion and Reason." In *Culture Theory: Essays on Mind, Self, and Emotion*, edited by Richard Shweder and Robert A. LeVine, pp. 323–346. Cambridge: Cambridge University Press, 1992 [1984].
Staal, J. Frits. "The Meaninglessness of Ritual." *Numen* 26, no. 1 (1975): 2–22.
———. "The Sound of Religion." *Numen* 33 (1986): 33–64, 185–224.
Stange, Paul. "The Logic of *Rasa* in Java." *Indonesia* 38 (1980): 113–134.
Starrett, Gregory. "The Hexis of Interpretation: Islam and the Body in the Egyptian Popular School." *American Ethnologist* 22 (1995): 953–969.
———. "The Margins of Print: Children's Religious Literature in Egypt." *Journal of the Royal Anthropological Institute* (incorporating *Man*), n.s. 2 (1996): 117–139.
———. *Putting Islam to Work: Education, Politics, and Religious Transformation in Egypt*. Berkeley: University of California Press, 1998.
Stearns, Carol Z., and Peter N. Stearns, eds. *Emotion and Social Change: Toward a New Psychohistory*. New York: Holmes and Meier, 1988.
———. "Emotionology: Clarifying the History of Emotions and Emotional Standards." *American Historical Review* 90 (1985): 813–836.
Steedly, Mary Margaret. "The State of Culture Theory in the Anthropology of Southeast Asia." *Annual Review of Anthropology* 28 (1999): 431–454.
Steenbrink, Karel. "Recapturing the Past: Historical Studies by IAIN-Staff." In *Toward a New Paradigm: Recent Developments in Indonesian Islamic Thought*, edited by Mark R. Woodward, pp. 155–192. Tempe: Arizona State University, 1996.
Stoller, Paul. *The Taste of Ethnographic Things: The Senses in Anthropology*. Philadelphia: University of Pennsylvania Press, 1989.

Stowasser, Barbara. *Women in the Qur'an, Traditions, and Interpretation*. New York: Oxford University Press, 1994.
Strauss, Claudia. "Beyond 'Formal' and 'Informal' Education: Uses of Psychoanalytic Theory in Anthropological Research." *Ethos* 2, no. 3 (1984): 195–222.
———. "Models and Motives." In *Human Motives and Cultural Models*, edited by Roy G. D'Andrade and Claudia Strauss, pp. 1–20. Cambridge: Cambridge University Press, 1992.
Street, Brian. *Literacy in Theory and Practice*. Cambridge: Cambridge University Press, 1984.
Sudnow, David. *Ways of the Hand: The Organization of Improvised Conduct*. Cambridge, Mass.: Harvard University Press, 1978.
Sullivan, Lawrence E. "Sacred Music and Sacred Time." *World of Music* 26, no. 3 (1984): 33–52.
———. "Sound and Senses: Toward a Hermeneutics of Performance." *History of Religions* 26, no. 1 (1986): 1–33.
Sumarsam. *Gamelan: Cultural Interaction and Musical Development in Central Java*. Chicago: University of Chicago Press, 1995 [1992].
Sutton, R. Anderson. "Commercial Cassette Recordings of Traditional Music in Java: Implications for Performers and Scholars." *World of Music* 27, no. 3 (1985): 23–45.
———. "Concept and Treatment in Javanese Gamelan Music, with Reference to Gambang." *Asian Music* 11, no. 1 (1979): 59–79.
———. "Do Javanese Gamelan Musicians Really Improvise?" In *In the Course of Performance: Studies in the World of Musical Improvisation*, edited by Bruno Nettl and Melinda Russell, pp. 69–94. Chicago: University of Chicago Press, 1998.
———. "Performing Arts and Cultural Politics in South Sulawesi." *Bijdragen tot de Taal-, Land- en Volkenkunde* 151, no. 4 (1995): 672–699.
———. *Variation in Central Javanese Gamelan Music: Dynamics of a Steady State*. DeKalb: Center for Southeast Asian Studies, Northern Illinois University, 1993.
al-Suyūṭī, Jalāl al-Dīn. *Al-Itqān fī 'Ulūm al-Qur'ān*. 2 vols. Cairo: Maṭba'at Ḥijāzī, 1910.
Sweeney, P. L. Amin. *A Full Hearing: Orality and Literacy in the Malay World*. Berkeley: University of California Press, 1987.
———. *Reputations Live On: On Early Malay Autobiography*. Berkeley: University of California Press, 1980.
Sy. Aliyah. "MTQ Sebagai Sarana Pengembangan Kebudayaan Islam." S1 (B.A.) thesis, IAIN "Alauddin," Ujung Pandang (Makassar), 1996.
Taher, H. Tarmizi. *Aspiring for the Middle Path: Religious Harmony in Indonesia*. Edited by Azyumardi Azra. Jakarta: CENSIS (Center for the Study of Islam and Society), 1997.
Talbi, Muhammad. "*Lā Qirā'a bi'l-Alhān*." *Arabica* 5 (1958): 183–190.
Tambiah, Stanley. "A Performative Approach to Ritual." *Proceedings of the British Academy* 65 (1979): 113–169.

Team Tadarus "AMM." *Pedoman Pengalolaan, Pembinaan dan Pengembangan "M3A" (Membaca, Menulis, Memahami) al-Quran*. Yogyakarta: Team Tadarus "AMM," 1995.

Thoits, Peggy. "Managing the Emotions of Others." *Symbolic Interaction* 19 (1996): 85–109.

———. "The Sociology of Emotions." *Annual Review of Sociology* 15 (1989): 217–242.

Tibawi, A. L. "Is the Qur'ān Translatable? Early Muslim Opinion." *Muslim World* 52 (1962): 4–16.

Tolbert, Elizabeth. "Theories of Meaning and Music Cognition: An Ethnomusicological Approach." *World of Music* 34, no. 3 (1992): 7–22.

Touma, Habib Hasan. *Der Maqam Bayati im Arabischen Taqsim*. Beiträge zur Ethnomusikologie no. 3. Hamburg: Karl Dieter Wagner, 1976.

———. "The *Maqām* Phenomenon: An Improvisation Technique in the Music of the Middle East." *Ethnomusicology* 15 (1971): 34–48.

———. *The Music of the Arabs*. Portland, Ore.: Amadeus Press, 1996.

Turner, Victor. "Dewey, Dilthey, and Drama: An Essay in the Anthropology of Experience." In *The Anthropology of Experience*, edited by Victor Turner and Edward M. Bruner, pp. 33–45. Urbana: University of Illinois Press, 1986.

———. "Encounter with Freud: The Making of a Comparative Symbologist." In *The Making of Psychological Anthropology*, pp. 558–583. Berkeley: University of California Press, 1978.

———. *The Forest of Symbols*. Ithaca: Cornell University Press, 1967.

———. *The Ritual Process: Structure and Anti-structure*. Ithaca: Cornell University Press, 1969.

Ulfah, Maria. "Hukum Melagukan al-Qur'an Secara Bersama." *Media al-Furqan* 5, no. 7 (1996): 19–28.

———. *Pedoman Praktis Belajar Lagu Tilawatil Qur'an*. Sound recording (two cassettes). Jakarta: Dian Records, 1986.

Versteegh, C. M. H. *Arabic Grammar and Qur'anic Exegesis in Early Islam*. Leiden: Brill, 1993.

Vygotsky, Lev Semyonovich. *The Collected Works of L. S. Vygotsky*, vol. 1: *Problems of General Psychology*. Translated by Norris Minick, edited by Robert W. Rieber and Aaron S. Carton. New York: Plenum Press, 1987 [1932].

———. *Mind in Society: The Development of Higher Psychological Processes*. Edited and translated by M. Cole, J. Scribner, V. John-Steiner, E. Souberman. Cambridge, Mass.: Harvard University Press, 1978.

Wagner, Daniel. "Memories of Morocco: The Influence of Age, Schooling, and Environment on Memory." *Cognitive Psychology* 10 (1978): 1–28.

Wagner, Daniel A., and Abdelhamid Lotfi. "Learning to Read by 'Rote.'" *International Journal of the Sociology of Language* 42 (1983): 111–121.

———. "Traditional Islamic Education in Morocco: Sociohistorical and Psychological Perspectives." *Comparative Education Review* 24 (1980): 238–251.

Wagner, Daniel A., Brinkley M. Messick, and Jennifer Spratt. "Studying Literacy in

Morocco." In *The Acquisition of Literacy: Ethnographic Perspectives*, edited by Bambi Schiefflin and Perry Gilmore, pp. 233–260. Norwood, N.J.: Ablex, 1986.

Wagner, Daniel A., and Jennifer E. Spratt. "Cognitive Consequences of Contrasting Pedagogies: The Effects of Quranic Preschooling in Morocco." *Child Development* 58 (1987): 1207–1219.

Waldman, Marilyn Robinson. "Tradition as a Modality of Change: Islamic Examples." *History of Religions* 25, no. 4 (1986): 318–340.

Wansbrough, John. *Quranic Studies: Sources and Methods of Scriptural Interpretation*. Oxford: Oxford University Press, 1977.

Watt, W. Montgomery. *Bell's Introduction to the Qur'ān*. Edinburgh: University Press, 1990 [1970].

Waugh, Earle H. *The Munshidīn of Egypt: Their World and Their Song*. Columbia: University of South Carolina Press, 1989.

Wegner, U. "Transmitting the Divine Revelation: Some Aspects of Textualism and Textual Variability in Qur'anic Recitation." *World of Music* 26, no. 3 (1986): 57–78.

Weintraub, Andrew N. "Theory in Institutional Pedagogy and 'Theory in Practice' for Sundanese Gamelan Music." *Ethnomusicology* 37, no. 1 (1993): 29–39.

Weix, G. G. "Islamic Prayer Groups in Indonesia: Local Forums and Gendered Responses." *Critique of Anthropology* 18, no. 4 (1998): 405–420.

Wensinck, A. J. *A Handbook of Early Muhammadan Tradition*. Leiden: E. J. Brill, 1927.

Wertsch, James V., ed. *Culture, Communication, and Cognition: Vygotskian Perspectives*. Cambridge: Cambridge University Press, 1985.

———. *Vygotsky and the Social Formation of Mind*. Cambridge, Mass.: Harvard University Press, 1986.

White, Geoffrey M., and J. Kirkpatrick, eds. *Person, Self, and Experience: Exploring Pacific Ethnopsychologies*. Berkeley: University of California Press, 1985.

Wikan, Unni. "Beyond the Words: The Power of Resonance." *American Ethnologist* 19 (1992): 460–482.

———. *Managing Turbulent Hearts: A Balinese Formula for Living*. Chicago: University of Chicago Press, 1995.

Williams, Ron G., and James W. Boyd. *Ritual, Art, and Knowledge: Aesthetic Theory and Zoroastrian Ritual*. Columbia: University of South Carolina Press, 1993.

Wittgenstein, Ludwig. *Remarks on Frazer's "Golden Bough."* Translated by A. C. Miles, edited by Rush Reeves. Norfolk, England: The Brynmill Press, 1993 [1979].

Wolters, O. W. *History, Culture, and Region in Southeast Asian Perspectives*. Rev. ed. Ithaca, N.Y.: Cornell University Southeast Asia Publications, 1999.

Woodward, Mark R. *Islam in Java: Normative Piety and Mysticism in the Sultanate of Yogyakarta*. Tucson: University of Arizona Press, 1989.

———. "The *Slametan:* Textual Knowledge and Ritual Performance in Central Javanese Islam." *History of Religions* 28 (1988): 54–89.

———. "Textual Exegesis as Social Commentary: Religious, Social, and Political Meanings of Indonesian Translations of Arabic *Hadith* Texts." *Journal of Asian Studies* 52 (1993): 565–583.

———, ed. *Toward a New Paradigm: Recent Developments in Indonesian Islamic Thought*. Tempe: Arizona State University, 1996.
Wright, Owen. *The Modal System of Arab and Persian Music, A.D. 1250–1300*. London: Oxford University Press, 1978.
Wulff, Donna. "Religion in a New Mode: The Convergence of the Aesthetic and the Religious in Medieval India." *Journal of the American Academy of Religion*, vol. 54, no. 8 (1986): 673–688.
Yampolsky, Philip. "Forces for Change in the Performing Arts of Indonesia." *Bijdragen tot de Taal-, Land- en Volkenkunde* 151, no. 4 (1995): 700–725.
Yates, Frances. *The Art of Memory*. Chicago: University of Chicago Press, 1966.
al-Zarkashī, Badr al-Dīn Muḥammad bin 'Abd Allāh. *Al-Burhān fī 'Ulūm al-Qur'ān*. Edited by Muhammad Abū al-Fadl Ibrahīm. 4 vols. Cairo: Dar Ihyā' al-Kutub al-'Arabiyah, 1957–1958.
Zen, H. A. Muhaimin. *Tata Cara / Problematika Menghafal Al Qur'an dan Petunjuk-petunjuknya*. Jakarta: Pustaka Alhusna, 1985.
Zoetmulder, P. J. *Pantheism and Monism in Javanese Suluk Literature*. Translated by M. C. Ricklefs. Leiden: KITLV Press, 1995.
Zuckerkandl, Victor. *The Sense of Music*. Princeton: Princeton University Press, 1959.

Index

'Abd al-Bāsiṭ 'Abd al-Ṣamad, 37, 189, 282n.30. See also *qāri'*
Abdel Haleem, M., 89, 97, 291nn.98, 107
Abdullah, K. H. M. Sayyid, 148–149, 160, 184, 187, 189, 193, 199–200, 243–245, 256, 275–276, 301n.51
ability, 36, 111–112, 115, 159–160, 165–166, 196, 275–276, 310n.5; competence, 126, 166, 172–174, 212, 274–275; as developmental, 4–5, 39, 55–57, 60–61, 87, 121, 170; self-assessment, 36, 58–59, 102, 133, 214–215; talent *(bakat, kemampuan)*, 113, 180, 212–215, 259, 304n.84; trying too hard, 199–200, 218–219. *See also* competition; *da'wah;* education; ideals; *kiai; lagu;* memory; music; orthopraxy; pedagogy; personhood; piety; *qāri'*; sociality; Sufism; *taḥfīẓ; tajwīd*
acara. *See* ritual
adab (cultivated comportment), 25, 61, 75, 82–84, 110, 148, 253, 261; definitions, 76–77; literature on, 77–78; of recitation, 29–30, 77, 138, 179, 204. *See also* competition; competitions; education; "Islamic," perceptions of; personhood; piety; sociality
aesthetics. See *rasa*. *See also* attention; competition; emotion; humor; "Islamic," perceptions of; motivation; music; orthopraxy; pedagogy; piety; Qur'ān; Qur'ān, structure and style; ritual; sociality; *tilāwah;* weeping
affect. *See* emotion; *rasa*. *See also* attention; competition; humor; laughing; memory; motivation; music; orthopraxy; pedagogy; piety; Qur'ān; ritual; sociality; *tilāwah;* weeping
Ainun Najib, Emha. *See* Emha Ainun Najib
alphabet, 46, 83, 117; and affect, 121, 137–138, 140–141, 143–145, 150; books to teach and learn, 144–145, 149; and esoteric *(ḥurūfī)* piety, 124, 138, 145; orthography, 121–122, 141, 144, 185, 293n.13, 296nn.52, 53; songs to teach and learn, 141–143; and *tajwīd*, 127–131. *See also* Baghdadi method; Iqra'; "Islamic," perceptions of; KKN; language; orality; pedagogy; reading; song; *tajwīd*
Ambon. *See* Moluku
animals, 137, 141, 144, 145, 160
Arabian peninsula (Ḥijāz): music, 183; and networks of scholars, 32, 63–64, 120; Saudi Arabia, 132, 166, 185–186, 248. *See also* Arabic texts, non-Qur'ānic; comprehension; education, institutions of; Ḥajj; language; music; pedagogy; Qur'ān; reading; *taḥfīẓ*

Arabic texts, non-Qur'ānic, 10–16, 32–33; Barzanji, 11, 13–14, 18–19, 124, 136, 146, 236–237; learning, 12–13, 124; Mawlid Al-Nabi, 11, 14, 18, 232; Salawat Nabi, 4, 14–15, 36; *tahlil*, 13, 237. See also *da'wah;* imitation; "Islamic," perceptions of; language; music; orality; piety; song; Sufism
"arts with Islamic flavor." See *da'wah*
Arung Palakka, 9
attention, 73–74, 82–83, 85, 87–88, 126, 131, 157, 160, 208; concentration for study, 108–111; getting and keeping others', 36, 65, 134, 199, 214, 257, 296n.44; and ritual, 73, 87, 89–90, 299n.26; and recitation of Qur'ān, 39, 91–94, 139. *See also* ability; comprehension; *da'wah;* emotion; gender; memory; motivation; music; piety; Qur'ān, structure and style; reading; ritual; sociality; *taḥfīẓ; tilāwah*

Baghdadi method, 117–119, 142, 148–151, 153; as "deep," 117–118, 147, 150, 152; *Qā'ida Baghdadiyya ma' Juz' 'Amma*, 147. *See also* alphabet; comprehension; "Islamic," perceptions of; language; orality; pedagogy; reading
Bahasa Indonesia. *See* language
Baitul Quran, 20–21
Bakan, M., 213, 301n.48
bakat (talent). *See* ability; education; music
Baker, J., 114
Bakhtin, M., 290n.90
Barzanji. *See* Arabic texts, non-Qur'ānic
Benjamin, W., 91
Berkey, J., 101, 147–148, 292n.119, 293n.11, 297n.63
Bohlman, P., 182
Bone (Watampone, South Sulawesi), 64, 119
Bourdieu, P., 68, 76, 224, 287n.18
Bowen, J., 89, 279n.3, 280n.20, 290n.81, 308n.53
Brinner, B., 173–174, 198, 310n.5
broadcast. *See* radio; television. *See also* cassettes; competitions; *da'wah*
Bugis. *See* language; South Sulawesi
Burhanuddin, H., 112, 131–132, 136–137, 166–168, 192–193, 201–202, 209, 248–249, 263

calligraphy, 20–21, 230, 281n.26. *See also* alphabet; Baitul Quran; competitions; Festival Istiqlal; Ministry of Religious Affairs; *muṣḥaf*
cassettes, 3, 13, 22, 102, 183–187 *(passim)*, 189–193 *(passim)*, 198–199, 208, 253, 258, 300n.42, 301n.49. *See also* music; pedagogy; *qāri';* revitalization, religious
chant. *See* music. *See also* orality; reading; ritual; Qur'ān; song; *taḥfīẓ; tajwīd; tilāwah*
children, 61, 112, 119, 141, 144–145, 153–154, 160–163, 221. *See also* Baghdadi method; competitions; education; education, institutions of; Iqra'; pedagogy; song
clothing, 117, 142, 145, 155, 161, 171, 230, 253, 257
cognition. *See* emotion; ideals; motivation; music; *taḥfīẓ*
colleges. *See* education, institutions of
competence. *See* ability. *See also* education; music; pedagogy; sociality
competition, 102, 143, 153, 242; experiences during, 248–251, 258–262; memorizers and, 61, 249–251; reasons for competing, 22, 216–217, 221–222, 236, 246–247, 259–260; Southeast Asia, 219, 275; training for, 255–258. *See also* competitions; Dahlan, Syawir; *da'wah;* emotion; motivation; *qāri'*
competitions (Musabaqah Tilawatil Qur'an, MTQ), 14, 21–22, 113, 136, 153, 236–238, 275; *adab* and, 77, 251, 253, 259–261; contest types, 230–231; history of, 231–233, 263; judges, 251, 253, 256–257, 309n.74; judging, 85, 136, 251–253, 309n.74; in Malaysia, 228, 233–235, 305n.23; national contest, events at, 17–18, 155, 228–230, 237–239, 250; sponsorship, 228–229, 233, 235–236, 308n.56; Telkom, 237,

256; women's, 258–261, 263. *See also* cassettes; competition; controversy; *lagu;* LPTQ; motivation; patronage; *qāri'*
comportment. See *adab. See also* law; piety; Sufism
comprehension, 29, 47, 83, 85–87, 102–103, 115–116, 131–132, 139, 159, 224–226, 246, 275, 292n.2; and Baghdadi method, 147, 151. *See also* attention; Baghdadi method; language; memory; orality; piety; Qur'ān; reading; *taḥfīẓ*
contests, Qur'ān recitation. *See* competitions
controversy: about MTQ competitions, 19, 241–244, 246–247; about Qur'ān and Islamic practices, 18, 81–82, 180–181, 280n.21, 300n.33. *See also* Arabic texts, non-Qur'ānic; *da'wah;* law
corruption. *See* patronage
Csordas, T., 52–53, 73, 89, 227, 271
Cummings, W., 31, 296n.52
curriculum. *See* pedagogy. *See also* Baghdadi method; cassettes; education; education, institutions of; Iqra'; reading

Dahlan, Syawir, 247, 257, 259-261
dakwah. See *da'wah*
dance, 18, 142, 145, 219, 228, 305n.24
D'Andrade, R., 225–226
da'wah (Islamic outreach), 2, 16–23, 134, 216, 240–241, 245, 280n.16; "arts with Islamic flavor," 14–15, 17–19, 240–241; and MTQ competitions, 22. *See also* Arabic texts, non-Islamic; Baitul Quran; competition; competitions; Iqra'; "Islamic," perceptions of; motivation; piety; sociality; song; reading; revitalization, religious; women's groups
Denny, F., 25–28 *(passim),* 125, 281nn.28, 29, 294n.26
Departemen Agama. *See* Ministry of Religious Affairs
devotion. *See* Arabic texts, non-Qur'ānic; *dhikr;* piety; Qur'ān; Sufism
Dewey, J., 56–57, 72, 144, 178, 271, 286n.97
dhikr, 11, 62, 101, 102, 180; Qur'ān as a "Reminder," 38, 62. *See also* Arabic texts, non-Qur'ānic; music; orality; Sufism; *taḥfīẓ*
Diponogoro, Prince, 9, 279n.7
Drewal, M., 90–91
Durkheim, E., 71, 224

Ebersole, G., 287nn.12, 21, 303n.69
education: affect and systems of, 33, 117–118, 120–121, 132–133, 158–160, 293n.12; identities of learning, 123, 125, 133–136; institutions of, 21, 116, 154–155; institutions of, Al-Azhar (Cairo), 32–33, 64; institutions of, IAIN (Institut Agama Islam Negeri), 9, 33, 142–143, 244; institutions of, *pesantren* (Islamic boarding schools), 13–14, 30, 32, 63–64, 103, 236–237, 256, 292n.2; institutions of, *pesantren kilat,* 33–34; institutions of, Qur'ān colleges, in Indonesia (IIQ, PTIQ, STAI), 13, 33, 64–65, 112, 183, 192; institutions of, TPA (*Taman Pendidikan Anak-anak,* Qur'ān kindergartens), 21, 117, 143, 153–155, 160–161; and Islamic tradition, 63, 77–78, 101–102, 104, 113–114, 118, 147–149, 293n.6; Islamic, in Southeast Asia, 23, 31–33; teachers and students, 78, 103, 118, 142, 147–149, 151–153, 158, 193–194, 301n.50; "tradition" and "modern" categories, 33, 64, 103, 114, 117, 136, 138, 155–156, 158, 160; theory about, 12, 54–57, 87, 118, 123, 295n.37, 298n.7. See also *adab;* imitation; "Islamic," perceptions of; *kiai;* KKN; language; memory; music; orality; patronage; pedagogy; Qur'ān; revitalization, religious; ritual; sociality; *taḥfīẓ*
Egypt (Misir). *See* cassettes; music; pedagogy; *qāri'*
Eliade, M., 120, 175, 294n.14
embodiment. *See* alphabet; emotion
Emha Ainun Najib, 14
emotion: 49–51, 69–70, 73, 208; embodiment, 41–42, 47, 50, 70, 83, 87, 91, 138–140, 145–146, 178, 208, 284n.73,

emotion (*continued*)
286n.103, 299n.26; "emotion work / management," 65–66, 73–74, 105, 107–111 *(passim)*; moral sentiments, 75; Qur'ān, reaction to, 39–43; religious experience, 49, 53, 56, 285n.89; "sincerity problem," 68–69, 71, 206; "social constructionism," 71–72; theory about, 49, 51–54, 67–73, 176–177, 225–226, 270–272, 284nn.73, 75, 299n.26. *See also* alphabet; attention; competition; education; humor; ideals; language; laughing; memory; motivation; orthopraxy; pedagogy; personhood; piety; Qur'ān; *rasa;* reading; ritual; sociality; Sufism; *tilāwah;* weeping
envy. *See* sociality
eschatology. *See* piety; Qur'ān; Qur'ān, verses; Sufism
esotericism. *See* alphabet; Sufism
exegesis *(tafsīr)*. *See* Qur'ān
expectation. See *adab;* attention; ideals; *i'jāz;* "Islamic," perceptions of; music; orthopraxy; Qur'ān, structure and style; ritual

Faḍā'il Al-Qur'ān. *See* Qur'ān. *See also* piety; Sufism
faṣāḥah (eloquence, fluency). *See* reading. See also *kiai;* language; orality; Qur'ān; *taḥfīẓ; tajwīd*
Federspiel, H., 228
feeling. *See* emotion; *rasa*. *See also* attention; competition; humor; laughing; memory; motivation; music; orthopraxy; pedagogy; piety; Qur'ān; ritual; sociality; *tilāwah;* weeping
Feener, R. M., 279n.7, 280n.10, 296n.53, 297n.69
Festival Istiqlal, 19–20, 281nn.23, 26. *See also* Baitul Quran; calligraphy; *da'wah; muṣḥaf;* revitalization, religious
fiqh (jurisprudence). *See* law
food, 10, 106, 108, 221, 248, 257
Foucault, M., 68, 75, 224, 268
Freud, S., 70, 72, 176

gaya (style). See *qāri'*. *See also* ability; cassettes; competitions; *lagu;* music; pedagogy
Geertz, C., 25, 51–54, 89, 122, 170–171, 219, 271, 279n.3, 285n.82, 286n.6, 287n.9, 292n.2, 299n.12, 303n.67, 305n.21
gender, 3, 11–12, 15, 35, 64, 79, 100, 113, 116, 135, 142, 160, 187, 198–199, 205, 219, 221, 234, 243, 263, 275. *See also* personhood; sociality; women's groups
George, K., 275, 281n.23, 310n.4
Al-Ghazzālī, 28, 45, 47, 101, 116, 138–140, 142, 180, 205–207 *(passim)*, 283n.54. See also *ḥadīth; tilāwah*
Goffman, E., 73
Graham, W., 281n.28, 298n.8

ḥadīth, 26, 27, 29, 31, 38, 45, 47, 62, 78–79, 81, 83, 104, 106, 179, 242, 276, 310n.6. *See also* education; law; memory; Muḥammad, the Prophet; orality; piety; Qur'ān; *sunnah*
ḥāfiẓ (Qur'ān memorizer). See *taḥfīẓ*
Ḥajj, 11, 12, 155, 183, 185, 191, 229, 234, 249. *See also* Arabian peninsula
Al-Ḥallāj, 80, 155
Hasan Basri, H., 245, 280n.18, 308n.58, 309n.66
Ḥasan of Baṣra, 79, 81, 82, 204
Hochschild, A. R., 73
Holland, D., 173
hope. *See* competition; *da'wah;* emotion; motivation; piety
humor, 61, 133–136, 189, 253. *See also* emotion; laughing; pedagogy
Humphrey, J., and C. Laidlaw, 58, 89, 170, 174–175, 222–223, 271, 299n.26. *See also* orthopraxy
ḥurūfī piety. *See* alphabet. *See also* piety; Sufism
ḥuzn (sadness). *See* weeping. *See also* music; piety; Sufism

IAIN (Institut Agama Islam Negeri). *See* education, institutions of

ibādah (worship). *See* piety. *See also* motivation; revitalization, religious
Ibn 'Arabi, 296n.46
Ibn Ḥanbal, Aḥmad, 46, 47, 80, 84, 116
Ibn al-Jazarī, 27, 28, 125–126
Ibn Khaldūn, 76, 104
Ibn Mujāḥid, 27, 28
Ibn Mas'ūd, 45, 46, 82, 83
ideals: Islamic models, 5–6, 16, 172, 179; models of coalescence for ritual and for emotion, 56–58, 68–69, 72, 170–172, 174–178, 271–273. *See also* ability; *adab;* emotion; *i'jāz;* "Islamic," perceptions of; law; music; orthopraxy; pedagogy; personhood; piety; ritual; sociality; *sunnah*
IIQ (Institut Ilmu Al-Qur'an, Jakarta). *See* education, institutions of
i'jāz ("inimitability" of Qur'ān), 43–44, 45, 92, 168, 172, 178–179, 284n.62, 290n.92. *See also* "Islamic," perceptions of; language; orthopraxy; piety; Qur'ān; *rasa*
ikhlāṣ (sincerity). *See* piety. See also *adab;* emotion; Sufism
iltifāt ("switches" in register). *See* Qur'ān, structure and style
imām. See *kiai*. See also *ṣalāt*
imitation, 133–143, 157, 165, 192, 195, 198; "legitimate peripheral participation," 12, 123–124. *See also* ability; attention; *da'wah;* education; law; orality; pedagogy; sociality
improvisation. See *lagu;* music; ritual. *See also* ability; attention; cassettes; competitions; law; orality; orthopraxy; pedagogy; *qāri';* Qur'ān, structure and style; ritual; *tajwīd*
individual. *See* personhood. *See also* emotion; sociality
inimitability (Qur'ān). See *i'jāz*
Iqra' (teaching method), 118–119, 151–153, 155–157; "Team Tadarus 'AMM,'" 153–155. *See also* alphabet; comprehension; education, institutions of; KKN; language; orality; pedagogy; reading; song
Irama, Rhoma. *See* Rhoma Irama
Irvine, J., 133
"Islamic," perceptions of, 15–16, 36, 124, 136; Arabic, 12–13, 43, 124, 137–138, 184–186, 232, 238–239; musical systems, 35–36, 182–188 *(passim)*. *See also* controversy; ideals; *i'jāz;* law; piety; sociality

Jakarta, 15, 20, 64, 135. *See also* education, institutions of; *qāri*
Jakobson, R., 92, 291n.89
James, W., 56, 69–70, 270, 285n.89
Jennings, T., 90, 122, 171–172, 271
Johns, A., 31, 32, 291n.100
judge *(qādi')*. See *adab;* competition; competitions; law
Juz' 'Amma (last thirtieth of Qur'ān), 3, 62, 64, 92–93, 149, 154, 157, 297n.62. *See also* Baghdadi method; Iqra'; orality; Qur'ān; Qur'ān, structure and style; reading; *taḥfīẓ*

Kahar Muzakkar, 9
Katz, J., 58, 68–69, 72, 87, 176–178, 271–272, 298n.7
khushū' (earnest feeling). *See* piety
kiai, 13, 32, 53, 63–64, 77, 82, 86, 99–100, 102, 111, 113, 135, 148–149, 243. *See also* Arabian peninsula; education; education, institutions of; law; reading; *taḥfīẓ*
kindergarten, Qur'ānic. *See* education, institutions of. *See also* Iqra'
KKN (Kulia Kerja Nyata), 117, 143, 155. *See also* education, institutions of; Iqra'
Kratz, C., 73, 176–177, 294n.19

lagu (Indonesian melody), 34, 65, 183–191 *(passim)*, 200, 214, 300n.37, 302n.54; judging criteria, 252–253, 256–257, 309n.67; "Lagu Cikoang," 217–218, 253; *"lagu nangis"* (old, "weepy *lagu*"), 35–36; modulation and arrangement, 37, 183, 188, 190, 201–203, 218–219, 258; moods of, 304n.82; notation, 197–198; recognition of, 190–191, 253,

lagu (Indonesian melody) *(continued)* 309n.74; "seven *lagu*," 183–184, 188–190; styles, change in, 35–37, 183, 217–218. *See also* cassettes; *i'jāz;* "Islamic," perceptions of; Muammar, H., Z.A.; music; pedagogy; *qāri'; qirā'āt;* song; *tilāwah*
language: Arabic, 85–86, 92, 95–96, 114–115, 120, 125–126, 129, 136–137, 185, 231; Arabic, pronunciation, 12–13, 86–87, 115, 132–134, 136, 149; Arabic reading, regional variants, 11–12, 126, 185–186; Bahasa Indonesia, 132, 136, 137, 141, 142, 150, 293n.13; "*Bahasa Al-Quran*" (language of the Qur'ān), 43, 124, 185–186; Javanese, 132, 134, 137; South Sulawesi, languages of, 9, 11–12, 14, 132, 134, 136, 150–151. *See also* alphabet; Arabic texts, non-Qur'ānic; comprehension; *i'jāz;* "Islamic," perceptions of; orality; Qur'ān, structure and style; *tajwīd; tilāwah*
laughing, 40, 61, 136. *See also* emotion; humor
Lave, J., 12, 54–55, 122, 123, 274, 285n.92
law, 28, 76, 77, 193, 243; and memorization of Qur'ān, 62; and music, 30, 180–181, 300n.33. *See also* controversy; *ḥadīth; kiai;* music; Sufism; *sunnah*
learning, institutions of. *See* education, institutions of. See also *adab;* education; *kiai*
learning, practice of. *See* ability; education; imitation; pedagogy
learning, theory about. *See* education. *See also* ability; imitation; pedagogy
linguistic register. *See* language; pedagogy
literacy. *See* alphabet; comprehension; education; language; pedagogy; reading; *taḥfīẓ; tajwīd*
LPTQ (Lembaga Pengembangan Tilawatil Qur'ān), 22, 65, 142, 233, 238, 253; and *lagu* development, 188, 190; other reciters' associations, 232–233. *See also* competitions; Ministry of Religious Affairs; music; patronage
Lutz, C., 50, 70
madrasa. *See* education; education, institutions of
Makassar (Ujung Pandang), 9–10, 12, 23, 281n.26; first MTQ competition in, 10, 229, 235; recitation in, 31, 218–219, 232, 255–256. *See also* language; South Sulawesi
Makdisi, G., 102, 107–108
Malaysia. *See* competitions
maqām (Arabic musical mode). See *lagu;* music. See also *qāri'*
maqām (Sufi "station"). *See* Sufism
"Al-Markaz Al-Islami." *See* Al-Masjid "Al-Markaz Al-Islami"
Martin, R., 27, 281n.28, 290n.88
Al-Masjid "Al-Markaz Al-Islami" (Makassar), 7, 10, 155–156, 166, 254, 281n.26
Mawlid Al-Nabi (Birthday of the Prophet). *See* Arabic texts, non-Qur'ānic; controversy
Media Dakwah (magazine), 241–242
memorization. See *kiai; taḥfīẓ*. *See also* ability; competitions; *ḥadīth;* memory
memory: emotion and, 105, 107, 120–121, 158; faculty of, 78–79, 84, 99, 101–102, 105–106, 111–112; Qur'ān memorization and, 78–79, 101, 111–112, 289nn.70, 71, 293n.6; music and, 87–88, 189; nostalgia, 36, 120, 151, 158. *See* attention; emotion; music; *taḥfīẓ*. *See also* ability; *adab; dhikr;* education; *kiai;* pedagogy; sociality
Merleau-Ponty, M., 70, 87, 299n.26
Messick, B., 118–120
Ministry of Religious Affairs, 233, 238, 248; and Iqra' materials, 154, 157, 308n.56; Qur'ān texts and, 44
mistakes. *See* orthopraxy
Moluku, 12, 19
mood. *See* emotion; *lagu; rasa; tilāwah*. *See also* attention; competition; Geertz, C.; humor; laughing; memory; motivation; music; orthopraxy; pedagogy; piety; Qur'ān; ritual; sociality; *tilāwah;* weeping
"moods and motivations." *See* ritual. *See also* emotion; Geertz, C.; motivation

motivation: *motivasi* (Ind. "motivation"), 4, 17, 36, 48, 52–54, 78, 107, 113, 142–143, 162–163, 189, 214, 221–227, 247; theory about, 48, 52–54, 222–227. *See also* attention; competition; competitions; *da'wah;* emotion; personhood; ritual; sociality
MTQ (Musabaqah Tilawatil Qur'an, Qur'ān recitation competition). *See* competitions
Muammar, H., Z.A., 184–186, 199, 202–203, 208–209, 214, 247, 257–259, 301n.49
Muḥammad, the Prophet, 25, 26, 29, 42, 82, 93, 94, 134, 161, 179, 242. *See also* Arabic texts, non-Qur'ānic; law; piety; Qur'ān; Sufism; *sunnah*
mujawwad (style of recitation). *See* recitation, types. *See also* cassettes; music; *qāri'*; Qur'ān
murattal (style of recitation). *See* recitation, types. *See also* cassettes; music; *qāri'*; Qur'ān; *taḥfīẓ*
muṣḥaf (Qur'ān text), 20–21, 26, 44, 103–104, 149, 151, 230, 281nn.23, 26. *See also* calligraphy; Ministry of Religious Affairs; Qur'ān; reading
music, 29, 87–88, 90, 290n.82; Arab music, history of, 182–183, 186; chant, 87–89; *dangdut*, 14, 134, 142; "ideal recitation" and "ecstatic feedback," 25, 35, 165; improvisation *(variasi)*, theory and practice, 26, 30, 34, 88, 91, 130, 165, 168, 181, 192–193, 195, 197, 199–200, 203, 214, 257, 290n.82; *maqām* (Arab "modes"), 34–36, 182–191 *(passim)*, 192, 197–198, 200; *qaṣīdah*, 186–187, 300n.43; Qur'ān's structure as "musical," 91; *samā'* (spiritual audition), 31, 138–139, 180, 189, 300n.33. *See also* ability; alphabet; Arabic texts, non-Qur'ānic; attention; cassettes; competitions; *da'wah;* emotion; gender; *i'jāz;* "Islamic," perceptions of; *lagu;* law; memory; orality; orthopraxy; pedagogy; piety; *qāri'*; Qur'ān, structure and style; *rasa;* recitation, types; ritual; song; *tilāwah;* weeping
Muzakkar, Kahar. *See* Kahar Muzakkar

Nasr, Sayyed Hossain, 180, 182
Al-Nawawī, 81–82
Nelson, K., 25, 35, 91, 125, 165, 179, 180, 204–207, 282n.30, 291n.103, 298n.5, 300n.33, 302n.60, 303n.76
Nettl, B., 197
New Order, 7, 17, 23, 33, 133, 220, 228, 235–236, 238–239, 265, 307n.47, 308n.50; and *globalisasi*, 19–20, 234–235, 240, 307n.43. *See also* patronage; Suharto
Nurhayati, 36, 161–162, 209–210, 246, 251, 253, 254, 257, 301n.49

orality: and Islamic education, 32–33, 115–116, 121–122, 147–148, 150–151; and Qur'ān, 23–25, 26, 125, 281n.28. See also *adab;* Qur'ān; ritual; *taḥfīẓ; tajwīd; tilāwah*
orthopraxy, 57–58, 164–170, 178–179, 188, 264, 298n.8; as a feeling-state, 167–168, 211; and *lagu*, 184; mistakes, 61, 95–97, 100, 113, 137, 148, 157, 161–162, 170, 180–181, 192–193, 196, 203, 249, 252, 308n.63. *See also* ability; ideals; *i'jāz;* "Islamic," perceptions of; music; pedagogy; personhood; piety; ritual; sociality

Palakka, Arung. *See* Arung Palakka
participation. *See* competitions; imitation; sociality
patronage, 235–237; corruption, religious problem of, 78–81 *(passim)*, 84, 242. See also *adab;* competitions; education, institutions of; motivation; New Order; piety
pedagogy, 32–33, 34, 124, 286n.4, 293n.6; competitions and, 255–258; handbooks for recitation and memorization, 86, 94, 104, 126, 309n.68; for *lagu*, 34–35, 160, 187–190, 195, 198–203, 255–258, 302nn.59, 63; linguistic register and,

pedagogy *(continued)*
133–134, 136–138, 150; performance as, 2–3, 22, 165, 188, 198; poems as, 118, 120, 293nn.10, 11; "proximate ideals" in, 172, 196, 288n.7; Qur'ānic and non-Qur'ānic learning contrasted, 12–13, 123–124; recording and broadcast, 2–3, 141–142, 254; song, *qaṣīdah*, and *tawshiḥ* and, 141–143, 186–187, 200–201, 302n.60; for *tajwīd*, 126, 131–132, 136–137, 153. *See also* ability; *adab;* Baghdadi method; cassettes; comprehension; education; education, institutions of; humor; imitation; Iqra'; "Islamic," perceptions of; language; memory; music; orality; *rasa;* reading; sociality; song; *taḥfīẓ*
Pemberton, J., 20, 298n.1, 304n.5, 308n.54
perception. *See* emotion. *See also* education; ideals; *i'jāz;* "Islamic," perceptions of; language; music; *rasa*
performance. *See* ability; Arabic texts, non-Qur'ānic; competition; competitions; controversy; *da'wah;* emotion; humor; ideals; imitation; "Islamic," perceptions of; *lagu;* music; orality; orthopraxy; pedagogy; piety; *qāri';* radio; *rasa;* ritual; television; *tilāwah;* weeping
personhood, 49, 57, 68, 72, 224–226, 274–275. *See also* emotion; ideals; sociality
pesantren (Islamic boarding schools). *See* education, institutions of
piety: and eschatology, 46–47, 84; hope, a sin to lose, 107, 261; *khushū'* (earnest feeling), 51, 167, 205, 210, 214–215, 260–261, 298n.5; as progressive, ongoing, 4–5, 39, 57, 89, 173; Qur'ānic, 29–31, 38, 45–48, 80–84, 138–140; sincerity *(ikhlāṣ)*, 92, 124, 134, 141, 239, 260. *See also* ability; *adab;* alphabet; Arabic texts, non-Qur'ānic; attention; comprehension; *da'wah; dhikr;* emotion; *ḥadīth;* "Islamic," perceptions of; law; orthopraxy; patronage; personhood; Qur'ān; sociality; Sufism; *sunnah;* weeping
poetry. *See* pedagogy; Qur'ān
practice, religious. *See* ritual. *See also* education; orthopraxy; pedagogy; piety; *tilāwah*
prayer: for memory, 106. *See also* Arabic texts, non-Qur'ānic; *dhikr;* piety; *ṣalāt*
pronunciation. *See* language. *See also* alphabet; Baghdadi method; humor; Iqra'; "Islamic," perceptions of; *kiai;* orality; *qāri';* reading; *tajwīd; tilāwah*
Prophet Muḥammad. *See* Muḥammad, the Prophet. *See also* Arabic texts, non-Qur'ānic; *ḥadīth;* law; piety; Qur'ān; Sufism
Prophets, 42, 80, 84, 93–94, 96, 98, 107, 142, 280n.16, 291nn.100, 101. *See also* Muḥammad, the Prophet
PTIQ (Jakarta). *See* education, institutions of

Qā'ida Baghdadiyya ma' Juz' 'Amma. *See* Baghdadi method
qāri' (Qur'ān reader), 78–79, 112, 135, 139, 231–233, 246–251, 255–262; Egyptian, 22, 25, 126, 186–187, 189, 191–194, 207, 296n.44, 300n.42, 301nn.46, 49, 302n.60; payment of, 63, 81–82; *qari musiman* (seasonal reciter), 246–247; styles of, 188, 191–195. *See also* 'Abd Al-Bāsiṭ 'Abd Al-Ṣamad; Abdullah, K. H. M. Sayyid; ability; Burhanuddin, H.; cassettes; competition; *da'wah;* gender; "Islamic," perceptions of; *lagu;* motivation; music; Muammar, H., Z.A.; Nelson, K.; Nurhayati; pedagogy; Ulfah, Hj. Maria
qaṣīdah (Arabic song). *See* cassettes; gender; language; music; pedagogy; *qāri';* song
qirā'āt ("readings"): history, 26–28; and *lagu*, 184; "seven readings," 27, 282n.38, 294n.27, 295n.34. *See also* "Islamic," perceptions of; *lagu*
Qur'ān, 23–25; emotional reaction to, described by, 39–43, 88; Faḍā'il Al-Qur'ān (piety and the text), 45–47; history and transmission, 25–26, 44, 78–

79, 100; *Miḥna*, 43, 79, 80; *puitisisasi* (poeticization) of meanings, 44, 135, 218, 230; structure and style, 88, 90–99; structure and style, *iltifāt* ("switches" in register), 88–89, 97–98; structure and style, self-reflexive, 29–30, 37–39, 43, 181–182; translation and exegesis (*tafsīr*), 13, 44, 230, 275; verses, 13, 28–30 (*passim*), 39–44 (*passim*), 47, 86, 88, 92–98 (*passim*), 101, 107, 112, 130, 178, 202, 231, 237, 278, 280n.16, 282nn.33, 39, 42, 283nn.55, 57, 58, 284n.68, 291nn.101, 102, 292n.4, 295n.35, 298n.5, 309n.68, 310n.6, (see also *Juz' 'Amma*); verses, "compete in good works" (*fastabiqū'l-khairāt*, 2 al-Baqarah 148, 5 al-Mā'idah 48), 219, 231, 254; verses, Al-Fātiḥah, 97, 112, 124, 127, 129, 150; verses, "increases them in faith" (8 al-Anfāl 2), 35, 42–43, 178, 199, 243; verses, "*li ta'ārifū*" (49 al-Ḥujurāt 13), 16. *See also* calligraphy; controversy; education; *ḥadīth; i'jāz; lagu;* language; Muḥammad, the Prophet; *muṣḥaf;* music; orality; piety; Prophets; *qirā'āt;* reading; revitalization, religious; Sufism; *taḥfīẓ; tajwīd; tilāwah*

Qur'ānic Sciences (*'Ulūm Al-Qur'ān*). See *ḥadīth;* law; Qur'ān

radio, 189, 300n.42; Radio "Al-Ikhwan" (Makassar), 2–3, 23, 218–219; RRI (Radio Republik Indonesia), 232, 235, 254. *See also* competitions; *qāri'*

Ramadan, 10, 14–15, 31, 65, 82, 218, 231, 254

rasa (feeling), 51, 106, 108–109, 132, 201, 203–204, 208, 242, 303n.67; aesthetics, theories, 56–58, 70. *See also* emotion; music; pedagogy; piety; Sufism

Rasmussen, A., 279n.1, 302n.62, 305n.21

reader. See *qāri'*. *See also* reading; *taḥfīẓ*

reading, 13, 82, 87, 114–115, 126, 138–140, 160, 162; Baghdadi method and Iqra', compared and combined, 117, 125, 146–147, 151–152, 157–159; *faṣāḥah* (fluency, eloquence), 64, 85–87, 309n.72; methods, various, 292n.4, 294n.27. *See also* attention; Baghdadi method; comprehension; education, institutions of; emotion; Iqra'; "Islamic," perceptions of; language; orality; Qur'ān; *tajwīd*

recitation: terminology, in Indonesia, 30, 34, 131, 229; types, 30, 34; types, *mujawwad*, 22, 160, 164–166, 183, 282n.46; types, *murattal / tadarus*, 131, 134. *See also* Arabic texts, non-Qur'ānic; music; orality; *qāri'; qirā'āt;* Qur'ān; reading; *tajwīd; tilāwah*

religious experience. *See* emotion

repetition. *See* piety; ritual; *taḥfīẓ*. *See also* music; orthopraxy; pedagogy; *tilāwah*

revelation. See *i'jāz*. *See also* ideals; law; orthopraxy; piety; Qur'ān; Sufism

revitalization, religious, 1–2, 13, 21–23, 38, 44–45, 121, 154–155, 166–168, 275–276; as education, 23, 33–34. See also *da'wah;* education, institutions of; Iqra'; "Islamic," perceptions of; patronage; sociality; women's groups

Rhoma Irama, 14

ritual, 294nn.14, 19, 20; *acara*, 135, 199, 218, 219–220, 232, 258, 303n.66, 306n.32; meaning and, 52, 89–90, 122; moods, motivation, and, 48, 51–53, 168, 170–171, 222–223, 285n.82, 299n.12; repetition, education, and learning, 122–123, 174–178; structure, indeterminacy, invariance, dynamism, 88, 90–91, 98–99, 115, 219–220; theory about, 73, 87, 89–90, 122, 170–172. *See also* ability; Arabic texts, non-Qur'ānic; attention; competitions; *dhikr;* education; emotion; ideals; "Islamic," perceptions of; motivation; music; orthopraxy; pedagogy; personhood; piety; *ṣalāt;* sociality

Rosaldo, M., 71–72

Rosenthal, F., 76–80, 297n.57

rote learning. *See* Baghdadi method; comprehension; education; orality; pedagogy; *taḥfīẓ*

RRI (Radio Republik Indonesia). *See* radio

ṣalāt (canonical worship), 10, 30, 34, 60, 65, 89–90, 93, 113, 130, 145, 280n.21. See also *kiai;* piety; Ramadan
samā' (spiritual audition). *See* music. *See also* controversy; *dhikr;* law; piety; Sufism
Sartre, J.-P., 69, 175, 270, 293n.12, 310n.1
Saudi Arabia. *See* Arabian peninsula
Sayyid Quṭb, 45, 146, 155n.72
schooling. *See* education; education, institutions of. *See also* Baghdadi method; Iqra'; *kiai;* pedagogy; reading
Sejarah Melayu (Malay Annals), 31
Sells, M., 92, 281n.28, 291n.94, 295n.32, 302n.62
sentiment. *See* emotion; *rasa*. *See also* attention; competition; humor; laughing; memory; motivation; music; orthopraxy; pedagogy; piety; Qur'ān; ritual; sociality; *tilāwah;* weeping
shaikh. See *kiai; qāri'*. See also *adab;* education
Shalihah, Khadijatus, 282n.38, 300n.37
sharī'a. *See* law
Sheikh Yusuf, 9
Smith, J. Z., 73, 89, 90, 171, 271
sociality, 5, 42–43, 49, 62, 66–69, 71–74, 109–111, 123, 174, 220, 274; envy, 276–277, 310n.6; participation *(participasi),* 30n.50, 253–254; "technology of the self / community," 74, 112, 274; "zone of proximal development," 295n.37, 298n.7. *See also* ability; *adab; da'wah;* emotion; ideals; imitation; motivation; personhood; revitalization, religious; *sunnah*
Soeharto. *See* Suharto
song, 87, 141–143, 187, 301n.43; alphabet songs, 142–143; Iqra' method and 152–153; MTQ competition theme song, 237–238. *See also* alphabet; Arabic texts, non-Qur'ānic; cassettes; "Islamic," perceptions of; *lagu;* language; music; orality; pedagogy
South Sulawesi, 7–10, 31, 63–64, 113, 135–136, 142–143, 155–156, 166, 189, 194–195, 210, 230, 235–236, 243, 250, 283n.47. *See also* Bone; education, institutions of; language; Makassar
sponsorship. *See* competitions; patronage
Staal, J. F., 89
Strauss, C., 67, 87, 225–226 *(passim),* 285nn.82, 92, 289nn.70, 71
style. See *qāri'*. *See also* ability; cassettes; competitions; "Islamic," perceptions of; *lagu;* music; pedagogy; recitation, types
subjectivity. *See* personhood. *See also* piety; *qāri';* sociality; *taḥfīẓ*
Sufism, 23, 29–31 *(passim),* 35, 39, 44–45, 47, 76, 79–80, 82, 101, 116, 138, 179–180, 193, 205–206, 208; experience, Sufi theory about, 75–76, 81, 272–273. *See also* Arabic texts, non-Qur'ānic; controversy; *dhikr;* emotion; law; music; piety
Suharto, 228, 238–239. *See also* New Order
Sulawesi Selatan. *See* South Sulawesi
Sumatra. *See* competitions
sunnah, 29, 38, 42, 82, 113, 157, 178, 180. See also *adab;* controversy; *ḥadīth;* "Islamic," perceptions of; law; Muḥammad, the Prophet; orthopraxy; piety; Qur'ān; sociality; Sufism
Sutton, R. A., 280n.15, 298n.1, 302n.56
Al-Sūyūtī, 125, 206

tadarus (style of recitation). *See* recitation, types. *See also* cassettes; music; *qāri';* Qur'ān; *taḥfīẓ*
tafsīr (exegesis). *See* comprehension; Qur'ān
taḥfīẓ (Qur'ān memorization), 32–33, 61–62, 78–79, 84, 101–103, 105–106, 111–112, 157, 249–251; difficulty of, 62, 85, 93–98, 104–105; and educational institutions, 63–65; and *lagu,* 65, 262; study and techniques for, 93, 99, 101–103, 104–111; *suras* commonly memorized, 64. *See also* ability; attention; competition; comprehension; education; education, institutions of; *kiai;* memory; music; orality; pedagogy; Qur'ān, structure and style; reading; ritual

women's groups *(continued)*
310n.84. *See also* Arabic texts, non-Qur'ānic; gender; *lagu;* Nurhayati; piety
Woodward, M., 279n.3, 281n.27

Yogyakarta (Java). *See* Iqra'
Yusuf, Sheikh. *See* Sheikh Yusuf

Zainuddin, K. H., M.Z., 16–17, 134–135
Zen, Muhaimin, 103–111 *(passim)*
"zone of proximal development." *See* sociality. *See also* Vygotsky, L.